CITIZEN OF NO MEAN CITY

Archbishop Patrick Riordan of San Francisco

(1841-1914)

Patrick W. Riordan
Archbishop of San Francisco

CITIZEN OF NO MEAN CITY

Archbishop Patrick Riordan of San Francisco

(1841-1914)

James P. Gaffey

A Consortium Book

Library of Congress Card Catalog Number: 74-5435

ISBN: 0-8434-0628-3

In Loving Memory
of
My Mother

Preface

"I am a citizen of no mean city."

These words were recalled as the most inspiring invocation following the earthquake and fire in San Francisco. In 1906 they served as "the compelling phrase needed to arouse the civic pride of those present to the realization of the glory of their community which was fated to rise out of its ashes to new achievement and new glories." Drawn from the Apostle to the Gentiles, this stirring announcement — only hours after the disaster — was "the right phrase out of all literature to give to San Francisco."[1]

Their latter-day herald was Patrick W. Riordan, a citizen and churchman whose public life spanned the three decades around the turn of the twentieth century. During his stewardship the largest religious community in the West suffered its cruelest blows from militant nativism and physical calamity. Yet it succeeded in discarding the last vestiges of Spanish colonialism, built a formidable physical presence, took a notable role in the restoration of a broken city, and was the critical element in the first case litigated before the World Court at The Hague, one of the brightest minor adventures in American diplomacy.

Curiously, historians have neglected the late development of religious communities in the West. Serious study has been devoted largely to the Spanish and Mexican periods. Only recently has the biography of Joseph Sadoc Alemany, San Francisco's first archbishop and a remarkable pioneer, been

completed;[2] and the study of his successor has been limited
to brief notices. This default may be explained partly by the
inaccessibility of sources. Students are only beginning to exploit the rich quarry in the Archives of the Sacred Congregation de Propaganda Fide in Rome, which contain a vast
amount of material on the Catholic community in the United
States. A number of diocesan depositories, too, as well as
those of religious societies, are being reorganized for scholarly use.[3]

In the course of this work, I have incurred a number of
obligations and genuinely regret that I am able to record only
a few. A deep debt of gratitude is owed first to those who
have actively promoted the research, especially the Most Reverends Leo T. Maher, Bishop of San Diego; Mark J. Hurley,
Bishop of Santa Rosa. This biography was written under the
direction of Monsignor John Tracy Ellis, of the Catholic
University of America. I am scarcely able to express my
appreciation to this outstanding scholar whose
uncompromising judgment of each page immeasurably
strengthened the study. It was a distinct privilege to have
worked with such an accomplished and compassionate
churchman.

A number of individuals read and made helpful comments on the manuscript as a whole or in part. These include
the late Professor John T. Farrell; Monsignors Donnell A.
Walsh, John T. Foudy, Harry C. Koenig, Walter J. Tappe, J.
Stoffell; Fathers Robert Trisco, John J. Hedderman, Louis
Arand, S.S., James McVann, C.S.P., John B. McGloin, S.J.;
and Brother T. Matthew McDevitt, F.S.C. While the criticisms
of these readers have been invaluable, I am responsible for
the final product and any shortcomings. I am grateful, too, to
an unusually large number of librarians and archivists, but
space forbids me from mentioning more than a few. Among
these keepers of the records who assisted were Mrs. Helen
Brentnor of the Bancroft Library, University of California,
Berkeley; Monsignors Thomas J. Bowe of San Francisco and
Francis J. Weber of Los Angeles; Reverends J. Joseph Galla-

gher of Baltimore; the late Thomas T. McAvoy, C.S.C., of the University of Notre Dame; the late Nicholas Kovalsky, O.M.I., of Propaganda; the late Patrick H. Ahern of St. Paul; Maynard Geiger, O.F.M., of the Santa Barbara Mission; and particularly Robert McNamara of Rochester, who not only duplicated critical documents but read lengthy portions of the manuscript.

Capable and enormously generous secretaries have been indispensable to the conclusion of this enterprise. I want to express my keen appreciation to my friends, Virginia Trodden, Gloria Anderson and Gwen Sandstrom, for having volunteered hours of their own time in producing, often from scraps, a letter-perfect manuscript, as well as correcting the stylistic oddities of each paragraph. A special acknowledgement must be given to Dr. William E. May of the Catholic University of America who as a supremely amiable editor gave searching and helpful criticism.

I would also single out a notable benefactress of many causes, Mrs. Louise Davies, for having taken an interest in this one. Finally, I am pleased to note my greatest obligations: first, to my parents who sustained my determination to finish the project; and to the Most Reverend Joseph T. McGucken, S.T.D., Archbishop of San Francisco who generously subsidized the entire publication of his predecessor's life.

Photographs of the important persons and places in Riordan's life are a valuable part of this study. Unpublished, and sometimes unposed, pictures were preferred. This is the reason why several reproductions do not have as finished a quality as would have been desired. At times, too, the cast of characters becomes numerous and complex. Hence, an effort was made to keep identities clear, even at the risk of occasionally underestimating the reader's memory and patience.

Santa Rosa, California
September 1, 1976

KEY TO ABBREVIATIONS

AAB   Archives of the Archidiocese of Baltimore

AACL   Archives of the American College, University of Louvain

AALA   Archives of the Archdiocese of Los Angeles

AASF   Archives of the Archdiocese of San Francisco

AASP   Archives of the Archdiocese of St. Paul

ACUA   Archives of the Catholic University of America

ADR   Archives of the Diocese of Richmond

ADRO   Archives of the Diocese of Rochester

AGCB   Archives of the Generalate of the Brothers of the Christian Schools, Rome

APF   Archives of the Sacred Congregation "de Propaganda Fide," Rome

ASM   Archives of the Society of Mary, Rome

ASMS   Archives of St. Mary's Seminary, Baltimore, Maryland

ASP   Archives of the Sisters of the Presentation, San Francisco

ASS   Archives of the Society of St. -Sulpice, Paris

AUND   Archives of the University of Notre Dame

Cong. Gen. "Scritture originali riferite nelle Congregazioni Generali," in the Archives of the Sacred Congregation "de Propaganda Fide"

iv

Congressi, A.C. "Scritture riferite nei Congressi, America Centrale," in the Archives of the Scared Congregation "de Propaganda Fide"

DP — Papers of John T. Doyle, Bancroft Library, University of California, Berkeley

LB-1 — Archdiocesan Letterbook, Volume One, San Francisco

LB(1a) — Archbishop's Letterbook, Volume One, San Francisco

GARF — General Archives of the Redemptorist Fathers, Province of St. Louis, in Rome

NA — National Archives, Washington, D.C.

Lettere — "Lettere e Decreti della Sagra Congregazione e Biglietti di Monsignore Segretario," in the Archives of the Sacred Congregation "de Propaganda Fide"

SBMA — Santa Barbara Mission Archives

SP — Papers of William Morris Stewart, Nevada Historical Society, Reno

UND, MC — Manuscript Collection at the University of Notre Dame

USF, MC — Manuscript Collection at the University of San Francisco

WP — Papers of Stephen M. White, Division of Special Collections, Stanford University

TABLE OF CONTENTS

LIST OF ILLUSTRATIONS

1

The "Chicago Gentleman"

Canadians do not customarily make the national holidays of their large neighbor to the south an occasion for celebration. But on July 4, 1839, the sixty-third anniversary of American independence, there gathered at St. Patrick's Church, in South Nelson, New Brunswick, a wedding party consisting largely of Irish who were lately transplanted in the New World. On this day Matthew Riordan and Mary Dunne pledged to each other their troth before Father Michael Egan, their parish priest.

Simplicity and struggle characterized this marriage. It was like so many others among these Irish arrivals who had left the spare patrimony of their own country for a share in the bounty of this rich land. The new husband was a skilled shipwright who had made his home in Chatham. His fancy had been charmed by a young, possibly unschooled, girl living with her large family in the vicinity.[1] It was to be a blessed and fruitful union. Two years later in Chatham, on August 27, 1841, the proud mother presented her first-born son who was baptized on the day following in St. Michael's Church, newly built and dedicated, and christened Patrick William.[2] Such was the beginning in a humble eastern Canadian village of a commanding leader of American Catholicism. His destinies would span the continent, bringing him to Chicago, the metropolis of mid-America, and finally to San Francisco, mistress of the Pacific Coast.

Patrick Riordan, descended from two ancient Irish septs, combining within himself the traditions and sturdy qualities

of southern and eastern Ireland. His father's clan had originated in County Tipperary and had migrated southward to
County Cork at such an early date that they are regarded as
belonging to that county.[3] Matthew Riordan's own home,
where he had grown into manhood, was Kinsale, a busy market area and seaport of Cork, richly steeped in Irish history
and in the traditions of the sea.

It was natural for young lads to adopt for themselves
crafts and professions which would keep them close to water.
Kinsale had long been the chief port of southern Ireland
before the river approaches to nearby Cork City had been
dredged and reclaimed. In the early nineteenth century, as
young Matthew was learning the skills of a shipwright, Kinsale offered him a good future, still actively engaged with her
larger sister, Cork City, in supplying the fishermen and the
traders to the West Indies and in serving as a provisioning
station for the British navy. But despite its feverish bustle,
the town had not imposed a paralyzing hold upon Matthew.
The independent and enterprising Irishman, unmarried and
skilled in carpentry, was seriously tempted to abandon his
home and to risk his future in the new flourishing land
beyond the Atlantic. Three of his married brothers — Patrick,
John, and James — had, around 1820, sailed for Halifax,
Nova Scotia, and settled in Gloucester County in northern
New Brunswick. Genuine pioneers, they brought with them
their wives and large families and, on July 11, 1837, received
a 100-acre tract of thick wilderness along the Chaleur Bay
near New Brandon which they cleared for homesteads.[4] This
rugged, heavily wooded area became their new home. The
hard-working brothers soon invested in a number of important local projects which included farms, lumber and grist
mills, and a thriving general store. Inevitably the community
was dominated by this sturdy family from Cork and was
incorporated under the official name of "Riordan." Precious
letters to Ireland described the wonders of the province and
the rapid success of the brothers, sorely tempting Matthew to
join them. Eventually, the young shipwright took leave of his
parents on a vessel westward bound, hopeful and expectant.

After weeks at sea, he reached Chatham, some seventy miles south of Riordan, where the brothers gave the new arrival a warm welcome to the New World.[5]

Mary, or "Molly," Dunne, whom Matthew had chosen for his bride, was a farm girl who had accompanied her family to Canada from Stradbally, County Leix.[6] Her childhood world stood in dark contrast to that of Matthew. County Leix was inland and agrarian, removed from the magic and mysteries of the sea and far different from the jagged and wild southern coasts. Her homestead lay in the heart of rural Ireland, southeast of Dublin, in a region blessed with some of the richest land of the country. The limestone fields were largely level, rising gently to the Slieve Bloom mountains in the northwest, and the wet bog which had covered the area had long been draining, leaving behind fertile fields for pasture and tillage. In this abundant setting Mary had lived with her parents and several brothers. Like Matthew Riordan many miles to the south, however, she too had been stricken with the spell of transplanting her life to the New World. On May 16, 1831, Mary's father Patrick received a substantial grant of two hundred acres a little distance from Chatham.[7] And so in Canada, thousands of sea miles from their ancestral homes, these two young people fresh from Ireland met and married in 1839, both swept up in a gigantic movement of history.[8]

Chatham, New Brunswick, a small village situated on the estuary of the Miramichi River, where Matthew and Mary had chosen to raise their family, provided the young Irish craftsman security and employment. His brothers had dissuaded him from coming on to the more isolated region of Riordan, strongly recommending that his future lay in Chatham. It was at this time growing into a major fishing center and possessed an excellent harbor with shipping connections to other river and coastal points. Generous quantities of spruce, hardwood, and hemlock bark had made lumbering the major industry of the region. The Cunard brothers had recently settled in the village and developed an immense business in timber and shipbuilding, employing over four hundred.[9] In this prospering milieu, the Riordan family began to grow: first Patrick William in 1841, and then Catherine on March 17, 1844.[10]

Patrick did not have time to strike deep roots in Canadian soil. Evidently, like so many Irish of the period, Matthew Riordan either did not plan to finish his life in New Brunswick or decided on an extended visit to Ireland. For soon after Catherine's birth he transported his family back to his home in Kinsale, never to return to Chatham. Little Patrick was nearing only his fifth birthday in Ireland when a second son Daniel was born and baptized on August 6, 1846.[11]

But the great tragedy which crippled Ireland in the mid-1840's had a profound influence on the fortunes of the Riordans, perhaps accelerating their return across the sea and exposing them to another hazardous and wretched voyage across the Atlantic.[12]

In the autumn of 1845 the potato blight first struck, leaving diseased vegetation over the countryside, killing within six years a million Irish through starvation and the famine fever, and sending hundreds of thousands of émigrés abroad. The height of the famine in which the Riordans had been caught was reached during 1846 and 1847; and the British Parliament faced an incredible problem of administration. There was already a serious food shortage in England, and the hapless attempts by the ministry to institute public aid had to be replaced by outside relief on a gigantic scale. By the spring of 1847, some three million were being supported by public funds. So distressed and diseased, Ireland could no longer be the proper home for Matthew's family. Friends and opportunity awaited them in North America.

The famine had broken the spirit of the Irish nation, and such a shattering experience would be preserved in oral tradition, retold on countless occasions around the firesides of those who had experience the catastrophe. On occasion in later years Patrick referred to the tormented history of his ancestors, perhaps invoking a distant and fleeting personal memory of these bleak days, perhaps reflecting his parents' grief. Ireland's history, he would say, has for a long time "been one which has filled the heart with sadness as it has been a record of poverty and of suffering. . . ."[13]

As Patrick, not more than seven years of age, sailed with his family again into the Atlantic and watched the green shores gently dissolve below the horizon, he was caught up in another sweeping, merciless movement of history. The blight of the summer of 1846 had terrorized the island and forced, for the first time in Irish history, a heavy exodus hazardously late in the year. Thousands had panicked and would risk their lives upon a winter crossing, disposed to face any misery save that of remaining in Ireland. Unlike their first voyages to British North America in the 1830's, Matthew and Mary Dunne were thrown with their children among large groups of desperate people now compelled to flee. Onward into the west, in overcrowded vessels, sailed the refugees from the Irish famine, burdened with a sense of permanent severance and doom, leaving with an air of chilling finality.

With New Brunswick their likely destination, the ships that carried the Riordans had quite probably set course for St. John, the principal port for the maritime provinces. The weeks of such ocean travel were a nightmare. Common to all vessels of these times were the overcrowding in the steerage, the airless quarters, and the seemingly interminable passage. The Riordans had known similar inconveniences earlier; but what made this second voyage worse was the suffering of their children and the sense of utter hopelessness. Travelers on these ships were too apathetic even to take the simplest precautions against disease. Ships which left Cork City had a particularly fatal record: one passenger in nine perished at sea.[14]

The Riordans' nightmare did not end once they reached the safe harbor of St. John and disembarked from their coffin ship. This massive, new influx of famine refugees presented grave problems to New Brunswick. The new arrivals were first quarantined on Partridge Island, which soon became so overcrowded that a number were forced to live in the damp, open spaces. Before 1847 had passed, one-seventh of the Irish who had come to St. John had died; one-half had crossed over to the United States; and others were kept in almshouses and orphanages. Added to this crisis were the anger of the native New Brunswickers toward the survivors and a severe depression in the lumber industry that shook the provincial economy.[15] It must have been a severe blow to Matthew Riordan when he learned that the Cunards had failed in Chatham and that panic had momentarily seized the town.

Conditions were difficult, therefore, for a young man like Matthew who had hazarded the journey with his wife and very young children. Mary's family had fortunately escaped the disaster in Ireland, having remained in New Brunswick; and they welcomed the spent travelers. To the whole family, the Dunnes and the Riordans, the image of America had become all the more attractive when contrasted with the unpromising picture of nineteenth-century Ireland and Canada. The coastal belt along the Atlantic already congested and teeming with hapless refugees, their vision turned westward beyond the Rochester-Buffalo area of upper New York State, beyond the industrial regions of Pennsylvania to the new settlements growing in the lake region. Mary's brother, Dennis Dunne, a deacon in the Seminary of Quebec, had been accepted by Bishop William Quarter, first Bishop of Chicago, and would be ordained in 1848 in America. In the early spring of this year the Riordans and Dunnes thus began their last migration, braving first in an open boat, as family tradition has it, a horrendous trip eastward through the stormy waters of the St. Lawrence and Atlantic. Landing in New York, they continued their movement to the West by wagon along the lake shore into the grass-covered, treeless prairies of northern Indiana. By April they had reached their destination, the flourishing city of Chicago.[16]

* * * * *

Chicago fulfilled the dreams of a young Irish shipwright anxious to provide his family a secure and comfortable home. In only seven and a half years of life, his older son Patrick had already seen a great deal more of the world than his schoolmates would in a lifetime. His new home, Chicago,

was, in 1848, the year of his arrival, marking the beginning of
a new epoch in its history.[17] The city, as it approached the
mid-nineteenth century, was young and vigorous. Its traditions were not as old and historic as some cities along the
Atlantic and the St. Lawrence, the French having long used
the area only as an easy portage route between the Chicago
and Des Plaines Rivers. But the settlement had shortly begun
shape as a vital center for the upper Mississippi Valley.

By 1848, as the Riordans and Dunnes beheld Chicago for
the first time, the city was undergoing its transition from a
giant trading post to a bristling municipality. The frontier
had passed on.[18] When the Illinois and Michigan Canal
connected the Great Lakes with the river system of the valley, the downward current of trade was turned toward Chicago, soon establishing it as the leading market for the western farmers. A large number of Irish had worked on this
enterprise; and Patrick's uncle, Father Dennis Dunne, had
been assigned soon after ordination to care for them along
the waterway. The railroad, too, touched Patrick's life. One
of the young boy's earliest memories was playing in the
empty spaces around his home with young John Ireland, a
lifelong friend and the future Archbishop of St. Paul. And in
the fall of 1848 both lads were privileged to watch the first
steam locomotive, the "Pioneer," puff in and out of Chicago
along its ten-mile track west of the city.[19]

In early 1850, as Patrick approached adolescence, his new
home was also beginning to take on a genuinely cosmopolitan
atmosphere. The foreign-born population outnumbered the
natives, many of them driven like the Riordans by disasters at
home and a longing for security in this bustling city. The
"Garden City," with its enormous commercial potentialities,
had boundless variety, whole districts segregated according to
nationalities, and an endless stream of uprooted Americans
marching further westward pouring into its hotels and camps.
This complex city was Patrick Riordan's home, where he
would ripen into manhood, where he would spend the first,
and admittedly the happiest, years of his priesthood, and
whereto he would never, as long as he lived, return as a
stranger.

During these quickly paced times the Catholic Church was taking deep root in the Middle West. The infant Diocese of Chicago, created only five years before Patrick's arrival, was as polyglot as the community; and the Riordans and the Dunnes, coming to their American home by way of Ireland and Canada, made their contribution to the mixed complexion of the Church. The two largest foreign groups were the Irish and the Germans. This Irish-German polarity in Chicago was clearly reflected in the Church when the first bishop, Irish-born William Quarter, was succeeded in the transitional year of 1848 by James Oliver Van de Velde, a Jesuit whom Rome selected largely because of his fluency in English and German.[20]

Such was the complex environment of 1848 when Patrick Riordan, well-traveled lad of seven years, first settled himself in mid-America. The Catholic congregation had rapidly outgrown old St. Mary's Cathedral, Chicago's original parish, and Bishop Quarter created, in 1846, three new parishes, St. Joseph's and St. Peter's for the German-speaking faithful and St. Patrick's to serve the Irish immigrants clustered in west Chicago. The Riordan family settled within St. Patrick's parish, near 730 West Adams Street. Patrick virtually grew up with the parish. His home was characteristically only three quarters of a block from the temporary frame church where he served Mass, and eventually next door to him there would be a convent of the Daughters of Charity.[21] In 1854, when Patrick was thirteen years old, his uncle, Dennis Dunne, was named pastor and completed building the stone church. A year later Dennis was named vicar general of the diocese.[22] Only fragments record Patrick's attitudes during these early years, but the long passages of time, it is certain, did not dim his memory or fondness for this old Irish parish.[23]

The new University of St. Mary of the Lake had been established only four years when the Riordans came to Chicago, serving the diocese as a seminary and parochial school. It was this institution that provided young Patrick his earliest instruction and his first assignment as a priest.[24] Bishop Quarter was an enterprising spiritual leader who inaugurated an ambitious educational program. Scarcely a month after his arrival in 1844, he had converted an old frame church building into a boys' school which bore the inscription, "St. Mary's College of the Lake," and on December 19 he had succeeded in obtaining from the state legislature a charter creating the "University of St. Mary of the Lake." Thus began the first school for higher education erected in Chicago.[25]

A truly ambitious enterprise for the infant diocese, Patrick's school reflected the aggressiveness and invincible confidence of mid-century Chicago as it made its transition from frontier town into a fast-growing urban community. Its faculty was prepared to offer a full program in language, humanities, and the sciences. More importantly, several of Riordan's life-long associates were connected with this institution. One senior student was John McMullen who later, as rector and professor at St. Mary, would become a critical force in Riordan's life. Patrick's boyhood playmate, John Ireland, was enrolled for a time but was removed when his family moved to Minnesota. Of the two Riordan boys, Daniel had in the course of time developed a greater attachment to the school, intending in his later years to write its history and living on to the age of seventy-five as its "last priest alumnus." Patrick, however, stayed at St. Mary for a brief time only and then discontinued there, as it was said, "on account of the distance from his home. . . ."[26]

Patrick moved on to take a portion of his secondary studies at the University of Notre Dame, leaving South Bend after two years in 1858 when he was nearing the age of seventeen. This school, administered by the Holy Cross Fathers, was another pioneering institution in the Middle West, chartered and opened in 1844. Riordan's years at Notre Dame were happy ones, filled as they were with rich memories which deepened with the passage of time. Ably guided by Father Edward Sorin, C.S.C., Notre Dame was likewise on the threshold of a great expansion. Although the student body numbered usually 140, the central building was enlarged in 1853 to accommodate 300, and three years later St. Mary's Aca-

demy for young women was moved to South Bend from
Bertrand, Michigan.[27] Once young Patrick arrived at Notre
Dame, he found himself in an academic atmosphere which
lacked much of the sophistication and advanced educational
methods of eastern academies. There was, however, a strong
emphasis on religious and moral training, tempered with stern
French discipline as the essential ingredients of a Christian
education. Despite its limitations and rigors, Notre Dame was
a school to which Riordan remained faithful in later life,
grateful and genuinely interested in its fortunes.

* * * * *

It was at Notre Dame that Patrick cultivated a spiritual
life, regularly attending the monthly nocturnal hours of
adoration in the chapel, and decided that he was summoned
to the diocesan priesthood.[28] After announcing his decision,
he was selected to study in Europe and left Notre Dame in
1858 to begin his year of rhetoric in Rome.[29] En route to
the Eternal City, the young student encountered a personal
experience which he frequently recounted in later years. Perhaps in an effort to economize, the diocese secured for Patrick passage on a ship that in time proved unseaworthy. The
oceanic voyage was unusually slow and dangerous, taking
nearly seven weeks and providing many anxious moments for
the travelers. On a Sunday morning, in the cold hours of
dawn, a landing was finally negotiated on the west coast of
Ireland. The passage had deprived Patrick and his two companions of Mass for nearly two months; and they were determined to take advantage of the opportunity. Their clothes
ringing with seawater, the three young Americans walked
that brisk morning "six Irish miles" in search of a parish
church and assisted at Mass.[30]

His first year in Rome was spent at the Urban College
attached to the Congregation of Propaganda Fide, an institution founded by Pope Urban VIII in 1627 to educate
prospective missionary priests who would work in areas subject to Propaganda's jurisdiction. American bishops were eli-

gible to send candidates to the Urban College since the Church in the United States remained under this congregation until 1908. For this training neither Riordan nor his bishops paid any tuition. The Propaganda bore all expenses, accepting worthy candidates at least fifteen years of age. The course extended over seven years, with two of them devoted to philosophy and another four to theology. Already enrolled at the Urban College to greet young Patrick in 1858 was a fellow Chicagoan, James McGovern, an intimate friend of the newly ordained alumnus, John McMullen, both of whom would exercise a profound influence on Riordan in his early ministry.

This first year in the Eternal City must have imprinted upon Riordan's mind many precious and durable impressions. Here he was given opportunities to visit the ancient ruins and shrines, to see from time to time Pio Nono, and particularly to prepare himself with students who originated from and trained for all parts of the world — "all living under the same rule," described a contemporary of Riordan, "speaking Latin as the language of the school and Italian for common intercourse, attending the same classes, and dispersing year after year to their missions to engage in the work of God's Church on earth."[31] Student life in Europe would introduce him to many of the most promising ecclesiastics of his generation. His prefect at the College was Francis Silas Chatard, an older undergraduate from Baltimore and the future Bishop of Vincennes, Indiana, who would later assist at Riordan's own consecration.[32] One outstanding member of the faculty who deeply impressed the young rhetorician was the twenty-eight-year-old Father Patrick Francis Moran, nephew of Paul Cullen, Archbishop of Dublin, and vice-principal of the Irish College of St. Agatha. The future Cardinal Archbishop of Sydney, Australia, was in the course of spending eleven years in Rome, researching in the Vatican Archives for his publications in Celtic ecclesiastical history and at the same time attached to the Urban College as its professor of Hebrew.[33]

Patrick's second year in the Eternal City was a mixture of exciting adventure and disappointment. First, he had the dis-

tinction of being one of the pioneer band of twelve students
to leave the Urban College and to move to the new American
College in Rome. Although the institution could accommodate many more, Cardinal Alessandro Barnabò, Prefect of
Propaganda, would not admit more than this number, hoping
to leave room for additional newcomers from the United
States. The day of the formal opening occurred on December
7, 1859, when the "Original Jacobs" separated from the ten
American students who remained at the Urban College. Wearing the cassocks which were distinguished by their blue but-
tons and piping and the red sash they marched in a procession to the new institution located nearby on Via dell'
Umiltà.[34] Later on this historic day the young philosophy
student from Chicago was arranged with his confreres in a
semicircle around Barnabò and heard the cardinal prefect
proclaim:

> To the twelve Apostles was commited the charge
> of converting the Old World, and to-day twelve are
> they who have to commence their labors which
> will enable them to convert the New World. . . .[35]

The College was formally inaugurated on the following day,
the feast of the Immaculate Conception and, late in the day,
Pius IX received the students and their superiors in his private
library, delivering a fatherly discourse and then conducting
the young men on a rare tour of the papal gardens. The
memory of these historic experiences never ceased to be
treasured by Patrick Riordan. Even when the college was
close to a half century in age, he still preserved the three little
gifts which the pope had distributed to the "Jacobs" at their
first audience — a small filigreed holy picture, a copy of St.
Pius V's devotion to the Passion, and a large bronze medal
struck in 1854 to commemorate the definition of the
Immaculate Conception.[36] The Roman correspondent for
the London *Tablet* sensed the singular character of these
days. "Thus the Americans have taken possession of their,
from henceforth, 'Alma Mater,' and if the fruits correspond

to a beginning so full of hope, America will yet, in years to come, treasure the precious memory of the eighth of December, 1859."[37]

The original student body truly represented the expanses of their homeland, the twelve belonging to seven states and eight dioceses ranging from one coast to the other. Only eighteen years of age at the time, Riordan was during his only year at the new college exposed to an exceptional group of clerical students, some of whom would directly influence the destinies of the American Church. From New Jersey was Robert Seton, grandson of Saint Elizabeth Seton and a somewhat eccentric ecclesiastic who would serve in 1884 as chief notary of the Third Plenary Council of Baltimore and in 1903 be named titular Archbishop of Heliopolis.[38] Riordan remained rather fond of Seton with all his odd notions. Long after the two seminarians had parted, he advised a close friend of his to visit Seton when in Rome. "He is one of my oldest friends," he wrote lightly, some sixty years later,

> we entered the American College together, after having been together in Propaganda for one year, on the 7th of December, 1859. He was older than I was, and I suppose he has kept up the difference between our ages since, although like some people, he does not like to have his age alluded to.[39]

During this year Riordan lived with two other more important figures from the East, however, whose public lives would be inextricably and tragically entangled. From the Diocese of Newark was Michael Augustine Corrigan, the first alumnus to be consecrated, who would die in 1902 as the Archbishop of New York City. The prefect of the group was Edward McGlynn of New York. A brilliant upperclassman borrowed from the Urban College, he would be ordained within a few months and as the thirteenth man, was never considered as an "Original Jacob." Patrick knew these two churchmen from their student years. Decades later, when they clashed violently over theological and political attitudes, he looked upon the celebrated Corrigan-McGlynn conflict with an exceptionally sober understanding that derived from these impressionable days in Rome. "I exceedingly regret this whole affair," observed Riordan in those troubled days. "I have always had a very deep and tender affection for Dr. McGlynn, and had he been approached properly and by one who knows his character, he could have been steered into safe waters."[40]

* * * * *

During this first year of the American College, few institutions in Rome were so well-managed and graced with such conspicuous honors, especially when Pius IX paid a formal visit. But Riordan's plans to finish his course in this heady atmosphere faded as his health deteriorated. Ironically, the college itself was considered a particularly healthy location. The fastidious troops of Napoleon III had occupied the building, quartering their sick there. "So you see," observed the veteran correspondent of the *Tablet*, "the Americans have no reason to fear for their health as far as locality is concerned."[41] Unfortunately, however, the Roman climate and Riordan's own congenital weak health forced him on August 5, 1860, to withdraw and to continue his preparation in Paris. There Patrick first sought entrance into the Seminary of St. Sulpice, but the superior, Henri Icard, suggested that he was not robust enough to sustain the rigors of the Sulpician regime and was more suited for the Colonial Seminary of Paris conducted by the Holy Spirit Fathers. On August 10, 1860, he enrolled in this institution, remaining exactly twelve months and completing his year of second philosophy.[42] Patrick's theology courses were, however, to be taken at another infant institution, the American College at Louvain. There he formally entered on October 1, 1861, the traditional date of the opening of the scholastic year, and it was to be in the north where from a new perspective he was to observe the clashing movements helping to shape the Europe which he would know as a priest and bishop.[43]

Coming thus to Belgium in the early 1860's Riordan's alert and sensitive mind was exposed to one of the most vigorous and visionary Catholic leaders of this critical period, Cardinal Engelbert Sterckx, who guided the Belgian Church as Archbishop of Malines from 1831 to 1867. Sterckx's approach to these new forces, Riordan was to learn, did not quite conform to the reactionary energies of Pius IX. Rapid industrialization had introduced in the young kingdom an aggressive anticlerical liberalism aimed directly at the secularization of all national institutions, especially education. The genius and irrepressible spirit of Sterckx in confronting dechristianization were particularly evident to young Riordan at Louvain. It had been under the cardinal primate's patronage that the ancient university had been restored only in 1834 and designed to provide the Belgian Church with a powerful intellectual center. Nothing had been spared in making it a "free" university, absolutely independent of the state in its administration, teaching, and budget. Academically, it was to rival the Free University of Brussels and the state's University of Ghent, both of which had allegedly absorbed much of the subversion and godlessness of the day.

Midway through his term at the American College, the young Chicagoan, who was ever attuned to current trends, was given an intimate glimpse into the dynamic and militant spirit by which the Belgian people met the public issues and hostilities of the day and mobilized their forces in the defense of the Church's rights. In August, 1863, the first Catholic Congress met in Malines. This assembly might, indeed, have been the most important single event in Riordan's student life at Louvain. For there, the Comte de Montalembert, the French champion of Catholic liberalism, delivered one of the celebrated appeals of his lifetime, demanding with bold and persuasive eloquence that the Church adjust herself to the age of democracy and give courage and hope to Catholic professors the world over.[44] Like any resourceful seminarian, Patrick took full advantage of his base in northern Europe and attended several such congresses in Belgium and Germany. From this exposure he derived his life-long conviction that the close harmony between clergy and laity was the source of the Church's strength in these two countries. But the Church, he believed, owed its deplorable weakness in the Mediterranean countries largely to the unfortunate lack of cooperation between these two groups, a tragic condition which illustrated, he would say, the truth of the tested axiom: "divided we fall."[45]

Such was the vibrant and liberating environment wherein Patrick studied during these five years at Louvain. For the second time he was enrolled in a new institution which had been founded in 1857. Only two years before he had walked as a first philosopher in that unforgettable procession from the Urban College to Via dell'Umiltà. At Louvain he entered as a theologian since the American College was not yet equipped to instruct in the humanities and philosophy. Originally, theology was taught in the college building in probably a three-year course which had been abbreviated to accommodate the urgent need of missionaries for the United States. A few gifted students, Riordan included, were encouraged to take the complete theological course of the university with the intention of winning a baccalaureate or even a licentiate.[46] Soon another Louvain singularity confronted the young man. During the early administration of John De Neve as rector, the student body was steadily growing from eight students in 1860 to thirty in the following year in which Riordan entered.[47] The composition of this student body was substantially different from that which Riordan had experienced at the American College in Rome; it more closely resembled the multinational texture of the Urban College. While enabling American-born students to pursue in Europe courses of theology and to familiarize themselves with the languages and customs of the Old World, the rector of the American College at Louvain also admitted young Europeans, who were later adopted by an American bishop.[48] During the decade in which Riordan attended Louvain, most of the student originated from the German states, especially Prussia; and trailing the native Germans in numbers were the Belgians, Americans, Dutch, and Irish.[49] During his years at Louvain,

Patrick spent most of his vacation time in Germany, familiarizing himself with the language and meeting distinguished Catholic scholars in German universities.[50] This unusual opportunity may well have been a deciding factor in promoting, possibly engendering, Riordan's life-long compassion regarding the German problem and his restrained attitudes toward Irish nationalsim. And later, as Archbishop of San Francisco, he would have close relations with a goodly number of these young Europeans as ordinaries and priests of western dioceses like Oregon City, Nesqually, and Victoria.

For five years Patrick Riordan wholeheartedly entered into the regime and routines of the college, finding at Louvain one particular upperclassman, whose friendship would last a lifetime, John Lancaster Spalding, a superior student from the Diocese of Louisville. Living within such a diminutive community must have been quite intimate and informal. The meager evidence highlights and, in good fun, mocks his efforts at eloquent speaking. During his first year, there was begun a handwritten bulletin of four pages called *The Missionary*, the first issue appearing in January, 1862. Since such a great portion of the student body were European-born, the bulletin was intended to enable these men to practice and polish their command of the English language, as well as to preserve a record of incidents for an eventual history of the college.[51] In the second edition, *The Missionary* produced in the style of a student publication an amusing critique of one of Riordan's sermons. "Last Sunday," it read,

> we were regaled with a sermon by the distinguished Chicago preacher, Mr. Riordan. We regret that space granted us in the valuable columns of *The Missionary* does not allow us to give at least a summary of this eloquent sermon. Mr. Riordan has a style at once graceful, flowing, and melodious. His periods roll along like a silver river meandering through a lovely flower garden.[52]

Evidently, Riordan was a favorite in the community and a good sport insensitive to such innocent teasing. The same general theme appeared months later in a lengthy, unsigned article grandly entitled, "The Vacation of a Chicago Gentleman, Nephew of the Immortal Douglas." Though Riordan was never named in the article, it probably was a narration of his Easter holidays composed in outrageous hyperbole. The waggish author introduced his subject with this extravagant description:

> As the scene of those fleeting days of a pleasure and innocent enjoyment he chose a lonely rural village on the shady banks of our elongated lake whose beneficial waters glittering beneath the pearly beams of the joyous life giving sun of spring reflect the deep azure blue of the ethereal sky which instils a calm and pleasing sensation of repose and quiet joy into the souls. In this lovely spot the "nephew of Douglas" who scarcely allowed his mind to relax itself in the pursuit of knowledge in its most lofty regions and most abstruse points, who in passion overcome by the irresistible influence of the charming nature and the amiable friends by whom he was surrounded; so much so that during the entire vacation he opened one book and this was a book of poetry.... One of the Chief delights of this Chicago gentleman was to listen enraptured for hours and sometimes whole days to the song of the nightingale. He even rose several mornings so early as 10 o'clock in order to enjoy, as he himself expressed it, the first pure soul-awaking notes of this heavenly Enchantress. On such occasions, his soul full of joy, his heart full of love and his stomach full of pancakes, because the world was full of love, [he] would exclaim: Oh Milton! how couldst thou ... neglect this bird *most musical* and *most melancholy*.

The reporter persisted further in his mischief. Referring next to the Chicago gentleman's recent performance on a discourse on the United States, he compared — with notable license on American geography — "such an overpowering flood of Eloquence to the waves of the mighty Mississipi [sic] the father of the waters, as he proudly rolls into the Atlantic. . . ."[53]

Nevertheless, life at Louvain was not all frolic and amusement. It was foremost an institution seriously dedicated to the formation of missionary priests for the American Church. Patrick Riordan succeeded admirably in his preparation and was ordained at Mechlin on June 10, 1865, at the hands of Cardinal Sterckx and winning his licentiate in theology in the following year.[54] Before he left for Chicago on October 10, 1866, there had been fixed irrevocably in his heart a warm and filial affection for the college which would glow for the remaining fifty-three years of his life. Patrick certainly influenced his beloved younger brother's choice of seminaries, for Daniel had entered in October, 1863, the *petit séminaire* of Malines and the American College itself two years later.[55] He also persuaded another family to send their son to Belgium, Edward Michael Dunne, who later acknowledged this decision as a factor in preserving his vocation and who became the second Bishop of Peoria in 1909.[56] Even until the final month of his life, in December, 1914, the fortunes of the college weighed heavily on his mind. In the first days of World War I, when Germany invaded neutral Belgium and reports reached Riordan on the devastation of Louvain, the old alumnus was shocked. Deeply concerned over the fate of his alma mater and the rector, he was ready to make any recommended contribution to restore the institution and to relieve the sufferings of his dear Belgians. "These are sad days for those who spend years in Louvain, as I did," he wrote to Bishop Camillus Maes of Covington, Kentucky, another Louvain student who was a native of Belgium. "I do not think that anything ever affected me as much as the devastation of a noble country and a noble people." These last words were written less than three weeks before his death:

> I am personally willing to give all I can for the old College. It is a dreadful condition of things. It

makes my heart sick to read the papers every
morning and see what calamities have fallen upon a
noble Christian people by the Attila of the
North.[57]

A two-continent environment had thus ripened in young
Patrick life-long characteristics. From a burgeoning Chicago
he developed resources as an organizer and builder, a master
administrator to come. Through his Irish blood he kept a
common touch. Matthew and Mary's son would never lose
the reality of that immigrant America which had uprooted
itself, worked with its hands, kept its place and peace, and
viewed a religious vocation as God's greatest blessing. Yet
his second and longer sojourn in Europe introduced him to
wider horizons. There he met the most promising clerics of
his generation, received an education second to none in the
Church, and — above all — tasted the good life of a gentleman.

2

A Young "Garibaldian"

Father Patrick Riordan returned in 1866 to a Chicago that had undergone a number of profound changes during his absence of eight years. The years from 1848 to 1871 were a robust interval as the community evolved with frightening speed into a rangy, swollen metropolis. In his absence during the Civil War, Riordan's city had emerged the indisputable commercial emporium of the Middle West. When young Patrick had left in 1858 for the Urban College, it was still contending with St. Louis for economic control of the Mississippi Valley.[1] It was fortunate that the Riordans and the Dunnes, battered from their losses in Canada and Ireland, had, in the mid-nineteenth century, chosen Chicago as their home. The city had long been winning this mercantile contest largely because of the superiority of its railroads over the river transport upon which St. Louis depended. Ultimately, the Civil War, which Patrick had observed from afar, had resolved the issue decisively. At the end of the conflict, Chicago had become the mistress of western commerce through good fortune, initiative, and enterprise — strong virtues which local clerics like Father Riordan would themselves cultivate and exhibit in their priestly lives. Upon his return, therefore, the new theologian from Louvain found himself comfortably in a city vibrating with activity and growing at a startling rate: its population, having risen quickly to 109,260 in 1860, would in ten years nearly treble to 298,977; and finally in 1880 Riordan's city ranked as the fourth largest city in the United States at 503,185.[2]

The Catholic Church in Riordan's home diocese could hardly fail to boom in such surroundings. Governing this community which faced overwhelming problems in the continuous physical expansion of the city was James Duggan. This young Irish-born prelate had been coadjutor to Archbishop Peter Richard Kenrick of St. Louis and at thirty-four years of age had succeeded Anthony O'Regan as Bishop of Chicago in 1859. In his earliest assignments, Bishop Duggan gathered about him some of his ablest priests: Patrick's best friend, John McMullen, was appointed chancellor; Thaddeus J. Butler, secretary; and in the critical position of vicar general he retained O'Regan's choice, and Patrick's beloved uncle, Dennis Dunne.[3] Diocesan expansion during Duggan's administration was evident in the formation of five new parishes and the foundation of schools and institutions. The Redemptorists were given charge of St. Michael's Church in 1860 and the Benedictines took charge of St. Joseph's in 1861, two important parishes serving the large German congregations on the North Side. With strong leadership and the increase of immigration, the Catholic community of Chicago had thus expanded many times in the first twenty years in which the Riordan family lived in the booming city so that by 1868 the diocese had reported a total number of 108,500 souls, more than those claimed by all the Protestant denominations.[4]

Upon his return in 1866, Patrick was assigned to the seminary department at the University of St. Mary of the Lake and appointed professor of canon law and ecclesiastical history. This institution had at best been an object of Bishop Duggan's program to advance the diocese. In 1861, he had given its administration to Father McMullen, who was appointed president and undertook its reorganization. Lately, St. Mary's had deteriorated to scarcely more than an advanced high school emphasizing the classics and the natural sciences, closely identified as a parish school for the Cathedral of the Holy Name. A devoted alumnus himself, McMullen had welcomed this gigantic task of renewal, vowing: "If St. Mary of the Lake is worth anything, she shall have all

I can bestow upon her."[5] Despite the urgencies of the Civil War, he succeeded in revitalizing the school: the faculty and student body were enlarged, a new south wing constructed, and introduced were new courses in law, theology, and medicine.

The dynamic president, with whom Patrick Riordan would spend his formative years in the ministry, was an extraordinary figure able to evoke a hero-worship from many of those who knew him. Riordan's own brother Daniel, who had been a student in McMullen's early regime, was charmed by this intelligent and intensely zealous priest who had been ordained only three years when placed in charge. "Beneath a stern countenance there was a surprisingly tender heart," recalled the younger Riordan. He was a magnanimous individual, sensitive to every form of suffering and "unselfish to a degree seldom witnessed in actual life."[6] McMullen's gifts and strong personality were even to smite Patrick Riordan's closest American friend from Louvain, John Lancaster Spalding, who succeeded better than brother Daniel in focusing his enthusiasm. "His religion was one of deeds rather than of words," said Spalding later in summing up McMullen's character.

> Not a faultless man, indeed; not one whom either world or the church would canonize, not a great orator, nor a master of style, nor a profound thinker, nor an enthusiastic reformer, not a skillful organizer of philanthropic schemes; but a plain, brave and genuine man, the best type of the kind of men the West rears; men who saved the Union, and who yet may save our religion and christian civilization.[7]

There were other outstanding faculty members gathered by McMullen who warmly greeted the new recruit from Louvain. The rector of the seminary department was McMullen's devoted colleague, James J. McGovern, the first native-born priest of Chicago whom Patrick had known as an upper-

classman at the Urban College. Also on the seminary faculty
were Thaddeus Butler, professor of ethics and moral theology, and Joseph P. Roles, professor of sacred eloquence who
was also rector of the cathedral and a member of the bishop's
council. Eventually, young Riordan fulfilled early expectations and advanced to a professorship of dogmatic theology.

* * * * *

Unfortunately, however, Father Riordan's induction into
this institution introduced him to the greatest misfortune
that had yet struck the Catholic Church in Chicago. Severe
differences had arisen between Bishop Duggan and McMullen,
and in early 1866, shortly before Riordan's return to America, the university department had closed its doors. The public reason given for this action was that the institution could
not liquidate its floating debt of a paltry $6,000, a pretext
which masked the bishop's personal antagonism toward the
university's persident. This was an unexpected and shattering
blow to the faculty and student body and particularly for the
stalwart John McMullen, who, without shame, broke down
and wept. So sudden and decisive was this move, as one
contemporary wrote, that "there was not an audible groan
. . . but a dispersion, as silent as that of the conquered chief-
tain and his vanquished warriors who shared with him in his
struggles for a noble cause."[8] The seminary survived and continued to function under McGovern, while McMullen, still on
the seminary faculty, was given a new parish to found, St.
Paul's, and took up residence in the meantime with Patrick's
uncle at St. Patrick's rectory.

But the fatal hour was soon to strike for the seminary as
well. In the year following the closing of the university, Bishop Duggan's health collapsed and, upon the advice of his
physicians, he retired for a long retreat to Carlsbad in Bohe-
mia. "It was at the time," recalled Riordan's superior, James
McGovern, rector of the seminary,

that Bishop Duggan's brilliant mind began to show signs of incipient insanity, and his variableness of purpose and action in the administration of his Diocese was giving rise to complications which finally led to unpleasant results. . . .[9]

Difficulties mounted. The bishop was resolved not to leave the diocese's government in the hands of Riordan's uncle. Before departing for Europe, Duggan appointed as vicar general for the German parishes, Peter Fischer, the pastor of St. Peter's, to share with Dunne the spiritual administration of the diocese. He also placed Thomas Halligan, pastor of St. Mary's, in charge of the fiscal management of the diocese.[10] Dennis Dunne had been effectively shorn of his authority. Though only forty-three years of age, Dunne did have a history of poor health, but what precisely offended his colleagues, it was recalled, was that control of diocesan property had been given to a "young priest generally supposed to be incompetent in transacting business and more frequently made the butt of the bishop's table by the bishop for his incompetency."[11] The principal issue of contention was soon to center, tragically, upon the seminary which Halligan became reluctant to finance and whose direction had lately been placed under a board which included Dunne, McMullen, McGovern, and Roles.[12]

At this time, Father Patrick was deeply involved in his heavy schedule at the seminary, teaching dogmatic theology and church history eight periods a week and preparing each class with a perfectionist's care. Nevertheless, by reason of his position he found himself squarely in the midst of warring factions. The young professor noted his distress over the erratic and strange behavior of the bishop. To Father De Neve, who had appealed for payment at Louvain of bills long standing against the diocese, Riordan grimly replied that he was powerless. Even his uncle, "Dr. Dunne, the Vicar General," he added emphatically, "has nothing to do with the financial affairs of the Diocese. He received none of the money, nor has any voice in its management." The American College at

Louvain ever in a straitened condition itself, was at this moment far more secure than St. Mary of the Lake. "Our own seminary," he explained,

> with respect to money matters is in worse circumstances than you can imagine. When the temporal administrator cut off diocesan support several of the Parish priests of the city, in order that we might not be obliged to close our doors, raised a sum on their own personal responsibility. I am teaching here for one year and as yet have not received one cent of salary in any shape or form as if the Bishop thought I could clothe myself without money.

Yet Riordan was genuinely and selflessly committed to his work of preparing young priests for Chicago and professed his willingness to forego compensation if, as he said, "my teaching can be of any good to the Seminary whose continuance I believe to be of paramount importance to the interests of the diocese. We want priests badly here and if the Seminary closes I do not see how we are to procure them."[13]

These conditions sadly narrated by Patrick for his former rector were bound ultimately to provoke a disaster if no remedy was applied promptly. Eventually the Holy See was itself informed of them by the four men with whom he was most intimately associated, and there followed a sequence of tragic episodes.[14] After Duggan had left for a tour of Europe, Patrick's comrades first alerted Rome, accusing the Bishop of criminal neglect of duty, especially regarding the seminary. Evidently, too, in collecting parish assessments, Halligan had been forced to bring Patrick's uncle to the civil courts, an action which provoked the vicar general to suspend the procurator *a divinis*. Meanwhile, when the unsuspecting prelate arrived in Rome in June, 1867, the Prefect of Propaganda confronted him with the accusations, divulged the identity of the informants, and began a lengthy inquiry into the state of ecclesiastical affairs in Chicago. Archbishop Peter Kenrick of

St. Louis, Duggan's metopolitan and patron, was promptly called in to report personally regarding the complaints.

Throughout this first stage of the controversy the twenty-seven-year-old Riordan remained discreetly on the margins, supporting his uncle and seminary colleagues. The fight would be best left to the older and more experienced clerics who had position in the diocese and Roman contacts. While the Vatican had at first lent a benevolent ear to the four accusers, his uncle's own premonitions of impending disaster were well taken. Bishop Duggan, humiliated and thoroughly outraged by the charges directed against him in Rome, was determined to settle scores with those whom he considered character assassins. As soon as he reached home August 3, 1868, Kenrick went at once to Chicago, spending six days there in conducting his investigation. In his lengthy report to Barnabò, the metropolitan vindicated Duggan, declaring that the four priests had been summoned to appear before him and had failed to substantiate their charges, and, accordingly, the two closest to Patrick had performed in notably poor fashion. "Only two of them have hitherto presented themselves," Kenrick wrote,

> and they have not been able to offer even the smallest proof. . . . Messers. Dunne and McGovern left the city as soon as they heard the Bishop was to arrive; the one under the plea of ill health, the other giving no reason whatever for absenting himself.[15]

Kenrick's formidable defense of Duggan finally prevailed with Barnabò, who recorded Propaganda's satisfaction "that the accusations brought against him have been found to be false, and that its good will toward him has not in the least been diminished."[16] Barnabò had hoped to have heard the last of this affair, having strongly recommended to Kenrick that the latter as metropolitan of the province should treat such complaints, not the Congregation de Progaganda Fide. But his hopes were never fulfiled.

Meanwhile, Bishop Duggan elécted to take full advantage
of Archbishop Kenrick's benevolence. Incensed by the public
embarrassment, he quickly embarked on a policy of rigorous
and extremely severe recriminations against the four priests.
Upon his return to Chicago he not only suspended the four
culprits, who refused to retract, and removed them from office; but he determined also to expel them from the diocese.[17] Patrick was brought directly into the conflict when
the seminary was closed and the student body dispatched to
St. Francis Seminary in Milwaukee. Now a professor without
a school who had his uncle and closest friends all but banished from Chicago, the young priest had ended his teaching
career after two stormy years and was given his first pastoral
assignment. He was stationed briefly in a rural parish in
Woodstock, Illinois, and later given a new parish to establish
in Joliet.

* * * * *

This scattering of the principals, however, failed to finish
the affair, and Patrick was ready to become a more active
participant. Two developments in the last quarter of 1868
highlighted the excessive measures taken by Duggan and renewed Propaganda's interest in Chicago. Such severity first
prompted the four suspended priests to appeal at once to the
Holy See, for their future looked very dark, indeed. As advocate of their causes, John McMullen was selected to go to
Rome, and he discreetly obtained letters of introduction
from Archbishops John B. Purcell of Cincinnati and Martin J.
Spalding of Baltimore. In Rome Barnabò warmly greeted a
favored alumnus of the Urban College, assigning him to live at
the American College and allowing him to offer Mass as long
as he remained in Rome. The prospects for Riordan's comrades had brightened. "I was received in Rome as if I were
returning home again," wrote McMullen. "The Cardinal has
treated me with the kindness and confidence of a father."[18]
In his enthusiasm to assist the cause of his uncle and his
seminary colleagues, young Father Patrick inadvertently un-
dermined their position and the chances of a quiet recon-

ciliation. Scores of complaints demanding the removal of Duggan had meanwhile reached the Holy See, and McMullen's presence in Rome was having its persuasive effect, both factors already inducing Barnabò to re-assess Kenrick's recommendations.[19] Before his departure McMullen had entrusted to Riordan's care his library, manuscripts, letters, and other personal effects. Father John Kilkenny, who had succeeded McMullen as pastor of St. Paul's, Patrick had learned, had begun to circulate among the parishioners the report that McMullen had not gone to Rome but was living in Cincinnati, a "miserable degraded Priest." McMullen's friends--especially his brother James--were outraged at this false report. At James' request Riordan searched through McMullen's papers. With a little more heart than head, the young pastor allowed James to publish a letter that his brother had addressed to Bishop Duggan. The letter, dated September 20, 1868, established McMullen's plan to go to Rome, stating simply and reverently the reason for the journey. "You have done me the honor more than once of signifying to me," it began,

> that I am sincere, honorable, and laborious in whatever I think, say or do, in all matters of importance pertaining to religion. I hope, dear bishop, that you will accord me the same kind judgment, while I state to you that I am convinced that it is my sacred duty to God, religion, and my fellow-men, to do all that I can within the bounds of truth and justice, to remove you from the bishopric of Chicago.[20]

Instead of having a salutary effect as Patrick had anticipated, the letter caused a major sensation. It was now public that McMullen was working in Rome not merely for the restoration of the four expelled priests but principally to displace his ordinary.[21] This had about it the spirit of reckless insubordination. Up to this moment even his three colleagues, wishing merely to retain a foothold in the diocese, had been reportedly unaware of McMullen's direct intentions against Duggan.[22] In self-defense, the indignant Bishop of Chicago took prompt action by having printed a circular that he released to the daily press. It contained a translation of his earlier vindication sent to Rome by Kenrick and Barnabò unreserved acceptance of the verdict.[23] It was intended that this publication should demonstrate how the Holy See had already—with McMullen still en route to Rome—taken "the wind out of the sails of that gentleman, who has thus taken a long journey for naught."

The news of the stormy controversy had filtered eastward, and the impression soon arose that Patrick and his young confreres were part of a broadly based conspiracy against ecclesiastical authority. In the New York *Tribune* a very well-informed correspondent interpreted the controversy as basically a conflict between conservative and progressive factions within the church. Duggan's adversaries, it was claimed, "do not stand alone, unsupported by authority other than their own. . . . McMullen and McGovern, who were Roman-trained, were said to represent the new "American spirit" which was infusing itself into Catholicism in the United States; and Rome must, as the solution, remove this country from its missionary status and thereby reduce considerably the power of the Bishops, which is made absolute on foreign mission ground, while elsewhere it is much restricted."[24] The anonymous article alarmed a number of ecclesiastics, notably John McCloskey, Archbishop of New York, who perceived in these successive events a breakdown of discipline among some of the younger priests. As he told the Archbishop of Baltimore, he feared that "the hopeful clique whose sympathizers are ready to act with them in more dioceses than one are chuckling . . ." at this latest subversion of authority. McCloskey vowed never to send another student to Rome if Propaganda tended to sustain its alumni against their bishops.[25] It was at this time, too, that Archibishop Martin J. Spalding began to reconsider his recommendation of and association with Riordan's confidant, John McMullen. "I fear we were both a little hasty in giving that letter of introduction to Dr. McMullen," he confided to Purcell. "It really amounted to nothing, but I understand he has attached great weight to it. . . . His cause is lost. Roma locuta est." Patrick was unknowingly included in Spalding's final grave comment to Purcell: "I fear he and his colleagues are dangerous men."[26]

The Holy See was not to be neglected in this latest development. Bishop Duggan did not add Patrick to the list of suspended priests but had immediately forwarded to Propaganda McMullen's letter which the young pastor had allowed to be published. The printed letter seriously jeopardized McMullen's position at the Holy See, and he wrote to Patrick for an explanation. Advised in these new circumstances to make a complete confession to Barnabò, McMullen confessed his ignorance of the recent publication of his letter. For the first time, however, he candidly affirmed his chief responsibility in the whole affair. Although Patrick's uncle was the ranking accuser, McMullen acknowledged that he had directed the resistance movement.[27] Though Patrick Riordan's blunder had provoked a minor crisis in Rome, it had forced McMullen to face the issues squarely, making him submit a full and frank exposition of his views and a history of the controversy. His refreshing candor could hardly but win a measure of approval from Propaganda. Eventually Riordan's explanation arrived in Rome with its attempt to exculpate McMullen from any complicity in the publication. It was not, however, an entirely persuasive performance. Suspicions still lingered within Propaganda that such a controversial item could never have reached the secular press without McMullen's consent.[28] Rumors circulating wildly in and out of the diocese at home compounded the confusion; and many of the Chicago priests questioned the motives of their suspended confreres.

While the position of Patrick's colleagues was rapidly deteriorating, Propaganda was startled into more decisive action by a second unexpected development related to the young priest —the tragic circumstances surrounding the death of his beloved uncle. For some time Dennis Dunne had been afflicted with a heart condition. This had so weakened him lately that when Duggan had returned home and first summoned the accuser, the vicar general could not attend this meeting. Patrick would doubtless never forget the day when, after the suspension, his uncle was compelled to turn his parish over to

another priest, and to move from St. Patrick's possibly to the
home of Patrick's own parents some little distance from the
rectory. There were certainly few moments of joy among the
Dunnes and Riordans in the fall and early winter of 1868 as
they watched Dennis' grief over his disgrace hastening the
end. The Holy See was notified of his last days by an alumnus of the Urban College, Louis Laitner, the paster of Dixon,
Illinois, and one whom Rome accepted as an impartial observer. A few days before Christmas the priest who had administered the last sacraments sent for Bishop Duggan who
came with another to serve as a witness, expecting that his
former vicar general was about to issue a retraction before
dying. No doubt Patrick was present for the extraordinary
exchange to follow—an incredible scene that would be
remembered forever. On his death bed, Dunne remained
unchanged and pronounced firmly that his course of action
had been for the good of the church and of religion.
"Thereupon, the Bishop," narrated Laitner for Propaganda,

> instead of comforting the dying man by com-
> mending his spirit to the Creator, tried repeatedly,
> even to [Dunne's] last breath, to extort from his
> mouth the desired recantation, and in so doing,
> provoked an uproar to the scandal of those present
> when he saw that he would not succeed in his
> efforts. This we learned from the Priests present
> and it is said that the Vicar's brother wanted to
> throw the Bishop out of the house. Thus dies a man
> pious, charitable, and zealous, a man who after
> many years of work in the missions died not only
> with the censure of the Bishop upon his back and
> with the loss of his office of Vicar but also in such
> poverty that the clergy and people paid for his
> funeral.[30]

The funeral of Father Dunne, the Holy See was to learn
later, was conducted on the Sunday following Christmas at
St. Patrick's, the church which he had built, and the ceremonies evoked the love and unfeigned respect which the com-

munity held for him. Long before the beginning of the Requiem Mass which Patrick could have celebrated, one press report stated, every inch of the large building had been occupied, leaving hundreds, possibly thousands, on the streets. "Few men were more beloved by our citizens at large than the deceased." The press account alluded to Bishop Duggan's conspicuous absence from the obsequies which, it was said, was "much commented upon, and in many instances called for angry imprecations on the head of that Functionary. Especially was this feeling noticeable among the clergy who openly expressed their dissatisfaction. . . .".[31] According to Laitner's report to Propaganda, the procession to the cemetery was even more extraordinary. Following the body were seventy carriages and some 3,000 people who included non--Catholics and the highest public officials. On the days following these sad events, respectable Catholics in each quarter of the diocese had given expression to their disgust with the bishop, cursing him, calling him a cruel tyrant and a dolt unworthy of the episcopate.[32] Apparently Duggan, now well aware of a rebellion germinating against his authority because of his harsh treatment of Dunne, frantically sought some means to conciliate his enemies and to quiet the murmurs and discontent rapidly encircling him. On the day following the funeral, according to another report to Rome from McGovern, Duggan appointed Patrick Riordan, the nephew, as pastor of St. Patrick's Church, the parish, as it was said, "from which Father Dunne had been driven, in order to make some reparation. . . ." Only four days later, on December 30, 1868, he removed Patrick from his important assignment "for the simple reason that someone told him that Father Riordan had spoken badly of him—which is false."[33]

The Holy See persisted in its efforts to achieve a peaceful settlement of these difficulties, persuading Bishop Duggan to accept the three suspended priests and to place them in new stations within the diocese.[34] But the attempt to calm the discord seething in Chicago failed when Duggan's questionable management of diocesan finances became known and when he betrayed signs of behavioral disorder by twice attempting to take his life. Eventually in the spring of 1869,

Archbishop Kenrick as the metropolitan undertook the unpleasant mission of removing his protégé, Bishop Duggan, and
returning him to St. Louis to be placed in a mental institution administered by the Sister of Charity. "The insanity
of the Bishop of Chicago is but too true," wrote Kenrick in
sad acknowledgement.

> He is now in St. Vincent's Lunatic Hospital in this
> city whither he was brought in Thursday last. The
> first symptoms, that I know of, were exhibited by
> him after the death of Dr. Dunne with whom he
> had a trying interview a few days before. I hoped
> that travel would relieve him and as the symptoms
> were mild and had passed away, I induced him to
> go to the South, and planned to visit Havanna with
> him. On his return to Chicago, he discovered that
> a petition was in circulation . . . [addressed] to the
> Pope, to have the temporal administration taken
> from him. . . . Reports . . . were also in circulation,
> that the opponents [sic] of the Bishop were about
> to bring forward other and more serious charges
> against him, may have reached his ears. The result
> is an entire break down of one of the finest intel-
> lects I have ever known. [35]

This   bishop's   removal,   it was hoped,   would   end the
quarrels in Chicago, for there was little chance of his recovery. "Bishop Duggan is at the Asylum, Bishop William
McCloskey of Louisville told Purcell, "hopelessly gone men-
tally." [36]

* * * * *

For a priest of only four years, Patrick Riordan had already been at the center of a lifetime's share of ecclesiastical
conflicts, and he would see much more. The removal of Bishop Duggan merely marked the opening of a second stage in
the discontent within the Church of Chicago. For the factions
which had arisen during the first crisis now fixed their atten-

tion on the naming of a successor. Spalding and Kenrick seriously discussed the matter, but they tended to delay since Duggan's condition might hopefully improve and since, too, the Archbishop of St. Louis had been long preoccupied about first securing a coadjutor for himself.[37] As metropolitan, Kenrick had been considering a recommendation of Thomas Foley, Spalding's own chancellor in Baltimore and of Francis Silas Chatard, Patrick's student prefect at the Urban College and the current rector of the American College in Rome.[38] When Kenrick was in Chicago to remove Duggan, he had named Thomas Halligan as administrator, the young priest who had been Duggan's own procurator and whom Riordan's friends viewed as an incompetent. It was a selection that renewed the old dissension in the diocese, Halligan refusing to restore the three priests to their former parishes and McMullen telling Barnabò that conditions had remained as deplorable and dangerously unsettled as before. [39] Meanwhile, Propaganda was receiving elaborate petitions featuring long lists of priests' signatures and naming candidates to succeed to the vacant See of Chicago. Apparently Patrick was in charge of gathering the endorsements favoring McMullen as quickly as possible. The young priest sent to Rome, written in his own hand, a list of sixty names out of a possible ninety that supported the McMullen candidacy, a list which had at its head the names of two known alumni of the Urban College, Thaddeus Butler and Louis Laitner. It was almost impossible, Riordan regretted, to secure the actual signatures of all the Chicago priests since they were scattered throughout the broad reaches of the diocese. The remaining names, he promised, would be forwarded shortly.[40] The petition recommending McMullen did not stand alone; soon there was forwarded, again with Riordan's name attached, a list in favor of Peter Corcoran, the pastor of Wilminton, Illinois.[41]

Father Riordan's petition pressing McMullen's candidacy did not please the bishops who were watching Chicago carefully. Kenrick caught wind of it and forwarded confidential reports about it to Spalding.[42] "I have not been able to find out who the individual was," Bishop John Luers of Fort Wayne informed Spalding from Chicago, "that drew up the

petition in favor of Rev. Doctor McMullen; this much I have
learned that it was done by his most intimate friends and
with his full knowledge and approbation."[43]

The Holy See was even more distressed, for the
differences in Chicago, it appeared, were now evolving into a
second and even more serious crisis. Propaganda was first
surprised and genuinely alarmed to find affixed to the two
petitions signatures of reputedly responsible churchmen. This
question of succession was evidently either creating two
distinct factions within the diocese, each with its own
nominee and each ready to compete with the other; or these
priest signatories were usurping for themselves the righright
to present episcopal candidates to the Holy See, an exclusive
right which did not belong to them.[44] Secondly, the
congregation was in a quandary as to how to investigate and
crush this schism seemingly budding in Patrick Riordan's
Chicago. Archbishop Kenrick was in disfavor for several
reasons, most recently because his indifference and
shortsighted support of Bishop Duggan had helped the
disorders to grow disastrously in the diocese. On June 6,
1869, Pius IX granted to Cardinal Barnabò the power to
name any archbishop in the United States who enjoyed the
confidence of Propaganda and who could make a personal
report on Chicago.[45] This mission, Barnabò acknowledged,
was extremely delicate and dangerous; any slight
mismanagement could provoke greater problems in both
Chicago and St. Louis. For the first time the Holy See must
have an authentic, trustworthy report regarding this
long-troubled area. The prelate chosen for prudence and
dexterity was Martin J. Spalding, the Archbishop of
Baltimore.[46]

The cardinal prefect's strategy succeeded admirably. Spalding's diplomacy had won the support of Kenrick who
promised to lend any assistance and even to meet Spalding in
Chicago during the investigation. The investigation avoided
all public antagonism. In his report, however, Spalding severely repudiated the efforts of Patrick and his colleagues. The
root origin of the Chicago discord, argued Spalding provocative-

ly, was avarice: a number of the priests, particularly the older ones, were seeking certain parishes, not where they could best serve souls but where they could quickly accumulate a fortune. In discussing Duggan's successor, Spalding regretted the possibility of losing to Chicago his own chancellor, Thomas Foley, although he adamantly opposed the nomination of Patrick's champion, John McMullen, as "an immense evil." The petition which Patrick had forwarded to Rome, said Spalding, "means little; this kind of document is easily prepared. There are those who signed it through friendship, others through fear of offending, others through *self-interest,* others through various motives; it is of little value."[4 7] On September 27, 1869, the tormented Diocese of Chicago, it was hoped, would begin a new, brighter chapter with the appointment of Thomas Foley of Baltimore as Coadjutor Bishop-Administrator.[4 8]

A cautious man who through his life was uncomfortable with recording his opinions candidly, Patrick Riordan left not so much as a word that described his intimate thoughts during these critical months. Nevertheless, his reactions would most likely be reflected much later in the two priests who were closest to him during the conflict, remote yet certainly interested and well-informed observers — John Lancaster Spalding and his brother, Daniel Riordan. The younger Spalding had not evidently shared the views of his Uncle Martin on the Chicago troubles and his sympathies surfaced dramatically in 1881, at the dinner following the consecration of John McMullen as the first Bishop of Davenport. All the speakers, so reported Archibishop Elder of Cincinnati, including the newly elevated bishop, "had carefully avoided any allusion to the painful events of 1868 &c." But decorum yielded when, as Elder put it, "our good friend of Peoria broke thru all this becoming reserve and extolled the Bishop for his conscientious and fearless advocacy of what was right, and his faith in [leaving the consequences to God]"[4 9]

Time heals most wounds. Four years after Spalding's tribute offered a fuller but more restrained comment. The younger Father Riordan had followed his brother to Louvain and had been ordained in Belgium on May 22, 1869, the month in which Bishop Duggan had been relieved. Curiously, however, Father Halligan as the diocesan administrator did not summon the newly ordained home but allowed him another year in Europe, not enrolled in a graduate program but simply traveling through Germany and Italy.[50] Daniel's information therefore depended on news from family and friends. Sixteen years after Duggan's removal, Daniel Riordan elaborated his understanding of these events for a writer who was preparing a biographical sketch of his successor, Bishop Thomas Foley. "If there is to be any allusion to the events which let to the retirement of Bp. Duggan, etc., and the appointment of the Administrator and Coadjutor," wrote Riordan,

> I trust that these events will be placed in their proper light and that no blame shall be charged to the innocent. . . . I trust too you will not overdraw the picture of the disordered condition of the diocese at the time of the appointment of the Bishop [Foley]. The Clergy and people were united and working together for the one great purpose. The whole trouble originated in Bp. Duggan, and he was not responsible. His mind was affected, its impaired condition being due to a bodily ailment of long-standing. Without this there would have been no trouble of any kind. [51]

No doubt this gentle judgment was shared by his priest brother who had lived through every moment of the long trial but who at the time of its writing had moved from the scene of unhappy memories to another arena of conflicts and opportunities. Yet, within five years of ordination, fixed traits had already emerged in Patrick's character. Clashes were not sought out, nor were they evaded, regardless of the intensity or danger. Fidelity to friends was a paramount virtue, even at the risk of antagonizing authority. His judgment was usually sound, but at certain pressure points discretion yielded to impetuous and heedless action. By 1870, with all his strengths and weaknesses, Father Riordan was — at the tender age of twenty-nine — a tested veteran of a minor war within the American Church.

The transition from Duggan to Foley coincided with the wars of Italian unification. At the heart of the movement was Giuseppe Garibaldi whose red-shirted warriors had made attempts to take Rome and despoil the Pope of his historic domains. Little wonder that several American prelates perceived a kindred spirit of rebellion in Chicago. As clouds darkened over Italy and mid-America, it was that special student of Chicago affairs and the occupant of America's premier see, Martin Spalding of Baltimore, who made the connection. Churchmen must watch, he noted, the "Garibaldian tendencies" of Patrick and his generation.[52] The young man's road ahead was yet filled with twists and sudden turns.

3

... Now That Bill Is In

When Bishop Thomas Foley was installed in the Cathedral of the Holy Name on March 10, 1870, Father Patrick Riordan was nearing the completion of his fifth year in the priesthood. In this remarkable half-decade the young priest had been exposed to the inner trials and intrigues of a great diocese. The youthful idealism evoked during happy days at Louvain was tempered early by the realities of clerical conflict that touched not only his closest friends but the heart of his own family. He had rapidly matured as a priest, having accepted in quick succession the varied roles of professor, pastor, and controversialist. Patrick had survived this ordeal, but his future seemed very bleak indeed. Fortunately, however, the new administration opened a new stage in Chicago's ecclesiastical history, a welcome interval of tranquility and harmony. Foley, the city's first native American bishop, faced a gigantic problem of nearly chronic and ubiquitous discontent, and he promptly embarked upon a well-measured plan of reconciliation. The troubles which he had inherited did not annoy or bewilder the new bishop who ever remained a judicious and impartial manager. "A great change was noticed shortly after his arrival," recorded Daniel Riordan, who was to serve as Foley's secretary and chancellor.[1]

In this new climate, those like Patrick who had been allied with McMullen were not kept long in a state of humiliation or disgrace. McMullen himself, though not restored immediately to the bishop's council, was given, on October 29, 1870, the rectorship of the cathedral, the first important appointment in the new regime. His two colleagues were appointed to important pastorates outside the see city, Joseph Roles to St. Mary's Church in Rock Island and James McGovern to Holy Trinity in Bloomington.[2] A pastor, serving still in Joliet, Patrick was not long overlooked and was soon returned to the city of Chicago, when, in his thirtieth year, he was named in June, 1871, the pastor of St. James' Church.[3] Off to a promising start, Bishop Foley's administration would restore peace and efficiency to the diocese. "All things are going on as well as I could hope for," Foley reported to his beloved former superior, Martin Spalding. "I am beginning to know my work and my men, and when I get things well in hand with God's help, I trust all difficulties will pass away."[4]

St. James' Parish, the ninth established in the city, had been erected in 1855 when Bishop Anthony O'Regan appointed Father Thomas Kelly to organize all the English-speaking Catholics on the south side. At this time, sixteen years before Riordan's appointment, there were some twenty families living in the vicinity of St. Agatha's Convent of Mercy at the corner of Calumet Avenue and Twenty-sixth Street, an orphanage that later developed into Mercy Hospital. Father Kelly had held his first services in the convent enclosure until 1858 when he raised a frame church on Prairie Avenue and Twenty-seventh Street which became known as the "Mother Church of the Southside." Through the years, succeeding pastors had enlarged the original structure and built a rectory, and in 1871, Patrick Riordan became the fifth pastor of St. James and was to direct its development for over twelve years.

Father Riordan had hardly been installed in his new assignment four months when disaster struck Chicago.[5] On October 8, 1871, a fire broke out near the lumber district on the west side. The majority of the city's buildings were frame structures, a vast collection of ideal fuel made bone-dry and particularly combustible after a notably hot summer. In such conditions, the fire soon raged beyond all chance of control, quickly becoming a holocaust fanned by a high and veering wind and leaping the river to the south and north sides. When its fury was finally tamed after twenty-seven hours, the fire had demolished nearly 18,000 buildings and left some 90,000 people homeless. The Catholic Church at the outset of Bishop Foley's promising episcopate had suffered losses estimated at one million dollars. Churches, convents, schools, institution–the labor of two generations–had been suddenly consumed. In the midst of such broad devastation, the new pastor of St. James had been very fortunate. As the conflagration was spreading to the south side, its onrushing blaze was checked early by the use of explosives and Riordan's church was spared.

But Chicago, the "Garden City" that had built a commercial empire through aggressiveness and increasing enterprise, had not been mortally wounded by this tragedy. Chicagoans faced their losses with characteristic resilience, and introduced Patrick to invaluable lessons of rehabilitation that he would draw up elsewhere a third of a century later. A vast system of relief was organized, attracting generous contributions from all parts of the world; and, in the busy years that followed, a new Chicago began to arise from these ruins, a new and greater city of brick and stone, larger and wealthier and more prosperous. Bishop Foley was among the first civic leaders to work actively for the city's restoration by promptly dispatching a number of his priests on missions to collect funds. Within the week, John McMullen left for the Northeast and chose Patrick as his companion. "I have been very busy in procuring and distributing supplies," McMullen told a friend, "busy as ever in my life. This evening I leave with Father P. W. Riordan for New York, and we will collect through New York and New England. Dr. Butler with another takes Maryland and Pennsylvania; Father Roles goes to the Pacific Coast; others to Cincinnati, and others to St. Louis."[6] The tour took the two priests well into New England and even as far north as Halifax, Nova Scotia.[7] But Patrick's mission was too urgent and rushed even to allow a brief visit of his origins at Chatham, only 266 miles away. Helping thus to rebuild Chicago with his fellow-citizens, Patrick was unwittingly profiting from the experience, preparing himself for the day, thirty- five years later, when he would behold another city devastated by earthquake and fire. In the restoration of this city he would take a commanding role.

In the 1870's Father Riordan settled down quietly to the business of building St. James' Parish. In a strange twist of fate, the Great Chicago Fire had blessed his parish. For some years previous to the disaster, people of wealth and position were flocking into the parish, and the sand dunes and brush of the south side were being pushed back by brick and frame cottages. Proximity to Lake Michigan and to the business center of Chicago had made this locale a favored residential district. The fire of 1871 had destroyed large areas of the north side and thereby diverted people southward, making the area within St. James' Parish even more desirable. These swelling numbers, Riordan found, were overcrowding his frame church on Prairie Avenue. To meet the demands of the hour and to accommodate his fast growing congregation, he decided to relocate the parish in a more central site. In 1873 the *Western Catholic* printed this inconspicuous announcement: "Fr. Riordan of St. James has secured a site and intends building a new church."[8]   Eventually replacing the old wooden church was a large stone edifice rising slowly on the corner of Wabash Avenue and Twenty-ninth Street. There were serious handicaps in attempting such a project in these times: the effects of the fire were still evident in Chicago's recuperating economy, and the severe panic of 1873 momentarily halted the progress of construction. Nevertheless, through the tireless energy of the pastor and the generous response of his people, the cornerstone was laid in 1876, and on May 23, 1880, the new St. James was dedicated, a handsome Gothic Church built at the cost of $75,000 and long remaining a city landmark.

The dedication was an eleborate ceremony, with Bishop Joseph Dwenger of Fort Wayne officiating and Riordan's collegemate, Bishop John Lancaster Spalding, delivering the sermon. Spalding's theme subtly reflected the common scholastic roots which he had shared with the pastor. His thoughtful and carefully prepared address, "Religious Thought and Physical Science," discussed in heightened tones the scriptures and Darwinism, pointing out how there could be no valid conflict between science and the Church. But Spalding used the occasion also to underscore his genuine affection for Patrick and Louvain. "It fills my heart with joy this day," he concluded,

> to see this glorious temple consecrated to God. Many years of my life have been associated with your worthy pastor. We walked together in the shadows of that old university where science and religion walked hand in hand and where we lived with that grand old mother of our souls and enlightener of all our ways. [9]

As an administrator, Patrick was known in those days to be perhaps the most successful pastor in Chicago. To raise funds, he never yielded to such schemes as parish fairs or picnics, but simply invited each parishioner to pledge in monthly installments what he could afford. This method, accordingly, distributed the financial burden equitably within the parish and kept the debt at the barest minimum.[10] But as far as time would allow the work to progress under Riordan, the new church was unfinished. Patrick fully intended in his later years to complete the central spire and to install the chimes, permanent altars, an organ, and the pulpit. But he was forced three years later to leave these precious tasks to his successor, Father Hugh McGuire.[11]

Patrick Riordan's twelve years at St. James were a critical stage in his long life, a welcome interval in which he quietly grew into priestly maturity. They were gentle, peaceful years. No longer was he the priest student at Louvain distracted by graduate studies; gone, too, were those tragic years at St. Mary of the Lake and in Joliet when he was caught up by divisions within the diocese and the punishments heaped upon those whom he loved. His times at St. James were those in which he could be fully a priest, possibly for the first time in his life, devoting himself wholly to building his temple of worship and to shepherding the flock committed to his care. These years at St. James, he confessed always in later life, were the happiest of his life, ". . . too beautiful to last, and I have never ceased in memory to bless them."[12]

Throughout his life away from Chicago, Riordan watched closely the activities of the parish. Though miles away and involved with other responsibilities, Riordan took an unfailing interest in the choice of his successors. Father McGuire, the first priest who replaced him and administered the parish for twenty-eight years, was in Riordan's opinion, "a most zealous priest in the highest sense of the word." He rapidly climaxed the building program, and on May 26, 1895, Riordan returned to St. James and consecrated the edifice. McGuire not only completed his predecessor's blueprints but succeeded in a more ambitious educational program than Riordan's. In August, 1884, nearly a year after his departure Patrick's elementary school was finished and opened for instruction; and McGuire in time enlarged it and added an impressive high school. "No one could have succeeded me at St. James," Riordan told Bishop Thomas Conaty, Rector of the Catholic University of America, who preached McGuire's eulogy,

> who gave me greater pleasure than Father McGuire. I put the best part of my life into that parish, and in the Church, and I was naturally interested in having someone to carry out the work along the lines marked out by myself, and he was just the man to do it.[13]

When he soon learned that his cousin, Father Patrick W. Dunne, was appointed the next pastor of St. James, Riordan was delighted. In a nostalgic mood he sent his warmest congratulations to Chicago. For Father Dunne, the old ex-pastor described with tenderness and care his sentiments regarding the parish. "I cannot tell you how much pleased I am," he wrote,

> that you, who are so close to me by blood relationship, should be named Pastor of the church which I built myself years ago, and which absorbed the best years of my life and activity.
>
> Of course the parish is much changed from when I worked in it, and nearly all the old parishoners and friends have moved elsewhere, but it is still very dear to me. I remember distinctly the morning when I turned up the first sod on the vacant lot. It was the feast of the Sacred Heart in the month of June, and we had no resources with which to build the church except my youth and energy, to which the people responded most nobly. I never visit the city without paying a visit to the church and thanking Almighty God that I was instrumental in erecting so noble a building to His honor and glory.[14]

Patrick Riordan cherished his parish. As a true pastor, he loved those clerical and lay people with whom he worked at St. James. It was the old friends of St. James that he had taken closest to his heart; and later it was the old days in this beloved parish that were most often on his lips.[15] At the silver jubilee of one of his former curates, Father Dennis Tighe, he sketched the relationship which had commenced between the two when the young priest was first assigned to assist him, only twelve days after his ordination. It was more a partnership. "We lived in old St. James, not as a superior and an inferior," Riordan recalled, "but. . . we lived together, from the first day to the last, as two brothers, united in a common work and for the benefit of a common cause." In genuine esteem for his first superior, Tighe attributed whatever success he may have enjoyed in twenty-five years as a priest to what he termed the "apprenticeship . . .

spent with an ideal priest as my pastor, whose lessons, taught by example, have ever since left on my mind an impression of what a good, edifying, zealous and self-respecting priest ought to be."[16] At St. James, Patrick Riordan earned the respect and affection of the laity as well, forging among certain distinguished citizens of Chicago bonds of friendship which would break only in death. One close friend from these days was Adolphus W. Green, a leading attorney in Chicago who specialized in corporation law and who later in 1905 took charge of the National Biscuit Company in New York City.[17] Dr. John Guerin was another, who served as an active supporter of the parish. Irish-born, Guerin had taught science at the University of St. Mary of the Lake until its extinction, and he had taken his medical degree in 1868. A powerful civic leader, he was at death the oldest member of the city's school board.[18]

The most celebrated of these early friends was Michael Cudahy, the Irish-born magnate who had revolutionized the meat-packing industry. In the early 1870's he had moved to Chicago, accepting a partnership in Armour and Company and superintending the company operations at the Union Stock Yards. Through this decade, while Patrick was organizing and building, Cudahy was pioneering the epoch-making innovation of applying refrigeration to the curing of meats. Ties of affection between Riordan and Cudahy thus began in Chicago and deepened once the latter retired in Pasadena, California. "Outside of my brother," Riordan would confess many years later, "there was no one in the world nearer or dearer to me. . . . He had for me a sincere and true friendship, and I think that I reciprocated it fully."[19] In his last years far away, one of Patrick's great crosses was the occasional news that one of these beloved ones had passed away. He cherished to the end these memories and associations, and it deeply pained him to see them fade in the course of time. In his twilight years, he often epitomized these regrets when he mused: "All the old friends are dropping off, and there are very few now left whom I knew when I was in Chicago."[20] Toward the end, one theme repeating itself in his thoughts was that during his last visits to Chicago he felt "almost a stranger in what was once my own city.["21]

* * * * *

In the late years of his pastorate at St. James, Father Riordan was given the opportunity of witnessing the phenomenal growth of the Church in mid-America, a growth which would ultimately affect his destiny. As a pastor he was not intimately engaged in these events, but he watched from afar with immense interest this astonishing process around him. These developments in the late 1870's and early 1880's were eventually to shape his own future and that of his close friends in the hierarchy. A series of three developments had yet to take place before Father Patrick would be considered for an episcopal appointment. While still recovering from the great financial panic of 1873, the bishops of the Province of St. Louis were anxious that the church should keep pace with eastern progress and sought to consolidate the province. Confidently, therefore they sent to the Holy See a list of momentous recommendations, suggesting the immediate erection of new dioceses and of new ecclesiastical provinces. New sees, Propaganda was advised, should be created in Peoria, Leavenworth, Omaha, and Denver, and vicariates apostolic in Northern Minnesota and Montana. Two new ecclesiastical provinces were requested: one at Milwaukee which could comprise the dioceses in Michigan, Wisconsin, and Minnesota; and the other one at Santa Fe which would include Denver and the Vicariate Apostolic of Arizona.[22]

At the provincial meeting, Bishop Foley had succeeded in impressing his fellow bishops that a new see should be erected out of his own booming diocese and be located at Peoria. The promising area already numbered over fifty churches and some 80,000 faithful and whose see city would be one-third Catholic.[23] The division which brought the Diocese of Peoria into existence was long delayed, but finally in late 1876 Foley's duties were substantially relieved when Pat-

rick's school friend, John Lancaster Spalding, was named its
first bishop.[24] On May 1, 1877, the two Riordan brothers
attended the consecration of their collegemate and beloved
friend in St. Patrick's Cathedral, New York City. Although
Patrick had no leading role in the ceremony, his brother
Daniel, now the Chancellor of the Diocese of Chicago, read the
bull of appointment.[25] It was a rite that Patrick was never to
forget. One could hardly anticipate that Riordan's loyalty to
his episcopal comrade in Peoria would later be tested to the
point of breaking and that the exultant joy remembered in
spring, 1877, would eventually dissolve for Patrick to feelings
of sharp poignancy. Nearly four decades later and in his se-
venty-third year, he recalled for his brother in melancholy
tones the striking scene in which both had witnessed Spalding's reception of the mitre. "I was thinking last night of this
very day thirty-seven years ago," he wrote moodily,

> when I was present at the consecration of poor
> Archbishop Spalding at the Cathedral in New
> York. It seems a life time ago when I look back on
> it, so much has been crowded into these thir-
> ty-seven years. All the friends who were with me
> that day are gone except the Archbishop and my-
> self, and we are not in the very best health and
> strength.[26]

At the time, however, Spalding's appointment to Peoria
was of paramount importance to Riordan and to his colleagues. For the first time since the Duggan affair, there
would be active in the Province of St. Louis a prelate who
knew intimately from his Louvain background at least two
priests of Chicago and who alone had professedly sym-
pathized with John McMullen. The fortunes of Chicago actually improved after Spalding's appointment; and it would
be the young Bishop of Peoria who would be the key instrument in bringing Patrick to the episcopacy and to the Pacific
Coast.

Spalding's admission to the provincial councils in St.
Louis was only the first of three developments that would

climax in Patrick's promotion. For Father Riordan who had, as a young priest, identified himself with Dr. McMullen, there was yet to be settled decisively the problem of vindication by Rome. Bishop Foley, it was true, had himself acknowledged the high motives of those who had opposed his predecessor, duly restoring them to positions of dignity within the diocese. Bishop Duggan, however, had had his ecclesiastical origins in St. Louis and had been a favorite of Archbishop Kenrick. As long as Chicago remained within this province, the Holy See would hardly receive an official recommendation of McMullen, Riordan, and their associates, particularly on a list of episcopal candidates. Ironically, the impasse was dissolved at Bishop Foley's death. When the fifty-one-year-old prelate died on February 19, 1879, having on his death bed named McMullen as diocesan administrator, Propaganda confronted a new series of uncertainties relating to Chicago, fortunately of a different nature from those which it had faced a decade earlier.

With the death of Bishop Foley, the bishops of the province were summoned to St. Louis to discuss the vigorous Church in Illinois and in the Mississippi Valley generally. The most important recommendation sent to Rome was that the See of Chicago should be elevated to archiepiscopal status, becoming the center of a new ecclesiastical province which would include as suffragan sees Alton and Peoria. Such a proposal would insure Chicago's independence of St. Louis. To achieve this, the bishops suggested that James Duggan, still living in St. Louis as the nominal Bishop of Chicago and showing no sign in the past ten years of recovering his mental balance, should be given a titular see and a comfortable pension of $2,000 a year. Next was the question of who should be named to the new metropolitan see. Shortly after Foley's death, the diocesan consultors and irremovable rectors of Chicago had submitted to the bishops' council the names of three candidates for the vacant see. The ballot was to reveal the mind of the Chicago clergy. John McMullen, the vicar general who had been consistently missing from several previous lists compiled at St. Louis, received a nearly unanimous endorsement of ninety-six votes. His younger associate, Patrick Riordan, appeared for his first time on a *terna*, named second with thirty-three votes; and Patrick J. Conway, who had succeeded Riordan's uncle as pastor of St. Patrick's, was given last place with twenty-six votes.[27] But memories were long in St. Louis. No Chicago priest had ever appeared on a St. Louis *terna* except Patrick's brother, Daniel. In the previous year, he had been named at Spalding's insistence for Council Bluffs, Iowa, a newly proposed and ill-conceived see to be separated from Dubuque.[28] The bishops of the province thus discarded this latest list of Chicago candidates and dispatched to Rome a new one which was headed by a former rector of the archdiocesan seminary at St. Louis, Bishop Patrick A. Feehan of Nashville.[29]

The cardinals of Propaganda examined the proposals very carefully. Chicago had accumulated such a checkered history that raising it to a metropolitan see could be hasty and premature, granting to it a dangerous sense of independence. Yet the facts could not be challenged. As a commercial emporium and an immigrants' center, it had rapidly evolved into "one of the first cities of the world." Its Catholic population had grown phenomenally to a total of 230,000 souls despite the scandals and divisions during Duggan's episcopate. In regard to Catholic numbers, in fact, Chicago was inferior only to the Archdioceses of Baltimore, Philadelphia, New Orleans, and New York. The proposal met with favor at Propaganda; and on August 29, 1880, Pope Leo XIII created the new Province of Chicago, naming Patrick A. Feehan as its first archbishop.[30]

Chicago's elevation to the rank of a metropolitan see was the second step in the direction of total vindication of the priests who had publicly opposed Bishop Duggan's regime. As Archbishop Feehan inaugurated his administration, he evidently elected to renew his predecessor's policy of quiet conciliation. He reappointed McMullen as vicar general and Patrick's brother Daniel as chancellor and secretary. Nevertheless, there remained in the archdiocese an anonymous but articulate group who had not been reconciled to McMullen and his associates whom they secretly defamed through lurid and scabrous letters to Rome. The unidentifiable "several priests of Chicago" welcomed Feehan's arrival, for it ended what they described as the scandalous McMullen administration. "Very Reverend Dr. John McMullen, Administrator, Rev. Patrick Riordan, and Rev. Joseph P. Roles," they argued in part,

> must now stop their champagne suppers which they had so very frequently during the interregnum. We have heard some lay people talk of their mid-night carouses at which they played cards and drank their bourbon whiskey and french wines to one and two and sometimes three or four o'clock in the morning. These men scandalized Religion by the abuse and vituperation which they flung, through the infidel Press upon the Church Authorities, when they denounced poor Bishop Duggan, and went from mission to mission stirring up sedition, to the grief and shame of all true Catholics. They eventually finally drove the Bishop mad. He is now hopelessly insane in a hospital at St. Louis. These men Dr. John McMullen, Rev. Patrick W. Riordan, and Rev. Joseph P. Rolles [sic] are leaders of a clique or ring (seven or eight) of priests with them composing the body — these seven or eight are remarkable for nothing but being their underlings or satellites. The object of this clique or quasi-secret society is to hamper and fetter the action of the Bishop or Archbishop and by every other influence corruptly endeavor to ensnare him in their toils, and make him entirely subservient to them, and thus render his life miserable. We have seen what they did to Bishop Duggan.[31]

Within a fortnight, another sensational report followed to Cardinal Giovanni Simeoni, new Prefect of Propaganda, charging that these three favored pastors, "that ring which gave such scandal to Catholicity in former times, and still threatens . . . ," had for years defaulted on paying their diocesan taxes. "These Reverend gentlemen," continued the second letter,

> could afford to get up costly champagne suppers, smoke choice cigars, and while away the time card-playing, but could not afford to pay their diocesan taxes. Whereas the poor, honest conscientious priests who struggle hard to support good Catholic schools . . . , and who find it difficult to make ends meet, strive, even by pinching themselves, to pay their diocesan taxes. . . .[32]

These anonymous communications disturbed Simeoni sufficiently to prompt him to request Feehan to report as quickly as possible on these "very many and very grave" accusations. The prefect considered the charges as spurious since, he said, McMullen and Riordan had already been mentioned for the episcopate, but he revealed his plans to resolve the slightest doubt within the congregation before these two names were again proposed to the Holy See.[33]

Rome's final vindication of McMullen, Riordan, and their colleagues was slow in coming, but it was eventually achieved in 1881 when the forty-nine-year-old vicar general was named the first Bishop of Davenport.[34] It was an extraordinary nomination in that bishops of St. Louis selected a priest residing beyond its jurisdiction, in the new Province of Chicago. In this way they gave the first tangible sign that McMullen had been forgiven for his exposure of Bishop Duggan. No one welcomed this promotion more than Patrick Riordan; this was the second of his closest friends elevated to the episcopate. For the prospective consecration in Chicago on July 25, the new prelate assigned to the pastor of St. James a place of particular honor which reflected the bond and affection between the two: Riordan was one of the two chaplains to Bishop McMullen.[35] This happy conclusion bore deep significance for Riordan's own future. It had been a painful

experience from the sad beginnings at St. Mary of the Lake
to this evident acquittal from censure in McMullen's elevation. This was the climax of a graduated process of justi-
fication of those priests who had risked their reputation and
the severest recriminations and dared publicly to oppose
what they perceived to be the unfortunate policies of their
ordinary. McMullen's fortunes, since he was the leader and
soul of the movement, best measured the stages whereby
these priests gradually achieved unreserved vindication. Probably Daniel Riordan had best described his brother's sentiments of fulfillment as he assisted the newly consecrated
bishop at the Cathedral of the Holy Name on that feast of St.
James the Great:

> In the East particularly there was and perhaps is a
> strong feeling against these priests with whom Bp.
> Duggan quarrelled. But no men were activated by
> higher motives in their actions than were these
> priests in their efforts to have Bp. Duggan re-
> moved.[36]

* * * * *

Riordan's eighteen years in the Archdiocese of Chicago
had led him to some of the gravest ecclesiastical crises of his
generation. Only the strangest and most illogical chain of
events would bring this midwesterner to the Pacific Coast.
His parochial success at St. James was bound likewise to
recommend him for advancement and fortuitously entangle
him in the long and wearing effort to provide a successor for
Joseph Sadoc Alemany, Archbishop of San Francisco. Curiously, the nomination of a successor, normally a fairly
prompt and predictable process, was to prove a formidable
problem for the Spanish-born prelate, a problem that would
drag on for nearly one-third of his lengthy episcopate.[37] Involved would be a number of outstanding younger members
of the American hierarchy, and eventually the fortunes of
time and need would bring Patrick to the Golden State.

Even after the division of the old Diocese of Monterey, in 1853, the Archdiocese of San Francisco still comprised an enormous area, including all the territory between the Colorado River and the Pacific Ocean and between Pueblo San Jose and the Oregon border.[38] This sprawling territory stretching over northern California and parts of Nevada was nearly half as large as France, and Alemany was spiritually responsible for the whole of it. The continuous growth of the state, particularly in the northeast mining belt, and the difficulties in communication and visitation had prompted his first thoughts of a coadjutor. As early as 1859, he sought the counsel of various prelates as to whether he should request the Holy See for a coadjutor or for another division of territory. The erection of the Vicariate Apostolic of Marysville in 1860 lightened Alemany's burden, removing from his care three-fifths of the archdiocese.[39]

But Alemany's prompt success in obtaining help in the scattered mining region was not so handily repeated in his later attempts to secure his own coadjutor. As early as 1868, he had expressed his intentions to retire from San Francisco, hoping to spend his remaining active days in his native Spain, where he planned to establish missionary colleges to train priests for Spanish America.[40] When his fourth list was rejected, Propaganda hesitated to direct Alemany to begin a fifth time, wishing to end the unpleasant business and to salvage one candidate from the score already proposed for San Francisco. On July 4, 1882, the cardinals of Propaganda reached the decision to urge Patrick Riordan's friend, John Lancaster Spalding, to accept the coadjutorship, and if he refused, to appoint Bishop John J. Kain of Wheeling.[41] At this point it was highly unlikely that a relatively unknown pastor in Chicago would be named to succeed Archbishop Alemany.

While the Congregation de Propaganda Fide had been for eight years stymied over the choice of a successor for Archbishop Alemany, it had also experienced minor difficulties in other areas of the United States, significantly in the southern sees of Nashville and Charleston.The name of Patrick Riordan

appeared seriously as an episcopal candidate. At the time of
Bishop Feehan's promotion as the first Archbishop of Chicago in 1880, the Diocese of Nashville had been joined to the
Province of Cincinnati and remained vacant for three years.
On July 27, 1881, Archbishop Elder and his seven suffragans
convened in Cincinnati and recommended Patrick Riordan as
second choice for Nashville. Among the comments on his
character the Cincinnati bishops noted that Riordan was
known to have "built a great and most beautiful church in
Chicago" and had been a most successful pastor in both spiritual and temporal administration. Inquiries on his fitness had
solicited only the most enthusiastic approval, and the bishops
concluded by saying that they believed he "had already been
proposed for Chicago and other dioceses."[42]

But after thirteen years the shades of the Duggan affair
still tracked Patrick. Two weeks after the official list had
been dispatched to Rome, Archbishop Elder as acting metropolitan submitted his own views, though after so many years
isolated in Natchez he carefully confessed he knew none
of the candidates personally. While Riordan was unquestionably qualified for the episcopate, an unnamed informant who
was not a suffragan of Cincinnati had brought it to
Elder's attention, after the provincial meeting, that there was
"some suspicion that Father Riordan had participated in the
conflict against the Bishop (Most Rev. Duggan) in 1868." A
scrupulous churchman, Elder had immediately communicated his misgivings to Archbishop Kenrick who was well-versed
in this affair and who replied that he knew nothing against
Riordan, reckoning that in 1868 he was a younger priest and
had taken no active part against Duggan.[43] In any case, the
Holy See judged it expedient to request a new list for Nashville.[44]

During these lengthy negotiations Father Riordan was
also seriously considered for Charleston which had been vacant since the death of Bishop Patrick N. Lynch in February,
1882. On March 22, the bishops of the Province of Baltimore
made their selections for this historic diocese.   Again Patrick occupied second place on the list.[45] Reports of Rior-

dan's place on this *terna* had already circulated broadly, even
as far as Davenport, where his close friend, Bishop John
McMullen, learned the news from Bishop Kain. Curiously,
McMullen reacted with a provocative suggestion which he
sent to the Metropolitan of Baltimore. He recommended his
old schoolmate at the Urban College, the ill-starred Edward
McGlynn of New York, to replace Riordan's candidacy. "You
most Rev. Archbp. know Father P. Riordan well," he told
Gibbons,

> and I know of no one who would be likely to make
> a better Bp. than Father P. Riordan — a graduate
> of Louvain — a successfull [*sic*] worker, a good
> priest, in every respect. But why not appoint Dr.
> McGlynn, Bp of Charleston. There is a big debt
> there, if I understand rightly. Well, Dr. McGlynn
> will be more likely to pay that debt than any Bp.
> of the country. It is true that he went in debt in
> N.Y. but it will be quite different when his mission
> is to pay debts. He is a truly spiritual man, and will
> sacrifice himself for the good cause. Appoint him
> by all means and his heroism will not let him re-
> fuse.[46]

What prompted this curious exchange is a mystery. Perhaps
McMullen preferred to see his comrade in Chicago advanced
to another, more prominent see. Riordan nonetheless remained Gibbons' favorite. To assist the Holy See in its selection, Gibbons had been requested to elaborate upon the attitude of the bishops toward each candidate. In response, the
Archbishop of Baltimore confidently described Riordan as
one who possessed all the "virtues required in candidates for
the Episcopal burden."[47]

* * * * *

Despite the tributes, Patrick Riordan was to reach the
episcopacy by the most circuitous route. In the summer of

1882, as his star was fast rising over Charleston, the Holy See was applying heavy pressure on his friend, John Lancaster Spalding, to accept the post in San Francisco. In July, Cardinal Simeoni strongly urged him to bow to the decision of Propaganda, even if the congregation's reasons to move west did not seem to him to be sufficiently sound. "Your praise and merit," advised the prefect gravely, "will increase considerably if for the benefit of the Church you follow the will of the Em. Fathers. I do not doubt that . . . you will send to me as soon as possible a reply of acceptance. . . ."[48] The subtlety of the tones had not beclouded the force of this request. As soon as this message reached Peoria, Spalding seemed to have gone into a state of mild panic, frantically drafting letters to Simeoni, Gibbons, and Alemany. It would be difficult, if not disastrously impertinent, to decline for a second time the promotion as Alemany's coadjutor. Spalding was well aware of the prolonged difficulties regarding this appointment, and the Holy See, hard-pressed and anxious to settle the succession, appeared determined to assign the gifted Bishop of Peoria to San Francisco. But Spalding's attitude had not changed. In devising his respectful refusal, he shrewdly suggested a substitute, namely, his collegemate from Louvain. First, he had to forestall Patrick's appointment to Charleston. Immediately Spalding sent to Gibbons, whose assistance as metropolitan he needed in this personal crisis, the firm suggestion that such an appointment would be a great mistake since Riordan had the capacity to fill a more important post. A second mistake, he insisted, would be to induce himself to leave Peoria and to accept the coadjutorship under Alemany. His present responsibilities in Illinois exceeded his ability, and his conscience would not allow him to go to San Francisco. "Now I have a wide acquaintance with the priests of the U.S.," continued Spalding,

> and I know no one so well suited to the position of Co-adjutor for San Francisco [than] the Rev. P. W. Riordan. Of course I do not imagine that you will think of proposing his name to the Archbishop;

but his appointment to Charleston would shut out
all hope of getting him into a position where he
can do far more good.

In closing, Spalding mildly warned Gibbons that if Riordan
were named to Charleston he would more than likely decline
it, an indication that Riordan had already discussed this prospect with him.[49]

Thus it was Bishop Spalding who, through indirection,
made the first association of Riordan's name with the Archdiocese of San Francisco. On the day following his letter to
Gibbons, he submitted to Cardinal Simeoni his regrets at
being unable to yield to the wishes of the Holy See. The
California climate, the Prefect of Propaganda was told, would
impair his health already delicate and poor. After more than
five years of work and struggle in his new diocese, he planned
to journey to Europe for a rest and, he promised, he would
visit the Eternal City, where he hoped to explain more fully
in person to Simeoni the several reasons for his position on
the coadjutorship. "If it is not officious on my part," he
concluded, "I dare say that the Rev. P. W. Riordan of Chicago is the man most worthy of the post of Coadjutor to San
Francisco and is most capable of filling its needs"[50]

The last recommendation of the Bishop of Peoria, however, was technically inappropriate since Patrick had never
been officially considered for Alemany's succession. According to Propaganda's decision of July 4, Spalding's written
refusal should have automatically given this important appointment to the Bishop of Wheeling and destroyed any
chance of Riordan's coming to the Pacific Coast. But John
Kain's notorious brusque manners had already so offended
Rome that the congregation confidently decided that before
they would proceed to send the bull to Wheeling, they
wished to gather more data on his fitness. While there seemed
to be no question of Kain's exceptional ability and fitness for
San Francisco, Bernard McQuaid, the fulminous Bishop of
Rochester, firmly disapproved of his promotion. In a
thoughtful reply to Propaganda he revealed a close under-

standing of the peculiar conditions in northern California, submitting a report that did not injure Spalding's championing of Patrick Riordan. The important Archdiocese of San Francisco, he pointed out, needed a "skillful Prelate . . . possessing a certain independence of character, who would not contentedly allow affairs to go along on their own course, but who would be ever ready to direct and lead. . . ." This unusual see, isolated in the West which formed an empire in itself, had a mixed and curious population because it was formed of a great many nationalities. Harmony among such divergent elements, judged McQuaid, could be achieved only by an American who could be just and impartial to each group. In distant California, where suffragans were known to have occasionally antagonized their metropolitan, the archbishop must not only be a man of virtue but, too, he must possess serenity and prudence as well as courage and consummate diplomacy. John Kain, he insisted, was too young and inexperienced to govern such an important and complex see as San Francisco. The Bishop of Wheeling, in McQuaid's opinion, was "childish in his manner, frivolous in spirit, and lacking this dignity and gravity in his behavior so necessary to impress the Clergy and the People." The one prelate who conformed to his ideals for San Francisco, McQuaid concluded, was a sophisticated Roman-trained prelate and Riordan's old prefect at the Urban College, Bishop Francis Silas Chatard of Vincennes. While McQuaid never promoted Riordan's candidacy directly, his unflattering commentary succeeded in eliminating Kain. His comments, noted Propaganda, corresponded exactly to the impression which Kain had left with some ecclesiastics during a visit to Rome.[51]

While the problem of San Francisco's appointment had again been momentarily halted toward the end of 1882, the movement for Riordan's assignment to Charleston grew increasingly stronger. By September seven long months had passed since Bishop Lynch's death, and Archbishop Gibbons was impatient to see the diocese filled. Prompted by his anxiety for Charleston and by Spalding's recent letter on Riordan's fitness for San Francisco, Gibbons wrote to Simeoni urging action and recommending the appointment of the pastor of St. James' Church. Spalding's intervention had not had the desired effect on the Archbishop of Baltimore, who now all the more wanted the Chicago priest in his own province. Gibbons repeated for the cardinal prefect that Riordan was altogether worthy of the episcopate and the Diocese of Charleston. "Lately, I received a letter from a Bishop of the Province of Chicago," he wrote, "who, in extolling the gifts and virtues of this Candidate, judged him to be both worthy of becoming a bishop and fit to rule any diocese even the greater ones."[52]

Early in 1883, Bishop Spalding, who had completed his fifth year in the Diocese of Peoria, arrived at the Holy See for his first *ad limina* visit. There he made himself available for direct consultation on matters related to the United States. His presence in Rome then was opportune for Patrick's future and for the Church in California. During five critical days of January, Propaganda made determined attempts to reach satisfactory decisions on Charleston and San Francisco. Into Rome had come McQuaid's letter championing Bishop Chatard and confirming Propaganda's doubts about advancing Kain, as well as the glowing recommendation of Riordan by Spalding and Gibbons, the former for San Francisco and the latter for Charleston. On January 11 the congregation appointed Henry Northrop, Vicar Apostolic of North Carolina, to Charleston and had all but assigned Riordan to the vicariate just vacated. At the same session, the cardinals could reach no decision over San Francisco, some electing Kain, others wanting another *terna*, and five voting to consult Spalding then in Rome.[53]

In the meantime, Spalding had been given a gracious reception in Rome, where he had been received by Leo XIII on January 14, and where he found everyone eager to hear about the United States. His views on Riordan were bound to have their effect; and his timely influence might be seen in Propaganda's next decision on January 15. After a lapse of four days, the congregation committed to Northrop the responsibility of the Vicariate of North Carolina and decided to delay a decision on San Francisco in order secretly to ascertain Archbishop Alemany's opinion on Riordan and Chatard.[54] A week later, Spalding was still in the dark as to the effect of his intervention, but his role was clear. "They do not insist upon my going to San Francisco," he wrote to John Ireland, Coadjutor Bishop of St. Paul, "and I have urged them to appoint our friend who I conscientiously think would be the better man."[55]

Meanwhile, the weary Archbishop of San Francisco welcomed the latest proposal from Rome, having been spared the ordeal of again hunting up candidates; and in one of the most important letters of his busy episcopal career, he made his choice. Chatard of Vincennes would not suit his archdiocese, he replied, because he reputedly did not have much talent for temporal administration, and too, it was felt that his "elevated manners" would annoy and alienate a great many westerners. Riordan, however, seemed to be the favorite, evidently a "superlative administrator who is averse to debts, an excellent preacher, learned and good-living, zealous, esteemed and respected by all." Bishop Spalding had already written to Alemany the previous August, explaining his refusal to come to California and urging Riordan's appointment in his place. "I would believe," added Alemany, "that the opinion of Monsig. Spalding carried great weight, for I know him well many years." Earlier in the year, Alemany had accidentally come upon the considered views of Bishop McMullen, who had been stricken with a terminal malady and had spent a few weeks in the West. The Bishop of Davenport seconded Spalding's suggestion, contending that Riordan was "most fit to govern a great diocese like that of San Francisco . . . ," at the same time helpfully submitting to Alemany a written report.[56] Alemany's enthusiastic acceptance of Patrick Riordan ended a long winter campaign which had begun nine years earlier. On June 18, 1883, the Sacred Congregation appointed Riordan coadjutor to Archbishop Alemany with the right of succession, and this Leo XIII approved and sanctioned on June 25.[57]

Evidently, there were few secrets in Rome. Making his quinquennial report to the Holy See at this time was another celebrated young prelate who, like Spalding, had declined the assignment. Only a week after the congregation's decision, on June 25, the very day on which Leo XIII sanctioned the promotion, Bishop John Keane of Richmond caught wind of it and at once dispatched the good tidings to Baltimore. "And so San Francisco is provided at last with a coadjutor in the person of Father Patrick Riordan," he reported to Gibbons with unfeigned relief. "I trust he will accept, and that so an end will be put to this long vexed question."[58] Five days later, when Cardinal Simeoni in Rome had hardly addressed an official letter to Alemany informing him of Riordan's appointment, the Chicago press broke the news to the public. The *Monitor* of San Francisco sniffed at the item suspiciously, unconvinced that this frustrating affair had at last reached its climax. The editor cautiously alluded to it "merely as a matter of news, not that we are credulous enough to take it by any means as true." Catholics of the West have been victimized by overzealous newspapers, recalled the writer, having already raised a score of ecclesiastics to the presidency of the archdiocese,

> ... and it is only necessary to remind *reflecting* Catholics that Rome moves slowly but surely in all such matters, and it is very, very rarely that she permits even Chicago to dictate to her whom she shall select for the Episcopate.[59]

In the meantime, Patrick Riordan was at first aware only of the public accounts, professing his disinclination after twelve years to leave his beloved parish. When Edward Sorin, C.S.C., Superior General of the Congregation of Holy Cross, prematurely congratulated him Riordan expressed his thanks. "I know nothing of the appointment," he added, "except what I have seen in the papers, and would not be at all displeased should it prove to be a mere rumor. I am perfectly happy where I am and had no thought of being disturbed.[60] In late July, Archbishop Alemany was the first to learn officially from Cardinal Simeoni who was so delighted with this arrangement that he could not wait to send first the apostolic bull. Thereupon, Alemany immediately published the appointment in the *Monitor* [61]

After nearly a decade of searching for a coadjutor, the Archdiocese of San Francisco was disposed to give the archbishop-elect a generous welcome. In mid-September, a week before Riordan's consecration, Alemany circulated a pastoral letter to be read in all the churches on the appointment, warmly describing the event as ". . . a day for many years expected and desired by us, not so much for our partial rest as for the welfare of the Church." The coadjutor's consecration, Alemany continued, bespoke the "unexampled vitality of the Church and the goodness of the Holy See to provide a young pontiff in the decline of the archbishop's life." Riordan's election came now as a "previous present from the hands of the Vicar of Christ and of Christ Himself." One characteristic of the new coadjutor's background which particularly impressed Alemany was his opportune training in Europe, whereby he had become, the letter claimed, an accomplished linguist and would thus be able to shepherd the various national groups in the archdiocese. [62]

In early August, both Archbishop Feehan and Father Riordan were formally notified by Simeoni. In his acknowledgement, the latter accepted the appointment with this pledge:

> Although altogether unequal to such an important office, I hope nevertheless that with the help of divine grace, I may faithfully discharge my work . . . and may never leave anything untried so that our divine Religion, scattered in these regions which embrace the province of San Francisco may ever grow and increase. [63]

The bulls arrived ten days later, announcing Riordan as titular Archbishop of Cabasa in Egypt. [64] The archbishop-elect chose his own parish church of St. James as the scene of his consecration which took place on September 16, 1883, with

Archbishop Feehan as the consecrator. One friend to whom
Riordan had been conspicuously devoted was missing from
the solemnities, namely, John McMullen, who had died at
fifty-one on the previous July Fourth. The Bishop of Davenport had certainly anticipated his comrade's elevation, for he
had given to him a plain pectoral cross which Patrick would
wear nearly every day for the next thirty-one years.[65] St.
James' Church was thronged to its capacity. Some 1,500
tickets had been issued but fully 2,400 persons were present and occupying every inch within the vast edifice. Archbishop Alemany did not attend the ceremony but sent in his
place his secretary, Father George Montgomery, who acted as
chaplain to Riordan. The ceremonies began shortly after ten
o'clock, lasting four hours. At the conclusion of the consecration rite, John Lancaster Spalding, the prelate whose written appeals and timely presence in Rome had probably been
the determining factor in Riordan's appointment, delivered a
short and eloquent sermon. At one point he detailed his personal relationship with the newly consecrated. "The man to
whom has been given the episcopal vestments," he proclaimed vividly,

> had been associated with my life in the most in-
> timate and tender manner; otherwise I would not
> now stand before you, for it was upon earnest
> solicitation that I consented to appear. When in
> the springtime of his youth, he left home, true and
> honest and upright, believing in the holy Catholic
> Church, I met him in a foreign land, and found him
> always noble and true, as marked for his senti-
> ments as for his learning. And for five years so he
> proved, sincere in his faith, true in all he did, earn-
> ing ecomiums from those with whom he was
> brought in contact without seeking the praise of
> those who were his superiors, but quietly and con-
> scientiously discharging all his duties. Oh, that
> God-like privilege of youth — the faithfullness,
> the feeling of dependence, the vigor of mind and

of body, the enthusiasm! This young man never
changed. He grew in my life and became so sweet
to me . . . . Since we first met, we have exchanged
no protestations of friendship, going each his own
way, seeking nothing from the other. Still, it is
not without emotion that I see him here, believing as he does, starting afresh to do the work of
God.

Despite his own refusal to come to California, Bishop
Spalding, highly articulate champion of colonization and efforts to redistribute Catholics out of the teeming cities and
into the more abundant farmlands, perceived on this occasion
great promise in the territory to which Riordan was assigned.
"The great province of the mighty West," he called it, "rich
and undeveloped, whose healthy air may be breathed, where
new life is imparted in bathing in the God-given sunshine.
. . ."[66] Present at the festivities was Patrick's mother Mary.
One unnoticed but cherished ceremony was her presentation
of a gift to her son, a gold watch inscribed, "From My
Mother," a memento which he would hold dear for the rest
of his life.[67] Indeed, the day was to become a legend of
sorts: Riordan was long thought to be the first American
priest raised directly to the rank of "archbishop" and the
first to be consecrated in his parish church.
    His days in Chicago fast drawing to a close, Archbishop
Riordan bade a simple, unaffected farewell to his congregation at St. James on October 1, preaching on the virtue of
faith and imparting a final blessing.[68] Before leaving for his
new post, he visited, on October 28, his *alma mater*, the
University of Notre Dame, where he was presented with a
gold chalice. On the following day he departed from Chicago
for San Francisco in a special train provided by the Cudahy
family. His large entourage including his brother Daniel,
Fathers Edward Sorin, C.S.C., and John A. Zahm, C.S.C., of
the University of Notre Dame; his old comrade, Father
Joseph Roles, pastor of St. Mary's Church in Chicago; and
Father Benedict Spalding, Bishop Spalding's brother and
Chancellor of the Diocese of Peoria.[69] Archbishop Alemany

did not wait until Riordan would reach San Francisco to welcome him personally to the archdiocese. As his coadjutor traveled westward, the sixty-nine-year-old prelate proceeded to Ogden, Utah, in the eastern extremity of the archdiocese. There with Father Lawrence Scanlan, who administered this territory, he met Riordan and his companions. The young coadjutor was deeply moved by the archbishop's extraordinary courtesy in coming to the borders of his jurisdiction to greet him. "I am only following a tradition of the Spanish people," Alemany was remembered to have replied, "that when a prince visits a province, he is always met at the frontier."[70] This encounter in Ogden on November 3 was the first time these two churchmen had met, and they remained one day in the city to visit the local Catholic institutions. Their next stop was Salt Lake City where, on Sunday, the congregation of the little church of St. Mary Magdalene experienced a rare solemn service as Riordan celebrated a pontifical Mass and Alemany preached and introduced his coadjutor.[71]

Once arrived in San Francisco, Patrick Riordan was presented to the people, preaching at the cathedral soon after to an overflowing crowd who wanted a first glimpse of their new spiritual leader. Later a large number of clergy and laity, numbering nearly 200, gathered at St. Mary's College. After the banquet, John Prendergast, representing the clergy and laity, welcomed him to his new home, describing in a particularly moving way, the unalloyed joy with which the archdiocese could receive its new archbishop. The appointment of a young prelate has so often brought with it an accompanying sense of sadness and gloom, remarked Prendergast, since in the transition there were "recollections of a glorious life brought to a close," either by death or by physical exhaustion. Frequently the old bishop was worn out with labors, long years having traced their mark upon the brow and perhaps the intellectual powers were "somewhat decayed, owing to the cares and anxieties of his episcopal office, so that an appointment of this kind is only a half joy to the people. . . ." But on this occasion, there was nothing to mar or compromise the joy of the Catholics of San Francisco. The senior archbishop was alive and alert, appearing, as Prendergast said, to "grow younger as he grows older. . . ." Why was it, asked Alemany's vicar general, necessary to appoint a coadjutor? "It is because there is more work to do," he answered emphatically,

> because new churches have arisen on every side, because the number of Catholics has increased, that our venerable Archbishop needs the assistance of a coadjutor to fulfill the duties of his high position. . . . Again, I beg to greet our most reverend coadjutor Archbishop. He crossed the Sierras and became a citizen of our State; we wish to take him now to our hearts to testify to him our affection and esteem, to promise our fidelity and our prayers, and wish him many years of happiness in this glorious land of California.[72]

While formal greetings and comments were solemnly exchanged these days, one member of the new archbishop's family reflected a more whimsical attitude toward the honor. His cousin, Peter Finley Dunne, one of the widely read humorists and political commentators of his day, the creator of "Mr. Dooley," whom Riordan had baptized at St. Patrick's, was only a sixteen-year-old high school student at the time of the consecration. Not a practicing Catholic in later life, Dunne recalled a visit which he had with his older relative, Patrick William, and noted the necessity that his branch of the family produce its share of episcopal leaders. "He is a creditable member of the family," Dunne told his sister puckishly. "We [Dunne's] need a few archbishops to keep up the average now that Bill has come in."[73]

PORTFOLIO 1

Bishop James Duggan in 1861

Courtesy of Diocese of Davenport, Iowa

John McMullen as Bishop

Courtesy of Msgr. Francis J. Weber

The Young Archbishop

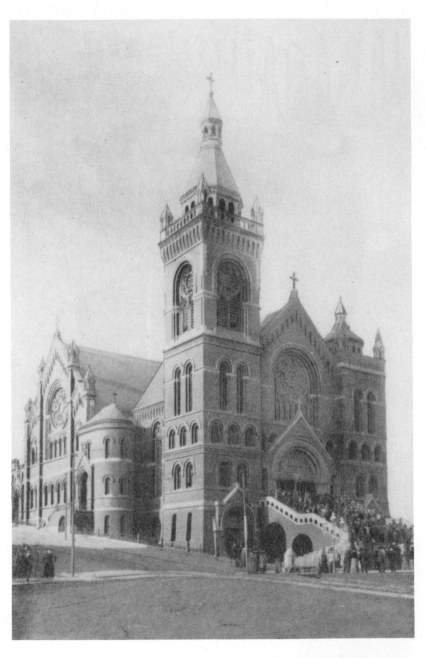

St. Mary's Cathedral

St. Thomas Aquinas Seminary
Mission San José, California

St. Patrick's Seminary
Menlo Park in 1898

The Archbishop at the Seminary Dedication, flanked
by Monsignor Prendergast, Bishop Montgomery,
Bishop Grace and Father Vuibert

Father Henry Amans Ayrinhac, S.S.
Rector 1904 - 1930

Bishop Francis Mora

Bishop Thomas J. Conaty

Bishop Thomas Grace

Reverend Denis Kiely

Bishop Lawrence Scanlan

Bishop George Montgomery

Bishop Patrick Manogue

Bishop Eugene O'Connell

Courtesy of Nevada Historical Society

Courtesy of Rev. John J.

4
Chicago Gothic

The arrival of a second archbishop in San Francisco naturally aroused curiosity. Who was this midwesterner newly transplanted to the West, the first native of North America destined to rule a California diocese? Contemporaries noted that in him dignity did not bring with it a finicky fastidiousness and was somehow harmonized with an unaffected simplicity. Even on solemn occasions Patrick seldom wore all the vestments of the episcopal office. During his long years in San Francisco, a whole generation of Catholics would grow up never to see an archbishop's skull cap and buskins.[1] There was more, however, than his easy adjustment to Western casualness. The press and several welcoming testimonials had highlighted his priestly spirituality, his success in building and organizing, his eloquence and charm, his effective ways with the laity. But these qualities were publicly attributed in some degree to most prominent ecclesiastics of the period and scarcely distinguished the essence of Patrick Riordan. Even the lengthy confidential appraisals sent to Rome were less than satisfactory in unveiling the real character of this man. But almost at once Propaganda was to be given glimpses into this remarkably complex and reserved individual.

There would be no question, Rome was first to learn, that Riordan would not allow himself to be eliminated from national affairs. The remoteness of San Francisco was certainly one of the factors which dissuaded several of the

most gifted ecclesiastics of Riordan's generation from
accepting Alemany's invitation to succeed him. Such a move
westward might deprive them of an effective voice in national
issues. While Riordan never demonstrated any personal
ambition to move eventually to a more prominent see in the
East, even when the opportunity would present itself in
Chicago, San Francisco during his episcopate would be heard
on public and confidential issues beyond its boundaries. Even
before he was given his own diocese, Patrick Riordan did not
hesitate to intervene in an extraordinary situation well
outside his jurisdiction in which he had no proper place and
his counsel had not been solicited. Throughout his three
decades as a bishop, Riordan devoted serious thought to
appointments to the episcopate, ever ready to comment on
candidates and one of his earliest acts in his new role was to
disqualify one whom he believed unfit for promotion.

Riordan had been consecrated hardly four months when
on his own initiative he interceded on the question of succession in the Diocese of Davenport where McMullen's death
had left a vacancy. In his first letter to Rome from San
Francisco, Patrick displayed this sturdy determination that
his removal to the Pacific Coast would not isolate him from
the Church's development elsewhere in the United States.
Rumors were circulating in the press and by word of mouth
that Father Patrick Conway, vicar general of the Archdiocese
of Chicago and its administrator in Archbishop Feehan's
absence, had been proposed to succeed McMullen. From his
Chicago days, Riordan was well-acquainted with Conway,
who had preceded him as pastor of St. James and was now in
charge of St. Patrick's, the historic parish where his uncle had
been pastor for fifteen years. Possibly, Riordan explained to
Cardinal Simeoni, this rumor favoring Conway's promotion
had no foundation, but it would be of no harm to "prevent
in time an elevation to the Episcopate which would be a
scandal to the good and zealous Priests of the diocese of
Chicago and disastrous to the good of the Church of Davenport." For the present, he declined to elaborate his motives
for this protest against Conway's candidacy. "I have known

him for twenty-five years," he wrote, "and I am not deceived in my judgment of his character." As long as the good of religion did not force him, the young archbishop preferred to keep to himself the counts which disqualified the vicar general, but "if there is a question of naming him a Bishop," he told the prefect with conviction,

> I would not hesitate to give your Eminence such grave reasons which would make his nomination impossible.
> I well know that he occupied a very high position in the Church, that is to say, that of Vicar General of the great and rich diocese of Chicago. How and why he has been raised to this important position, I cannot explain without entering with details which would serve no purpose. I therefore take the liberty of asking Your Eminence, if there be a question of his promotion, to inquire of me the reasons of my protest.[2]

The young prelate had no right to comment on the Davenport succession since he was not a member of the Province of St. Louis. And as long as he failed to specify charges against Conway, no response was forthcoming from Cardinal Simeoni. The only comment that can be made of the source of the archbishop's grievance is that there is no evidence to link it with the Duggan affair. During that crisis Father Conway had not openly aligned himself against Riordan's friends, and as pastor of St. James' Church he had even signed Patrick's celebrated petition in favor of McMullen as the best prospect to succeed Bishop Duggan.[3] Whatever his secret reasons, more likely they were not directly associated with the memory of McMullen or Dennis Dunne; nevertheless, they were important enough to prompt Riordan to pursue his communication to Rome without detailing the complaint. The rumors persisted and alarmed Riordan into writing four months later to Rome a second appeal which was neither solicited nor acknowledged.[4] At the same time, Bishop Spalding supported his efforts at blocking the nomination. He, too, had been disturbed by the newspapers, and in a confidential letter to Propaganda he described the vicar general as a "man of little knowledge, one who is said to be almost ignorant."[5] These reports from San Francisco and Peoria may have had their effect, for the Holy See appointed as Bishop of Davenport, Henry Cosgrove, the administrator of the see since McMullen's death. This scrupulous care regarding episcopal advancement both in his state and beyond would characterize Patrick Riordan for the next thirty years.

But problems in the Midwest never superseded the immediate question of Archbishop Alemany's retirement. As soon as the young coadjutor had been settled on the Pacific Coast and had undertaken his first tour of the many institutions of the archdiocese, Alemany began the negotiations with the Holy See for his withdrawal. In late October, even before he had met Riordan, the old prelate had been anxious to resign in favor of the younger man. A third of a century earlier, he had accepted his position only out of obedience, and he was now impatient to conclude his active episcopal ministry. "Since the [coadjutor] is relatively young, lively, learned, prudent, and able to manage affairs," he informed Simeoni, "I believe that he could easily rule this diocese by himself and that my presence and advanced age could serve him but little, and possibly even disturb his efficient administration." With these generous sentiments, Alemany professed his readiness to leave.[6] He was physically fit, a doctor having recently assured him that he would live another twenty years. But the old archbishop strongly preferred to leave his American home and to spend his last days in a Dominican convent or college in Spain, guiding young novices[7] But the prefect absolutely refused to consider Alemany's immediate departure from San Francisco and conceived a compromise. Since Riordan was as yet unaccustomed to the archdiocese, it would be far more opportune, Simeoni shrewdly observed, that Alemany for the present govern through the coadjutor; and for this purpose, the prefect allowed the archbishop to delegate all his faculties to Riordan. "In this way," said Simeoni, "Yr. Ex. will be able to enjoy the desired rest and be useful to the Church with your wisdom and experience." Later there would come the acceptable moment to withdraw entirely from the burden of administration." [8]

As it turned out, this arrangement continued satisfactorily until early July, 1884, when simultaneously Propaganda dispatched an inquiry to Riordan regarding Alemany's withdrawal and the latter mailed from San Francisco his formal resignation. Anticipating that Alemany would soon make another attempt, the congregation wished to learn from the coadjutor whether in his judgment he had acquired sufficient experience and familiarity with the archdiocese to undertake its management himself.[9] Cardinal Simeoni had timed his inquiry well, for one week after his letter to Riordan was posted for San Francisco, Alemany took the bold step of addressing his resignation directly to Leo XIII. He had borne episcopal responsibilities for thirty-four years, he said simply, and was disposed to hand them over to his coadjutor; his final days he would spend in Spain, assisting the Dominican Fathers to whom he belonged.[10]

This communication came as no surprise to officials of the Roman Curia, but before they would act upon it, they must first hear from Archbishop Riordan. As soon as the letter of inquiry was received from Propaganda, Riordan immediately drafted a lengthy report which gave proof he had not remained aloof and idle during his first months in San Francisco, and he quite candidly detailed the precise conditions of the archdiocese. First, regarding spiritual affairs, there were no exceptional problems, except the usual shortage of priests. In the city itself, only thirty-two priests served a Catholic population of 150,000, some with parishes that were too large and falling into "indifferentism." There was a critical need of priests for the German people. They numbered, observed Riordan, some 10,000 subjects of the archdiocese of whom 500 attended Mass on Sundays and holy days. A German religious congregation, possibly the Redemptorists, must be introduced for the Germans. Two religious communities, the Jesuits and Dominicans, were managing churches within the city which, Riordan recommended, should be converted into parishes, with fixed boundaries and responsibilities. All the parochial churches, excepting three, were wooden structures and hardly designed to last for a long time; new buildings must, therefore, be built of more solid materials. Reaching his last point under the rubric of spiritual affairs, Riordan severely criticized the condition of the parochial schools which, he said, were poorly constructed, too few in number, and too poorly attended. Out of some 20,000 Catholic children, 16,000 were enrolled in the public schools, and this figure, he observed, revealed a corresponding spiritual decline among Catholic youth.

Passing to a minute analysis of the temporal state of the archdiocese, Archbishop Riordan alluded to some "very grave" problems which demanded patience and labor. Recently, he had himself computed the archdiocesan debt at $600,000, apart from the additional liabilities of parishes, schools, and other institutions. The slight income, which derived from the cemetery and the Pious Fund, an endowment paid annually by the Mexican government, was scarcely enough to pay the interest. This precarious financial situation, the coadjutor urged, could be extinguished if the archdiocese kept faith with its creditors and took steps at once to liquidate its debts. In a final word, Riordan attempted not to present himself as too anxious to succeed to the See of San Francisco. "I must add finally," he carefully told Simeoni, "that although unworthy for many reasons, I am ready not to solicit the administration of this burden but rather to submit to the will of Your Eminence in all things."[11] This report would certainly win Propaganda's confidence. Riordan had not glossed over any relevant detail or spared his judgment, describing a challenge that he seemed capable and eager to undertake. Only one item now remained to be solved. In submitting his formal resignation, Archbishop Alemany had suggested an annual pension of $500, and in a subsequent message, Riordan told the congregation that the Archdiocese could easily afford such a slight sum.[12]

While Rome was moving slowly toward a decision, the two archbishops had gone east to attend the Third Plenary Council of Baltimore, which was in session between November 9 and December 7, 1884.[13] In the previous spring, while preparing various assignments, Archbishop Gibbons had asked Alemany to inform his coadjutor that he would preach on some day during the council, and this task, remarked Alemany, "I have no doubt he will do, and do it well, for he is very gifted."[14] Impressed by the archbishop's enthusiasm for his coadjutor, Gibbons decided to give to the forty-three-year-old prelate the prominent office of speaking on the final day of the council. This would afford an opportunity for the American hierarchy to view one of its newest members. A man who was unquestionably endowed with forensic ability but who was characteristically disinclined to public speaking, Riordan reluctantly accepted this invitation. "I hope that more judicious solutions have been made for the other sermons," Riordan told Father John S. Foley, one of the council secretaries. "I wish you could manage to have me appear on an off night and have an older and abler preacher for the closing Sunday."[15] Although scheduled to preach December 7 on "The Perpetuity of the Church," Riordan was taken ill and in the sequel was replaced by his friend, Bishop Spalding.[16]

Two weeks after the conclusion of the Baltimore council, Rome was ready to grant Archbishop Alemany's long-standing request. Satisfied at last that his coadjutor could rule the Church in San Francisco, Pope Leo XIII, on December 21, 1884, accepted the resignation, and one week later, on December 28, formally granted to Riordan all faculties to govern the archdiocese.[17] Returning leisurely from Baltimore, Patrick had stayed for Christmas with his brother Daniel in Chicago. He had reached Salt Lake City when he was notified from San Francisco that the Holy See had accepted the resignation and that he was to replace the archbishop.[18] Approaching mid-life, Patrick Riordan had received his last assignment, and it would last exactly thirty years. Official word of Alemany's resignation from Rome did not reach the

Pacific Coast until January 25, 1885, and the open secret
ended early the next month when the *Monitor* carried a
public announcement of his retirement.[19] Now, fully in
charge as metropolitan, Riordan petitioned the Holy See for
the pallium, the sign of full archiepiscopal authority. The
new ordinary personally thanked the cardinal prefect for the
trust which he had exhibited toward him and prayed that
with divine help he might ever be ready to succeed in this
awesome responsibility. In reply Cardinal Simeoni faintly referred to Riordan's candid report on the church in San
Francisco but expressed his confidence when he wrote,

> You know indeed that the Archdiocese is
> pressed by important difficulties, and yet I trust
> [your] prudence, knowledge, and ability of admin-
> istration. . . . shall be so overwhelming that all
> Archdiocesan business can grow and flower under
> your regime.[20]

Simeoni made arrangements to send the pallium to Riordan
and a papal bull to Alemany naming him to the titular See of
Pelusium, thus climaxing the exchange of authority.[21]

Alemany was determined to leave as soon as he heard
from Rome and the Master General of the Dominican
Fathers. "If I had my choice," he said in a press interview, "I
would rather remain here and die here than go back again to
the sunny fields of Spain."[22] Though he was welcome to
remain in California, his motives to depart were prompted
probably from a deep longing to see his native Spain before
he died and from his desire to present not the slightest interference or distraction in the administration of his successor,
even if it be only his quiet presence in San Francisco. On May
24, 1885, Patrick Riordan and the archdiocese bade farewell
to the old churchman who, in his seventy-first year, had labored for over a third of a century in California and would
spend his last years vainly trying to establish a missionary
college in Spain.

The new archbishop had thoughtfully remained in the

shadows during the elaborate farewells and testimonials addressed to Alemany. But two decades later, when an older
and wiser Riordan had more than tasted the rigors of archdiocesan administration, and his tender impressions of his
predecessor had mellowed and deepened through the years,
he submitted to the *Catholic Encyclopedia* a biographical
sketch of Alemany, recording the deep affection that had
grown while they worked together during this year and a ½ yrs
half. The article was remarkable not as a biographical exposition but rather as a reflection of Riordan's affection and
genuine respect for his predecessor. When, after a lengthy
wait, a coadjutor was given to him, "which was not until he
had reached the scriptural age of three score years and ten,"
wrote Riordan,

> he lovingly transferred to his successor the burden
> which he had borne long and faithfully for his
> Master's sake. Whilst he had ever the greatest
> consideration for the comfort of others, his own
> life was one of austerity. . . . No one ever saw him
> manifest anger; he was ever gentle, but firm when
> duty called for him. So considerate was he for the
> feelings of others that certainly he never intention-
> ally or unjustly wounded them. Most thoughtful
> and courteous in all he did, he journeyed a
> thousand miles to Ogden, Utah, in November,
> 1883, to meet for the first time, to accompany
> thence and to welcome to San Francisco his coad-
> jutor and successor. . . . From the first meeting and
> until his death the closest and tenderest friendship
> existed between them.[23]

The year 1885 offered several milestones to the Church   – 85
on the Pacific Coast. For then two new metropolitans were
due to receive their pallia, Riordan of San Francisco and
William H. Gross, who had been appointed in February as
Archbishop of Oregon City. Gross and Archbishop Gibbons
had been intimate friends since their early years in Baltimore,

and Gibbons had consented to make the trip to the Far West
to confer the pallium on Gross. Riordan, too, admired the
Archbishop of Baltimore. When Gross told him that he expected Gibbons in Portland in early September, Riordan immediately invited Gibbons to invest him as well with the
pallium, promising to fix the date so that the bishops who
would go to Portland could come on the following week to
San Francisco. Visiting ecclesiastical dignitaries being so rare
in California, the archbishop hoped to arrange an appropriate
public display for this ceremony. He told Gibbons: "I am
confident that the presence of many Prelates on that occasion will do great good to our people, and make them feel
that they are part of the great American Church."[24]

But these ambitious plans were forced to give way when
Gibbons learned in May that he would be elevated to the
cardinalate and decided to postpone the trip until after the
ceremonies in Rome.[25] Gross was willing to wait the two
years when the cardinal would make his first trip west, but
Riordan was anxious to get on with this task and, therefore,
settled for a less imposing ceremony that attracted only the
two bishops of the province and the new Archbishop of
Oregon City. On September 20, 1885, just four days past the
second anniversary of his consecration in Chicago, he received, with Bishop Patrick Manogue of Grass Valley
attending, the pallium at the hands of Francis Mora, Bishop
of Monterey-Los Angeles, the oldest prelate in the province.
Archbishop Gross, who had at one time as Bishop of
Savannah been suggested for San Francisco, preached on the
order of the episcopate, and he concluded with this
exhortation to the newly invested metropolitan:

> You are the successor of a venerable prelate who
> was dearly and deservedly beloved by his flock,
> and whose absence leaves a vacant seat in the cere-
> mony of this day. The memory of Archbishop
> Alemany will be ever in the hearts of his children
> who will not cease to thank God for his thirty-five
> years of labor in their midst. May the same merci-

ful God grant to you, dear Archbishop, who now
presides over this Diocese in all the vigor of youthful manhood, the grace and strength necessary for
the great task imposed upon you.[26]

Thus began the tenure of the second Archbishop of San
Francisco which was to last one short of thirty years. At the
age of forty-three, San Francisco was his first and last major
appointment. Patrick Riordan would remain these three
decades irrevocably identified with his beloved see, never to
resign from it, never to transfer from it, never to lose it. The
remarkable history of his appointment included the nine
years in which Archbishop Alemany failed repeatedly to have
any of those named whom he had himself placed on several
ternae, but succeeded at long last in acquiring a true
churchman who would come willingly and confidently to
continue his own work in the remote reaches of the West.
There were at first the fears in Rome of his youth and
inexperience. Archbishop Riordan had come to San
Francisco from a wealthy Chicago parish, not thoroughly
tested and seasoned in diocesan affairs as would have been
Keane of Richmond, Chatard of Vincennes, Kain of
Wheeling, or Spalding of Peoria. This was the calculated risk.
Yet Patrick Riordan began his administration, self-possessed
and unfrightened, an ecclesiastical statesman who would
move through the passage of time quietly, without excess or
flamboyance, but move productively and effectively, ever
consolidating and enlarging what had been handed to him,
willing also as a national leader *ex officio* to contribute his
experience and views to the problems and issues confronting
the American Church of his generation.

* * * * *

From the beginning, Patrick Riordan had made no secret
of his awareness of the problems and responsibilities which
he faced in this new assignment. When William J. Onahan, an
old Chicago friend from days at St. Patrick's and a prominent

lay leader, congratulated the new archbishop upon succeeding Alemany, Riordan had confessed: "The diocese is
heavily encumbered and for some years to come the burden
placed upon me will not be lightly carried." In these early
years Riordan had hoped to renew a spirit of generosity
which had all but disappeared in San Francisco and, he said,
to "kindle a love for the Church which so far has not reached
that point where a sacrifice is sweet."[27] The first three years
of his administration had largely fulfilled his expectations.
When he made his first quinquennial visit to Rome in
November, 1888, he made no effort to conceal his fervid
enthusiasm in presenting a formal report on the archdiocese.[28] There was, he informed Propaganda, an unbounded hope that the community committed to his care
would advance day by day because, he said, the "citizens of
these regions are, generally speaking, of such a peaceful
nature." Within the archdiocese lived 600,000 non-Catholics
reflecting all possible shades of belief and unbelief and, along
with them, more than 200,000 Catholics. Although these
faithful were scattered through a large territory, continued
Riordan buoyantly, they were easily accessible by land and
water for instruction and visitation; and 180 priests were
actively engaged in 127 churches and chapels, whose number,
he added confidently, "grows daily." Riordan made his
schools an important item in this first report. A troublesome
handicap in advancing the church within his jurisdiction was
the wretched poverty of the people who lacked the wealth to
sustain an extensive educational system but, said the archbishop, "this and other obstacles we are trying either to
remove wholly, if possible, or at best to lessen gradually." In
the see city and neighboring towns, there were six academies
for boys as well as sixteen for girls; and his parochial-school
system for younger children, he insisted, showed even more
promise, each "solid" parish having its own separate school
and the total enrollment in the archdiocese reaching 8,000.
In addition, Riordan proudly alluded to the Young Men's
Institute, a thriving new organization of many thousands
which spread through California and whose principal objec-

tive was to shield Catholic youth from secret and Masonic organizations. The one glaring weakness which he planned to remedy was the absence of a seminary. His theological students numbered twenty-nine, fifteen of whom were at St. Mary's in Baltimore and fourteen divided between two Irish seminaries, All Hallows College in Dublin and St. Patrick's in Carlow; but, Riordan added, he intended to take steps as soon as possible to build his own minor seminary.

These figures and exultant comments had displayed the young Archbishop of San Francisco as a man of large and ambitious projects, and Rome marveled even more at his financial skill. While he had inherited a large debt of $600,000 and was in the midst of building a cathedral, Riordan had not only met the interest, but within four years he had paid $500,000 of the principal. The remaining obligations, he promised Propaganda, "will be dissolved shortly so that there is no cause for fear or anxiety regarding the state of temporalities in the Archdiocese." Riordan's first report was an exuberant performance, and the Roman officials were impressed. His descriptions, extravagantly observed one consultor of Propaganda, were

> stupendous. His territory is a true paradise in which everything flourishes with a marvelous prosperity, and gives abundant fruit from the cultivation directed by this most vigilant Prelate.[29]

In this report of 1888, Archbishop Riordan suggested two large projects which were dear to him. They were to occupy the next ten years of his episcopate, namely the erection of a cathedral and of a seminary. Ever since Christmas Eve of 1854, the archdiocese had been served by St. Mary's Cathedral on California Street which Archbishop Alemany had built on the edge of the young city soon after taking up his residence in San Francisco. Through the years, the city had unexpectedly expanded in the direction of the cathedral which was eventually engulfed in the Chinatown district. St. Mary's had in time ceased to be the center of

Catholic life in San Francisco. Its relocation had become one
of the most pressing needs of the archdiocese. The edifice
was itself commodious, its construction having cost in its
time more than any other building in the city; but the old
Chinatown, which predated the fire of 1906, flourished in
vice, opium dens, gambling houses, and slums. In 1866
Father Herbert Vaughan, later Archbishop of Westminster,
had visited San Francisco and had been appalled at Alemany's
residence and its neighborhood. "To the left," he wrote

> are a number of little yards, and the backs of the
> windows of the houses in which Chinamen are
> swarming. Broken pots and pans, old doors.... . To
> the right adjoining the Cathedral . . . is where the
> Archbishop lives. . . . No man is more poorly
> lodged in the whole city; and no man preaches in
> the spirit of evangelical poverty, a detachment in
> the midst of this money-worshipping city like this
> Dominican Spanish Archbishop of San Fran-
> cisco.[30]

Conditions had not improved a decade later when
another visitor contrasted the cathedral to the more fashion-
able Grace Church where, he recorded, "the wealthiest and
most aristocratic Episcopal congregation in the city worships.
. . ." But only blocks away, the visitor continued, where the
Catholic cathedral stood, "the streets are lined with houses of
prostitution; and a stone's throw beyond is the Barbary Coast
reeking in infamous filth."[31] Alemany had been well aware
that to approach his pro-cathedral from any direction had
been a source of embarrassment to his faithful, and in his last
report to Rome he had acknowledged that the building was
"now located in a very inconvenient and improper place."[32]
Near the end of his administration, he found a desirable site
in the western portion of the city, and in May, 1883, he
purchased for $71,250 the northwest corner of Van Ness
Avenue and O'Farrell Street.[33]
    The gigantic task of building the new cathedral, however,

remained for the young successor who was eager to begin it as the first major work of his episcopate. Construction was not new to Riordan, for his stone Gothic Church of St. James in Chicago was considered one of the most splendid religious edifices in the area. The site chosen by Alemany was a section on an inclined slope. Less than a year after he had succeeded to the see, Riordan announced in December, 1885, that he had awarded the contract for excavation and had developed a systematic plan to collect funds for the project. First he would appeal to the wealthy laity, intending to visit personally every Catholic whom he considered able to subscribe a sum of $500 or more. Once the goal of this initial stage would be reached, hopefully $100,000 in 100 days, he would lay the cornerstone, and then, he continued, he would appeal to the general Catholic body, asking them to donate any sum from $5 to $100. A number of objections to such an ambitious task so early in his episcopate had come to Riordan's attention, but he was determined to proceed, reminding his people that "even in the unsettled districts of Colorado and Wyoming there were magnificent structures, erected by faith and love of Catholics in honor of Almighty God."[34]

Unexpected delays attended the work. It was not until May 1, 1887, fourteen months tardy according to the original scheme, that Riordan laid the cornerstone of the unfinished building. This ceremony signaled the beginning of another campaign to raise funds, consisting variously of direct appeals, concerts, lectures, and even bazaars. Every dollar contributed to the new cathedral, the *Monitor* pleaded, would be spent on a "building wherein the praises of God may be sounded in a pure atmosphere and without the disagreeable accompaniment of Chinese gongs and other disturbing annoyances."[35] Finally on January 11, 1891, hardly more than five years after the groundbreaking, Riordan dedicated his new cathedral to St. Mary of the Assumption in elaborate ceremonies which reflected the importance which he had attached to this first major enterprise. Bishop Spalding, his Louvain schoolmate who had preached at his consecration, came again from Peoria to deliver the serman at the Mass of the dedication; and later at pontifical vespers, Riordan had Bishop Lawrence Scanlan from Salt Lake City preside and Archbishop Gross preach a second sermon. From his experience of the Chicago fire twenty years earlier, Riordan deplored wooden, combustible churches and had constructed his cathedral of brick in a design called "Modern Romanesque." Not an extravagant building, it was designed by two Chicago architects whom Riordan had known as a priest; its final cost reached only $350,000, nearly one-third of which had been invested in the excavation of the site. Its red-brick exterior was distinguished by two tall flanking towers and an imposing flight of forty granite stairs. The interior was spacious, able to accommodate a congregation of 3,000 and designed with the absence of pillars to give an unobstructed view of the altar and the pulpit. Its appearance, noted contemporaries, differed entirely from the styles of the other churches in the city; and it was not long until it was described in some less reverent circles as a model of "Chicago Gothic."[36]

The first major act of Archbishop Riordan's episcopate had fulfilled what was the dream of many a bishop. Some years later, however, his views shifted to the position that a more modest building best served a diocese as its cathedral. Fourteen years after the dedication, he counseled his suffragan, Bishop Thomas Conaty, to discard his plans of erecting a large and imposing structure in Los Angeles. Even though his opinion had not been requested, the archbishop emphatically advised Conaty that his "contemplated building will be very expensive and entirely too large for twenty-five years to come," inflicting upon the diocese a debt which would become a millstone about your neck for many years to come." "What you need," Riordan advised,

> is a good serviceable working Church, a little larger, especially in the Sanctuary, than the ordinary parish Church, and one which will not cost more than $120,000 or $150,000 when entirely completed.

Conaty's diocese was rapidly growing and, an easterner, he had been in southern California less that two years. Riordan's own experience had taught him that in a quarter century population movements had rendered obsolete the most magnificent cathedrals and forced bishops to relocate them. And he awaited no invitation to express his views. "I take the liberty of saying these things," he continued,

> because I have seen so much trouble come from Churches that are too expensive and Cathedrals put in wrong places. In nearly all large cities of the East the large Cathedrals built are now useless. For instance, Boston, Buffalo, Pittsburg, Chicago, and other cities. It is in my judgment better to have a Church a trifle too small than one much too large, and then it is absolutely desirable that the people assembled for worship can distinctly hear a Priest of ordinary voice. This is especially true in our Country where preaching is an absolute necessity.[37]

* * * * *

The establishment of a seminary, Patrick Riordan was soon to discover, was a far more complex and frustrating business than the building of a cathedral. One pressing problem that his predecessor had never solved was that of native vocations which most American bishops found were cultivated chiefly through a parochial-school system and a diocesan seminary. Under Archbishop Alemany the archdiocese had depended upon volunteer priests from Europe and the eastern United States. In his final report to the Holy See, the old prelate confessed that of his eighty-eight priests only four were native Americans, while the great majority, sixty-four, were Irish-born.[38] While Alemany was regarded as a sincere and adequate administrator, Rome officials were bewildered at his failure to establish a diocesan seminary to serve the church on the Pacific Coast. "It is not easily understandable," noted the alert official who studied the report, "how one zealous Bishop is unable to keep open a Seminary successfully while the Jesuits have opened two Colleges in this Diocese!"[39]

Alemany had not neglected the matter of a seminary and from the beginning had made heroic efforts at establishing such an institution. A small seminary had existed at Mission Santa Barbara and later at Mission Santa Inés, serving all of California since 1840. When Alemany was moved from Monterey to San Francisco in 1853, he also brought his seminary northward, naming Father Eugene O'Connell, a former dean at All Hallows College, rector of the new St. Thomas Aquinas Seminary which was located at Mission Dolores, a parish a short distance from the heart of the city. But this pioneer seminary, which was also the seat of a parish, was forced to close in 1866 under the rectorship of Father John Prendergast.[40] The lesson of this failure was that the archdiocese was unable to supply from its own ranks a seminary staff free from parochial responsibilities. Alemany enlarged his plans, deciding to secure a religious community for this important mission and to establish a large institution that would serve his province, that is, the archdiocese and his two suffragan sees. When his first overtures to obtain the Sulpicians failed, he began in 1879, with the help of Propaganda, to negotiate with the Marists.[41] Once the Marists reluctantly committed themselves to a major seminary, he taxed both his own archdiocese and the Diocese of Grass Valley, and built a new St. Thomas Seminary near Mission San Jose in the southern edge of the archdiocese.[42] On January 13, 1883, the institution opened with four Marists, who had been trained for a major seminary and had as their superior John Francis Regis Pestre, S.M., a priest of tested ability.[43]

Within a matter of months after Archbishop Riordan's arrival as the coadjutor, the infant seminary appeared as an unfortunate and premature foundation with little chance to survive. In detailing a report to his superior general, Father Pestre first noted that its location had placed it in virtual isolation, situated thirty-six miles from San Francisco and accessible only by a burdensome three-hour journey. For these reasons the superior was unable to attend meetings of the archbishop's council and had no voice in determining the admission of students. His staff, commented Pestre, could endure these and other handicaps if they had a substantial student body to instruct, but such would never be realized in this seminary. The parochial-school system, first, was inadequate to foster many native vocations, and the few local candidates presented by Alemany were ill-equipped for serious work in theology. Since the collapse of the seminary at Mission Dolores, the program of preparing these young men consisted largely in pre-law Latin courses taught in the schools of the Christian Brothers and Jesuits, a preparation hardly satisfactory for the ecclesiastical sciences.

Archbishop Alemany's institution, Pestre continued, never had more than five students, only one of whom was able to take theology; and there was little chance that a major seminary could then be sustained in the Far West. The bishops of the province were too impoverished to pay the support of a large number of seminaries, and two prelates, Bishops Mora and Manogue, were adamantly opposed to its foundation. Nor was there any hope to be derived from the Archbishop of Oregon City and the Vicar Apostolic of Colorado, both of whom expressly preferred the eastern seminaries which were far less expensive and better organized. The situation had become more alarming when two professors abandoned the seminary for other less frustrating posts. "Here we are," Pestre lamented, "isolated from the rest of the world and reduced to a single province of San Francisco, where two suffragans are against us."[44]

Archbishop Riordan learned these facts personally from the Marist superior when he visited St. Thomas Seminary on December 5, 1883, during his first tour of the archdiocese. In their initial meeting he struck Pestre as being "very amiable and very open." During the inspection, Pestre was further impressed by what he termed Riordan's "frank American speech" which frequently described the situation as "absurd" and "impossible." The young archbishop had

been himself a seminary professor and had never forgotten
his sad experience fifteen years earlier at St. Mary of the
Lake, where the faculty had been forced to struggle without
adequate support. In a confidential interview with the superior, Riordan registered his shock at these conditions, agreed
that a major seminary could succeed only with at least sixty
students and declared that it was "absurd" to have seques-
tered two qualified professors for five students. The archbishop likewise acknowledged that Mission San Jose was a
poor site for a seminary. He inquired whether the Marists
could operate a minor seminary if the major one were suspended until a sufficient number of pupils were trained.
Though his community did not regularly staff minor seminaries, Pestre was enthusiastic over the proposal, and Riordan
promised to approach Alemany as delicately as possible.[45]

Riordan's promise to work for a minor seminary had convinced Pestre of his "good sense," but the project was
indefinitely delayed since Alemany resolved to do nothing
before consulting the bishops of his province. The Marist
superior was alarmed at this tactic. A provincial council, he
reported to the superior general, might not be convened for
many months since Bishops O'Connell and Manogue, it was
understood, had been offended at Alemany's failure to invite
them to a public dinner for Riordan when the coadjutor first
arrived in San Francisco. Once the bishops could be assembled, Pestre noted, it would be no easier to predict the seminary's future. The old archbishop earnestly intended to continue the seminary at any cost; and O'Connell, "half fallen
into infancy, would say amen to each word of Mgr.
Alemany." Since his sparse diocese was hardly a source of
native vocations, Manogue was inflexibly opposed to any
local seminary, major or minor, and emphatically claimed
that the best trained priests came only from Ireland. Only the
new coadjutor, observed Pestre, had adopted a reasonable
position. From the beginning Riordan had declared everywhere, the rector informed his superior general in France,

that the suspension of the Seminary is a necessity. Even before visiting us . . . he had already announced this idea elsewhere, as I since learned. So that when I myself mentioned this plan to him, it was not new to him: he favored it since his arrival. And this is not astonishing: he had seen the suspension of the Major Seminary of Chicago, where he was a professor, although it was . . . in better condition than our seminary. All the clergy, secular as well as regular, know of his project of suspension and highly approve of it and expect its fulfillment next year.

But as a coadjutor he would have to proceed cautiously and diplomatically without offending the two principal supporters of St. Thomas Seminary, namely, Alemany and his vicar general, John Prendergast.[46]

While the seminary rector eagerly waited for Riordan's opportunity, Alemany remained unalterably opposed to suppression, appealing even to the Holy See to save the institution and to remove Pestre who, he charged, was "always dissatisfied."[47] Despite the archbishop's strenuous efforts, the Marist superior general decided in May, 1884, to abandon the seminary and to assign the two remaining professors to other posts. This withdrawal, at the moment when Alemany was about to submit his own resignation, had deeply wounded the old prelate who had witnessed the collapse of two seminaries, a failure which he regretted to pass on to his successor. Refusing to capitulate, he operated St. Thomas Seminary for one heroic year after the Marists' withdrawal. It was headed this time by a German refugee priest who had taught in Europe. During his last days in California, as he watched the problems multiply, the old prelate's thoughts centered on the preservation of the seminary. In his farewell to his clergy, he emphatically recommended the struggling institution to their spiritual and material charity. But his hard-headed successor was out of sympathy with the

whole enterprise. One month after Alemany's departure from
San Francisco in May, 1885, Riordan announced that it
would not reopen; its nine students transferred to the Sulpician seminary in Baltimore. St. Thomas', the new archbishop
was convinced, had failed through poor planning. A stronger
parochial-school system and minor seminary must precede
the foundation of a house of theological studies. The Marists
were not responsible, but rather the victims of unreasonable
demands.[48]

Soon after Riordan succeeded to the See of San Francisco, Pestre's congratulations from Dublin came as a most
agreeable surprise, revealing, the archbishop replied, that
"you still bear in kind remembrance a diocese that did not
prove to be very grateful to you for services rendered. . . ."
The archdiocese, continued Riordan, had suffered by the
Marists' departure, and he planned temporarily to close the
seminary and to send the few students to the Sulpicians in
Baltimore. "I am of the opinion," he wrote,

> that the project was premature, and the only and
> proper thing to be done is to open as soon as
> means will permit a preparatory Seminary includ-
> ing perhaps a course of philosophy. For some time
> even that is impossible, burdened as I am with an
> immense debt. . . .

But the archbishop had his eye on the future, suggesting that
when conditions would permit a minor seminary, he might
request the Marists to return to San Francisco, and hoping
that the "memory of the past will not be an obstacle to your
aiding me in carrying out so important an enterprise."[49]
Later that same year, partly in a gesture of conciliation, he
invited the Marists to take charge of the French national
church, Notre Dame des Victoires. On July 24, 1887, the
Holy See granted its approval of this arrangement.[50]

* * * * *

Although preoccupied in these early years with the construction of the cathedral, Riordan had not abandoned his intention to establish a seminary, and he vigorously renewed his predecessor's efforts to secure a community to staff it. He preferred the Sulpicians in place of the Marists, possibly because their European and American seminaries had earned a distinguished reputation, and probably, too, because they accepted the administration of minor seminaries. At this time, too, his household included several Sulpician alumni, notably his secretary, George Montgomery, who, as a Baltimore seminarian, was reputed to have kept the rule flawlessly. Riordan's campaign to found such an institution soon was, therefore, inaugurated in 1888 during his first *ad limina* trip to Rome. En route, he stopped briefly at Paris to visit Henri Icard, P.S.S., the ancient superior general who had, over a quarter of a century earlier, directed young Patrick away from St.-Sulpice and who was well-versed in San Francisco affairs through long correspondence with Alemany. When this personal appeal failed, the archbishop went on first to Lourdes, where he made the seminary his special intention at the Marian shrine, and then to Rome where he enlisted the assistance of the Holy See.[51] In a strong appeal to Icard, Cardinal Simeoni of Propaganda invoked "special" reasons why a seminary was imperative in this archdiocese which was ever growing in importance "through the continuous and increasing immigration" generated "by the delightful climate and fertile soil." His congregation, he continued, not only applauded Riordan's initiative, but had also encouraged him to undertake the project of building a seminary which would serve not merely his archdiocese but the entire province. "I am certain," Simeoni concluded firmly, "... Yr. Ex. will favorably receive the Archbishop's invitation which I urgently recommend to you."[52]

This was not the first instance in which the cardinal had personally intervened in behalf of a Sulpician seminary for San Francisco. Ten years earlier, Icard had himself encountered the same emphatic request from Rome with the inspiration at that time furnished by Archbishop Alemany. On the

previous occasion, the superior general had declined
Simeoni's proposal on the plea of insufficient manpower, but
as a compromise he had offered to train as Sulpicians any
diocesan priest of San Francisco whom the archbishop would
appoint to the seminary faculty.[53] The Sulpician governing
body had, however, expressed interest, deciding:

> It is a great center where the action of the Com-
> pany could have a very extensive influence. A large
> number of providential signs, among them the very
> significant intervention of the Cardinal prefect of
> Propaganda, seem to strengthen the Bishop's pro-
> posal. It will be excellent, we believe, if the Sup.
> Gen. can do anything in favor of this worthy and
> holy prelate.[54]

A decade later, while Icard was reluctant to refuse Cardinal Simeoni a second time, the Society of St. Sulpice was
again hard-pressed in resources for another commitment in
the United States. Yet it was no secret that it had recently
taken charge of two American institutions whose original
appeals had come long after Alemany's request — St. John's
Seminary in Brighton, Massachusetts, and Divinity College at
the new Catholic University of America. Furthermore, Archbishop Corrigan of New York had at this time unearthed a
promise of twenty-four years before, that the Suplicians
would manage the seminary for his archdiocese.[55] Riordan
returned to Paris for another confrontation with Icard and
his consultors and, with some artful diplomacy, won a verbal
agreement that the society would come to San Francisco
some day.[56] But heavy pressures weighing on them from
elsewhere, the Sulpicians eventually decided to grant priority
to Corrigan and to give Riordan vague assurances for the
future. The appeals from San Francisco, the society noted,
were supported by several emphatic letters from the Prefect
of Propaganda, but the long-standing promise to New York
must be honored first.[57]

Evidently this tenuous pledge was ample for Riordan, who boldly began at once the remote preparations for his seminary. Though he experienced little difficulty in securing spiritual and material support in the archdiocese, he was haunted by the fear that the Sulpicians might indefinitely postpone their coming to San Francisco. "I hope," he eventually told Father Alphonse Magnien, S. S., the Sulpician superior at St. Mary's Seminary in Baltimore,

> that your Superior in Paris has not forgotten his promise to establish a foundation in this diocese. The people will be disappointed unless I am able to open the Seminary before long. As I explained before, two or three Fathers would suffice for a beginning. I need not dwell again on the importance of this work. It is more than important. It is absolutely necessary. Please when you are writing to Paris put in a strong word in favor of it.[58]

Viewing the needs and resources of the archdiocese from a broad perspective, Riordan was unwilling to repeat his predecessor's mistake of trying inordinately to accelerate the development of a native clergy. The decision whether to institute a major or minor seminary was crucial and, wishing to plant deep roots, the archbishop was favoring the latter. "I am more and more impressed," he informed Magnien a fortnight later, "with the absolute necessity of opening a Petit Seminaire. It is impossible to keep up the supply of Priests until that is done. I must ask you to 'instare opportune et importune.' "[59] For five years, nevertheless, the Sulpicians remained aloof and virtually disengaged until October, 1896, when their consultors acknowledged their commitment and recorded: "The Seminary of San Francisco has already been built. It should open in September, 1898, and will commence as a minor seminary."[60] With this modest entry, the historic Society of St.-Sulpice was preparing to begin its last foundation of the nineteenth century.

The undefined position of the Sulpicians did not deter Archbishop Riordan from pursuing his objective with characteristic energy and orderliness. In December, 1890, the month before he dedicated the cathedral, he instructed his attorney, John Thomas Doyle, to investigate how the projected seminary could be best incorporated in the State of California. The best legal way to incorporate this institution, advised Doyle, required the names of the donors and a precise description of their contributions. "You cannot incorporate," he informed Riordan, "until you have your foundation donations in tangible, realizable shape, and the necessities of the case require that you incorporate at once. Hence your unavoidable hurry."[61] This counsel to hasten suggested, or confirmed, the archbishop's immediate course of action. He first approached a small number of wealthy and interested laity who eventually subscribed $300,000.[62] "I am hard at work," Riordan told Magnien during the campaign, "getting a large endowment fund for the maintenance of the Seminary, and shall succeed beyond expectations."[63]

Meanwhile, Doyle instructed the archbishop that the statute which would incorporate the seminary required as well a statement of location. [64] A large factor contributing to the recent failure of the effort at Mission San Jose was its isolation and distance from San Francisco, and Riordan himself had favored a seminary in or near the see city. But these plans were modified when Doyle's sister, Mrs. Kate Johnson, a well-known Catholic benefactress, offered "a plot of ground near Menlo Park of about eighty acres," situated thirty-two miles south of San Francisco and directly accessible by railroad.[65] This site was, in Riordan's judgment, ideal for the institution, a rich, oak-filled meadowland nestled between the country estates of Atherton and the newly opened Leland Stanford Junior University near Palo Alto. Before the archbishop could accept it from Mrs. Johnson as a seminary campus, he confronted two difficulties. One concerned the water supply. This was solved when Governor Henry Markham personally interceded in Riordan's behalf, and Senator and Mrs. Leland Stanford guaranteed the supply.[66] This point being easily settled, John Doyle was ready to prepare a deed for the property, but Mrs. Johnson, he had noted, had presented it under two conditions: that it never be "alienated or converted to any other uses than those of the Seminary" and its construction commence within a year. The archbishop was also anxious for a prompt start, and the donor allowed this construction to consist merely in the "excavation of a basement, the making of a concrete wall, or even the dumping of building material on the ground."[67] But the requirement of permanent inalienability handicapped the gift; and before he would accept it, Riordan requested that no such restriction be effective after fifty years.[68]

To provide for a seminary building and its endowment was a most formidable undertaking for a young prelate who had worked vigorously to dissolve a huge diocesan debt and to erect a cathedral. But for the next five years Riordan promoted his campaign, largely through organized parish collections.[69] There was a serious hidden problem: while the seminary began as a personal project, it could not succeed without the support of his priests. The majority of the San Francisco clergy were Irish-born who had originated since Alemany's time largely from All Hallows College and St. Patrick's College in Carlow. They had proved themselves indispensable to the church in the West, providentially combining the spirit of the adventurer and the hardy zeal of the missioner. After the Civil War, California with its vast religious needs and the romance of the rugged West had become a favorite outpost for the products of Irish seminaries. Replacements were steady as young Celts followed older uncles, cousins and friends to missions in the faraway "land of gold." In time the Irish-born clergy had developed into a notable group, some having assumed important roles in archdiocesan administration. Generally they were industrious and reliable but, in the eyes of native Americans, many had retained unchanged certain strict ways of the Irish ecclesiastic, often accenting their authority, clannishly drawn to each other, and occasionally indulging in blistering criticism from the pulpit.

As a whole, Riordan's Irish-born priests did not at first
approve of the new seminary; and possibly his decision to
dedicate it to the patron of Ireland was, in part, an effort to
make conversions. The American youth, they felt, were con-
stitutionally and temperamentally too delicate to bear the
rigors of seminary or priestly life. There was among these
priests the suspicion that the California boy was congenitally
weak, living in a warm and debilitating climate and often
bred from parents who had sought the West for reasons of
health. This factor accordingly contributed to the collapse of
Alemany's seminaries. The best prospects, it was believed,
were to be found in the Irish seminaries where the faith was
deeper and the weather more invigorating. Some particularly
sensitive Irish priests regarded Riordan's seminary as a
monument to the alleged inadequacies of foreign clergy.
Others disfavored it because it was too magnificent and
expensive. The archbishop had, in their opinion, taxed the
parishes too severely for a project that was dubious and had
failed in the past.[70]

On August 27, 1898, Riordan nonetheless dedicated "his
crowning work," which was inaugurated as a minor seminary. St. Patrick was chosen as its patron not for personal
reasons but because, he declared, this saint was

> the patron. . . of a great Catholic race to which the
> vast majority of our people belong, that has suf-
> fered more than any other for religion's sake, and
> the most devoted, the most generous and the most
> priest loving race within the fold of the Church of
> Christ.

At the time of the dedication, two-thirds of the brick structure had been completed, the administrative wing, junior college, and refectory. The building was spacious, endowed with
wide corridors, high ceilings, and large windows. A quiet dignity graced the entire complex, its exterior trimmed in stone
and the interior moderately comfortable for the inhabitants.
He expressly did not wish the institution to harden its stu-

dents or deprive them of a cultural rearing: this western seminary, commented a contemporary, was "to train clerical gentlemen."[71] In addition, his archdiocese, Riordan was convinced, had more sick priests than any other in the country;
and this phenomenon could be traced largely to the austere
regime in seminaries.[72] St. Patrick's would, therefore, not
only train clerical gentlemen but keep them healthy and
physically sound. For the first faculty, the Sulpician superior
general had sent four priests, naming as its first president,
Father Jean-Baptiste Arsène Vuibert, S.S.[73] With Bishops
Montgomery of Monterey-Los Angeles and Grace of Sacramento present, Riordan kept the ceremonies as simple as
possible, restricting its attendance to the clergy alone. At the
banquet following the dedication, Riordan betrayed his
awareness that the institution was not wholly popular with his
clergy. He took advantage of the occasion solemnly to vindicate his campaign and his recent heavy demands on the
parishes. He underscored not only the evident value of the
seminary but also that he had borne his share in the campaign, expecting as much from his clergy. "Never have I
found a people so zealous for the advance of the Church," he
told his priests.

> They responded readily to my representations with
> regard to this Seminary. I have asked friends to
> meet the expenses incurred in sums proportionate
> to their needs. In some cases I have requested
> $50,000 and have always met with a response. In
> no case has the answer been "No." My experience
> has confirmed me in the opinion that the people
> are generous and willing to make sacrifices for the
> honor of God and the good of religion when an
> appeal is properly placed before them.

This pioneer institution, which Riordan had also conceived as
serving "all districts west of the Rocky Mountains," having
granted two free scholarships to each diocese of the Pacific
Coast, inspired a number of flattering tributes. But Bishop

Grace best described its significance as the "crowning of a most important and useful life," an epithet which the archbishop warmly acknowledged for the remainder of his episcopate.[74]

In the next few years, Archbishop Riordan began construction of a permanent chapel and a wing for senior students. The benefactress who financed the erection and furnishing of the chapel was Mrs. Jane Lathrop Stanford, the trustee of nearby Stanford University. In October, 1901, when she returned to Palo Alto after an absence of nearly a year and a half, her business troubles had been solved and her extensive building program at the university was well on toward completion. Though a communicant of no organized church, she was a profoundly pious Christian and, at this time, was erecting on the Stanford campus a memorial church as her personal gift to the university.[75] While the university, according to the founding grant and her wishes, would remain nonsectarian, she promoted the erection of denominational churches in the vicinity of Palo Alto. As soon as she learned that Archbishop Riordan had no funds to build the seminary chapel, she offered the necessary $50,000 and requested the project to begin at once. In the negotiations she enjoined Riordan's attorney that the donation would remain confidential. "Very funny reason she assigned for silence," John Doyle told the archbishop, "viz., all the professors, at Stanford, wanted something or other and if they heard of this they would be jealous and each more urgent for his own particular desire than before." Stanford University had been founded in memory of her son, and when Riordan's offer to call the chapel after Leland Stanford Junior was communicated, Doyle reported ". . . she said no! no! If that was done people would think that she gave the money to have that done which I thought a pretty shrewd thought on her part."[76] Construction was to have begun immediately. On August 4, 1904, Riordan's coadjutor, Archbishop George Montgomery, dedicated the crypt of the new permanent chapel.[77]

Aside from the progressing construction, no one expected the first years at Menlo Park to be easy. From the beginning Riordan shrewdly exercised prudent restraint in developing his institution, never pressing for hasty growth. First, he discouraged a large enrollment. "The fewer the better," he told the rector. "The first year should be a year of organization and preparation. . . . I am convinced that the seminary will grow from year to year, and it is better that it should grow slowly."[78] But there soon arose two developments that mildly threatened the institution and handicapped the archbishop's campaign to win his priests over to it. Many of the original candidates had been hastily enrolled and unscreened, at best altar boys who had not developed a particular conviction regarding their vocation. The defection in the first half decade was viewed as "ominous," some classes falling off as much as seventy-five per cent. While the faculty insisted that this was to be expected, these departures appeared to many as conclusive proof that the native Californian was unsuited for the priestly life.[79] The greater source of tension, however, arose within the Sulpician community itself when control of the seminary finances was unfortunately divided between an American and a Frenchman who could not learn English. The situation had become so intolerable during the first scholastic year that Riordan confidentially recommended faculty changes to Father Magnien, adding a revealing comment: "The trouble at the Seminary is that there is no head to the institution, that is, no business head."[80] Friction among the instructors persisted until January, 1904, when Father Edward R. Dyer, S. S., the Sulpician vicar general in the United States, visited the archdiocese and was himself distressed over the clash. Dyer was nonetheless ready to discuss the possibility of expanding the school and establishing a faculty of theology. Perhaps, it was thought, this addition might dissolve the tensions at Menlo Park. Even at these prospects, Riordan was disposed to postpone this development. If the congregation could not send superior instructors to Menlo Park, he would send his major seminarians elsewhere for theological studies.[81] After his tour, Dyer decided that only a change of rectors could remedy the dissension and assuage the archbishop's apprehension about a theology department. He nominated, therefore, a man of "light and power," Father Henry Amans Joseph Ayrinhac, S.S., formerly superior of the philosophy department at St. Mary's Baltimore, who later distinguished himself as a canonist.[82]   Under his strong administration of twenty-six years, harmony was restored, and the seminary began to strike deep roots.

The principal reason why Patrick Riordan had established the seminary was to free himself from dependence upon foreign-born priests and to encourage native vocations both in his own archdiocese and also in the entire Far West. As a former professor himself, he devoted great personal interest in St. Patrick's and regarded highly the specialized work of the Sulpicians. "While the work of a good Priest in the Diocese results in very great profit to the enumerable [sic] souls," he told a young priest whom he had released to the congregation,

> yet the work of preparing Priests is a higher and more meritorious work. The former is the work of the Apostles and the latter the work of Our Lord Himself.[83]

Until his death, his great pleasure was the frequent visits to the grounds, living in a large house on campus provided by his good friend, Michael Cudahy. The faculty was pleased with the confidence that he placed in their program; and though he never delivered formal talks to the students, he did consider giving a course on pastoral theology.[84]

The seminary grew in importance to the archdiocese as Riordan became progressively critical of the two traditional sources of clerical training since Alemany's time, namely, All Hallows and St. Patrick's in Carlow. While All Hallows alumni dominated the archdiocesan council, Riordan once complained to its rector, William Fortune, of the heavy brogue of his students, suggesting too that the college intensify its train-

ing in the public reading of the scriptures. Relations were
further strained when Fortune was reported to have replied
that his students could read and explain the scriptures better
than the archbishop.[85]   Riordan was likewise distressed at
the curriculum offered at Carlow. Instead of the classic four-
year course, this college provided only three years of theology; and Riordan eventually took steps to reduce the
number of Carlow students adopted for San Francisco.[86]

St. Patrick's Seminary did not develop rapidly; and the
archbishop remained undaunted when it had but a handful of
young men. Only after he scheduled the clergy retreats at
Menlo Park did many of his priests begin to accept it. In the
later years of his episcopate, the student body increased in a
promising way from the original twenty-eight. A decade after
its opening, Riordan witnessed the fulfillment of his dreams
when he ordained Father John M. Byrne, the first priest who
had received the full course at Menlo Park.[87] And two years
before his death, the archbishop expressed unfeigned satisfaction at the prosperity of his seminary, his "crowning achievement," whose new admissions each year had begun to reach
twenty students. "Of course, we shall lose a good many of
them before they get through," he told his brother.

> But it is encouraging to see vocations increasing
> year by year.When I came here, there were very few
> vocations to the priesthood, and, now in a few
> years if things continue as they are going, we shall
> be able to supply the Diocese with our own priests.
> It has been a long work, and a hard work, but what
> succeeds always gives pleasure. [88]

* * * * *

Patrick Riordan's two major projects, the cathedral and
the seminary, were built and operating when, at the age of
fifty-eight he started for Rome in 1899 to present his second
ad limina report. This marked precisely the midway of his
thirty-year episcopate. More importantly, this report would

most clearly reflect his ability as an administrator. This time there would be no reporting to Propaganda on the successes and failures of his predecessor; Riordan had been solely responsible for the archdiocese for the last fifteen years. The Catholic population of the archdiocese, his report began, had increased since his original report of eleven years earlier from 200,000 to a total of 225,000, a growth of another one-eighth; and the see city alone now numbered as Catholics one-half of its 360,000 inhabitants. Riordan spoke of the minor seminary newly erected and entrusted to the Sulpicians, adding that there were forty-two major seminarians preparing elsewhere in America and Europe. Introducing impressive financial figures, the archbishop then forcefully indicated that an investment of over six million dollars accounted for the extraordinary progress since his first report of 1888. Since then, the 125 churches of the archdiocese had collectively spent $2,468,000 in expansion while incurring a manageable debt of $432,450. Another $2,990,000 had been expended in educational institutions, accumulating a token debt of $193,000. These figures, Riordan estimated, represented both the munificence of his laity and the industry of his clergy. Although it was impossible to build parochial schools in the country districts, their enrolllment in the urban areas had increased in this interval over fifty per cent to 12,027 in forty-seven separate institutions. For the second time, Riordan's detailed report gave satisfaction at Propaganda. Cardinal Miecislaus Ledochowski, who had succeeded Simeoni as prefect in 1892, alluded to the "flourishing condition" of the archdiocese, and especially commended the archbishop on his parochial schools and the new seminary.[89]

But Riordan's success as an administrator was known not merely within the Roman congregations. His ability in such affairs was evident also to those who worked with him. On occasion, even visitors to San Francisco were introduced to this dimension of the archbishop. One traveler was Father Walter McDonald, a noted theologian from St. Patrick's College, Maynooth, Ireland. In the summer of 1900, less than a year after Riordan had submitted his triumphant report to

Rome, Father McDonald made his first tour of the United States which included San Francisco. One of the most vivid impressions from this trip, which he expressed a quarter century later in his memoirs, was Riordan's exceptional and highly efficient approach to diocesan administration. At the archbishop's invitation, the Irish educator visited the San Francisco chancery which, according to his account,

> had struck me greatly; the broad, thick, well-bound and much ruled books; the many pigeon-holes, one for every parish, convent, and other instituitions in the diocese; the apparatus of seals, stamps, type-writers, such as one sees in a book. It was, certainly a great business office, in first-class business fashion: I came away in admiration.[90]

Patrick Riordan had been lauded as a student and a gifted preacher, but actually it was McDonald's alert observations that touched more closely upón his most striking talent, namely, an ability at management and organization. This would hardly be a surprise. Before his appointment to San Francisco, his direction of St. James' Parish had earned him the reputation in the judgment of one writer of being "the most conspicuously successful pastor, perhaps in Chicago." For twelve years he had conducted St. James in a systematic and "well-disciplined" way, the name of each parishioner recorded and his background kept vital. A resourceful fund-raiser, Riordan had never yielded to outlandish schemes like carnivals or picnics. "Whenever money was needed," a contemporary noted, "the parishioners met in the basement, were informed how much was needed, assessed themselves proportionately. . . and paid monthly to collections; that was all."[91]

The secret of Riordan's success in San Francisco was his years in Chicago. He had inherited the midwesterner's spirit of independence, shrewd enterprise, and a sense of the future — qualities which had quickly raised that city from the ashes of the fire of 1871 to the business center of the Mississippi

Valley, and which was building what was to become the largest Catholic community in the United States. He had come to San Francisco when the city was yet limited by what a contemporary described as a "village cast of mind."[9][2] Everybody, accordingly, knew everyone else and had taken his measure as narrowly as possible. Having come, however, from a city of vibrant growth and sound business practices, Riordan had given first priority to details of the internal organization of the archdiocese. Parochial finances were systematized, according to sound procedures, and the archdiocesan credit improved so rapidly that shortly, noted one who knew, "the mere name of Archbishop Riordan was sufficient security with the monied men of the State."[9][3]

Riordan himself attributed his success to his origins in Chicago. On his way to Rome to present his triumphant report of 1899, he visited his home. Filled with the exuberance that comes from accomplishment, he publicly expressed his debt to Chicago for the lessons which he had learned there, describing it as "the greatest, the most progressive, the most catholic city. . . in the world." Riordan further acknowledged that he held this city up as an example to his people on the Pacific Coast. ". . . if I have succeeded in inspiring them with a love of religion," he professed,

> and inducing them to bring out of their treasures large sums for the building of Holy Church, I attributed it in great measure to the lesson and spirit I have received in this Archdiocese.[9][4]

5

The King's Men

When Patrick Riordan succeeded Archbishop Alemany, he inherited as metropolitan an immense ecclesiastical empire. It covered 351,521 square miles, a territory larger than France and Italy combined and embracing the States of California and Nevada as well as the Territory of Utah. Under previous bishops, the Catholic Church had been long established and rooted in the Far West. Each diocese had met the needs of sudden movements of population and each had claimed origins which predated the Civil War. By 1885, when Alemany had departed and left a successor in charge of affairs, it had been fully forty-five years since a bishop had first come to Monterey, and San Francisco had had its archbishop for nearly a third of a century. Even the poor and scattered reaches of northern California and Nevada had been given its resident bishop a quarter of a century earlier, based first at Marysville and then at Grass Valley.

The arrival of Archbishop Riordan, however, coming from the Midwest with its flourishing dioceses and provinces, introduced a new era not merely for his own see but for the entire church in the Far West. Of the three prelates whose dioceses lay within the Province of San Francisco, he was the only native North American; and the fact that he was also the youngest and least experienced in the West and in diocesan administration did not deter him from overseeing the development of the suffragan sees. An able and strong executive,

Riordan had cultivated and brought with him to San Francisco that sense of initiative and keen alertness characteristic
of nineteenth-century Chicago. During his episcopate he took
seriously the responsibility of his office as metropolitan,
never hesitating to exercise his limited but prescribed rights
throughout the vast province.

As soon as he took charge, Riordan found himself entangled in a long-standing discussion over a boundary adjustment between the Sees of San Francisco and Grass Valley.
The Diocese of Grass Valley, the youngest in the province,
was headed by Bishop Patrick Manogue, a universally respected churchman who had first come to California as a
miner. After a successful pastorate in Virginia City, he had, at
the age of fifty-one, succeeded Bishop Eugene O'Connell in
1884.[1] His see, founded first in 1860 as the Vicariate of
Marysville and elevated nearly eight years later into the Diocese of Grass Valley, was much poorer and more diffused
than San Francisco, stretching through northern California
and Nevada between parallels of latitude 39° and 42° and
between the Pacific Ocean on the west and the Colorado
River on the east.[2] "To give an idea of the extent of this
laborious mission," Manogue had written to a French mission-aid society,

> it will suffice to say that it contains about 197,000
> square miles — England, Ireland, Scotland, and
> Wales, united, contain but 119,600 . . . the Diocese
> of Marysville exceeding Great Britain and Ireland
> by 77,400 square miles —. From this calculation
> you are unable to infer that our Vicariate is almost
> equal in extent to the Empire of France — the
> latter exceeding it by only 7,800 square miles.[3]

Though the diocese had since its beginning recorded a
numerical growth, its ministry in these remote portions had
been carried on as late as 1881 under missionary conditions.
In his last report to Rome twenty years after his appointment, Bishop O'Connell numbered only thirty priests actively

engaged, the majority of whom were Irish missionaries from All Hallows College. "Alas!" commented O'Connell, "there are no missionaries from religious communities 'because of the difficulties of the region'!" So scattered was his territory that he had kept his residence in Marysville although the cathedral was located in Grass Valley.

In the 1880's a dark future loomed for this northern diocese whose communities like Virginia City, Downieville, and Grass Valley had boomed during the gold rush but had suddenly declined with the eclipse of mining. Even before Riordan's arrival, the bishops of the province had sought a solution through a change in boundaries. The logical move to ease the church's struggle in the north was to transfer O'Connell's see to Sacramento, the state capital and a bustling city that survived the passing of the mining era and belonged to the Archdiocese of San Francisco. Alemany had been willing to give up this city because it was growing rapidly in a rich agricultural area and, as the center of the state government, needed more direct spiritual attention.[4]

To Patrick Manogue the transfer of the see to prosperous Sacramento seemed to be the only reasonable hope for the languishing Church in northern California. After O'Connell's retirement in March, 1884, he earnestly campaigned for the geographic changes, introducing the newly arrived Archbishop Riordan to the problems of his diocese. At Manogue's insistence, Riordan toured the northern country and, judged Manogue, was intimately acquainted with its problems. "Archbishop Alemany is about to retire and Msgr. O'Connell is *hors de combat*," he observed,

> and I would know no better source in which to place confidence than in Msgr. Riordan and myself, because on us depends in large measure the prosperity . . . of the Church on the Pacific Coast.[5]

By the end of 1884, the Holy See was impressed with Manogue's argument that for its survival his diocese needed a see city like Sacramento, endowed with stability and permanence. This thriving center already numbered 20,000 inhabitants, and as the state capital it needed the close attention of the church which could be best achieved through a resident bishop. Since Manogue and Alemany had differed over the boundaries proposed, the Holy See on November 23, 1884, granted to Manogue and the new Archbishop of San Francisco the faculty to arrange between themselves the new line of demarcation between San Francisco and Grass Valley.[6] Even in these initial stages, there appeared signs that the two men ruling these sees were strong-willed and tenacious prelates. Cardinal Simeoni's letter was welcome news to Manogue, who anticipated Rome's final decision and immediately purchased property in Sacramento for a new cathedral.[7]

Riordan, however, who had been in California less than a year and a half, frowned upon his suffragan's impetuous and unauthorized action. It was obvious now and in later developments that the new Archbishop of San Francisco would not be intimidated by the pioneer Bishop of Grass Valley. Beneath the negotiation of borders raged a deeper contest of wills. "The Young Archbishop would seem to think Californai was made for himself," Manogue confided to a friend,

> and has the whole say about any and every spot of it. He would also seem to disregard the Cardinal's letter as ambiguous and devoid of any weight because he hasn't been officially and personally consulted by the Cardinal; in a word, he thinks the question even about Sacramento is merely reopened for him to assent or not assent just as he pleased and therefore keep us indefinitely at his nod and good pleasure.

In presenting his plan of apportionment, Manogue favored either a simple line running east to west through the state or the original plan that the California bishops had drafted in 1881. He was astonished, however, when the younger Riordan rejected both schemes. "As Archbishop Riordan seems reluctant and stubborn about the lines," Manogue continued,

> I think my long life of work and position among people on this coast should be my excuse from going again on my knees to him. Having always attempted to do my duty, I have not been accustomed to being snubbed by even an old man.

Riordan's youth and lack of temporal seniority in the California hierarchy irritated Manogue, who mused that one of the two lines of demarcation recently excluded by Riordan had been proposed by the bishops of the province "before even Abp. Riordan was thought of for San Francisco. . . ." Even the Holy See's late action in reconsidering the boundary question, he added, "was made before he succeeded to the San Francisco See. . . ."[8]

By June 15, 1885, an agreement was reached. Riordan had taken the initiative in this apportionment, bent on consolidating his jurisdiction territorially and not hesitant in slicing off remote areas.[9] The new scheme differed substantially from the originals of both Manogue and of the provincial council. It assigned most of the interior of northern California to Grass Valley, placing each prelate relatively in the center of his own territory whereby he was no longer forced to pass through the other diocese en route to a station within his charge.

As soon as Archbishop Alemany in Rome learned of the new arrangement, he protested vigorously, fearing that the archdiocese had been too sharply reduced in size, now much smaller in area than the two suffragan sees.[10] But Riordan's generosity had not been incautious or reckless. "Well have I studied the question," he reported to Simeoni in defense of the scheme, "especially in regards to the near future. . . ." If these remote areas should ever attract a large population, two new dioceses could be created to accommodate these increases, one in the north and another in central California, but the plan submitted, urged Riordan, best fitted present conditions in the state. "I am inclined to believe," he added,

> that the venerable Archbishop Alemany was slight-
> ly displeased in seeing his old diocese dismem-
> bered, and because he does not agree with my
> ideas, and with me [he assumes] that being new
> and a stranger I do not have that affection which
> he has always had for his diocese.[11]

Riordan's sturdy confidence was persuasive, and the Holy See accepted the arrangement as a sensible compromise. Manogue acquired not only the spare mountainous regions of the arch-diocese but also the promising and wealthy vicinity around Sacramento. Adding minor adjustments recommended by Propaganda, Pope Leo XIII approved on December 13, 1885, the new boundary between San Francisco and Grass Valley whose new see was Sacramento.[12]

The relationship between Riordan and Manogue soon be-trayed evidence of serious strain. Their most important mis-understanding centered upon the disposition of the Santa Inés Ranch, located in Santa Barbara County within the Dio-cese of Monterey-Los Angeles.[13] In 1844 the Mexican Government had given this extensive estate to Francisco Gar-cia Diego y Moreno, Bishop of Both Californias, and its in-come had been used to help support a seminary. In 1857, when it had been decided to sell the holdings, Garcia Diego's successors, Archbishop Alemany and Bishop Thaddeus Amat, had tentatively agreed to divide the property into five equal parts, two going to San Francisco, two to Monterey, and one share to the Vicariate Apostolic of Lower California. Com-plications emerged, however, when Marysville was erected into a vicariate apostolic. Alemany wished to renounce the former agreement and to assign a full share to Bishop Eugene O'Connell, the new vicar.

When Amat balked at Alemany's proposal, the matter of apportionment was forwarded to the Holy See which, in 1882, denied any share for Marysville. The establishment of a new diocese, it ruled, did not entitle it to the benefits of the old. Rome had also granted the permission to sell the proper-ty, but Alemany and Amat elected to wait for a more pro-pitious moment.

In 1883 Alemany and Francis Mora, Amat's successor, finally divided the holdings of the Santa Inés Ranch between themselves without consulting Manogue or the failing O'Connell. This private transaction, which virtually abandoned the claims of Grass Valley, had embittered Manogue. A plain-speaking individual, he rarely tempered his expressions and in this action sensed the essence of conspiracy. He was desperate for any sort of income for his struggling diocese, and nothing would dissuade him from pursuing his claims on the Santa Inés Ranch. Cardinal Simeoni had hoped that this dispute could be settled quietly between Riordan and Manogue, but in 1888 the former had already left for his first *ad limina* report to the Holy See before Manogue could approach him regarding it. Anticipating that Riordan would be questioned in Rome about the ranch, Manogue planned to have his diocese fully represented on his occasion if only through lengthy reports detailing his position.[14] But Riordan had no intention of conceding to the Bishop of Grass Valley any rights over the ranch. During his sojourn in Rome, he was shown the documents sent by Manogue. The archbishop directly challenged the claims, imploring Simeoni to uphold Propaganda's original decision and to restore peace within the Province of San Francisco. Manogue's charges regarding duplicity were harsh. The large number of Catholics, contended Riordan, whom Manogue alleged to be scandalized by this injustice was hardly possible. All the prominent members of the laity in Sacramento were personally known to him, and no one of them had ever alluded to this dispute. "Besides . . . ," added the archbishop regarding his suffragan,

> he always operated with such great secrecy that even though I had seen him almost every month during this past year he has never spoken to me one syllable on the "rights" of his diocese.[15]

By late 1888 the controversy over the Santa Inés Ranch was fast descending into a heated quarrel partly because the two principals were articulate and irrevocable in their posi-

tions and partly because Cardinal Simeoni in his efforts to
render a fair judgment followed an exceptional procedure.
The prefect abandoned his policy of secrecy and allowed
both prelates to see a number of their unvarnished statements
regarding the other. Simeoni's decision of November, 1888,
which was documented with many of Riordan's choice comments, was promptly sent to Sacramento where the unfavorable judgment left Manogue outraged and furious. If the
bishop wished to raise the question of dividing the income of
the Santa Inés Ranch, there could likely be raised a concom-
itant question of proportionately dividing the archdiocesan
debt. Equity and justice would demand, observed Simeoni,
that after its creation in 1861 the new Vicariate of Marysville
should have been held responsible for the long-standing obligations contracted by the archdiocese for those areas detached from it at that time. In confronting Manogue with this
dilemma inspired by Riordan, the prefect advised the Bishop
of Sacramento to forget his claims.[16]

If Simeoni's letter quieted Manogue, it did not subdue
him. At first intent on dispatching a scorching protest, he
reversed his decision. Instead, he elected to brood "in secret
anguish and silent patience" for a year and a half until he
could visit Rome on his *ad limina* journey and make a personal representation of his rights in this conflict. On his return to San Francisco, Riordan uneasily noted his suffragan's
resolute silence. "The Ranch question seems to be settled,"
he wrote Denis O'Connell, Rector of the American College in
Rome, "not a word is said about it." Again, to O'Connell two
months later:

> Bp. Manogue has never spoken to me since I re-
> turned about the Ranch difficulty. Of course I
> shall not speak to him about it.[17]

Had the Bishop of Sacramento, however, committed to paper
his honest reaction upon receiving the instruction, his expression and conduct, he feared, would have been considered
"obstinate and rebellious." Nevertheless, once he presented

himself at Propaganda in 1890, Manogue spared few feelings and delivered a merciless rebuttal of Riordan's arguments, hotly describing them as false and unfounded, and demanding the congregation to reopen the issue to consideration. The Diocese of Grass Valley under Bishop O'Connell, Manogue declared had discharged all liabilities owed to the archdiocese. When O'Connell retired in 1884, Alemany himself congratulated him that his resignation left the diocese free from all debt to San Francisco. Riordan's insistence of this counterfeit debt, Manogue charged, was merely a clever ruse designed to becloud the genuine issue and to raise "arguments not real but imaginary." "If this debt is so burdensome," he acidly protested,

> why did he not pay it instead of building a new Cathedral at an enormous expense, while the old one was yet able to serve for many years? The present one, that is, the new Cathedral under construction, has thirty-six stairs to climb to the two doors in front; stairs which are a terror to the old and weak. There was neither prudence nor judgment in choosing the site.

Rehearsing his own unique competence and experience in California, the pioneer bishop reminded the congregation that after nearly forty years he was "no stranger to priests and prelates, to Catholics and Protestants, to Jews and Gentiles. . . ." As a pastor and vicar general he had built churches, schools, monasteries, hospitals and orphanages and had paid for them all. As Bishop of Sacramento he had purchased land for a cathedral, an episcopal residence, a retreat house; and all these debts, it was hoped, would be fully liquidated in two years. His own newly constructed cathedral, he claimed proudly, "is the largest and most beautiful church of California, admired by all and attracting to the Church many non-Catholics and indifferent Catholics."[18]

Manogue's defense in Rome had moved Simeoni to reconsider the merits of the case, and in an extraordinary pro-

cedure he informed Riordan of the vigorous refutation and
forwarded a signed version to him.[19] This development depressed the relationship between the archbishop and his suffragan to a new nadir. Once Manogue's signed statement
reached San Francisco, Riordan was acutely incensed on
seeing with his own eyes the blunt and often insulting charges
made by his suffragan. His reply to Propaganda evoked some
of the harshest sentiments ever expressed during his long episcopate. Though he could dismiss the document in a few lines,
he told Simeoni, he judged that his character had been questioned and that he must compose a careful defense of himself. "During the seven years of my administration," he
wrote,

> my relationship with the Bishop of Sacramento
> was most amicable; and though I have never been
> invited to his house, he has ever been a frequent
> visitor in mine. Whenever he came to this city, with
> few exceptions, he always came to see me, dined at
> my table, and consulted me on diocesan points re-
> garding the interests of Religion in this vast area.
> There never passed between us a single word which
> could in the least indicate the state of mind which
> finds expression in the letter of the good Bishop.

Evidently astonished at Manogue's hidden sentiments,
Riordan maintained that during this whole period the Bishop
of Sacramento had never alluded to the matters mentioned in
his report to the Holy See. Even as he wrote these lines to
Rome, the archbishop had in his possession two flagrantly
contradictory documents written by Manogue: one a private
letter addressed to him that was solicitous and affectionate
and the other his notorious report to the Holy See which
teemed with contemptuous and arrogant language. "I am
unable," continued Riordan, "to understand the reason for
this sudden change . . . ," why he had kept an obstinate silence regarding these inequities to his diocese and, particularly, why he had secretly appealed to Rome in order to obtain

justice from his metropolitan. To Riordan, moreover, Manogue's criticisms of the new cathedral in San Francisco were beyond reason — "the style of architecture, the many stairs, and the small door," none of which items was relevant to the issue under consideration. After a detailed and convincing explanation of the financial histories of the two dioceses, Riordan sternly demanded full satisfaction for what he termed this "false and scandalous" behavior. "Not satisfied with accusing the saintly Archbishop Alemany, the founder of this See, of cunning and dishonesty . . . ," he concluded,

> not content with vilifying the character of his Predecessor, Bishop O'Connell. . . , he turns against me, who, on every occasion during the last seven years, always treated him with uniform courtesy and kindness. Such improper and anti-Christian conduct must be stopped, and for my part I respectfully and emphatically pray that the accuser be admonished that Bishops be treated with the courtesy due to their dignity and in a fashion suitable for a Christian gentleman.[20]

Bishop Manogue's personal recourse to the congregation had proved disastrous. The archbishop's spirited defense persuaded Simeoni to close the affair, passing on to Sacramento Riordan's warning to observe the "due character and dignity" of the accused.[21] But more grief awaited Manogue. To his consternation he next learned from San Francisco that Riordan had seen every word of his charges sent to the Holy See; and the archbishop insisted upon an apology from him through Propaganda. Manogue was struck by the force of Riordan's reaction; it was, in the bishop's eye, full of "passion and great excitement . . . bitter beyond expression." The suffragan was further puzzled about how his confidential document fell into the archbishop's hands. "Why he should have received my letter or a full copy thereof from Rome is incomprehensible to me," he desperately asked Archbishop Domenico Jacobini, secretary to the Roman congregation.

Everything I said was true; but it seems the truth is
sometimes distasteful. As I have always esteemed
Archbishop Riordan and as it is only diocesan
matters coming down from Archbishop Alemany
that have caused misunderstandings, I hereby make
the apology demanded if you consider me guilty.
The Archbishop is hasty and impetuous and some
examination on his part would avert many misunderstandings.

Manogue further regretted his remarks about the two cathedrals, never intending, as he said, to "injure feelings." "There
was laudable pride on my part," he explained,

to show that our Cathedral was not inferior to that
of San Francisco, notwithstanding the great and
rich population there while I was compelled to
travel through mountain regions in heat and cold
to collect and meet bills of expense.[22]

* * * * *

When the hardy and virile Patrick Manogue approached
his fifteenth year in the episcopate and at the age of sixty-
three began to give signs of serious physical decline, it was
Riordan's duty as metropolitan to arrange for a successor. In
early January, 1895, less than two months before his death,
Manogue, acutely suffering from poor health, petitioned
Archbishop Francesco Satolli, the apostolic delegate, for a
coadjutor with the right of succession.[23] Riordan had approved of the request and in a letter to Propaganda expressed
his doubt that Manogue would live much longer.[24] Meanwhile, the Holy See asked for more details about the prospective appointment, and Riordan's foreboding was fulfilled
when, after a reign of eleven years, Manogue died on the
morning of Ash Wednesday, February 27, 1895.[25]

Riordan named Father Thomas Grace as diocesan administrator and celebrated the pontifical Mass at the obsequies in

Sacramento.[26] Manogue had died without nominating his co-adjutor and thereby left the issue of succession entirely to the living. Promptly, in Riordan's residence in San Francisco, the five diocesan consultors commenced the business of selecting names for the successor, their choice falling upon four priests of the Diocese of Sacramento.[27] In turn, the bishops of the province met on April 18, including Riordan, Lawrence Scanlan of Salt Lake, and George Montgomery, the new coadjutor of Monterey-Los Angeles. Absent was Francis Mora, who had been detained in Spain because of poor health.

Only one name of the four chosen by the Sacramento consultors, Thomas Grace, was put on the bishops' *terna*. Evidently through the metropolitan's persuasion, the bishops added in second place Thomas James Conaty of Springfield, Massachusetts, and in third place James Cleary of St. Paul. This was the first instance wherein the Holy See would assign a bishop directly to Sacramento. This appointment, Riordan's provincial council emphasized, was critically important since it was the state capital and thereby required a polished and gifted prelate who would best represent the Church in California to the government. Of the three candidates, Grace was clearly the preference. A popular priest who had labored in the area for twenty-three years, he best knew the local conditions and was expected by the people to be Rome's choice. And since the diocese, reported the bishops, embraced such a scattered and mountainous region, the favorite should be an ecclesiastic like Grace who had been long accustomed to the long journeys and physical hardships of the diocese.[28] The apostolic delegate seconded the recommendation of Grace, adding that this priest not only enjoyed the confidence of the bishops, the clergy, and the people, but also was intimately acquainted with the management of this diocese.[29]

When Grace, however, secretly informed the Holy See of his poor health and incapacity to make visitations, Propaganda delayed the nomination and provoked a minor upset in Sacramento. The press in San Francisco had sorely distressed

the diocesan consultors by publishing rumors that Riordan
had been actively campaigning in favor of one of his own
priests. With Manogue's passing, there was no Sacramento
representation on the bishops' council, and not quite two
years had passed since the archbishop had pressured the appointment of his secretary, George Montgomery, as Bishop
Coadjutor of Monterey-Los Angeles. Evidently the presence
of Manogue was still felt in his see. The leaders of the Sacramento clergy feared that Riordan might send another personal favorite to their diocese. In August they felt it worth
their while to make a direct appeal to Rome, demanding a
bishop who would be openly independent and "free from all
bond of particular friendship between him and the metropolitan of San Francisco."[30] These groundless fears were finally
dispelled when nearly a year after Manogue's death Leo XIII
approved the appointment of Thomas Grace on February 22,
1897. On June 16, in Manogue's Cathedral of the Blessed
Sacrament, he was consecrated by Archbishop Riordan, assisted by Bishops Scanlan and Montgomery.[31]

* * * * *

West of the Rockies, midway between Canada and
Mexico, lay the forbidding Territory of Utah, long a no man's
land within the Province of San Francisco, to which as metropolitan Riordan gave a permanent and independent ecclesiastical government. An enormously diversified area, Utah presented exceptional problems for the establishment of the
church. Bisected by the rugged Wasatch Mountains, its irregular physical setting had made colonization and settlement
immensely difficult. In the eastern half of Utah stretched
broken and deep-cut plateaus too rugged for farming, a
boundless and lonely wasteland; and in the west, encircled by
highlands, lay the Great Basin with its arid valleys and sage-
brush deserts.

By the time that Riordan succeeded to the spiritual administration of this land, the Mormons had dominated it politically, economically, and religiously for nearly a half cen-

tury, that is, since Brigham Young led a pilgrim host into the valley of the Great Salt Lake. In the next fifty years the Mormons developed into a self-conscious and tightly sealed community, wrestling a hard living from the desert. Their numbers increased as Mormon converts poured into the territory. Communal settlements quickly spread along a promising river-crossed strip between the Great Salt Lake and the Wasatch Mountains, and under Young's genius for organization these pioneers began to prosper, engaged in the lively commerce on the overland trail routes, and succeeded in forcing the sterile land to yield to their irrigation projects. The stark aridity of the area had first left the Mormons in virtual isolation, but by reason of the railroad and mining enterprises, substantial number of newcomers or "Gentiles" were attracted to Utah, who resented Mormon exclusiveness and felt, in turn, despised as undesirable and unregenerate intruders. Though the Mormons composed seven-eighths of the population, the antagonism endured beyond the turn of the twentieth century.[32]

No Catholic bishop would be inclined to welcome responsibility for this area; and Patrick Riordan was no exception. In February, 1868, the Holy See had erected a vicariate apostolic which included the Territories of Colorado and Utah and had named as vicar Bishop Joseph P. Machebeuf.[33] Very soon after his commission the new vicar undertook the more than 600 miles to Salt Lake City, the center of the Mormon Church and the home of Brigham Young. In dispatching his first impressions to Rome, Machebeuf reported that the territory was inhabited by a great majority of "fanatics" numbering more than 100,000 souls. Their center was Salt Lake City, a beautiful township well-planned and garnished with a multitude of gardens and trees. The city's population ranged between 25,000 and 30,000 among whom, said Machebeuf, there were "less than 1,000 *Gentiles* as the Mormons call all those who do not belong to their sect." In his tour of two weeks the French-born missionary had found in the whole territory not more than thirty Catholics, and in a heart-rending farewell he had promised them a resident priest.[34]

Although Bishop Machebeuf had sent in succession two priests to the desolate mission in Utah, the work had proved too taxing for the struggling vicariate. Through his intercession the Holy See on February 23, 1871, had entrusted the care of this territory to the Archbishop of San Francisco, and Alemany accepted the responsibility with considerable reluctance.[35] The first pastor of Utah Territory named by Alemany was Father Patrick Walsh, who built the historic church of St. Mary Magdalene, the only Catholic edifice then in the entire region. He was succeeded in mid-1873 by Lawrence Scanlan, an outstanding Irish missionary who, for forty-two years, was destined to guide the Catholic Church in Utah.[36] When Scanlan arrived in Salt Lake City to assume his parish which, he claimed, covered 84,916 square miles — equal in size to England and Scotland combined — he found "only about a dozen individual Catholics in this City then having a population of 25,000."[37]

Under Scanlan, who was ably assisted by another Irish-born missionary, Father Denis Kiely, the Catholic Church in Utah had begun to take root. Their community developed rapidly enough that only thirteen years after his arrival the territory was ready for its own government. The administration of Utah from the edge of the Pacific Coast presented awkward problems, tautly stretching the archdiocese 1,200 miles across two states and a broad territory and making episcopal visitations very difficult. Riordan had made a serious effort to study first-hand the conditions in the territory. In his first three years in the west he paid at least six visits to Utah, acquainting himself with each mission station and prominent lay leaders. No one, he believed, knew the religious situation in Utah as intimately as he, except for priests working in the territory.[38] Heavy pressures were applied at Propaganda when Riordan renewed an old Alemany policy of requesting a vicariate for Utah. Alemany himself personally advanced the cause. Stopping in Rome after his resignation, the old prelate strongly added his support to the proposal.[39] Under Simeoni's instructions, Riordan assembled a provincial meeting, and the bishops submitted a vicariate which would include not only the whole Territory of Utah but also six counties of eastern Nevada. Within this large area, Riordan himself estimated a probable total of nearly 9,000 Catholics, 5,300 in Utah, and 3,500 in this portion of Nevada. The three candidates suggested all belonged to the Archdiocese of San Francisco, each Irish-born alumnus of All Hallows College. Named first was Lawrence Scanlan, the vicar general of the Archdiocese of San Francisco for Utah. Only forty-three years of age, he had been working in the distant missions of the archdiocese since his ordination nineteen years before, twelve years of which had been spent in Nevada and Utah. Richly qualified in every respect, Scanlan was, in Riordan's opinion, his most experienced priest in practical affairs, gifted with good sense and very popular among the people of Utah, Catholics and non-Catholics. Having served since Alemany's administration as vicar forane in Utah, Scanlan knew the whole territory intimately, and the church's successes there were due directly to his leadership and zeal.

Completing this *terna* were Thomas Grace, then the pastor of St. Rose's Church in Sacramento, and William O'Connor, pastor of St. Mary's Church in Stockton. But, as Riordan told Simeoni, the one candidate specially recommended by the bishops of the province was Scanlan since, he said, "we are convinced that there is no part in this vast territory, no matter how remote and difficult to approach, which he could not promptly visit, straining in every way to provide for the spiritual needs of his people.[40] These and other considerations which had been proposed by Alemany in Rome moved Propaganda on September 6, 1886, to name Scanlan the first Vicar Apostolic of Utah and titular Bishop of Larandum, an action sanctioned six days later by Leo XIII.[41] One remaining delicate responsibility for Riordan at this time was to make certain that his new suffragan had some clergy since the priests serving in Utah had the right to return to San Francisco. The archbishop himself made the trip to Salt Lake City and personally begged them not to leave their missions in the territory. He succeeded admirably as each priest consented to remain with the new vicar apostolic; and the intrep-

id nucleus of the church in Utah was preserved intact.[42]
Scanlan's consecration was delayed, however, as another decree was needed from Rome to clarify that the new vicariate
belonged to the Province of San Francisco.[43] Assisted by
Bishops O'Connell and Manogue, Archbishop Riordan imposed hands upon him on July 29, 1887, in San Francisco —
the thirty-fourth anniversary of the province.

The elevation of the Utah vicariate into a diocese four
years later was far more complicated an episode, and it better
revealed Riordan's firm commitment to the courageous work
there. Curiously, this development became entangled in swift
ecclesiastical movements in the Middle West, and Riordan
soon found that the larger issue was not to gain a new diocese
but to retain the invaluable Lawrence Scanlan in this crucial
post within his province. After two heroic years in the unpromising Diocese of Cheyenne, Bishop Maurice Burke submitted his resignation in 1889 and suggested that his territory
be committed to the Vicariate Apostolic of Utah.[44] Even
though he would acquire from Burke's administration a scattered Catholic population of 2,100 and only five priests,
Scanlan welcomed the additional charge and keenly took this
opportunity to petition the Holy See to raise his vicariate to
the status of a diocese. Since the pioneer foundation of its
first permanent mission in 1871, the church in Utah, he
informed Simeoni, had expanded at an extraordinary rate,
numbering after only nineteen years ten priests and sixty
sisters, fifteen churches and eleven schools instructing nearly
1,000 students, and a growing Catholic population of
6,000.[45]

While the Utah question was pending, it so happened that
a coadjutor was requested for James O'Connor, Bishop of
Omaha, whose health had seriously failed. Planning to meet
two needs in a single appointment, Cardinal Simeoni preferred to send to Omaha Bishop Burke, who possibly would
keep in this new appointment the administration of Cheyenne. The metropolitan, however, Archbishop Kenrick of St.
Louis, was not in favor of this arrangement. Since delays
were compounding problems in Bishop O'Connor's diocese,

an unauthorized diocesan council was summoned by the vicar general in Omaha and recommended the name of Riordan's colleague in Salt Lake City, Lawrence Scanlan.[46]

Though far removed from these developments in the Middle West, Archbishop Riordan remained intensely interested in these complications in mid-America for two reasons. Bishop Burke had been his friend since their days as priests in Chicago. As a newly ordained priest, Burke had been assigned first to Riordan's close friend, Father Joseph Roles, and had later succeeded to the archbishop's old parish of St. Mary's in Joliet, Illinois.[47] When, at this time, the suggestion had been made to send Burke from Cheyenne to the Diocese of Monterey-Los Angeles as coadjutor to Bishop Mora, Riordan heartily opposed as an "injustice" the removal of his friend from independent authority to a secondary position. "If Los Angeles were vacant," he wrote to Father John P. Farrelly of the American College in Rome,

> I would say, "Yes, certainly." He would be extremely popular and he would work splendidly. He has always been a perfect priest and gentleman.[48]

Riordan agreed with Simeoni that Burke should be appointed to Omaha, but he disapproved entirely of the six candidates recommended for that see by the Province of St. Louis. It had been more than two decades since the tragic Duggan affair in Chicago, and Riordan evidently bore deeply rooted grievances against Archbishop Kenrick who had defended the ill-fated prelate and concurred in the punishment of Riordan's dearest friends in the priesthood. "I would be glad for many reasons, exclusive of personalities," he confessed freely, "to see sent to Omaha someone who has not grown up in the atmosphere of St. Louis. An infusion of new blood would do no harm."

But this new blood, the Archbishop of San Francisco also made clear, would not come from his province, particularly from Salt Lake City. This was the second reason why the Omaha succession interested Riordan: he had heard what he termed an "absurd" rumor that Scanlan was being seriously considered for this diocese. Not a member of the Province of St. Louis, Riordan had no direct way of communicating his views to Propaganda. But this handicap did not eliminate him from these developments. The best way to alert the Roman authorities, he knew, would be through a familiar unofficial medium, his friends at the American College in Rome. "I cannot understand it," he openly confided to Denis O'Connell.

> Monsig. Scanlan is in his due position, and does his work better probably than another could do it. It would be a great mistake to transfer him. I would protest against [such a removal] in the most energetic manner. Inform me if there is some rumor of this kind in Rome.[49]

By June, 1890, Propaganda was disposed to consider these three interrelated issues — a new diocese to be erected at Salt Lake City, the troubled conditions at Cheyenne, and a coadjutor for Omaha. The congregation, however, elected to defer any decision until additional information reconciled a number of conflicting proposals.[50] An inquiry from Simeoni was sent to San Francisco, asking for Riordan's opinion on the creation of a diocese at Salt Lake City.[51] The proposal, the archbishop replied, was "most agreeable to the Bishops of the Province." For one reason rarely considered, according to Riordan, the civil courts in the United States that protected property rights were unaccustomed to titular sees and vicariates apostolic. In the instance of succession, there would be less danger in losing ecclesiastical property if it were registered in the name of the Bishop of Salt Lake.[52]

Meanwhile, however, Riordan had not succeeded in removing the danger that he might lose Scanlan. In October the Omaha consultors again placed him at the head of their *terna*, but the bishops of the province replaced his name with that of Richard Scannell, Bishop of Concordia, Kansas, and in so doing, they announced that ". . . it would be a great calamity for the Church to move Mons. Scanlan from Utah, where he is working so well and ... difficult to find another who would labor with success in this poor vicariate."[53] Possibly Riordan had informally communicated his strong views to St. Louis. Propaganda examined both lists of candidates for Omaha and compromised, returning Scanlan to the position of *dignissimus* and naming Scannell *dignior*. Riordan could have done no more to prevent Scanlan's removal. But his worst fears for the eastern portion of his province failed to materialize when on December 16, 1890, the congregation erected a diocese at Salt Lake City and named Scanlan its first bishop.[54] Only through his persistent intervention did Riordan succeed in keeping the one man whom he felt to be indispensable for the singular mission in Utah.

* * * * *

The third suffragan see under Patrick Riordan was the venerable Diocese of Monterey-Los Angeles, which comprised the southern portion of his province. Originally his predecessor had begun his episcopal ministry in this territory when he had been appointed in 1850 Bishop of Monterey. Three years later, however, when Alemany was promoted to the archiepiscopal See of San Francisco, the new Diocese of Monterey-Los Angeles had been created, and Thaddeus Amat, C.M., named as its first bishop who, in 1859, moved his residence from Santa Barbara to Los Angeles. This diocese embraced an area of 86,632 square miles, equivalent, the Holy See would be told by Riordan, to two-thirds of the area of Italy, and it included those parts of southern California and Nevada below 37°6′N. Lat., from the Pacific Ocean to the Vicariate Apostolic of Arizona.

During the quarter century of Amat's episcopate (1853-1878), this territory had remained the "cow counties" of California, developing at a sluggish rate in comparison to the constant economic and industrial advance around San Francisco. Amat's greatest problem then was simply the visitation of his diocese. Whenever he was scheduled to inspect the north, he had first to entrain directly to San Francisco, a distance then of 484 miles, and thence to make his

way to the northern portions of his diocese. About the time
of Amat's death in 1878, however, the diocese had been
struck with a boom that suddenly transformed southern California into a major population area. As the predominantly
Irish- and Spanish-born secular priests discovered, these new
immigrants originated largely from the Middle West where an
Anglo-Saxon, nativist culture abounded. By the turn of the
century, though San Francisco remained heavily Catholic, the
south had discarded its early traditions and had become
predominantly Protestant.[55] It was in this fast developing
Diocese of Monterey-Los Angeles that Archbishop Riordan
was most forcefully to exert his rights as metropolitan.

Thaddeus Amat had been a sturdy, strong-minded prelate, described by Bishop William Ullathorne of Birmingham
as the "shrewdest" man at Vatican Council I. He was known
to have, on occasion, clashed with his metropolitan, Archbishop Alemany.[56] After a rule of twenty-five years, he left
at his death a legacy of administrative problems for his successor, Bishop Francis Mora. In his first report to Propaganda
in 1881, Mora recorded the early stages of the non-Catholic
influx into his diocese, noting that out of the 13,000 living in
Los Angeles only 5,000 were Catholic. The diocese possessed
a total of forty-three priests of whom only twenty-two were
resident pastors serving a Catholic population of 25,000. The
real weakness of Mora's diocese lay in two related areas, finances and education. In such a developing territory there
were no parochial schools except two in Los Angeles. Although Mora had managed in three years to scale the diocese's debt to $60,000, he was sorely plagued with an exorbi-
tant annual interest of nine per cent. The only evident
solution for liquidating this liability and for constructing
schools, he felt, would be to allow him to sell the extensive
mission properties which were unproductive and virtually
worthless.[57]

From his earliest days in California, Riordan had been
acutely aware of the phenomenal growth in the south. Before
he left in 1888 for his first *ad limina* journey to Rome, he did
not disguise from Mora his intention of personally informing

the Holy See of the pressing need of a coadjutor for the
Diocese of Monterey-Los Angeles. At first Mora was not enthusiastic about this prospect. He could yet rule effectively
without such help, but, he told Propaganda, if it so judged,
he would accept a coadjutor with whom he could work agree-
ably. Evidently Riordan's description of the demands of
southern California had moved the Prefect to instruct Mora
to nominate a coadjutor. "Your Diocese is too large," added
Simeoni, "and the number of inhabitants increases day by
day, so that it is extremely difficult to see how one person
however industrious can effectively provide for the demands
and necessities of the Church." In reply, Mora recommended
Joachim Adam, a pioneering Spanish-born priest who was
fifty-one years of age and who had served for five years as
Mora's vicar general, a priest whom the bishop earnestly desired as his successor.[58]

The candidate, a former student of the Urban College in
Rome, was not unknown to the congregation. He had shortly
before, through Mora's intervention, declined the Vicariate
Apostolic of Brownsville on the excuse of poor health.
Simeoni was apparently perplexed at Adam's sudden recovery of health. Having nonetheless promised to send Mora
an agreeable coadjutor, Simeoni turned to Riordan for his
personal views on the candidate.[59] This invitation gave Riordan an opportunity to submit a detailed and forthright analysis of the Diocese of Monterey-Los Angeles, a generous opportunity in which he displayed his most active intervention
in the affairs of a suffragan see. It entangled him in a knotty
problem of succession which occupied a good deal of his time
and energy for five years. A radical adjustment must be made
for the southern portion of his province, replied the archbishop. A coadjutor would be the short-term solution, but
plans must also be made for a division of the diocese in two
or three years. The new coadjutor, Riordan indicated, must
be a man "rather young in age but endowed with talent,
energy, and strength of character so as to be able to infuse
vitality into that diocese which is presently weak and in-
firm."

Riordan knew Adam well, first as a schoolmate at the Urban College and then as a priest in California. "He is a great friend of mine," he wrote: "an excellent and most worthy Priest, but wholly unfit to be made a Bishop." The vicar general, first, suffered continuously from asthma attacks which often forced him to leave Los Angeles for long intervals. Father Adam, added Riordan from personal experience, had "no more ability in managing the temporal affairs of a diocese than a baby," being unable to administer even his small parish. Though an amiable gentleman, he also lacked the strength of character that was indispensable as Mora's successor, and he would tend to be governed by the clergy rather than to rule himself. If consulted, the priests of the Diocese of Monterey-Los Angeles, the archbishop advised, would overwhelmingly prefer Adam in their desire to preserve the status quo. "They care not to see change," he explained,

> which introduces new life in the diocese. They want a Bishop whom they can manage as they wish. Many of them want only to be left in peace and free to do what they please. The laity, forming a truly strong part of the Church in the diocese, would be immensely discontented since, if he were promoted, they would be entirely deprived of all hope, at least for many years, of seeing our Holy Religion prosper and progress in this region.

Southern California, Propaganda was further informed, had been inundated by immigration from the eastern United States. Protestant groups, particularly the Methodists and Baptists, had nearly taken command of this portion of the state. In such a desperate situation, this diocese needed a "strong, active, energetic Bishop, who has good use of the English language," and, Riordan warned, "if we do not wish entirely to lose our present position, we must send some help as soon as possible." Though not requested to suggest alternate candidates, he mentioned that he had in mind two or three priests suited for this emergency, and if the congregation were interested, he would assemble a provincial council to submit a formal *terna*.[60]

Riordan was determined to prevent Adam's appointment and to have his say as metropolitan. Riordan certainly resented Mora's direct communication with the Holy See regarding his successor and his tendency of eliminating his provincial council of bishops from reviewing the candidates. As soon as his own letter was dispatched to Rome, Riordan enlisted the services of Denis O'Connell to whom he remarked that

> . . . of all the names Adam is the most incompetent. He is an excellent poor man, and is rather suitable to be a chaplain in a community of nuns.

If the question be referred to the bishops of the province, he continued, they would all, Mora excepted, disqualify Adam, and the cardinal prefect must be induced to send to the south a "brave and energetic" man. "You must see to it," he directed O'Connell in a second letter, "that no appointment is made until the Bps. of the Province have a meeting. It would not be fair to us."[61]

Cardinal Simeoni had promised an agreeable coadjutor to Bishop Mora and had allowed him even to make a selection, an exception to procedure. Now alarmed, however, by this strong and uncomplimentary appraisal from the metropolitan, the prefect was stunned. Eventually he accepted the metropolitan's recommendations to conform to regular procedures. Directives were sent to San Francisco and Los Angeles, ordering a regular *terna* to be drawn up.[62] According to prescription, Mora convened his diocesan consultors who proposed Joachim Adam; Polydore J. Stockman, pastor of St. Bernadine of Siena Church in San Bernardino; and Laurence Serda, pastor of Sacred Heart Church in Oakland. In turn, the four bishops of the province met in San Francisco in September, 1889, results of which reflected the archbishop's domination. The bishops' meeting must have been a stern encounter between Riordan and Mora. First, the *terna* from Los Angeles was discarded. The new list of candidates was a curious document which kept Adam in first place with a special recommendation but added Edward Dunne, Riordan's friend and pastor of All Saints Church in Chicago, and George Montgomery, chancellor of the Archdiocese of San Francisco.[63] When the bishops next discussed the division of the Diocese of Monterey-Los Angeles, Mora protested vehemently and left the meeting. After some hesitation, he had consented to additional candidates, but not to the partition of his territory. Yet despite his opposition Riordan, together with Manogue and Scanlan, sent separately to the Holy See a detailed plan of the prospective division.[64]

Eventually, as a compromise, Riordan endorsed Adam and proposed as well the division of Mora's diocese. These developments in California only confused the Holy See, and Riordan's labored explanations did not help. In addition, by 1890 Propaganda was beginning to show signs of irritation toward Mora for his evident incapacity to develop an adequate parochial-school system. Only twelve schools had been opened by 1890 along side forty-three churches.[65] Propaganda had begun to lose confidence in Mora's administrative ability. Mora's persistent contention that most places were too impoverished to afford a parochial school had become unconvincing. In February, 1892, Mora was, therefore, sternly instructed that Propaganda was considering partition and was taking from him virtual financial control of the diocese. He was then forbidden to alienate any property or to incur new debts without special permission from Rome.[66]

Riordan had never anticipated that his original recommendations would provoke the loss of fiscal control in the south, a harsh action which came as a staggering blow to his senior suffragan. In a confidential letter to Rome, Mora deplored the severe restriction over diocesan finances. There was in the province, he insisted, a movement among the "American bishops" against him because of his Spanish origins. With this prohibition he was likewise uncertain how to go about paying taxes and improving the diocese. This was a reasonable defense, and in another effort to learn the exact state of the diocese, the prefect consulted Bishop Peter Verdaguer, Vicar Apostolic of Brownsville, who had been a priest of Monterey-Los Angeles.[67] This Spanish-born prelate assured Propaganda that Mora's diocese was genuinely straitened simply because his taxes were high and his revenue low. As long as he lacked the authority to sell property, his taxes would place him more deeply in debt. But the wretched condition of the diocese, added Verdaguer, was bound to improve with the continuous stream of immigrants into southern California. Prompted by these recommendations, in August, 1890, the congregation partially lifted its restrictions imposed on Mora.[68]

Riordan had meanwhile withdrawn from the question of a coadjutor or partition for the Diocese of Monterey-Los Angeles. His letters to Denis O'Connell in late 1891 had recorded his last views until early 1893 when Bishop Mora himself reopened the issue. This time he wanted to resign from the see. Informing both the Holy See and Riordan, the sixty-five-year-old prelate attributed his decision to broken health. For a year and a half his physical and mental powers, he said, had progressively declined, his memory failing and his mind unable to co-ordinate ideas. Even at present, he noted, he was scarcely able to stand upright while celebrating Mass.[69] The new Prefect of Propaganda, Cardinal Miecislaus Ledochowski, tried to console the stricken bishop in his sufferings, inviting him rather to accept a coadjutor than to resign.[70] A man who had shortly before suffered the loss of the financial administration of his diocese, Francis Mora was immensely grateful to the Holy See for this unexpected expression of solicitude. Though he yet preferred total abdication, he would welcome any arrangement by Rome and recommended a hasty appointment.[71] Even his tenacious metropolitan was hasty to add his own word of encouragement. A bishop's life, Riordan told Mora, would tax the strongest constitution; and if he were older than his fifty-two years he would request a coadjutor for San Francisco to share the responsibility. "I have made up my mind," he further confessed, "that should my life be spared seven or eight years longer to ask permission to retire and let someone else carry on with the work."[72]

The heavy immigration into southern California had been fast transforming the racial complexion of his see. Bishop Mora, even after offering his resignation, favored the continuance of Spanish-speaking prelates. But Riordan had long disapproved ·of perpetuating such a succession, convinced that his own advent to the west had ended the Spanish ascendancy in the province. This spirit was reflected officially for the first time in the southern diocese when its consultors met in August, 1893, and chose a *terna* for the coadjutorship. The Los Angeles consultors selected George Montgomery as *dignissimus*, Riordan's own chancellor in San Francisco; Thomas Grace as *dignior*, then chancellor of Sacramento; and William O'Connor, pastor of St. Mary's Church in Stockton — each of these candidates English-speaking.[73] Within the same month Riordan summoned his suffragans to San Francisco where they endorsed the consultors' *terna*.[74]

Through the newly appointed apostolic delegate, Archbishop Francesco Satolli, Riordan renewed his efforts at having a coadjutor appointed at once to Monterey-Los Angeles. Montgomery was the logical choice, Riordan told the delegate. By any comparison he was far more able and worthy than the other two candidates on the *terna*: "We put their names on the list because we had no others."[75] During these anxious days the archbishop again enlisted the aid of Denis O'Connell in Rome, urging him even to "volunteer without being asked a strong word in his behalf."[76] After an uncomfortable delay Propaganda was ready to end this thorny issue and on December 18, 1893, named the forty-six-year-old chancellor-coadjutor to Bishop Mora with the right of succession. The nomination was sanctioned by Leo XIII on January 7, 1894.[77] O'Connell immediately telegraphed the news to San Francisco, and Riordan registered his supreme delight at Montgomery's promotion. "The appointment," he reflected,

while it deprives me of one of the best men I have
ever known, and one [of] the most loyal and devoted workers, gives a most excellent Bishop to
Los Angeles, and so I am resigned to lose him for
the greater good of all California. Deo Gratias for
this grace.[78]

The California hierarchy thus acquired its first native-born
American.

* * * * *

The effectiveness of any society, religious or civil, is
largely dependent upon a reasonable flexibility, its capacity
to sound the current tendencies within its environment and
to make discreet accommodations. Coming from Chicago
with its traditions of enterprise and efficiency, Archbishop
Riordan devoted a good portion of his first decade in San
Francisco to promoting enduring changes in his province. The
struggling church in the northern portions of the state was
first stabilized when its see was moved from the dying mining
regions to the prospering capital of California. Through Riordan's assistance the future of the Church was secured to the
east when the Territory of Utah gave signs of promise and
was rewarded with an independent administration. To the
south, the languid Diocese of Monterey-Los Angeles formally
ended its Spanish period and was given its first native American bishop.

The first third of Riordan's episcopate had recorded an
extraordinary transition for the Catholic community in the
West. He had begun this period as the youngest bishop in
California: Mora was his elder by nineteen years and Manogue by fifteen. But under Riordan a new generation of suffragans had evolved, each hand-picked not by their episcopal
predecessors but for the first time by the Archbishop of San
Francisco. Three notable priests, who at one time belonged
to the archdiocese, now occupied the satellite sees; and each
had been Riordan's candidate. Grace and Scanlan would sur-

vive their metropolitan at their posts; and Montgomery would return to San Francisco as coadjutor, never to succeed.

Evidently, Patrick Riordan's instincts had not allowed him to confine his energies to his own see. He was an archbishop in the fullest sense, a religious leader who viewed seriously his responsibilities as metropolitan and who alerted himself to the critical changes affecting his vast province. As a strong executive, he was determined to pilot the church's development in the Far West. It is ironical, too, that in his province Riordan would soon exercise the tight control of episcopal appointments which had characterized St. Louis during those lean years in which Chicago priests like himself and his friends had little hope for advancement.

6

Collision Course

The middle years of Archibishop Riordan's episcopate were plagued by an acute epidemic of nativism, a relentless antagonism toward the foreign-born.[1] In the turbulent 1890's, the American Protective Association emerged prominently in northern California, exploiting the anti-Catholic and anti-alien feelings there and provoking the rise of one of the church's most brilliant and irrepressible defenders, Father Peter Christopher Yorke.

One of the major factors for this conflict was the numerical predominance in Riordan's see city of the foreign-born residents of any of the thirty-five principal cities of the United States, an extraordinary 42 per cent.[2] The city's principal immigrant group, the Irish, whom Riordan regarded as the backbone of his laity, composed more than a tenth of the city's population.[3] In playing a conspicuous role in labor movements and politics, they had long aroused the ethnic suspicions of respectable middle-class folk. The boisterous and chauvinistic celebrations on St. Patrick's Day annually revived a stinging resentment against the Irish revelers. "What has given most offense to most Americans, native and naturalized," commented one veteran journalist,

> were the efforts of the Irish to have the banner of their race take the place of the national flag on public buildings . . . efforts to secure a more formal recognition of the supremacy of one class of for-

137

eigners over not only all other classes of foreigners,
but the natives as well.[4]

Had Patrick Riordan been possessed of clairvoyance in
the first decade of his episcopate, he might have perceived
slight but dangerous manifestations of nativism. In 1886, a
year after he had received the pallium, a disgruntled politician, Peter D. Wigginton, proclaimed in Fresno the birth of a
new American Party, whose platform demanded a restrictive
immigration policy and the repeal of naturalization laws.[5]
The work of Frank Pixley as an editor and debater fore-
shadowed the religious tempest which would rage during the
archbishop's middle years. The *Argonaut,* Pixley's highly influential San Francisco weekly, was distinguished for its brilliant writing and range of interests, having earned the reputation of being the "most original, most readable, and most
widely read weekly west of New York."[6] But beneath its
sophistication it was intensely anti-Catholic; and from 1878
to 1896, more editorial space was devoted to the Catholic
question than to any other single issue. Themes which Pixley
invoked would become very familiar to Riordan: Catholic
interference in politics, the antagonism between public and
parochial schools, the church's conspiracy for world domination.
     One direct attack on Riordan that betrayed the vitupera-
tive character of religious controversy centered on the
church's discipline on marriage. In 1886, the archbishop ordered the reading of a pastoral letter which repeated the
grave penalties for Catholics who married without a priest as
witness. Outraged by the silence of the daily press, Pixley
misrepresented the letter as an indictment against the sanc-
tity and integrity of non-Catholic marriages. Archbishop
Riordan had dared to state, he wrote savagely,

    that American citizens who marry . . . according
    to the laws of this country are living in horrible
    concubinage and their off-spring consequently bas-
    tards unless they pay so many dollars and buy the

gracious consent of the foreign Prince to whom
they owe allegiance.

    . . . Is there another man in San Francisco ex-
cept Patrick Riordan or some of his Irish crew,
who dares to step forward in public. . . and call the
daughters of America harlots and their sons bas-
tards.[7]

But the archbishop did not view Pixley with alarm or as a
serious menace to the religious tranquility of San Francisco.
In his *ad limina* journey of 1888, he informed Propaganda that
though he had encountered some written and spoken hostility against the church, his faithful enjoyed peace and were
exposed to no form of persecution.[8] Pixley's significance,
nevertheless, was first to reveal a nativist minority evolving at
this time in California. It would develop into an articulate
segment that would attract prominent figures and not hesitate to engage the church publicly. Pixley's style of argument
also previewed the gross tactics invoked by religious controversialists, tactics that Riordan and his apologist, Father
Yorke, would later confront and adopt in their fullest fury. A
penetrating analysis of these tactics was offered by Arthur
McEwen, an independent newspaper man himself whose
forthright opinions spared neither persons nor institutions.
McEwen conceded Pixley's journalistic abilities. "California,"
he admitted, "has never had a more vigorous newspaper
writer. . .never. . .equalled for the sonorous force and masculine swing of his style." But, insisted McEwen, his strategy
was cruel and dishonest. Pixley was "not fair," he continued,

> He did not pretend to be. It was his glory to be a
> headlong partisan. He left it to the other side to
> correct his mistakes and misstatements. If history
> did not meet his momentary requirements he
> amended history . . . he accused, vituperated, ridi-
> culed, insulted, outraged, inflaming himself with
> the clangor of his own style as if it were a battle

drum. He planned a campaign to smite the Catholic
Church anywhere and everywhere, and to hit an
Irish head wherever it had the misfortune to be
within reach of his bludgeon. He was out for indis-
criminate war, war that recognized none of the
ameliorations of civilization.[9]

This described a style of polemic that even clergymen would
adopt in defense.

The force which ignited and sustained the religious controversy during Riordan's episcopate was the American Protective Association. Founded in Iowa in 1887, this militant
anti-Catholic movement had been rooted in California by
1893.[10] As the A.P.A. gained momentum, Archbishop Riordan and other Catholic leaders had at first perceived little
danger. The *Monitor* dismissed it as another "simple Orange
movement," and comforted itself with the conviction that
eastern bigotry would never cross the Rockies.[11] The archbishop did not record his views in these early stages, but in
February, 1894, Father William Gleeson, a seasoned polemicist who had debated with Pixley himself, made the "first
public notice" of the association in California. To a large
audience he explained that it could not survive in the enlightened nineteenth century and could be extinguished by
mere exposure.[12] While these sweet words were comforting
the Catholic community, the first A.P.A. local council had
been founded in September, 1893, rapidly expanding in membership and planning for the moment in which to leap upon
the public scene.[13]

The incident that eventually brought the association out
of the shadows was a minor dispute in which Archbishop
Riordan protested the use of an allegedly anti-Catholic
textbook in the public schools of San Francisco. In February
an unsigned report was submitted to the Board of Education
denouncing the *Outlines of Medieval and Modern History* by
Philip Van Ness Myers.[14] The document was meticulously
prepared, extracting a number of quotations from the textbook and arguing in great detail that it was offensive to Cath-

olics and had no place in nonsectarian schools. The origin of
this protest was uncertain; and though no signature was affixed to it, the board presumed that the complaint came
from the Catholic clergy with official sanction. The situation
became increasingly confused, however, when in an interview
Riordan refused to involve himself directly and denied any
knowledge of the document. "I know nothing of the book or
the protest," he said. "I have never seen the history or heard
of it." He was even too busy, he added, to read the protest.
His denial prompted the board to create a committee to investigate the complaint.[15]   In the following weeks the committee considered statements from various quarters which included the publisher, the American Patriotic League, and
several Protestant ministers. In mid-March, the controversy
again flared up when the *Examiner* published Riordan's own
lengthy report to the committee which detailed his objection
to the *Outlines* and to the publisher's explanations. After
enumerating a large number of what he termed exaggerations
or falsehoods, Riordan demanded the suppression of the
book. "There are many more and even worse things in the
volume," he emphatically concluded, "and after a careful
examination I consider it utterly unfit for use in a school
patronized by children of various creeds."[16]

   Alert nativists, exploiting the high tension, viewed the
archbishop's strong condemnation as an affront to American
institutions. Immediately there appeared in San Francisco the
first public lectures sponsored by the American Protective
Association. On March 18, John Quincy Adams Henry, a
zealous nativist and the pastor of the First Baptist Church,
inaugurated a series of anti-Catholic meetings that ran on
indefinitely on Sunday afternoons. His lectures drew packed
audiences, according to press accounts, as he pointed his first
arrows against Riordan's report and loudly declaimed against
"Rome's Hand in Our Public Schools."[17]   At his first
meeting, A. P. A. officers appeared publicly on the platform
with several clergymen, the unveiling of an alliance that
would endure during the entire life of the association in California.[18]   Meanwhile, the pressure mounted day by day, and

the Board of Education had hoped that a compromise would
settle the dispute. On April 11, the board ruled that Myers'
Outlines was to be retained in the public schools, but the
teachers were authorized to omit passages of the text that
they judged prejudicial.[19] This decision was a smarting
rebuff to Riordan, who had publicly demanded its
suppression.

*   *   *   *   *

Riordan was reluctant to encourage a religious controversy by personally responding to broadsides from the American Protective Association. The medium through which he
chose to present a Catholic defense was the *Monitor,* the
official Catholic paper whose circulation extended throughout the Pacific Coast. Throughout his administration, he
spared no effort in promoting a strong Catholic paper. So
vigorous were his convictions regarding this press that he was
willing even to discontinue the *Monitor* if it failed in competence and effectiveness.[20] "The most powerful educational
agency of our day and country is the press," he reasoned.

> Our age is predominently an age of newspapers.
> Millions, old and young, look to them as the only
> source of knowledge. . . . In large measure they
> occupy the place once held by the pulpit and plat-
> form.

The Catholic press was, in his judgment, an indispensable
instrument in dispensing Catholic teaching and supplement-
ing what was lacking in sermons and classrooms.[21]
Before the outburst of the A.P.A., however, Riordan
had been silently critical of the *Monitor,* and contemplated
drastic changes in its management and structure. The *Monitor*
had become an old and familiar feature of Catholic life in San
Francisco, having been founded in 1858 by three Catholic
laymen. But as a weekly that reported Catholic and Irish
news, it had had for nearly two decades no official

association with the archdiocese although Alemany encouraged its support.[22] In 1880, the Monitor Publishing Company was created originally as a "partnership," including several clergy and a layman. Eventually the Archbishop of San Francisco headed the organization.[23]

The opportunity for change came in 1891 when Stephen J. McCormick, the venerable editor of eleven years, died. A temporary editor, Bryan Clinch, was appointed, and the partners discussed the possibilities of tightening of the *Monitor's* organization by legally incorporating it. One partner, Bishop Patrick Manogue of Sacramento, particularly favored this action because, in his judgment, the weekly

> has been allowed to droop and decay under the old regime. It was merely a family arrangement . . . and in want of new blood, decayed and almost died. On the coast, there are many souvenirs connected with the Monitor from early days, and today the only good thing about it is its old time name — 'The Monitor.'[24]

Almost a month later, he repeated his dissatisfaction to Riordan's secretary, Father George Montgomery. "The *Monitor* has nothing but a name, an old name; it requires new life . . .," he wrote emphatically. "To be able to recommend it, it must be improved."[25] This view reflected the sentiment of the other owners who had, under Riordan's leadership, converted the proprietorship of the *Monitor* in February, 1892, from a partnership into a joint-stock company. Under the incorporation, a new board of directors was formed, electing Riordan as president.[26]

This action marked an important departure for the *Monitor*. Riordan now took a greater personal interest in the paper, determined now to eliminate its substantial annual deficits and making its success an archdiocesan project. Thus it became the official organ for the Archdiocese of San Francisco and for the Diocese of Sacramento. The clergy was asked to support it; sermons on Catholic literature were

preached in every church; and the archbishop invested every
dividend into its improvement.[27] The board of directors desired, above all, a fresher spirit in the *Monitor,* and while the
legal changes in organization were being arranged, it hired a
new permanent editor. Under the new articles of incorporation, Riordan was responsible for the selection and had
formed definite views on the requirements of a lay editor of
the *Monitor.* "As the majority of our Catholics who support
Catholic papers are of Irish birth or Irish origin," he held,

> it is necessary that the editor should be in sym-
> pathy with the national aspirations of the race,
> otherwise there will be trouble on that head at
> once, and secondly he should be th[o]rough Cath-
> olic having the spirit of the Church in his writings
> . . . a man may be a very good editor of a secular
> paper and a total failure as editor of a Catholic
> paper. A Catholic Editor must know the principles
> of his religion and the history of his Church and be
> in a word a fairly good theologian besides that he
> must in all his writings be filled with the spirit of
> his religion. Of course he should be a practical
> Catholic in his attendance at Mass and in the recep-
> tion of the Sacraments.[28]

A man who fulfilled these detailed qualifications in Riordan's
judgment was Francis J. McGuire, editor of the Portland
Catholic Sentinel, who was engaged and took charge of the
San Francisco paper on April 1, 1892.

While the new *Monitor* showed considerable change, introducing a welcomed new format and pursuing a strongly
Irish policy, there was still need for further editorial strength;
and Riordan was soon to learn the unalloyed sentiments of
his tough-minded suffragan in Sacramento. The *Monitor*
needed more than an attractive layout, insisted Bishop Manogue, a persistent critic who placed the highest priority on
improvement in content. "Even gilded edges," he warned,
"will be of no avail if there be a lack of intrinsic worth." He

even favored the temporary employment of an editorial assistant who would be an able writer and would strengthen the message of the *Monitor*. In his frank judgment, the new editor hired from Portland was not the "one to elevate the paper in the modified form or any form." And Manogue, whose Diocese of Sacramento was also the capital of the state, unequivocally demanded that the new *Monitor* must remain neutral in public matters. Under the former system, before it had become an official organ, the editors did not hesitate to write on the public issues and on men of the day. "Let me, from late experience say," Manogue counseled,

> that no favorite in politics should be held up by the Monitor. . . . Except in a crisis of great magnitude a Catholic paper should be cautiously neutral. Catholics are on both sides of politics. This. . . is private and only my own suggestion.[29]

In November, 1892, Archbishop Riordan, intent on completing his program of reform, met in Chicago a Canadian writer, Francis A. Quinn, and engaged him as "editorial writer." This action, it was hoped, would make the weekly a self-sustaining enterprise, but new problems arose. For some time, unfortunately, the relationship between the editor and the editorial writer had never been clearly defined, a situation that bred strong internal dissension. The paper continued to operate on a deficit; and after only ten months on the *Monitor* staff, McGuire submitted his resignation. "Mr. Quinn," he complained to the archbishop,

> has taken entirely control of affairs when it was thoroughly understood that I would have the management of the paper. . . . It would, in my opinion, be perfectly honorable to pay Mr. Quinn $500 and provide him with a ticket to Chicago. He will never do for this Coast.[30]

In December, 1893, Quinn, the son-in-law of the Irish patriot,

Thomas D'Arcy Magee, succeeded as editor, continuing to stress Irish news but failing to enlarge the editorial vision and interests of the *Monitor*. Possibly, Bishop Manogue's instructions to be neutral on current issues had made his position impossible. Although circulation was increasing, disturbing reports regarding Quinn reached Riordan. The new editor, it was charged, was temperamentally unstable, his budgets uneven, and his editorials notoriously weak and infrequent. "Time and again have I complained of the narrowness of the editorial work," the manager, Charles B. Flanagan, reported,

> . . . the Monitor should be a first class Catholic paper. The editor receives very liberal pay, he receives high pay contrasted with other offices and little return is made for it . . .the paper has been conducted in a narrow groove. Unlike other leading Catholic papers, it has not touched on questions of the day.[31]

Since its reform under Riordan, the *Monitor* had thus suffered an unprecedented series of grievances among its lay personnel. Quinn wished desperately to have his contract renewed and offered to be rehired as editor at half his salary.[32] But Riordan decided to dispose of this internal weakness, especially at a moment when the American Protective Association was growing bolder and more articulate. He began to look among his priests for a man who might edit his weekly, and his eyes fell upon his young chancellor, Father Peter Christopher Yorke.

The priest who succeeded Quinn in the *Monitor* was born on August 13, 1864, in Galway, Ireland, where he had attended various schools in his home district and at the age of eleven had entered St. Jarlath's College, Tuam, to begin preparation for the priesthood.[33] In 1882, Yorke began his first year of philosophy at St. Patrick's College, Maynooth, as a student for the Diocese of Galway and there for four years pursued his studies with a measure of brilliance, winning a modest number of scholastic prizes but receiving no ecclesias-

tical orders.[34] In May, 1886, he had left the college to study
for the Archdiocese of San Francisco, his mother having emi-
grated to the Bay Area. There had been a touch of confusion
in the negotiations which brought Yorke to the United
States, for when Archbishop Riordan had merely written for
the student's testimonials without formally accepting him,
Yorke presumed his adoption and prepared to study for San
Francisco. Riordan was displeased at this impetuosity, and
only York's reply and a statement of the student's own
mother who resided in Hayward, California, satisfied the
archbishop. The cleric was then adopted and directed to go to
Baltimore, where he would begin in September, 1886, his last
two years of preparation at St. Mary's Seminary.[35] On September 3, he arrived at the seminary where he lived with two
students who were in later years intimately associated with
Archbishop Riordan's administration, Patrick E. Mulligan and
Charles A. Ramm. On December 1887, Cardinal James
Gibbons ordained Peter C. Yorke to the priesthood.[36]

In the early months of 1888, the newly ordained priest of
twenty-three years arrived in San Francisco, where Riordan
assigned him to St. Mary's Cathedral on California Street,
thus beginning a vigorous ministry of thirty-seven years. In
November, 1889, the Catholic University of America was inaugurated under the rectorship of Bishop John J. Keane.
Riordan, a strong supporter of the institution who was most
desirous to have the archdiocese represented and to develop
his gifted priests, dispatched the young Irish priest to Washington for graduate study. This was the first such assignment
from San Francisco, and the archbishop regarded it as a handsome compliment and opportunity, much like his own at
Louvain nearly a quarter century earlier. At first, however,
Yorke experienced great difficulty in adjusting to his new
environment in Washington. Riordan was deeply distressed at
his unenthusiastic response to the appointment, calling upon
him at the university and personally encouraging him to stay.
Bishop Keane and Father Alphonse Magnien, Yorke's recent
superior at St. Mary's Seminary, were likewise puzzled at his
contrary attitude. There were even early suggestions of his

dismissal. Riordan's secretary confided to Magnien Riordan's disappointment after having visited Yorke at the university. The archbishop "told me when he came home," explained Father Montgomery,

> that he feared Father Yorke was not going to do much good at the University and explained--in this way. He visited Fr. Yorke, I think *twice* before coming away, the first time only a day or so after the University opened — and he dropped a word or two by which he seemed to be displeased with the food. He said he felt disappointed in Fr. Yorke at once, but did not intimate to him, and told him that everything was new and fresh, and he must expect some little friction for awhile.
>
> The next time he visited Fr. Yorke it was the same thing. He then inquired carefully into the matter of food, and was convinced that anybody that would find fault deserved not to be there. And he came away quite disappointed in the start Fr. Yorke had made — and especially for that reason — the trivial excuse or grievance even if it existed at all.
>
> So that if Bishop Keane should feel necessitated to write to the Archbishop he may know just how the Archbishop himself felt. He used the very word you use — "sorehead." Of course it would be a disagreeable thing should Fr. Yorke come home before his time. . . the Bishop will write fully to His Grace before doing anything should anything be inevitable.
>
> The Archbishop felt it all the more because Fr. Yorke knows the sacrifice that is made for him. We are really scarce of Priests, and it was to encourage the great work and give Fr. Yorke an opportunity that many a young priest ought to be grateful for. And besides, we are still in debt and every dollar is needed.

> It is a shame that some smart men have no
> sense.[37]

Montgomery had alertly perceived that ineluctable polarity
of brilliance and stubborn independence in the young Irish
priest, a strange disequilibrium that would both advance and
harrass Yorke's future. In time, however, Yorke redeemed
himself at the university, weathering this personal crisis. Riordan's confidence was restored in him as glowing reports from
Bishop Keane began to reach San Francisco. "I cannot tell
you," Riordan replied to the rector,

> how grateful I am at all you write about Fr. Yorke.
> When I came to Chicago from Boston I found him
> anxious to return with me to San Francisco. But I
> concluded it was better for him to go back to the
> University and live down the somewhat unfavor-
> able impression he had made during the year. He
> took my advice and has . . . kept his promise.[38]

In 1891, Father Yorke was thus one of the first five students to attain at the institution a licentiate in theology,
thereby becoming part of what was described as "the first
fruits of the University's work."[39] The young priest's ability
in Scripture had impressed Father Henry Hyvernat, professor
of Semitic languages, and the rector even appealed to Riordan to release Yorke to the university. But the archbishop
did not comply with the request, for he already had a position waiting for Yorke in San Francisco, "I am badly in need
of priests," he told Keane, "for several months I am getting
along without a secretary, having been compelled to send my
sec. to a mission for which I had no other priest. Fr. Yorke is
very much needed here."[40] Undaunted, Bishop Keane made
a second plea for Yorke, but the archbishop's refusal was
final, stressing that the straitened condition of his archdiocese demanded his services. "I cannot open my mind to you
in a letter," Riordan added cryptically, "but I am confident
were you to see things as I do, you would be in accord with

my views. When I go East this fall, I will give you my reasons." Whatever may have been the special message he was
saving for Keane, Riordan was, nevertheless, delighted in the
excellent record achieved by his young priest, and he concluded warmly, "Fr. Yorke's success is a great consolation to
me."[41] On his return to San Francisco, Yorke was assigned
to the newly finished St. Mary's Cathedral, where before long
he distinguished himself as an eloquent speaker.

The archbishop could hardly fail to notice the exceptional gifts and industry of this Irish cleric. At the cathedral,
Yorke displayed a variety of interests, directing the League of
the Cross and organizing a choir of boys. In 1893, he took
entire charge of the archdiocese's contribution to the Catholic Educational Exhibit, which was displayed in Chicago at
the Columbian Exposition. In April, 1894, when Montgomery
was consecrated Coadjutor Bishop of Monterey-Los Angeles,
Riordan selected Yorke to succeed him as chancellor and
secretary, a choice that was well-received. "The reverend
gentleman," commented the *Chronicle,* "is universally popular and his new office is one that is generally considered to be
in line to higher honors."[42] Indeed, Riordan had perceived
great promise in the new chancellor. But in time his association with Yorke would grow strained and awkward, eventually erupting into a costly misunderstanding that extinguished
any possibility for higher honors.

* * * * *

In the same year, too, there appeared in San Francisco
the first public attacks against the Catholic Church by the
American Protective Association, and the *Monitor* appeared
helpless to respond. Its staff, at this critical moment, was
divided with internal discord, and its editor, the scholarly
Francis A. Quinn, whose interests were not given to the lively
issues of the day, was unsuited to direct an effective campaign. To compensate, there arose at this time a curious
weekly, the *Arthur McEwen Answered,* which struggled to
refute any anti-Irish or anti-Catholic insinuations in

McEwen's own *Weekly* and other publications.[43] Although the *Arthur McEwen Answered* survived for only seven issues, it revealed a general dissatisfaction with the *Monitor's* sluggish policy as the A. P. A. offensive mounted during early 1894. Though several of the *Monitor's* board of directors wished to ignore the association, fearing that a direct Catholic response would only serve to gain it publicity, Archbishop Riordan became convinced that a stout defense of Catholic principles must be made. He felt it would be unfitting, even hazardous, for him to make rejoinders personally. The solution in his judgment was to use his gifted and tireless young chancellor as spokesman. Riordan quietly attached Yorke to the editorial board, and he published the majority of the unsigned front-page editorials on the early activities of the A. P. A.[44] Though no priest had previously been in charge of the weekly, the archbishop named Yorke as editor-in-chief in the autumn of 1894, six months after his appointment as chancellor.[45]

At the time of Yorke's assignment to the *Monitor*, the American Protective Association marshalled its growing forces for a direct encounter with the Church by sponsoring public lectures by a former priest and an ex-nun and establishing its own weekly, the *American Patriot*. The November election of 1894 provided the occasion for the first pitched battle. As it approached, religious animosities rose to a high pitch as both A.P.A. and Catholics fired heavy broadsides. Archbishop Riordan himself took no public notice of the conflict; but under his personally chosen editor, the *Monitor* returned blow for blow, first by the conventional tactic of name-calling and then by a series of public exposures which developed into the most lethal weapon against the association. Yorke's exposé began in late August, 1894, by publishing highly secretive oaths and rituals, and it continued until the election with detailed reports of internal dissensions, correspondence, extensive membership lists, minutes of meetings, and a sensational disclosure of the association's business directory. The objective was to indict the A.P.A. as a treacherous and clandestine group whose aims were political and ir-

reconcilable with the American principle of religious freedom.[46] The results of the election settled nothing, both sides
claiming victory, but the *Monitor* acknowledged that the
A. P. A. controlled more votes than anticipated, possibly
6,000 alone in San Francisco.[47]

While, as has been noted, Riordan did not personally
engage the American Protective Association, a close study of
the archbishop's life-long relationship with Father Yorke
requires an understanding of the latter's activity in this
religious controversy, an activity which Riordan fully
supported and appreciated. After the election of 1894, the
A.P.A. began to work with greater purpose and confidence,
joining crusades for local political reform and tightening the
efficiency of its organization.[48] During these months,
Catholic leaders in San Francisco were not inactive but quite
ineffective. The most aggravating problem confronting them,
as the A.P.A. skillfully mobilized, was their inability to
publicize the Catholic position and to win a hearing in the
columns of the daily papers. This aborted the strategy of
presenting to the uncommitted American public the true
nature of the association. The general policy of the local
press was to treat public lectures, such as those arranged by
the A.P.A., as legitimate news which deserved reporting.
Post-mortem letters from Catholics to the editor that offered
elaborate rebuttals or attempts to correct false impressions
were strictly barred from publication. A fracture of this rule,
it was feared, could lead to an endless religious feud and
destroy a newspaper.

In late November, 1895, there occurred a sensational
breakthrough which Yorke had been long hoping for. This
development inaugurated what contemporaries called the
"Great Controversy," a lengthy religious debate which extended to mid-1896. The spark that ignited the Catholic offensive was a bitter diatribe delivered on November 25 by
Donald McDugald Ross, a militant A.P.A. leader who was a
Presbyterian minister and a citizen of Canada. In his philippic
against the church, Ross attributed certain quotations to official Catholic authorities in order to establish the intrinsic

incompatibility between Rome and democracy.[49] When a
summary of his lecture was published in the *Chronicle*,
Father Yorke sought to publish a complete rebuttal, proving
that Ross' quotations were forgeries and offering to pay $100
if Ross could prove to the satisfaction of three non-Catholic
lawyers that his quotations embodied authentic Catholic doctrines. The *Examiner* ever intent to increase its circulation,
broke its rule and printed Yorke's rebuttal with the introductory remark that its rival, the *Chronicle,* had refused to
print it.[50] Yorke's published letter marked the beginning of
the Great Controversy and enabled him to introduce a more
offensive type of warfare.

The Presbyterian minister was profoundly embarrassed
by Yorke's challenge, a masterfully conceived package which
allowed no honorable escape; and after much hesitation, he
accepted, withdrawing for three months to corroborate his
statements. Ross' retirement, however, signaled no lull in the
controversy, as Father Yorke's letter to the *Examiner* invited
an avalanche of attacks on the Catholic Church by Protestant
ministers and A.P.A champions. A great many antagonists
eagerly engaged Yorke, forcing him to discuss an enormous
variety of subjects which ranged from Archbishop John
Hughes and the public schools to the assassination of Lincoln,
from the Sacrament of Penance to the Jesuits, from poverty
in Spain to the temporal powers of the pope, from Catholic
missions among the Indians to persecution in Brazil, and
others.

Peter Yorke, virtually alone in his efforts, faced an
ambuscade of adversaries who sniped simultaneously from
every direction. During the next fourteen months of open
controversy from November 28, 1895, through January 11,
1897, Yorke had published over twenty-five lengthy defenses
in the daily press. His replies bristled with facts and figures,
threatening his antagonists with a thoroughness of research
and with a pungency of expression that allowed no
unfounded syllable to escape exposure.

Few salutary results could be derived from a religious
dispute waged on the terms and in the spirit of the Great

Controversy. Even within the Catholic community, Yorke's vinegary approach had not won unanimous approval. Catholics in general deplored the controversy while heartily supporting the editor's militancy. They had become weary of the false statements about the church which had hitherto been published regularly in the secular press and nearly as regularly had gone unanswered. To many Catholics, therefore, Yorke had arisen opportunely as a redoubtable apologist. By the force of his character and intelligence, he stood like a "giant among swarms of dwarfs." While Riordan had recorded no public judgment, a number of Catholic leaders lionized Yorke as their champion who held his ground in a controversy which others had provoked. Yet there appeared some reservations. "The Archbishop," one pastor commented obliquely, "has sanctioned the stand of Father Yorke and is, from what I can learn, in perfect sympathy with him. We priests of the diocese are with the Archbishop."[51] Several other Catholic spokesmen more openly disapproved of Yorke's belligerent approach. Father Michael D. Connolly, pastor of St. Paul's Church and an intimate friend of Riordan, publicly deprecated his "carrying on a warfare" with the A.P.A. because, he felt, it did not represent a genuine Protestant body and thereby merited no such attention.[52]

Though he tried to remain aloof, Archibishop Riordan was known to have encouraged and supported Yorke's direct attack on anti-Catholic bigotry since 1894 when the first rumblings were heard. In these early days, when some of the stockholders of the *Monitor* protested that the weekly's language was "unfit for a bar room," Riordan had decided that a forceful stand must be made against the association. He formally took upon himself full responsibility and ordered Yorke to publish a manifesto explaining the paper's strident policy. In a significant article entitled, "A Plea for Plain Speaking," the young editor faced the charge that his use of words like "liar" and "forger" were improper for a Catholic publication but argued at length that the dishonest, cowardly, and treasonable tactics of his adversaries deserved to be so stigmatized. "Grave expostulation or tearful pleading," he insisted,

will have no effect upon a slanderous tongue that
remains unbridled, and civil discussion is ineffective with disputants who argue from counterfeits.
The horsewhip is the only corrective for such
abuses. . . .[53]

Yorke remained faithful to this conviction, and at this
moment his ways were also those of his archbishop.

* * * * *

Through events occurring in the Northwest, the Holy See
itself received early in 1896 its first reports on the dynamic
and irrepressible Father Peter Yorke, and these did
not conform to the general enthusiasm of the Catholic community in San Francisco. On December 26, 1895, Bishop
Aedidius Junger died, the Prussian-born prelate who had
ruled for seventeen years over the Diocese of Nesqually,
Washington.[54] Nesqually was a promising diocese comprising
the entire State of Washington in which there were forty-
one parishes and a Catholic population of 42,000. In the last
two decades of the nineteenth century, the Northwest
had been witnessing a whirlwind of settlement and
prosperity. Washington, Archbishop Riordan believed with
many contemporaries, would very soon be the wealthiest and
most densely populated state on the Pacific Coast, and therefore, he thought it was of paramount importance that "a
man, first class in every sense" be selected for the See of
Nesqually.[55]

For Bishop Junger's successor the diocesan consultors
recommended three clerics from the Northwest, but the bish-
ops of the Province of Oregon City disqualified this list.[56]
The consultors' candidates having been set aside, the bishops
presented to Propaganda an entirely new *terna,* nominating
Edward J. O'Dea of Oregon City, Peter C. Yorke of San
Francisco, and Edward H. Brown, S. J., of Gonzaga College,
Spokane, in that order.[57]

One week after this *terna* reached Rome, the congregation directed Francesco Satolli, the apostolic delegate, to

gather promptly more information on the nominees.[58] In this report, Satolli first eliminated Brown since two of his confrères, one being his superior, believed that his delicate health and lack of administrative experience would make him an unwise choice. In the case of Yorke, Satolli had directed his inquiry to Archbishop Riordan, but since the latter was absent at the time from San Francisco, the delegate was forced to consult with Father Henry Imoda, Provincial of the Jesuits' California Province.[59] Imoda knew nothing against Yorke's priestly conduct, but he assigned another Jesuit who, he felt, was more experienced in the sacred sciences, to comment on his "theological standing," particularly regarding the tracts on the church and the Roman Pontiff. The unnamed Jesuit, a thorough ultramontanist, presented a lengthy and elaborately detailed account which severely criticized Yorke's pronouncements in theology and philosophy. The volatile talents and achievements of the young chancellor, began the report, are those more "of a popular orator, eloquent lecturer, journalist, of a priest able to found, foster, and keep up Catholic clubs and other like societies, of a parish priest, than of a Bishop." His philosophy, moreover, was weak and antiquated, betraying an ignorance not only of St. Thomas Aquinas but even of what were called the "petty Cartesian [ideas] once found in the philosophical courses of the first part of the century. . . ."

Satolli was further informed that Yorke's theology, examined largely from his current encounters with the American Protective Association, was no better. It was described as

> bold, somewhat flippant, at the time crude and shallow, not from the study of the grand doctors of the Church and solid modern theologians, but from the reading of books and reviews wherein there are *vera mixta erroneis.* . . .

In trying at first to present a comprehensive critique of Yorke's thinking, the Jesuit commentator invoked an

ominous expression that would horrify most Roman
ecclesiastics. He pictured the young editor as having a
"tendency to modernize and americanize Theology, as some
of the clergy do modernize and americanize the Church."
Most of his heated exchanges with the A. P. A. served the
church well in the public eye, silencing the adversaries and
producing in San Francisco a "real good." But from the
perspective of "faith and absolute worth," the report
continued, Yorke's pronouncements were dangerous and
offensive, especially on the relationship between church and
state. As an apologist, he had explained away many "rights"
of the church sanctioned by popes and ecumenical councils,
such rights as "the immunities of the Church, her coercive
power, her rights — to some extent, at least, over temporal
matters, her authority on those civil rulers who were Catholic
or governed Catholic nations, etc." Such rights, according to
Yorke's view, added the commentator, did not have a divine
or ecclesiastical origin, but are "expressly and repeatedly
supposed by him to come exclusively from the State , which,
therefore, can take them away whenever it thinks fit to do."
With such liberal views as these, Yorke was presented as a
"Gallican, an old Parlementaire." Even his adversaries, said
the anonymous critic, believed that he had deliberately
diluted Catholic teaching in order to make Catholicism
appear "decent in the eyes of the American people."

Thus was Riordan's champion introduced to the Holy See
as a headstrong and chauvinistic American who had conceived
unsafe political notions. The report soundly condemned his
alleged remarks on the American principle of "separation
between State and Church, not only as relatively, but
absolutely good. . .the best of all." On the question of a legal
conflict between church and state, Yorke had failed to
concede a priority to the church and was quoted in the
report as holding: "In such collisions grievous mistakes may
have been made on both sides" and "each case must be
decided on its merits, _no_ general answer can be given to such
a question. . . ." In conclusion, the Jesuit conceded that

Yorke seemed unaware of committing these "serious jumblers" which had jeopardized the sacred sciences, but this lack of perception had not exculpated him from occasionally "twisting, mutilating, perverting, or otherwise garbling the text he is quoting."[60]

This lengthy document eventually reached the highest authorities, and it was in many ways an unfortunate and unfair analysis. Studying largely Yorke's recent exchanges in the press, the author had extracted quotations out of context and had ignored the spirit in which they were written. The report failed to mention that these writings were polemical in character, composed sometimes overnight in the white heat of religious controversy, not intended to be scholarly, definitive tracts or to sustain themselves under close professional scrutiny. In making certain questionable emphases, Yorke was trying to fashion a theology intelligible to a non-Catholic, American mentality. He had no idea of presenting material for analysis for professional theologians.[61] In spite of that fact, however, the report influenced Archbishop Satolli's judgment, and Edward O'Dea ultimately emerged as the choice for the Diocese of Nesqually. Yorke, Satolli informed the Holy See, still very young, was, it was true, full of zeal and intelligence, but his knowledge of philosophy and theology was deficient, even inaccurate on occasion. [62]

Though Riordan remained on the periphery of these confidences, the report was significant. It revealed that endorsement of Yorke's crusade was not unanimous within the Catholic community; and it served to measure Riordan's own views — whenever they would be unveiled. Tardily, the archbishop was impelled to provide for Propaganda a second assessment of Yorke's contribution. Originally, Satolli had tried to sound Riordan out on his editor's candidacy, but by the time he concluded his investigation and dispatched his report to Rome in early May, 1896, no word had come from Riordan. By May, too, Propaganda was ready to make its choice. As soon as the archbishop returned to San Francisco toward the middle of the month and examined his mail, he hastily addressed a series of letters to the delegate and to Rome. Aside from Yorke's nomination, Riordan had another profound interest in this appointment to Nesqually. He had long deplored the conditions in the Province of Oregon City and feared that a local candidate would again be selected, perpetuating in his judgment an ecclesiastical inbreeding. As soon as he learned of Bishop Junger's death, he had asked Cardinal Gibbons to use his influence with Archbishops Gross and Satolli in securing men for this province who, he said, "are really capable to give the Church some dignity and standing in the Northwest."[63] The problem had been unexpectedly compounded when Peter Yorke, his young chancellor, had been named *dignior* on the *terna*.

In offering his judgments to Satolli and the Holy See, Riordan announced first his own special competence in expressing an opinion in ths matter. Not only did none of the bishops of the Province of Oregon City know Yorke, he noted, but he knew the candidate singularly well as his own diocesan priest and also as one who shared the same home. The young priest, observed Riordan, was talented but had had no experience in managing temporal affairs. Since the Diocese of Nesqually had labored under difficult conditions and now gave promise of a rich development, it needed a man not merely knowledgeable but endowed also with "tact, prudence and experience." So impressed was Satolli by Riordan's interest in the nomination that he asked the archbishop to prepare a longer report not only on the Diocese of Nesqually but on the whole northern province.[64]

All this time, Riordan devoted his energies to considering the whole situation in the Northwest, seeing to it as well that his chancellor would not receive the assignment. In his own hand, he addressed a confidential letter to Cardinal Camillo Mazzella, a Jesuit member of the Roman Curia who had for years taught theology at Woodstock College, Maryland. He was, in the archbishop's opinion, better acquainted with conditions in the United States than the other members of Propaganda, and Riordan further acknowledged, "I feel you have special affection for the American Church." The See of

Nesqually was an appointment of the greatest importance, he explained, since the present tide of immigration running in that direction would soon make the State of Washington more populous than many other states. For this reason, this diocese needs as its chief pastor a "Bishop of mature age, sufficient knowledge, a good public speaker and large experience in matters belonging to the spiritual and temporal administration of the Church" — qualifications which Father Yorke, argued Riordan, did not sufficiently possess. Though gifted and already an accomplished public speaker, he was too young, only thirty-one years of age and a priest of seven years, and too inexperienced in the work of administration. His work as chancellor and editor of the diocesan paper had not sufficiently groomed him for a promotion to the episcopacy. Even his position as chancellor, Riordan insisted, involved no management of the archdiocese and was "in this diocese a mere title without any responsibility or work connected with it."

Yet Riordan's judgment on Yorke was not purely deprecatory but conscientious and paternal. "He lives with me," he added,

> and I confess that I am much attached to him, and
> have every hope that in the time to come say eight
> or ten years from now, when his mind matures,
> and his judgment is strengthened by years and experience, he will be a suitable candidate for the
> dignity and responsibility of the Episcopacy.

The promotion at this time, he felt, would be a grave misfortune for his chancellor personally and for the church in the Northwest. The Archbishop of San Francisco was dissatisfied not merely with Yorke's nomination but with the entire *terna,* urging that Edward O'Dea, *dignissimus,* was not qualified, and he strongly recommended that a new *terna* be submitted and composed of easterners. The pioneering Far West, Riordan was long convinced, had not yet developed a clergy sophisticated and mature enough to produce its own bishops. Rome had had a tendency, in his opinion, prematurely to promote western priests who were too young and unripe, as Yorke and O'Dea.[65]

Within a week, Riordan had finished his report on the Province of Oregon City and sent fuller and stronger suggestions on the Nesqually succession. In it he pressed upon both Propaganda and the delegate the importance of this see which was at present moderately small with 50,000 Catholics but growing rapidly into the most densely populated state on the Pacific Coast. The new bishop must be a native American, he argued, not a Belgian or a German as were nearly all the priests of Nesqually. He must also be a proven administrator, zealous and experienced, knowledgeable and articulate. His own Father Yorke, repeated Riordan, able and promising, was yet too young and unseasoned for a bishopric. In the previous year, 1895, when the bishops of the Province of San Francisco considered candidates for the vacant See of Sacramento, these prelates, who knew Yorke more intimately than the bishops of the neighboring province to the north, had not considered him eligible and had nominated an older, veteran churchman. But if Yorke continued to develop, under the guidance of older men, "I have every hope," Riordan added,

> that he will develop and become a priest endowed with the greatest talent and prudence. At the moment he is little more than a boy to whom it would be dangerous to give the care of a diocese.

Father Magnien, it was known, had written to Rome an enthusiastic letter in Yorke's favor, but, the archbishop warned, the Sulpician superior had not seen the young priest since he left St. Mary's Seminary. His argument concluded with his repeated suggestion that the successor to the Diocese of Nesqually come from the East.[66] Already, however, the congregation had secretly selected O'Dea as the third Bishop of Nesqually, and since the news of the appointment had not been released, it assured Riordan simply that its choice had not been Yorke.[67] Not only did Riordan show that he had

not been drawn into the Yorke vortex, he also betrayed his
strong opinions regarding ecclesiastical developments elsewhere in the nation, as well as his lifelong tendency of commenting extensively on episcopal prospects, even well beyond
his own province.

* * * * *

Despite the optimism of many Catholics in early 1896,
the Great Controversy had not delivered the death blow to
the American Protective Association. Catholic leadership,
spearheaded publicly by Father Yorke, was at long last on
the offensive, but neither side was disposed to capitulate. In
administering the *coup de grâce*, Yorke chose the November
election of 1896, thereby entering more overtly into the area
of politics. The *Monitor* opened the campaign, in a sensational maneuver, by exposing an alleged alliance between the
A. P. A. and John Diedrich Spreckels, a state leader of the
Republican Party who aspired to become a United States
Senator.[68] This scandal, richly detailed in the weekly, succeeded in impressing voters that the association was not the
organization to purify American politics. Troubled also with
organizational collapse on national and local levels, it began
to decline noticeably. The November election reflected this
regression, and Yorke announced an unconditional triumph,
telegraphing Archbishop Riordan in Chicago that the enemy
had been "busted."[69]

The political victory of 1896 signaled a new stage in the
life of Peter Yorke. During the Great Controversy, he had
displayed exceptional promise. Only thirty-one years of age
and already the chancellor of a large archdiocese and editor
of a formidable Catholic weekly, his reputation had spread
along the Pacific Coast. Yet an individual whose temperament flourished in a conflict or crusade, he found it impossible to divest the martial spirit which had sustained him for
three years. And it was equally unfortunate that his archbishop neglected to adjust this young, robust priest to a more
conventional ministry at a time when he was approaching the
height of his energies and mental prowess.

In the months following the evaporation of the A. P. A. in San Francisco, Father Yorke made efforts to fill the vacuum, first by looking elsewhere for the slightest trace of its activity. He first attacked the Free Library of Oakland for excluding the *Monitor* and militantly crusaded against the association in that city's election of March, 1897.[70] Unwilling to allow the past to be forgotten too quickly, in May he began a weekly publication of a nearly linear refutation of Myers' *Outlines of Medieval and Modern History,* the public school textbook which Riordan had censured three years earlier.[71] At the same time, Yorke himself undertook a series of lectures outside San Francisco, frequently using this opportunity to rehearse the highlights of the Great Controversy and to justify his tactics. There have come to our country, he repeated to large audiences, those claiming that Catholics are enemies of American institutions and slandering everything sacred to them. For a time Catholics bore this abuse in silence, he declared, but as the clamor grew louder and fouler, "we are compelled to speak out in defense of our rights and of our sacred honor. We shall have been less than men if we had not done so."[72]

In the aftermath, Father Yorke's most promising and substantial project was the formation of the Catholic Truth Society. The notable success of this organization in England had long interested Riordan, who had suggested that a similar society be established in San Francisco to spread Catholic teaching through public lectures, books, and tracts. An effort to mobilize the laity who could more readily reach the non-Catholic, the society was designed to prolong the spirit of the Great Controversy, keeping the Catholic community vigilant and militantly disposed to crush any renewal of APAism. The force behind the movement was Father Yorke, and in autumn of 1897 it was announced that the archbishop would institute in November a permanent Catholic Truth Society in San Francisco.[73]

In the weeks before its official beginning, Riordan was in the East, and Yorke undertook a series of six lectures under the broad title of "Ghosts" to provide funds for the society and to explain its general purpose.[74] These celebrated lectures stimulated a good measure of public interest, and as soon as he returned to San Francisco, Riordan, on November 27, 1897, formally inaugurated the Catholic Truth Society. Addressing a mammoth audience at the Metropolitan Hall, he announced the precise purpose of the new group, to make known the doctrines of the Catholic religion, "as they are taught by the Church." Such an objective demanded an organization relatively independent of parish administration since even the most zealous pastor, in addition to his spiritual obligations, was charged with expanding and supporting the "material edifices for efficient parish work, the church, school, and institutions of charity." This new, vital society, the archbishop continued, would succeed only if the laity would be "educated in a strong, robust, masculine Catholicity," and be bound to the Church by grace as well as by intellectual conviction." Eloquently and compellingly, Riordan challenged the young men of the archdiocese to adopt the society as their special mission. What was needed, he said, were

> men of fresh hearts, bold and energetic characters, men of enterprise, of daring enthusiasm, of positive virtues who can act . . . not simply good, easy men whose chief merit was their ability to do harm and whose chief study is to keep things quiet and as they are.

In intensity and bold eloquence, the archbishop's summons to apostolic action matched the many which his chancellor had hurled to the faithful of San Francisco. "Life is better than death," he added,

> and it is better sometimes to blunder, if we blunder through zeal and generous devotion, than never to act. We don't want to keep things as they are. We want progress. We want to excite activity, and stir up to energetic and continued efforts, to advance

the cause of truth, charity and civilization. As Catholics we must go forward, or cease to hold our own in the country. We can maintain our position only by advancing.

Applying this moving theme to the Great Controversy, he recalled the mixed blessings of organized bigotry. The bitter antagonisms of recent years, he pointed out, have succeeded in strengthening the faithful and in attracting uninterested Americans to the church's claims far better than "a hundred years of quiet unattacked existence." The archdiocese has itself experienced the lesson of persecution and has gained from it. "Attack brings into line the careless and the indifferent," he concluded in a ringing passage,

and makes more vigilant the loyal and devoted, and outsiders view in astonishment the spectacle of a world-wide society, ancient but ever new, attacked but ever triumphant, energetic, persuasive, progressive, "always dying," always "showing the death of the Lord," that His Divine Life may be more clearly manifested in her indestructible vitality.[75]

The launching of the Catholic Truth Society had given Peter Yorke purpose and direction as the critical year of 1898 dawned. Riordan himself was enthusiastic over the project, and Yorke generously supported it, chiefly through lecturing. Yet it offered no substitute for the thrilling days of the Great Controversy, and the youthful chancellor-editor never lost touch with the public scene, ever wary of a revival of the A. P. A. Even though in 1898 he would find himself ensnared in public issues, Yorke genuinely believed that he had never violated the sane tradtion that Catholic priests must not interfere in politics. He belonged to no political party, viewing Democrats and Republicans, Socialists and Populists, with what was termed "benevolent neutrality." The *Monitor*, he argued, was politically impartial and nonpartisan, its policy bound to the fortunes of no party and its columns available to advertise any worthy candidate. Nonetheless, Yorke never hesitated to review individual politicians and issues insofar as they related to his conception of religious liberty. One sacred responsibility of a priest-editor, he was convinced, was to mobilize public opinion within the Catholic community whenever its political rights were in jeopardy. "Whenever we find a man who is dragging religion into politics," warned a *Monitor* editorial,

> whenever we find an organization that is worked on the line of bigotry, whenever we find a measure that discriminates against citizens because of their belief, then we are heard, and we are conceited enough to believe with some effect.[76]

The issue which particularly interested Father Yorke at this time was the administration of the historic Sailors' Home in San Francisco. This public institution, he claimed, in a long series of editorials, had been managed by a genuinely sectarian, even anti-Catholic group. A vicious controversy ensued when in May the Board of Supervisors, led by a Catholic, Doctor Charles L. Clinton, renewed the lease for this group and Mayor James Duval Phelan, also a Catholic, endorsed it. When this action was announced, the *Monitor* reacted angrily, describing it as an "open and shameless adhesion to the forces of bigotry" and blacklisting the supervisors who had favored the lease's renewal as "Judases who have betrayed the sacred cause of religious liberty."[77]

In these weeks before the November election, Archbishop Riordan would have certainly noticed signs of a profound change in Peter Yorke. After four years of relentless activity as a polemicist, his health had suffered immensely, and during the summer he was briefly placed under medical care. His writings at this time reflected a severe emotional strain. His rhetoric and literary cleverness persisted, but fast disappearing were the mental discipline and discretion which had characterized his earlier work in the Great Controversy. He was no longer, in Riordan's judgment, the apologist,

judiciously correcting the misrepresentations of Catholic
teaching. He was fast evolving into a formidable political
commentator whose outspoken views on public issues and
men influenced a large portion of the Catholic community.
Riordan disapproved of his recent political statements and in
July reprimanded him so sternly that the young priest
offered to resign from his archdiocesan offices. "After your
statements this morning," he wrote to the archbishop,

> nothing remains for me but to place my
> resignations formally in your hands. Therefore I
> hereby resign from the Direction of the Catholic
> Truth Society. I hereby resign the merely honorary
> title of Chancellor of the Archdiocese. I hereby
> resign the Editorship of the Monitor. All these res-
> ignations I wish to go into effect at once. It is the
> right of a retiring editor to say a few words of
> farewell to his readers. In Saturday's Monitor I
> shall say these words as briefly and impersonally as
> I can, barely announcing the change. As I am pen-
> niless it will be a favor to me to be put to work in
> the ordinary ministry at once.[78]

Evidently Riordan did not desire Yorke's abdication at this
moment. While his resignation was apparently not accepted,
the priest was resolved to make his withdrawal a public
matter and two days later again threatened to announce his
resignation. "It is most extraordinary," he repeated to the
archbishop,

> that you should appeal to my honor as a gentleman
> after the shameful charges you made against me on
> Monday morning. In justice to my good name, I
> cannot reconsider my determination. Whether you
> accept my resignations or not I will not recall
> them. I will therefore... announce the fact of my
> resignation in Saturday's Monitor. That announce-
> ment will be as brief and impersonal as I can make

> it. But it will be well to understand that in the
> event of the not unlikely comments and false sur-
> mises as to my resignation, I reserve the right of
> making public all my reasons for my action at such
> time and in such manner as I shall judge best to
> protect my name and the integrity of my
> motives.[79]

While rumors began to circulate, Riordan would not be intimidated and no notice appeared in this issue of the *Monitor*.
This ambivalent situation was in the meantime compounding
the strain on Yorke. After steady support from Riordan he
could not fathom the causes for this newly negative attitude.
"The Bishop gave me his blessing when I started on my
work," Yorke confided to a close friend, "and he has but to
raise his hand to have me discontinue."[80]

There is no explanation why Archbishop Riordan failed
to clarify his thinking for Yorke or to place heavier controls
on him as the autumn elections approached and the young
editor was expressly determined to be heard regarding two
important candidates. On the ballot for re-election was Mayor
Phelan of San Francisco, who had alienated Yorke over the
Sailors' Home. Even more insufferable to the priest was
James George Maguire, Democratic candidate for the gover-
norshop of California. A well-known champion of Henry
George's single-tax theory, Maguire had distinguished himself
as a liberal congressman. But what genuinely offended Yorke
was not his political creed but his view of Irish history and
his undefined relationship with the Catholic Church. Ten
years before, Maguire had written a provocative book, *Ireland
and the Pope,* whose thesis was that the subjugation of Ireland
by Great Britain was due not to English arms but chiefly to
the political intrigues of certain medieval popes.[81] Maguire's
book had created a mild sensation among Irish Catholics and
had even been cited by Yorke's adversaries during the Great
Controversy. Yorke's suspicions of this gubernatorial candidate were further quickened when the latter added to his
campaign committee Charles L. Clinton, the supervisor who
had strongly opposed the priest over the Sailors' Home.

As the political campaign entered its final stage, Father Yorke intended again to use his editor's prerogative of instructing the Catholic electorate. His intentions were expressly not to support particular candidates or issues but merely to indicate those who, in his opinion, were the unworthy individuals by reason of their sympathy or unhealthy inclination for APAism. He planned judiciously to unsheath his most effective and lethal weapon in the columns of the *Monitor*, namely, the exposure technique. "We endorse no man. Let that be carefully understood," he editorialized.

> We stand by our policy which time has proved. Every candidate who is in our belief a member or a friend of the proscriptive society the A.P.A will be published in this paper.[82]

Meanwhile, Riordan was fast losing patience with the independent action adopted by his chancellor. He reconsidered Yorke's offer to resign and return to the "ordinary ministry," and had quietly at this time begun to search for a new editor of the *Monitor*.[83] The precise reasons for Riordan's dissatisfaction remain obscure. It is possible that Yorke's long involvement in the Sailor's Home dispute had aroused public indignation over ecclesiastical interference in politics; or possibly his outspoken and nearly defamatory attitude toward Phelan and Maguire had convinced the archbishop that is was unworthy of the priesthood and divisive within the Catholic community.[84]

At any rate, Father Yorke never published the promised list of candidates whom he believed to be soiled with APAism. The final break between him and his superior occurred unexpectedly shortly before mid-October, so unexpectedly, in fact, that when Yorke was removed from the *Monitor* Riordan had not yet secured a permanent replacement for him, commandeering Bryan Clinch to take temporary charge while he continued negotiations for a permanent editor.[85] On October 15, York formally ended nearly five years with the *Monitor* by publishing a predictable "valedictory," his last editorial. Recalling the anti-Catholic agitation that had swept San Francisco, he reminded his readers of their long-standing debt to the *Monitor* for having risen gallantly to their defense. A Catholic paper which existed "only to record fairs and funerals" and remained discreet and silent in emergencies would be a fraud, he argued, because of its failure to instruct, warn, and protect its supporters.[86]

Though there had arisen an irreconcilable disagreement between them, Archbishop Riordan had no intention of annihilating Father Yorke. After his removal from the *Monitor*, Riordan allowed the priest to retain the nominal office of chancellor and granted him a year's leave of absence. In the last days of October, Yorke made preparations for a lengthy sojourn in Europe, and as he had no funds, a number of his friends contributed to a purse to finance the trip.[87] His departure from San Francisco was scheduled for November 8, the day of the election. Although he had lost his most convenient medium of communication, the archbishop's reprisals had not subdued the former editor who did not plan to vanish from the public scene with an innocuous "valedictory." As the political campaign neared its climax, he was inflexibly determined, as he had warned Riordan, to vindicate his reputation and to lay before the Catholic people his judgment, particularly on the two principal candidates, James Phelan and James Maguire.

One week before the election, the opportunity presented itself at a benefit lecture in Oakland for Father Yorke to make his last public appearance before departure and to deliver what strikingly resembled a fiery political harangue. In a most controversial address, he first condemned Mayor Phelan by name for his complicity in the dispute over the Sailors' Home and association with Supervisor Clinton, describing Phelan as standing "in the forefront of the ranks of bigotry and intolerance." His public condemnation of Maguire was even more severe, largely for having failed to take a position during the Great Controversy and for having accepted Clinton as a member of his campaign committee. "Ah, James

G. Maguire," declaimed Yorke in a memorable apostrophe, "false to your mother's creed, false to your father's people, you needed but this crowning infamy that you should be false to your own plighted word."[88] In these final moments of the campaign, Yorke's address caused a stir in San Francisco, and the question of the hour came to rest upon Archbishop Riordan's reaction. The *Bulletin*, a daily newspaper associated with Phelan, charged that the address in Oakland had not been sanctioned by Catholic authorities. Though as editor of the *Monitor* Yorke had become a "power in this city," his recent erratic conduct, noted the *Bulletin*, "had caused displeasure in certain quarters and his resignation followed." Yorke's word, divested of Riordan's support, no longer commanded its former influence among the clergy and laity; and "he will not," the daily warned, "be endorsed in his present action by those without whose approval he is nothing."[89]

As a seasoned polemicist, Father Yorke was prepared in the next few days to trade blows with the *Bulletin*, but the real issue was Yorke's precise position in the Archdiocese of San Francisco. As he prepared to depart on a year's leave, it was not publicly clear what office he retained and how much confidence Riordan yet placed in him. The *Bulletin's* express purpose was to deprive Yorke of all prestige derived from his past years as a successful controversialist in the *Monitor*. Hinting at having inside information, it also suggested that his Oakland speech did not represent an official Catholic position but was due simply to a spirit of insurgence and "insubordination."[90] Though he had lately published his "valedictory," Yorke emphatically denied his severance from the *Monitor*, a position that confused issues more. "I am as much editor of the [Monitor] to-day as I was a year ago," he replied in several papers.

> It is true that I am preparing to take a vacation from my many duties and that the labor of settling many details of business has left me no time to wirte for the paper; but I am still its editor....[91]

This conflicting testimony magnified the importance of a public statement from Archbishop Riordan, who alone could measure the weight of Yorke's views. As soon as Yorke's Oakland speech had been published, Charles McClatchey, editor of the Sacramento *Bee* and enemy of the priest, inquired of Riordan by telegraph whether the Catholic Church sanctioned Yorke's attack on Maguire.[92] The archbishop merely replied: "Father Yorke is alone responsible for his utterances."[93] So brief a statement from Riordan, however, failed to clarify the priest's official position, and there were reports that the Republican Party planned to circulate 100,000 copies of Yorke's address. Confronted with this critical situation, Riordan consented to a rare newspaper interview. In a masterful display of diplomacy he succeeded in avoiding a perplexing dilemma. Instead, he used the opportunity to teach a lesson on civil liverty which in the end neither condemned his chancellor and his admirers nor offended the indignant Mayor of San Francisco. "The Catholic Church," he began, "never dictated a political policy to its clergy and laity." Under his regime, each priest was "perfectly free" to support any party, Republican or Democratic, and his office as a priest did not deprive him of the citizen's right "to make public his views if he should so wish on the rostrum or in the newspapers of the country."

In this careful statement, Riordan unequivocally demonstrated his public loyalty to Father Yorke, controverting the well-known allegations that the priest had lately become recalcitrant and defiant. "There is not in this diocese, and under my jurisdiction," the archbishop solemnly announced,

> a priest more obedient to his ecclesiastical superior than Father Yorke. He is a man of splendid abilities, untiring zeal and devotion to the interests of his church, and for four years defended its doctrines and its practices with an eloquence and learning for which all our Catholic people should be forever deeply grateful.

Riordan was at pains to register his displeasure at the *Bulletin's* obvious efforts to diffuse the impression that Yorke had been guilty of insubordination. "Nothing can be farther from the truth," he insisted, "his whole priestly life has been one of great devotion to religion and perfect obedience to the commands of his ecclesiastical superior." The pertinent question before the public, continued Riordan, was not Yorke's behavior but the choice among the mayoral candidates to be decided within the week. Mayor Phelan, the archbishop noted as a private citizen in a subtly partisan comment, had for two years, "given an honest and capable administration, and his little known opponent has had very little experience, if any, in municipal affairs." Though Father Yorke might reasonably disapprove of Phelan, Riordan himself expressed a preference for his candidacy, allowing, as he said, that "others may think differently. This is a free country in which everyone is entitled to his views. I have given you mine"[94] Riordan's statement was an attempt to repair the damage inflicted by Yorke's address and to emphasize in the last days of the campaign the fact that the Catholic Church was politically detached. Though he had avoided a public disavowal of the priest's action, the archbishop nevertheless "cheerfully" accepted his resignation as chancellor on the day before he left San Francisco.[95]

This dramatic confrontation between two unflinching ecclesiastics was equally unfortunate as it was dramatic. Engulfed too long in polemics, Yorke, in these latter months, had imperceptibly allowed the theater of conflict to shift to partisanship, finding himself at grave odds with his own superior. The adversaries of the A.P.A. had long tried to silence him and failed. In the end it was his former patron who had lost confidence in him and forced him to abandon religious controversy. Once a champion of uniting and mobilizing great numbers in the Catholic community, Yorke had lately developed into a threat to divide it from within over political questions which he would transform into religious issues. To an archdiocese, of which neither was a native, providence had brought together two strong leaders, not quite a generation apart in age – the older, a quiet, restrained, highly efficient administrator; the younger, a brilliant and perhaps charismatic, unpredictable, and utterly fearless spellbinder. Yorke at one time represented for Riordan one of the highest hopes of his episcopate, a promising young priest whom he could cultivate and fashion into a leading churchman. He was also the object of one of the severest reprisals ever administered by Riordan, a reprisal which deprived him of his important position in the archdiocese as editor and chancellor and of all serious consideration for advancement to the episcopacy. Perhaps Riordan shared the responsibility for this break. If brilliance and zeal needed to be tempered, the archbishop may have given too much rein, failing to provide opportunely a firm hand of guidance for his protégé. The priest had fallen into the venomous spirit of old Frank Pixley, a spirit that needed a gentle exorcism.

Yorke's essential critique of his superior lay in the latter's reluctance in "grappling with the great questions that are now troubling the minds of men." The archbishop's duties embraced more than efficient administration. Though Riordan's chancery, Yorke confided to a friend, might be a "well-managed business office," he was, like other prelates, "too much engaged in ledgers, or writing letters to priests and religious, about paltry matters that could be well-arranged by vicars." While Riordan accordingly held himself aloof from the issues of the day, "the whole Pacific slope is waiting, open-mouthed, for every word that falls from our Archbishop . . . ."[96] Yorke conceived his mission in terms of alerting him to these realities.

Evidently Peter Yorke did not encounter the fulness of Riordan's displeasure until his return to California. His tour through Europe had been highlighted by a private audience with Pope Leo XIII and a lengthy visit in Ireland. In November, 1899, after an absence of exactly one year, he returned home for a new appointment. Neither his diversion abroad nor Riordan's disfavor, it was soon evident, had mellowed the ex-chancellor's spirit, for he remained quite impenitent of his past actions. "Tonight I stand on the same platform I did twelve months ago," he said in his first public appearance. "If I have ever been wrong I should be glad to acknowledge it. But I must say this, that I have yet to see any disproof of any charge I ever made." The happy return home had made the old Yorke sparkle. "I am ready again for work of the same kind," he vigorously declared, "and I feel strong and proud to be beginning again." [97] But Archbishop Riordan had no assignment awaiting Yorke, and this omission was a severe reproach. Riordan had, in fact, successfully evaded the issue of his ex-chancellor's return, having left San Francisco weeks before for Rome to present his second *ad limina* report. Offers from eastern publishers had invited him to leave San Francisco and to devote himself to writing. But Yorke declined, explaining: "I have given my vows of obedience to the Bishop of San Francisco." [98] It was Yorke's close friend, Father Peter S. Casey, the ailing pastor of St. Peter's Church, San Francisco, who soothed the pain and embarrassment. Casey invited the unattached priest to be his assistant and to administer the parish in his absence. Riordan thus left Yorke as a curate at St. Peter's until March, 1903, when he granted him the permanent rectorship of St. Anthony's Church in Oakland.

This exile to the East-Bay city did not end Peter Yorke's activity in public affairs. With his singular personal dynamism, he would ever remain a factor in San Francisco. He would soon rise to defend trade unionism, Irish independence, and other causes; but influence with his former patron had been forever forfeited. Complete restoration and reconciliation would wait until the final years of Riordan's episcopate.

The archbishop had had his fill of champions.

PORTFOLIO 2

Cardinal Alessandro Barnabò
1856 - 1874

Cardinal Giovanni Simeoni
1878 - 1892

PREFECTS OF
PROPAGANDA FIDE

Cardinal Girolamo Maria Gotti
1902 - 1916

PREFECTS OF
PROPAGANDA FIDE

Cardinal Miecislaus Ledochowski
1892 - 1902

Archbishop John Ireland
1836 - 1918

bishop John Lancaster Spalding
- 1916

sy of Msgr. John Tracy Ellis

Archbishop John J. Keane
1839 - 1918

The Archbishop and Father Yorke - Later

Special Tribunal at The Hague which adjudged the Pious Fund case. Seated L.H. Ruyssenaers, secretary of the Tribunal; Emilio Pardo, agent of Mexico, J.S. de S. Lohmann, arbitrator for Mexico; Mr. de Martens, arbitrator for the U.S.; H. Matzen, umpire of the Tribunal; T.M. C. Asser, arbitrator for Mexico; Sir Edward Fry, arbitrator for the U.S.; Jackson H. Ralston, agent for the U.S. Standing, Walter S. Penfield, bursar; Mr. Koell, secretary; Louis G. Pardo, secre-

tary for Mexico; Hon. A. Beernaert, chief counsel for Mexico; Hon. W. L. Penfield, counsel for the U.S.; Wm. M. Stewart, counsel for the U.S.; W.T.S. Doyle, asst. secretary; Archbishop Riordan; Henry B. Ames, asst. secretary; Chas. J. Kappler, asst. secretary; Garrett W. McEnerney, chief counsel for the U.S.; Leon Delacrois, asst. counsel for Mexico; Ad. Dauby, secretary; Emile Decaisne, secretary.

Garrett McEnerney

Father Peter S. Casey
1851 - 1913

Father Patrick E. Mulligan
1865 - 1928

Senator William Morris Stewart

James Duval Phelan
1861 - 1930

The Young Father Yorke
1864 - 1925

John Thomas Doyle in 1901

Courtesy of Lawrence L. Johnston

7

Other Giants

In the three decades between the Third Plenary Council of Baltimore and the start of World War I, the Catholic community in the United States encountered a series of convulsive internal problems which drew into combat its most articulate personalities, including the Archbishop of San Francisco. By 1885, the first year of Patrick Riordan's episcopate, issues of national importance had rapidly crystallized. In the years to follow, there erupted such varied and complex issues as secret societies and the acculturation of immigrants, organized labor and the McGlynn case in New York City, the establishment of the apostolic delegation, the disapproval of Americanism and the question of parochial schools. As Riordan surfaced as one of its leaders, the Catholic community could ill afford disturbances and public argument that were to keep it in open view and divide its leadership. Its hopes were focused on uninterrupted, quiet harmony in a modern democracy.

But the transition of the American Church to the twentieth century was to be exceedingly eventful. In the ecclesiastical generation to which Riordan belonged, there arose a number of conflicts that destroyed his hopes for tranquil, undisturbed growth. These public controversies, particularly during the ten years after Riordan's appointment to San Francisco, were national in dimension and related generally to the question of the church in society. In a word, Riordan's generation confronted the classical question which

177

had tormented Catholic France after the liberal revolutions
of the mid-nineteenth century. How, asked the historian of
the church in that period, ought the ecclesiastical order
"respond to a regime of modern freedom, of political
freedom, freedom of the press, of conscience, of worship:
Ought it *encourage* progress to exploit an inevitable,
historical situation for the good of the Church — or *combat*
progress without compromise as an evil."[1] As a Louvain
student, Riordan had already confronted a phase of this
question when Cardinal Sterckx was progressively
accommodating the Belgian Church to the liberal
constitution of 1831 and keeping intact his loyalty to Pius IX.
The dilemma often split the American heirarchy and
succeeded in polarizing two schools of thought.[2] Neither
group developed into a self-contained faction, neither
expected its members to act with ruthless loyalty and logic.
But basic to each side were certain definable principles and
attitudes which generally governed its response to crises.

One school was sympathetic to the spirit of Pius IX, who,
as a teacher of truth, reminded the faithful of the purity and
changelessness of their faith, at times dogmatizing and
condemning new liberal trends without full awareness of the
Church's growing isolation in the late nineteenth century.
Among its American leaders were Archbishops Corrigan of
New York and Katzer of Milwaukee, Bishop McQuaid of
Rochester, and a number of influential members of the
Society of Jesus. Generally, Riordan was not sympathetic to
this traditionalist group. On the contrary, his closest friends
were numbered among the so-called progressives or
"americanizers," such as Gibbons, Ireland, Keane, and
Spalding. This latter school was more flexible, more
adaptive to the conditions and demands of American democracy, more attuned to the spirit of the pontiff of its day,
Leo XIII. Fundamental to their position was the fear that
a purely legalistic approach would alienate the society in
which the church must work and which it must reconstruct.
Despite occasional harshness in expression among these
vigorous protagonists, each school was sincere, genuinely
committed to its principles and devoted to the Holy See.

As an archbishop of an important and historic western see, Patrick Riordan was directly exposed to the national problems which seemingly dissolved the harmony within the American Church in the decade following the last plenary council. Even as early as his consecration in 1883, he revealed an overall sympathy with the progressives, selecting among the officers of his own consecration ceremony, Ireland as co-consecrator and Spalding as preacher. But his liberal tendencies were not exclusive or ideally consistent since Bishop Francis Silas Chatard of Vincennes, a conservative and Riordan's former prefect at the American College in Rome, had assisted with Ireland as co-consecrator. A year and a half later, Riordan recorded his admiration for Gibbons when he invited him to confer the pallium. In the first ten years of his episcopate, during which these controversies gained national attention, the young Archbiship of San Francisco regularly struck a liberal stand on issues, while at the same time hesitating to engage himself directly in the disputes. Among the reasons for this reluctance was the fact that he devoted his initial years in San Francisco to concentrating on the demands of his archdiocese and province, and his work on the Pacific Coast thus insulated him from the eastern and midwestern centers where the controversies originated. San Francisco had removed Riordan by thousands of miles of difficult railroad travel and had thrust upon him domestic affairs of a character largely different from those troubling the more settled and sophisticated dioceses east of the Rockies. Yet, as a churchman, he remained intensely interested in the trials of American Catholics. Throughout his episcopate he was kept well-informed through monthly letters from Ireland and a weekly correspondence with his brother, Father Daniel Riordan, a prominent Chicago pastor who was intimately associated with the progressives and was possibly Bishop Spalding's closest friend.[3]

* * * * *

One social phenomenon of the late nineteenth century which constantly concerned the American bishops was the swelling ranks of the secret societies. In these closing years, Riordan's episcopate entered into what one of his contemporaries styled "the Golden Age of fraternity." A curious vogue of belonging to exclusive fraternal orders had swept the country so irresistibly that by the turn of the century well over five million citizens had been initiated and remained active, possibly one male adult in every five identifying himself with some oath-bound brotherhood. In a culture being rapidly transformed by industrialization and urbanization, secret societies responded to a basic human instinct. They offered a convenient medium whereby the common man's leisure was organized and his place in the community assured. Amidst the anonymity of urban living, a sense of belonging and self-esteem was recovered largely through the extravagant regalia and rituals. Another factor for the phenomenal popularity of these brotherhoods was that most were able to invest their resources and to offer to their members sickness and death benefits.[4] The American hierarchy faced a perplexing problem in determining its policy toward them. Their rituals and strict requirements of secrecy and obedience had evoked in the minds of many bishops dark suspicions of irreligion and conspiracy. Essentials were so concealed, or confusing by conflicting testimony that it was nearly impossible to uncover precise character and objectives of the fraternities. Moreover, the directives of the Holy See governing such groups had arisen from the vigorous condemnation of the Masons and other subversive, anticlerical factions common in Europe, but it was open to question whether they were applicable to the majority of American societies.

Patrick Riordan was introduced to the problem of secret societies at the start of his episcopal career when the Ancient Order of Hibernians came under attack at the Third Plenary Council of Baltimore. In January, 1877, the Holy Office had declared that since it had found nothing reprehensible in this society "it must not be disturbed." The case was reopened seven years later, however, when in May the same Holy Office published general norms condemning societies which resembled Masonry, Bishop Chatard inquired in August whether the A.O.H. would thus merit condemnation, to which he received the answer that it "must not be tolerated" as long as it was considered a Masonic sect.[5] In one of the most agitated sequences in the plenary council, Chatard invoked this decision of the Holy Office, and Riordan witnessed two California bishops rise to a firm defense of the order, Manogue claiming that in his diocese this society was of a far different character, its members being loyal Catholics, and Alemany citing the previous instruction not to disturb it.[6] Since no solution had been reached to ensure uniform action in the various dioceses of the United States, the council significantly transferred from individual bishops to a newly invested commission of all the metropolitans the authority of judgment over secret societies, with the proviso that if the archbishops could not arrive at a unanimous decision on a given society, the final judgment was to be rendered by the Holy See.[7]

Under this new arrangement the year 1886 was devoted chiefly to gathering information on these fraternities. Archbishop Corrigan, for example, made a thorough investigation of the Ancient Order of Hibernians, first extracting certain favorable replies from its New York State secretary and then sharing in a circular letter to the metropolitans the results of his researches and requesting their opinion whether Catholic chaplains might be assigned to the order. While the majority approved such appointments, few responded with an endorsement more emphatic than that of the young Archbishop of San Francisco, who reflected a strong liberal attitude toward all such societies. "I have always been of the opinion," he told Corrigan,

> that we should treat such organizations in as large a spirit as the discipline of the Church will permit us. There is no use keeping aloof from them, and speak of them only in words of caution and criticism. If we would save them for the Church, we must give them recognition.

The Ancient Order of Hibernians, continued Riordan, was a strictly benevolent society, neither conspiratorial nor anticlerical. The appointment of Catholic chaplains to its lodges would be a wholesome step in introducing a strong Catholic spirit.[8]

But Riordan was distressed over the puzzling, even contradictory, position that the Holy Office had taken regarding the Ancient Order of Hibernians since in one instruction it had decreed that the order not be "disturbed," whereas in another it decreed that it ought not to be "tolerated." Although Rome was evidently most reluctant to make a decision in this matter, Riordan elected to use the occasion of his first *ad limina* journey in 1888 in appealing to Archbishop Domenico Jacobini, Secretary of Propaganda, to elicit a clarification from the Holy Office. Riordan's distress centered on the fact that by October, 1886, the American archbishops had surveyed the nation, having given careful consideration to the Ancient Order of Hibernians, and recommended to the Holy See that its members be "not annoyed." But in the following year and a half no acknowledgement had come from the Holy Office. The exact status of the Hibernians was further obscured, in Riordan's view, on the golden jubilee of Pope Leo XIII's priesthood in 1887. On this solemn occasion when along with so many others the Hibernians had sent their gift to the Holy Father, it had been duly returned to the society because, it was told, the Holy Office had censured it in the past. In Rome, therefore, Riordan personally requested Jacobini, "for that love which you always bear for the American Church," to avert an apparently impending condemnation of the Ancient Order of Hibernians. Since its Irish members "are so numerous in the United States," explained the Archbishop of San Francisco,

> and these last years they have been highly commended because of their Catholic conduct, the Bishops are frightened lest from this grievance there arise some very harmful consequences for the

American Church, considering especially the intense irritation which Irish Catholics suffer in America.[9]

Jacobini immediately referred Riordan's strong sentiments to the Holy Office, where the matter continued to rest undisturbed, especially after Chatard, the most articulate foe of the Ancient Order of Hibernians, relaxed his hostility and without special approval or privileges formally tolerated the society in his own diocese.[10]

In the following years, churchmen of the East and Middle West hotly debated the status of the secular societies, but the varying attitudes of the archbishops had been so inflexible and irreconcilable that decisive action had become impossible. In an attempt to reach a judgment on the disputed fraternities, a committee, to which Riordan was appointed, was created at their meeting of 1892. The other members were Corrigan, Ireland, Katzer, and Patrick J. Ryan of Philadelphia, who would compile the data for Gibbons to forward to the Holy See for a final decision. Despite Gibbons' efforts at delay and his reluctance to allow Rome to make a decisive judgment on these American societies, the reports of the committee were sent to the Holy See in 1893, and it was in the late summer of the following year that the decision was given.[11] On August 20, 1894, a decree was dispatched to Archbishop Francesco Satolli, the apostolic delegate, whereby three of the disputed societies, the Odd Fellows, the Knights of Pythias, and the Sons of Temperance, were condemned. Although the archbishops were not to be officially informed until their meeting in early October, Riordan had prematurely learned of the condemnation and communicated to Gibbons his unfeigned regrets at Rome's decree, trying to dissuade the Archbishop of Baltimore from promulgating it. "Its publication," he wrote, "will produce incalculable mischief to thousands." Anticipating the unfortunate results that lay ahead, he expressed his fears for the Catholics in the West, thousands of whom, he estimated, had "drifted" into these condemned societies, a critical

situation that made it impossible for him to force these men
out of their membership or to levy severe penalties on them
and their families. A disaster could be averted, suggested
Riordan, if the two most articulate liberal prelates in the
American hierarchy, Gibbons and Ireland, would personally
intercede at the Holy See for a reversal of the decree. "You
are our only hope in this crisis," he wrote to Baltimore, "and
I hope that God will aid you to prevent a great mischief.
Archbishop Ireland should accompany you to Rome. He
would be a tower of strength in settling this important
question."[1 2]

When, at their meeting in Philadelphia in 1894, the
archbishops learned that the Holy Father had entrusted to
them the decision to promulgate or not, they unanimously
agreed that its publication would be inopportune and that
the decree should not be communicated to the suffragans.[1 3]
The prelates obviously feared that such a public
condemnation would add fuel to the agitation currently
provoked by the growing American Protective Association.
Their attempt, however, was frustrated when in December
Archbishop Satolli informed them that the pope wished the
condemnation to be properly promulgated and
communicated at once to the suffragans. As soon as
Riordan's close friend, John Ireland, learned of this latest
directive, he let Gibbons know how "amazed and saddened
beyond expression" he was because of it.[1 4] Promptly on the
heels of this letter from St. Paul came in rapid succession two
more earnest protests from San Francisco. "There is no
doubt in my mind," Riordan stated, "that these societies are
pure and simple benevolent organizations, in no wise hostile
to religion." The archbishop repeated his conviction that the
decree was destined for failure. As harsh as it was, this
condemnation would be hopelessly ineffective in either
persuading men to abandon the societies or preventing them
from joining them. The success of such measure depended
upon the ability of its executors to elaborate its reasons. This
decree, Riordan argued, with its virtually arbitrary statement
on the three societies, has handicapped and embarrassed the

American Church by calling upon it to implement it without explanation. The church would greatly suffer in California, especially in the work of conversions, where the number of mixed marriages was exceptionally high and in most cases the non-Catholic party was a husband who belonged to some society. Gibbons was further informed that Riordan had appealed to the delegate to use his influence, and the cardinal was urged to work for a new hearing. "All the Bishops of the Province," he concluded, "agree with me that the publication of the recent decision will work an immense harm to the Church in this part of the country."[1 5]

Less than two weeks later, the persevering Archbishop of San Francisco again besought the cardinal to come to their relief, insisting that a hearing in Rome was absolutely essential for a decision which would bar hundreds from the sacraments, would prevent scores more from conversion, and would antagonize large and influential bodies of citizens. For years, Catholic men had invested dues in these benevolent societies for death benefits, and to deprive them of these benefits, urged Riordan, would be "simply preposterous." The archbishop felt that he had performed his part by writing two letters to Satolli whose reply had given him no encouragement, and he now implored Gibbons to repeat his significant victory of 1887, when, through personal intervention in Rome, he had saved unionism from condemnation. "I pray you," he wrote, "for the sake of the Church to take up this matter and do again what you did for the Knights of Labor."[1 6]

In the general bewilderment which had arisen over the status of the societies, Archbishop Satolli soon yielded to the extensive protests. In the early delays of 1895, he elaborated certain principles derived from the decree. These judiciously removed a great deal of the sting from the condemnation and offered a practical norm for the bishops. A nominal membership was allowed, provided that the member had applied in good faith amd would suffer grave temporal injury by withdrawing. Though, in Satolli's judgment, Catholics were forbidden to join them, the ban would be lifted from these societies as soon as they removed all grounds for suspicion, and bishops were directed not to promulgate the decree but privately to instruct their clergy concerning it.[17] When word of this compromise reached San Francisco, Riordan was relieved, telling Gibbons: ". . . entre nous such an interpretation renders the condemnation null and void." But Riordan strongly preferred a reversal of the decree. This complicated and tenuous arrangement failed to solve the problem and was hardly intelligible to the average layman. And, he concluded ruefully, "the condemnation had done an immense harm in this Western Country."[18]

But Riordan's hopes were doomed to fade in the following months. Urged by prelates like Riordan and Ireland, Cardinal Gibbons went to Rome in the summer of 1895 but failed to have the decree abrogated. In the following February, Satolli circulated among the metropolitans the latest directive from the Holy Office. A passive membership, accordingly, would be tolerated provided that, in the delegate's judgment, there was no danger of perversion or scandal, the Catholic had joined in good faith, and his resignation would involve a heavy financial loss. Riordan was disinclined to publish this directive, and in the end he merely distributed it quietly to the "confessors of the Diocese."[19] True to his policy of moderation and leniency toward these societies, he acknowledged the condemnation in his own letter to his clergy but directed them not to make it public from the pulpits. It was sufficient, he judged, for each priest to know that he had no faculties to absolve members and that cases should be referred to the archbishop.[20]

* * * * *

Concurrently with the issue of Catholic membership in secret societies, Riordan manifested a broad and sympathetic concern for the working class although he could take no credit as an outspoken and productive champion, as was the case with Gibbons, Ireland, and Keane. When in 1884 a decree from the Holy Office condemned the Knights of Labor in

Canada, a quandry confronted the American hierarchy. The Knights of Labor formed an important labor organization that had been originated shortly after the Civil War in Philadelphia and that had been disfavored by a score of American prelates as another subversive secret society bound tightly to socialism and anarchism.[21] In San Francisco, Patrick Riordan had had direct experience with the Knights since they had been operating in California since 1878, and the Irish Catholic element of the state had long played a conspicuous role in early labor movements. A depression ending in 1886 had promoted trade unionism, and in the first two years of Riordan's episcopate, the Knights recorded its greatest increase in membership and influence.[22] Riordan was generally sympathetic to the organization, and though he was unable to attend the archbishops' meeting of 1886, he communicated to Gibbons his strong opposition to its condemnation in the United States. While conceding that an astute minority might be exploiting the organization for its own political objectives, most members, he argued, were honest men who knew of no other medium whereby to achieve economic and social redress. The intrigues of a few, therefore, did not warrant a wholesale condemnation and, he added, an attitude of moderation and waiting seemed best since there were signs, particularly in its unmanageable size, that the Knights of Labor's collapse was imminent. [23]

While in the spring of 1887 Riordan did not contribute substantially to the triumph of his more progressive associates, especially Gibbons, in preventing a papal condemnation of the Knights of Labor, he had applauded the result and had maintained a consistent attitude in a related controversy, the dispute between Archbishop Corrigan and Father Edward McGlynn. The latter, pastor of St. Stephen's Church in New York, was one whom Riordan had known from his student days as the prefect over the twelve "Jacobs" who constituted the pioneer student body of the new American College in Rome. McGlynn had long been an articulate champion of social reform, notably of the Irish Land League. He had been converted to the radical single-tax theory of Henry George, possibly the most creative American theorist in economics who was misrepresented by many as a socialist. In the fall elections of 1886, McGlynn had been forbidden by his superior, Archbishop Corrigan, to support George in public meetings as a candidate for the mayoralty, a directive which the priest disregarded on the score of his rights as a citizen. He thus incurred a brief suspension by the archbishop. Agitated by McGlynn's activities and encouraged by George's defeat at the polls, Corrigan then issued a pastoral letter which gave a traditional defense of private property, sounding an elaborate warning against "certain unsound principles and theories" which assailed its rights, and publishing what amounted to an open attack on George and his disciples. As an astute observer on the distant Pacific Coast, Patrick Riordan studied these developments in New York with concern. Although the Catholic press, and even Gibbons, welcomed the pastoral letter as opportune, Riordan was dismayed in the fear that Corrigan's blustering approach to this crisis would not merely hurt an old friend, Doctor McGlynn, but would inevitably alienate the Irish and working classes from the church.

The situation in New York had meanwhile become more critical when McGlynn continued his public appearances and Corrigan retaliated, first by suspending him a second time and then by removing him from his pastorate. As soon as this news reached San Francisco in early 1887, Riordan requested Bishop John Keane, Rector of the projected Catholic University of America, who was at the time doing business in Rome, to "put in a good word" for the censured priest. "The McGlynn affair," he wrote, "is taking in this country a very nasty phase." Corrigan, he told Keane confidentially, had no reason to insert his definitions on property in the pastoral letter 24 since "there was no occasion for it," the municipal elections having buried George out of sight. "I regret exceedingly the whole affair, " continued Riordan.

I have had always a very deep and tender affection for Doctor McGlynn, and had he been approached

properly and by one who knows his character, he
could have been steered into safe waters. Should
we lose the working classes and the Irish we shall
have no one left and be compelled to preach to
empty benches. For my part, I would wish that
this constant interference with societies and labor
unions should cease, and if some of the Bps. have
leisure time for pastorals let them attack, if they
must, some body, the gigantic corporation and
monopolies of the land and say a kind and tender
work [sic] for the great army of the labouring
classes, that in our large cities are being reduced to
the condition of slaves.

Keane was thus asked to intercede at the Holy See in
McGlynn's behalf for, Riordan added, "at heart he is all right,
though he may be imprudent and obstinate."[2 5]
In the years to follow, there was no evidence that
Patrick Riordan involved himself further in this dispute other
than merely to observe coolly from his remote see and to
register his disfavor of Corrigan's policy. He probably
rejoiced, therefore, when late in 1892 McGlynn was absolved
from the ecclesiastical penalties and restored to the exercise
of his priestly functions. An aristocrat by temperament,
however, and a prelate who numbered among his closest
friends and most generous benefactors several of the leading
capitalists of his generation, Riordan was at heart no social
reformer. As the passage of time mellowed his attitudes, he
developed a certain distaste for socially liberal movements,
and in his last years he never accepted or understood what
historians have styled the spirit of the "Progressive Era."
While he allowed Father Peter Yorke to defend labor's cause
in the teamsters' strike of 1901 and again in the streetcar
operators' strikes of 1906 and 1907, the archbishop never
personally committed himself to these organizations. In fact,
three years before his death, he privately castigated the
unions as a major cause for unemployment and economic
decline in San Francisco. "Times here are unusually dull," he

lamented to his brother, "the poorest and most distressing in
twenty-five years, wherein hardly a new building was under
construction and a score of others unoccupied." He
continued, "the dullness is attributable in large measure to
the attitude of the labor unions," which in his view had driven
from the city thousands of workers to less developed coastal
communities like Seattle, Portland and Los Angeles.[26] In
ecclesiastical affairs the Archbishop of San Francisco, with
few exceptions, favored the liberal wing. Yet, like John
Ireland of St. Paul whom he admired enormously, as soon as
these affairs resolved themselves into purely secular issues, he
was at best an enlightened conservative.

* * * * *

Another conflict which disturbed the equilibrium of the
American Church in these last years of the nineteenth
century centered on the question of nationalism, specifically
the position of German Catholics. Having for generations
been the beneficiary of waves of European emigration,
the American Church was a polyglot institution, combining
people of different races and nationalities, of distinct cultures
and heritages. Friction had gradually evolved between its two
principal immigrant groups, the Irish and the Germans,
especially after the Civil War when the former began to
occupy an ascendant position in the American Church,
notably in the hierarchy. Their background "as
English-speaking refugees" and their gravitation toward the
large cities had enabled the Irish to assimilate more rapidly
into the native American culture. It was the transplanted
Germans, however, who sought to preserve their ethnic
distinctiveness and strongly resented Irish dominance in the
church, and their convictions were soon shared by the Polish,
Italian, and French-Canadian Catholics. Reluctant to be
absorbed by their milieu, the Germans as a rule struggled to
retain their old-world customs and language and resisted any
effort at Americanization which might force them to
surrender their precious heritage.[27]

Yet Archbishop Riordan's persistent efforts to organize St. Boniface's Church, the German national church in his archdiocese, dispelled suspicions that this Irish-descended prelate harbored hostility toward the German language and customs. Long before Riordan's arrival, San Francisco had become a genuinely cosmopolitan city, and from the beginning of his administration, Archbishop Alemany had provided for the care of the German Catholics, scheduling a special Sunday Mass for them at the cathedral and securing a Tyrolese priest who was eventually given his own church. In 1860, Father Sebastian Wolf had been appointed the first resident pastor for the Germans, and under him the scattered congregation had been organized and property purchased for a church and school. His successor, Father Peter J. Kaiser, had within two years erected a modest frame church on Golden Gate Avenue which was dedicated in 1870 to St. Boniface, and six years later the parochial school was entrusted to the School Sisters of Saint Dominic.

But an intensive program for this community had not occupied a high position on Alemany's list of priorities. A great many of them, he felt, could profitably attend the services in English; and the Germans were not always known for their generosity toward the Church.[28] By the time Riordan came as coadjutor to San Francisco, however, he discovered that he had as his responsibility a German problem different from that in dioceses east of the Rockies. In many areas elsewhere in the United States, German Catholics had professed their faith aggressively and tenaciously, some having lately been victimized and driven from the homeland by Bismarck's *Kulturkampf* and others anxious to conserve their identity through national parishes, schools, newspapers, and benevolent societies. But Riordan found that the German Catholics in his charge were of a different character, listless and unconcerned. In a confidential report to Propaganda he deplored the lack of German-speaking priests and estimated that out of 10,000 German Catholics scarcely 500 fulfilled their Sunday obligations.[29]

Despite his Irish-dominated clergy, Patrick Riordan bore an understanding and reverence for German culture. As a Louvain student, he had befriended German schoolmates. He could speak their language and spent most of his vacations in their homeland. Hence, he did not yield to the pressures of the "melting pot," and from the beginning of his episcopate he was determined to restore the German congregation on his own initiative. For the project he preferred the Redemptorists, who had specialized in work with German Catholics and whom Riordan as a Chicago pastor had invited to give missions at St. James. Even as coadjutor, when he was in Baltimore attending the Third Plenary Council, he had approached the provincial who assured him that he anticipated no difficulty but advised him first to make a formal petition to the superior general in Rome. In April, 1885, he told a close friend, Father Louis Cook, C.Ss.R., of his plans to invite his community to take charge of St. Boniface's Church, now an old and crowded structure, guaranteeing further that a more amply German church would be built in any district selected by the Redemptorists. [30]

With Father Cook's encouragement Riordan now appealed to Cardinal Simeoni to endorse his request and presented his petition to Father Nicholas Mauron, C.Ss.R., the superior general, repeating his distressing estimates of German attendance at Sunday services and stating that he could find no better remedy for this crisis in his see city than the presence of the Redemptorist Fathers. [31] Mauron was favorable. Two Redemptorist priests were dispatched to San Francisco as soon as the Holy Father granted permission for a foundation at Mauron's request on June 21, 1885. [32] But the two Redemptorists sent were quickly discouraged by the work. As a consequence, the provincial, Father William Loewekamp, C.Ss.R., came in person to California. On studying Riordan's offer, he declined it in Mauron's name. The facilities, he judged, would not accommodate a community and were too distant from the provincialate — as Loewekamp told the archbishop, "the smallness of grounds and building thereon and the little prospects."[33] Riordan pleaded for reconsideration. So desperate was the archbishop for these priests that he made the exceptionally generous offer that the Redemptorists might choose in the near future as large a site as desirable for their convent and German church which, as soon as it was requested, he would make a territorial parish.[34] Meanwhile, conditions improved at St. Boniface's, and the Redemptorist missionaries there who had at first been unfavorable toward this mission earnestly pressed their superiors to accept Riordan's terms as soon as possible. One of them admitted, "Before I got here, I was of the opinion this mission would be a desperate work, but I am ever so happy to have been mistaken . . ."; and another added: "The good Archbishop is willing to help us in every reasonable way. . . ."[35]

The superior general was heartened by these glowing reports. Negotiations were reopened and proceeded hopefully until Loewekamp met the archbishop in Chicago and presented him with a very harsh contract. The community would receive, according to Loewekamp's new terms, not only the German parish but also another large English-speaking parish capable of supporting two priests and located within fifteen miles of the see city.[36] Riordan felt that he could not accept such heavy terms, and when the provincial showed the contract to the archbishop's friend, Father Cook, the latter was at pains to explain Riordan's position. "The priests will appeal to Rome against us and the Archbishop," he told Loewekamp, "and we will have to leave the Diocese . . . we could never do any good in California if that contract were carried out. The priests would hate the sight of us." Cook informed his superior general that when Riordan asked his advice, he had counselled the archbishop not to accept it, as he said,

> for his own sake and for ours. For his own sake because his priests would all arise in opposition to him and make his life a burden. . . . For our sakes because we would be a useless body of priests and

an object of contempt to the priests in the Archdiocese.[37]

If the Redemptorists were too slow in mitigating their demand, Riordan was still resolved to strengthen his failing German parish. The terms, he felt, forced him to seek assistance from other quarters, and he confided to Cook that the latter's provincial had "asked more than any Bishop could give him at least at the start."[38] Though he had preferred the Redemptorists for the mission, he next approached the Franciscans, who accepted his arrangement and promised to send three or more priests.[39] "This is the City of St. Francis," Riordan wrote to the Franciscan provincial gratefully, "and his children should have a home in it."[40]

The arrival of the friars on February 16, 1887, provoked the first open signs of the nationality problem in Riordan's own archdiocese. The archbishop had been compelled to act hastily in committing the Franciscans to St. Boniface since the pastor, Father Sebastian Wolf, was failing in health and anxious to resign. His assistant, however, Father Louis Reidhaar, a former missionary in the Orient who had been received by Archbishop Alemany, protested this action to the Holy See. Riordan, he charged, had no right, according to the legislation of the Third Plenary Council of Baltimore, to entrust a parish to a religious community without the consent of his diocesan consultors. The majority of the German faithful, explained the disgruntled priest, were hotly indignant at the removal of their venerable pastor, regarding it as some sort of expulsion. The parish had accordingly never flourished largely because of the opposition of the Irish clergy, and the archbishop himself had, on occasion, publicly expressed his disapproval of national churches, declaring that all must learn English. "It is an open secret," Reidhaar continued, "that Monsignor Riordan does not want the Franciscans so much for the care of the souls of the Germans as to have in his Diocese a religious corporation to be able to give missions." And for this end, it was charged, the archbishop was determined to sacrifice his German parish. The condition of German Catholics, he concluded grimly, had been most unfortunate throughout California. Both Riordan's suffragans, Bishops Mora and Manogue, have followed the metropolitan's example in refusing to give German priests to German Catholics and have thereby caused incalculable leakage from the Church.[41]

Father Reidhaar's mischievous letter carried little weight in Rome, especially when he later confessed to having learned that the pastor, Father Wolf, had resigned at his own request. Yet Cardinal Simeoni wanted an exact report on the German parish, gently reminding Riordan that a transfer of a parish to the care of a religious order required first the approval of the Holy See. [2] In a prompt reply, the archbishop submitted Wolf's own testimony that he was not forced to retire but had been in full awareness and concord with Riordan's negotiations with the Redemptorists and Franciscans. The coming of the latter community, Riordan added, could not be better received elsewhere than in his see city which, he said, was "founded more than a hundred years ago by one of their Fathers and called after the name of their Holy Founder, the City of St. Francis." Moreover, the friars had also remedied a critical situation, the collapse of the German faithful, so efficiently that the congregation had been rapidly growing under their direction and a larger church had been planned.[43] The archbishop's assurances, however, had not satisfied Simeoni's inquiry. It was not until his first *ad limina* visit to Rome that he formally requested and received the Holy See's approval of the Franciscan foundation at St. Boniface's Church.[44] Riordan was in time so pleased with this arrangement that he invited the order to found two more German parishes, St. Elizabeth's in Oakland in 1892 and St. Anthony's in San Francisco in 1893.

While he was accommodating the German congregations in his own charge, Riordan kept well informed on the national phase of the German-Irish tensions. Although he refrained from taking a prominent role in this controversy, his sympathies again lay with his liberal associates, opposing any

accusations by German leaders of discrimination by the Irish
majority. Early in 1887, when Bishop Keane printed a
document on the German question in reply to a memorial
submitted to Rome by Father Peter M. Abbelen of
Milwaukee severely critical of the Irish bishops, Riordan
highly approved of the Keane refutation, telling the
university rector that he had even stronger ideas on the
subject.[45]

A decade later, as a trustee of the Catholic University of
America, Riordan was briefly again exposed to the
controversy. Ever since his appointment to its faculty of
theology, German-born Monsignor Joseph Schroeder had
consistently espoused the conservative position of each issue.
Long a recognized leader of the German-Catholic faction in
the United States, he was lately suspected of working for
Keane's elimination from the university. After the rector's
dismissal in 1896, Monsignor Schroeder's enemies began to
consolidate their forces in a renewed campaign to remove
him from Washington. The issue was to be decided at the
meeting of the university's Board of Trustees. As Ireland
told O'Connell one month before, it would be Patrick
Riordan who would lead the fight against Schroeder.[46]
Although the trustees had voted for his removal ten to four,
the matter was not settled until late December when
Schroeder was allowed to resign in favor of a teaching post in
Germany. His withdrawal from the university had cheered
and vindicated Riordan's closest friends. Ireland was himself
convinced that the German professor's downfall marked the
end "of antiliberalism" and of German factionalism and had
registered a "great defeat for Corrigan."[47]

* * * * *

Although he had been able to remain safely on the
margins of such national controversies as the secret societies,
the McGlynn case, and the nationalities conflict, Riordan was
drawn into the acrimonious school question. He supported
his progressive colleagues in its early stages. But, in the first

recorded instance of his episcopal career, he broke ranks at the end and associated himself with traditionally conservative prelates. Education has even been a chief pastoral concern for the church, and in the United States a parochial-school system had been operating since the first half of the nineteenth century. A large network of elementary schools had developed since then, designed principally to safeguard the faith of the immigrant children from what churchmen termed the secularism and anti-Catholic hostility in the public schools. This separate system of primary education imposed very heavy financial demands upon the Catholic community, yet it had been endorsed and urged by the Holy See and successive councils of Baltimore until the Third Plenary Council made it mandatory to erect elementary schools in parishes where they had not been established.[48]

From the first days of his episcopate, Archbishop Riordan was an avowed advocate of parochial schools. One of his severest criticisms of his predecessor's administration was the inadequate educational system which he found upon arrival in San Francisco. He had confidentially reported to Propaganda that four out of every five Catholic children were attending public schools were they must, he surmised, be suffering an inevitable impairment of faith and morals.[49] On his succession, he inaugurated a program of expansion, introducing new teaching communities to the archdiocese and seeing to it that each large urban parish had its own grade school. It was not a perfunctory campaign for Riordan, for his Redemptorist friend from Chicago days, Father Louis Cook, C.Ss.R., meanwhile confided to his superior general that the archbishop "has much opposition on the school question . . . from the older prominent priests."[50] But according to his *ad limina* report of 1888, he had within four years doubled the attendance of his parochial schools to 8,000 students, and his policy would maintain this pace for the remainder of his episcopate.[51]

Through the nineteenth century there had surfaced a bristling antagonism over the issue of public vs. parochial schools, indiscreet Catholic zealots attacking the common

school as morally and intellectually inadequate, and their
opponents denying any right of public assistance to such
sectarian institutions. In the last decades, however, a new
stage evolved in the complex school controversy. A number
of Catholic communities, especially rural, found it financially
unreasonable to sustain a separate network of schools, and a
minority among Catholic leaders took courage to espouse a
reconciliation between the two systems. A compromise had
been amicably arranged in such cities as Savannah and
Poughkeepsie whereby local public school authorities
provided instruction in secular studies for Catholic children
without jeopardy to their daily religious training.

The Holy See had not been formally aroused to this
fragile situation until the prelate whom Riordan admired
most in the American hierarchy, Archbishop Ireland,
delivered in July, 1890, a significant address to the National
Educational Association, "State Schools and Parish Schools."
On this occasion, traditional Catholic educators were
shocked at Ireland's regret that conditions had forced a
parochial-school system to exist in this country. And they
were doubly shaken by his proposition that the state had
some rights in education, though secondary to those of the
parents, and should work out a compromise with Christian
denominations, possibly eliminating the need of such a
system.[52] Evidence soon appeared that this issue was
interlaced with the German-Irish tension. German Catholic
leaders, staunchest defenders of the parochial schools,
challenged Ireland's orthodoxy and asked a worthy advocate
in Rome, Cardinal Paul Melchers, formerly the Archbishop of
Cologne and now a curial official on the staff of Propaganda,
to submit a German-language newspaper account from the
American press and his own misgivings to Cardinal
Simeoni.[53] The following year Ireland implemented his
proposal in Faribault and Stillwater, Minnesota, where two
pastors let their parish school buildings at nominal sums to
local school boards.[54] Another outcry was raised, Rome was
to learn, when Father Thomas Bouquillon, professor of moral
theology at the Catholic University of American published in

November, 1891, a pamphlet, *Education: To Whom Does It Belong?* which argued for Ireland's position, assigning to the state a certain authority in education.

Patrick Riordan, an interested observer, had not participated in the early rounds of the school conflict. He was present, however, in the same November at the archbishops' meeting in St. Louis where Ireland unofficially but carefully explained to his fellow metropolitans the arrangements at Faribault and Stillwater. Riordan was among the several archbishops present who acquiesced in Ireland's explanation of the experiment.[55] But he was drawn into the controversy as the Archbishop of St. Paul's star began to rise. While the dispute was seething among prelates and in the American press, Cardinal Simeoni wished to be fully informed on Ireland's proposal, addressing a confidential letter to twelve American bishops, Riordan not included, who were asked to discuss the school question with as much freedom as their conscience and the good of religion demanded. Archbishops Williams of Boston and Janssens of New Orleans and Bishop Kain, as well as an unsolicited letter from Cardinal Gibbons, all supported Ireland without reserve; and Archbishop Elder of Cincinnati and Bishop Tobias Mullen of Erie approved of the specific experiment at Faribault and Stillwater, but they rejected on principle an extension of this arrangement as implied in Bouquillon's pamphlet. Ireland had meanwhile left for Rome, and when he arrived at the Holy See, he was given the arguments of the six prelates who had vigorously condemned his views. To these arguments, Ireland presented a brilliant and altogether satisfactory defense of his position that favorably impressed a special papal commission consisting of the five cardinals of Propaganda.[56]

In the spring of 1892, while Ireland was approaching success in the Eternal City, Patrick Riordan was innocently involved in a desperate counterplot initiated by Archbishop Corrigan, possibly the most persistent adversary of the Archbishop of St. Paul. In those anxious weeks before the Holy See's decision, Ireland had, without Gibbons' foreknowledge, published in the *Civiltà Cattolica* of March 19,

the influential Jesuit biweekly published in Rome, a private
letter from the cardinal to Denis O'Connell, suggesting in
enthusiastic terms the archbishops' collective harmony with
Ireland's views at their meeting of the previous November in
St. Louis.[57] As soon as this was made public in the United
States, Corrigan sent a sharp protest to Gibbons and
clandestinely approached each archbishop to endorse a
statement contradicting Gibbons' description of the
archbishops' meeting. Corrigan's memorial stated that on that
occasion Ireland had, at Gibbons' invitation, only informally
explained the nature of his contract with the civil authorities
at Faribault and Stillwater. In this way, the school question
had been "accidentally" raised at the meeting, as was most
evident from the minutes — recorded by Ireland himself as
secretary — that omitted this discussion. Contrary to the
misrepresentation in the cardinal's printed letter, the
archbishop's action, concluded Corrigan's document, must in
no way be construed as an "approbation of the laicization of
these [two] schools."[58]

    While Riordan had been surprised that Gibbons' letter
should have been published, he paid scant attention to it, and
he was now asked by Corrigan to telegraph an assent to the
latter's memorial. The Archbishop of San Francisco had
neither studied Gibbons' letter nor been given a full text of
the memorial; he had seen only a synopsis. Presuming from
Corrigan's message that the eastern metropolitans had already
signed, Riordan was disposed, without further investigation,
to present a qualified endorsement, wiring New York:

> Document vague and capable of misunderstanding.
> We did not meet in St. Louis as a judicial body. We
> listened out of courtesy to Archbishop Ireland['s]
> account of the Faribault question. We passed no
> opinion on it; in this sense you may add my
> name.[59]

A week later, Riordan explained his curious response to
Corrigan's request to Father Magnien, S.S., of St. Mary's

Seminary, Baltimore, a very close friend of Cardinal Gibbons. His telegram to New York, the archbishop wrote, accurately represented the archbishops' meeting. At St. Louis they had passed no judicial opinion, Riordan pointed out, since Ireland at his own request merely explained his experiment in Minnesota and expressly stated his willingness to abandon it if necessary. When he invited criticism, his colleagues voiced no objection, not even Corrigan. Neither had Ireland proposed it as the best or an ideal system but, judged Riordan, "as the best practical solution of a difficulty for a special place and for a special circumstance." The Faribault-Stillwater plan was thus not in conflict with the traditional parochial-school system, for, insisted Riordan,

> we all felt, at least I did, that man of his enlightened and apostolic zeal, knew as correctly and loved as warmly as any Bishop in the country the principles underlying the system of Catholic education and that no one had advocated them more vigorously and eloquently than he. . . .[60]

Riordan's reluctance to sanction the statement without reserve dissuaded Corrigan from affixing his name to it. The Archbishop of New York was able to add six other signatures before sending the original to the Jesuit editor of the *Civiltà Cattolica* for publication with a duplicate to Cardinal Miecilaus Ledochowski, the new Prefect of Propaganda who had lately succeeded Simeoni.[61]

Removed from the chief centers of action and genuinely committed to the parochial school, Archbishop Riordan was little aware of the deeper significance of Corrigan's efforts. He hardly anticipated that his hasty reply would be considered by his liberal associates a mortal breach of loyalty. He certainly rejoiced at Ireland's qualified triumph when on April 21, 1892, Pope Leo XIII gave his approval to the principle of toleration of the Faribault-Stillwater experiment, provided that it be not accepted elsewhere on

principle and that the legislation of the councils of Baltimore
on parochial schools remain effective.[62] In the wake of this
victory, two successive blows struck Riordan's closest friends,
Gibbons and Ireland. In early May, before the official
decision had been made public, Corrigan took advantage of
the confusion in the press at a public dinner in Albany in
honor of Henry Gabriels, the newly consecrated Bishop of
Ogdensburg, to rise dramatically and disclose a cablegram
allegedly from a high Vatican authority which read,
"Faribault-system condemned. Special case tolerated."[63]
Later in the same month, Gibbons was profoundly disturbed
at learning of Corrigan's memorial,[64] and was informed by
Ireland that their mutual friend, Patrick Riordan, had been
among the seven signatories.[65]

As soon as Riordan became aware of this, he was at pains
first to vindicate his action to the distressed cardinal,
emphatically assuring him of his sympathies in the dispute.
Had he studied Gibbons' letter in the *Civiltà Cattolica*,
Riordan insisted, he could have confirmed it as a valid
description of the archbishops' meeting in St. Louis and
peremptorily dismissed Corrigan's document. In what seemed
a somewhat frantic effort to recover Gibbons'
confidence, Riordan went on to laud the Faribault-Stillwater
experiment as a temporary accommodation for
emergencies — even though he had in his heart never accepted
it on principle. Significantly, he suggested further that it be
extended to his own territory and elsewhere, even to the
Archdiocese of New York, until the parochial system was
able to instruct all Catholic children. The archbishop
deplored how this question had provoked "such littleness of
mind, such acrimony of spirit, among those whose positions
in the Church demand and suppose exalted qualities of
character." The manner in which Corrigan had earlier in the
same month announced Ireland's defeat at Bishop Gabriels'
testimonial dinner in Albany had astonished Riordan, and
Rome would be told. "The saddest sight that the American
church has yet witnessed," he wrote,

was that when the Archbishop of its greatest see
stood up amidst the merriment of a banquet, the
clinking of glasses, and read with an air of triumph,
amidst the vociferous cheers of hundreds of priests,
a telegram from what he called a most trustworthy
informant . . . announcing the condemnation of
the Faribault plan.[66]

Within the same week, the beleagured Archbishop of San
Francisco was forced to face direct charges of betrayal from
Ireland himself. Throughout the school controversy, Riordan
had encountered what he viewed as an agonizing dilemma:
his personal affection for Ireland and his total commitment
to the parochial school. Before the decision on the Faribault
and Stillwater schools, Riordan welcomed the glowing press
reports of his friend's early successes at the Holy See, writing
to Denis O'Connell in Rome: "I hope that what I read about
him is true. Nothing would give me greater pleasure than to
learn that he has overthrown his enemies."[67] But following
the decision, Ireland complained that his allies had failed
him. Out of the American hierarchy, he seemed convinced,
only Gibbons had fought at his side. Indeed, he may have had
in mind one of his dearest colleagues in mind, Patrick
Riordan, when he wrote these words to Bishop Keane:

You will say, I had friends — yes, but friends who
were silent, who left me alone on the battle field —
while no one enemy held back his fire. . . . I have
won — so far; but by God — at what cost. I have
lost my faith in human nature.[68]

Archbishop Ireland had at first intimated Riordan's
apparent duplicity to Cardianl Gibbons, but shortly before he
began his return journey, he addressed his charges directly
to San Francisco. On June 3, 1892, Riordan received this
poignant message from Ireland in Rome.

Today I was informed that during the contest,
seven (7) of the Archbishops of the United States

had been on record in the Vatican and in the
Propaganda against me, among them the
Archbishop of San Francisco. Et tu quoque! The
man upon whose faithful friendship I would at any
time have pledged my head, whom rather than
betray I would have died. Tears fill my eyes as
your name rang into my ears.[69]

These words which suggested Brutus' treason to Caesar
unnerved Riordan completely. Believing that Ireland had
already left for the United States, he immediately drafted
two letters to his closest allies in the controversy, Gibbons in
Baltimore and O'Connell in Rome, knowing that news of his
pained and indignant reaction would thus eventually reach
the Archbishop of St. Paul. In both letters he included a copy
of a letter from Corrigan exonerating him from any
complicity in the memorial. Ireland had inflicted a cruel
injury upon him, he told O'Connell, when he classified him
with his enemies. "I love him," Riordan wrote, "more than I
do any man in this country, my brother excepted. . . . I
cannot bring myself to explain my conduct to a man who
should believe in me without an explanation." He
acknowldged his temptation to endorse Corrigan's memorial,
but, he added, "what kept me from doing it was my
knowledge of the character of New York. It struck me that it
might be a Trojan horse in its implication."[70]
    Cardinal Gibbons received much the same explanation
which, it was hoped, would be delivered to the returning
archbishop on his arrival in the United States. Riordan
strongly emphasized that in these accusations Ireland was
guilty of a betrayal of his own. No explanation of his
conduct, he vowed, would be sent to St. Paul since Ireland
had no right to suspect his loyalty. "Even if a thousand reports that I had sided with his opponents had reached him"
Riordan contended,

he was bound to disbelieve them, until he learned
from myself that I had done so. I am pained

> beyond what I can write at his letter. But I must
> remain silent towards him until he withdraws it
> and writes that he has been misled by reports to
> which he should not have given credence.

Unstinted support would have ever been available to John
Ireland, Riordan insisted, had he requested it, but the only
message received from him was this latest burst of sarcasm and
abuse. "His opponents showed excessive littleness and
meanness in the unseemly quarrle [sic]," the archbishop
concluded acidly. "He seeks to alienate his friends in his half
measure triumph."[7 1] The stratagem succeeded as the
cardinal provided for Ireland copies of Riordan's explanation.
In the following month, Gibbons' confidant, Father Magnien,
came to Riordan's archdiocese to deliver the priests' retreat
and also to bring with him "the first-hand details of Ireland's
campaign in Rome." Evidently by then conciliation had been
achieved between St. Paul and San Francisco, Riordan
reporting to O'Connell: "I am delighted that our friend has
come away ever victorious."[7 2]

The papal decision to tolerate the Faribault-Stillwater
arrangement had not settled the school controversy. In
November, 1892, when the archbishops convened in New
York to resume discussion, they were confronted with
Archbishop Francesco Satolli, a personal representative of
Leo XIII.[7 3] Reluctant to make the 6,400-mile round trip in
the early winter, Riordan had wanted this meeting postponed
until the following summer. This, he had told Gibbons,
would afford ample preparations for such crucial discussion
and "give healing time to the controversy of the past
year."[7 4] Nevertheless, Riordan made the dreaded
transcontinental trip to the meeting where Satolli presented
confidentially to the metropolitans a solution to the school
question in fourteen propositions which distinctly reflected
the liberal views of John Ireland. While they upheld the
parochial schools, demanding that this preferred system be
improved and enlarged, the propositions allowed Catholic

children in straitened conditions to attend public schools and expressly prohibited the denial of the sacraments to parents who sent their children to these schools. Satolli's scheme urged that Catholic educators co-operate with the state authorities, declaring with certain precautions that the former even promote the extension of public schools and that the prospect that Catholic children might learn in them the rudiments of art and natural sciences was not repugnant to Catholic doctrine. In sparse areas, it was further proposed, bishops might judge that insofar as adequate parochial schools could not be sustained, religious instructions might be best given through frequent catechetical classes, possibly arranged during the free time at the public school or even elsewhere if necessary.[75]

Regardless of his recent and emphatic protestations to Cardinal Gibbons favoring the Faribault-Stillwater experiment — even suggesting its extension — Riordan did not approve of Satolli's solution. Instead, he conceived it as a hazardous compromise, and the vast majority of the American hierarchy shared these views. Unfortunately the controversy broke once more in the secular press when the ablegate's proposal at the meeting was published without authorization. Aware of the mixed reaction in the United States, Pope Leo XIII wished to have recorded the hierarchy's opinion on the fourteen propositions, and in a circular letter of January 3, 1893, each ordinary was instructed to send to Rome his confidential and candid views.[76]

As the debate over the schools warmed again, Satolli's other suggestion at New York, the establishment of a permanent apostolic delegation, had meanwhile been subjected to the severest criticism among the archbishops, John Ireland being the notable exception in its favor. Opposition to such an institution in America was not new. Fifteen years earlier, George Conroy, Bishop of the Irish See of Ardagh, who was serving as a temporary apostolic delegate to Canada, had toured the United States primarily to sound out the hierarchy as to whether a delegation should be established there. During his visitation he had been able to question nineteen prelates from coast to coast. The response had not been enthusiastic. Only three bishops had then welcomed the proposal as a necessity, among whom curiously, had been two Californians, Eugene O'Connell of Grass Valley and Riordan's predecessor, Joseph Alemany. While there would be no serious protest, the consensus was that if the appointment had to be made, the delegate should, as a compromise, be an American citizen and reside far from the national capital, perhaps in New York City.[77]

In the years after 1878, Rome sensed additional problems developing within the American Church, particularly the quarreling among Irish- and German-American bishops and the need to watch and guide the growth of the educational system on all levels, from elementary schools to seminaries and even the Catholic University[78] In the meantime, too, the American hierarchy had deepened its opposition to a permanent delegation as a threat to its independence, and in its name Gibbons had, in late December, 1892, dispatched to the Holy See a letter expressing its displeasure. Before it reached Rome, Satolli was announced as the first apostolic delegate — a non-American who would elect to live in Washington, D.C. On consultation with the archbishops whether this crucial letter be delivered, the cardinal decided safely to withhold it. But the two metropolitans of the Pacific coast, William Gross and Patrick Riordan, the latter not sharing his predecessor's enthusiasm for a permanent Roman representative in this country, preferred its presentation despite the pope's wishes. Riordan telegraphed from San Francisco: "I am in favor of presenting the document — too brave a sentiment for most."[79]

Eventually the Holy See received word on the school question from the United States and carefully studied the secret opinions of the fourteen propositions. Of the eighty-four replies, only seventeen approved Satolli's solution, six of whom had reservations; and fifty-three registered various degrees of disapproval.[80] Among those in favor were, it was expected, Riordan's progressive colleagues—Gibbons, Ireland,

Williams, Kain, and Keane; but the only prelate in the
Province of San Francisco who stood with them was
Francisco Mora, Bishop of Monterey-Los Angeles.
Inconsistent with his professions in past correspondence with
Gibbons, Archbishop Riordan aligned himself with such
unconciliatory conservatives as Corrigan, Elder, McQuaid,
and Chatard, submitting to the Holy See one of the most
complete and argumentatively compelling critiques. He
objected to ten of the fourteen propositions. Satolli's plan,
he urged, was unrealistic and impractical in the American
situation and in virtual conflict with the directives of the
councils of Baltimore.

His document forcefully repeated the traditional
arguments for a separate school system, a learned and
legalistic presentation and coldly detached from personalities.
More significantly, however, Riordan was not the only
avowed liberal who broke ranks.[81] His Louvain collegemate,
Bishop John Lancaster Spalding,[82] an extremely able and
likewise independent observer of the national scene who
respected the public school but had recently disapproved of
the Faribault-Stillwater arrangement, summarily condemned
the delegate's proposal. He used the opportunity to articulate
his strong views on the liberal-conservative conflict in the
American hierarchy. This controversial proposal, he charged,
has already inflicted irreparable harm on Catholic schools,
designed "in the interest of Monsignor Ireland and his clique
[*coterie*]" and foolishly released by Satolli to the secular
press. The Faribault plan was, in his judgment, "truly
ridiculous, a senseless compromise which neither Protestants
nor Catholics accept." And even more scandalous has been
Ireland's publicized denunciations of Archbishop Corrigan as
an enemy of the Holy See. "It is impossible to understand
the course pursued by the prelate of St. Paul," Spalding
wrote with extraordinary candor to the pope.

> He [Ireland] has tried to excite hatred against
> German Catholics in the United States; he has
> proclaimed that the Jesuits are his enemies; he had

criminally attempted a *coup d'état* [*il a attenté un coup d'état*] against our religious instruction, and now he publicly announces that one of his confrères is a conspirator against the authority of the pope. He has made the Catholic University a center of agitation for his ideas, a fact which threatens the total ruin of this institution: and in whatever he does he represents himself as the special friend and authorized agent of Your Holiness. The danger is great, and it has become extremely urgent to put an end to the notion which the clique [*coterie*] spreads throughout the country, that Your Holiness approves of everything which the prelate of St. Paul does. I am American, he is Irish, and I am convinced that I know the American character as well as he: and I do not hesitate to speak to Your Holiness as I would speak were I at the tribunal of God, that his manner of behavior threatens a very great ruin.[83]

Had he seen this confidential document of Spalding, Archbishop Riordan would have concurred with his criticism of Satolli's plan and probably, in the strictest confidence, would have shared this trenchant condemnation of his closest episcopal friend and his partisans. Although he had told Gibbons that next to the cardinal he had been Ireland's "staunchest friend and loyal ally,"[84] Riordan's secret thoughts evidently were known neither in Baltimore nor in St. Paul. Like Spalding, he was repelled by the controversies, reluctant to engage himself publicly and regarding them more corrosive to the American Church than the popular antireligious harangues of the "great apostate," Robert G. Ingersoll. Early in 1893, when he was composing for Rome his secret report on Satolli's fourteen propositions, Riordan revealed his private thoughts to an old Chicago friend, William Onahan, a lay leader, who was at this time arranging the Catholic Congress to be held at the World's Columbian Exposition in 1893. The archbishop was so discouraged by

this internal feuding, he told Onahan, that he was tempted to
attend neither the congress nor the archbishops' meeting. "I
am sick at heart," he confided,

> and disgusted beyond measure at the sickening
> spectacle of that going on in the East. May God
> forgive the men who have brought on us such
> scandals. They have done more harm than
> Ingersoll. The man who would muzzle them and
> their newspapers would be a public benefactor.

John Ireland was certainly included in these words, for
Riordan next instructed his friend to see to it that the
congress fully treat the school question "according to sound
orthodox views." He told Onahan:

> There is no use in mincing terms on such a
> question. We must have a bold, strong Catholic
> utterance in favor of Catholic education for our
> children, and the sooner we tell the American
> people that any system of education that excludes
> God from the school room cannot have our
> blessing and approval, the better. Weak Catholics
> are not strengthened, converts are not made by
> half measures, by compromise, by a soothing syrup
> presentation of religious truth, but by the whole
> truth.

Riordan had thus become so irrevocably opposed to Ireland's
views on education and so deeply committed to the parochial
school that, he added, "I dare not trust my pen to run on in
this matter-and in this flourish he was, apparently, sincere.[85]
Onahan was a rare individual who knew intimately many
members of the American hierarchy and whom Riordan
trusted with his innermost convictions. Less than a month
later, the archbishop was even more explicit in his
accusations when he disengaged himself from the congress,
fearing, as he warned Onahan, that it would serve to prolong

the dissension by letting "those who love the vulgarity of demagoguery to give expression to their liberal views on social questions." The archbishop continued:

> To be candid with you I am so heartily disgusted and sick with all that has happened in the past year, that I see no hope for us, until men who are in authority have some idea of the dignity of their position, and walk in the footsteps of the great bishops of the past who laid the foundations of our Church.[86]

In any case, the school controversy was settled in the late spring of 1893, contrary to Riordan's preferences. In a compromise statement to Gibbons, Leo XIII sustained the disputed propositions of Satolli but added that the former legislation in favor of the parochial schools was in no way nullified.[87]

Despite his misgivings of the Catholic Congress, Riordan nevertheless remained genuinely committed to the parochial-school system; and soon after the pope's decision he had the opportunity of demonstrating this conviction in his home town of Chicago. The World's Columbian Exposition had scheduled for early September the Catholic Educational Exhibit. To organize the display from his archdiocese, Riordan had appointed a gifted young Irish priest, Peter Yorke, who had recently returned from graduate study at the Catholic University. Elaborate preparations were made under Riordan's patronage; and so thorough were arrangements that in Chicago the San Francisco parochial schools presented the third largest exhibit. On a visit to the Midwest, Riordan himself inspected the exhibition and many times later expressed his immense satisfaction that so many awards of excellence had been granted to the Catholic schools, including his own.[88]

* * * * *

His position as the Archbishop of San Francisco had
made Patrick Riordan *ex officio* a national leader of the
American Church, and his firm disposition and vigorous
opinions on various issues had earned for him a wholesome
respect from other members of the hierarchy. His attitudes
tended to be liberal, but as he faced these momentous
questions, he was neither a disciple nor a partisan nor a
member of the "clique" but manfully independent in his
views — closely similar to the position of his collegemate,
Bishop Spalding. Personal loyalty was critical to him in these
struggles as was evident by his shock at Ireland's distrust of
his conduct during the school controversy. This insistence on
such loyalty, however, on one occasion compromised his
honesty. For he never directly revealed to Ireland his candid
and extremely critical assessment of the school controversy.

Although he was a tenacious competitor who could duel
with powerful senators and attorneys as he would in the
Pious Fund settlement, Riordan declined to engage in the
great ecclesiastical disputes of his generation. Conscious of
his responsibility as a churchman, he tended to sacrifice
progress abroad rather than to implicate himself in any
movements that threatened his diocesan priorities, such as
parochial schools or secret societies, even if their leaders were
his closest friend, John Ireland, or beloved old schoolmates
like Francis Silas Chatard. More significantly, geography
shielded Riordan from exposure to the sharpest edges of
these controversies. His archdiocese was in the late
nineteenth century still an outpost of the American Church,
far removed from the rivaling centers at Rochester, New
York, and St. Paul. "We are . . . cut off from the great life of
the nation," Riordan explained to his satisfaction,

> by two ranges of Mountains, the Rockies and
> the Sierras, and a vast desert intervening, that we
> seem to belong to a Foreign country. . . .[89]

If there was a consistency in Patrick Riordan, it was that he
was first a shepherd at home, and only then a progressive
abroad.

8

The Hague's First Client

California history is blessed with an irony that a Canadian-born ecclesiastic reared in Chicago and educated in Europe would be a leading force in perhaps the most historic litigation of the Golden State, the case of the Pious Fund of the Californias. Patrick Riordan was the principal figure in this first case adjudicated at the Hague Tribunal.

The most attentive observer in the court building in the *Prinsegracht* was William Thomas Stead, the distinguished English editor and founder of the *Review of Reviews,* who was probably the most influential journalist of his generation. A jingoist in his earlier career, Stead had shifted to the peace movements, committed wholeheartedly to the principle of international arbitration as proposed by the first Hague Conference of 1899. With consummate interest, Stead observed the first adjucation three years later at The Hague's Premanent Court of Arbitration. "The figure around which the drama of the court revolves is Archbishop Riordan of San Francisco," he reflected. "He sits quietly at a table in the rear of the counsel. He does not speak, but one quickly discovers that Msgr. Riordan is the pivot around which the case resolves." [1]

The unusual history of the Pious Fund of the Californias ranges over two centuries, from the generous institution of a humble religious trust to an international controversy, from the earnest solicitations of seventeenth-century missionaries to the dogged determination of an astute churchman of the twentieth century. Archbishop Alemany had been able

213

legally to establish the rights of the California hierarchy to
this ancient legacy created in the days of the Spanish Empire.
It is under his successor that its cause became genuinely
celebrated, entangled with the complexities and delicacies of
foreign affairs and associated forever with the movement of
world peace.

Riordan's connection with the case began in the last
chapter of its history.[2] The fund had originated in 1697 as a
permanent source of income for the mission system in upper
and lower California. Difficulties arose in 1842 when the
Mexican government assumed from Francisco Garcia Diego y
Moreno, the first Bishop of the Californias, the trusteeship of
the fund. The properties were sold, but the government
respected its commitment to pay an annuity of six percent.
These payments ceased, however, after the war with the
United States when the Mexican government interpreted the
peace treaty as having extinguished its obligations to the
missions in Alta California, now under the American flag.

Succeeding Garcia Diego in 1850 first as Bishop of
Monterey, Alemany desperately needed revenue and refused
to abandon his claims to the fund. His first efforts were a
series of frustrations until the winter of 1853 when he
enlisted the talents of John Thomas Doyle.[3] For one half
century, this pioneer attorney would play an indispensable
role in the complex litigation. On examining the documents
that Alemany had inherited, Doyle reasoned that there was
no claim against the United States, but a possible claim could
be lodged against the Mexican government. This strategy
succeeded in 1875 when a Mixed Claims Commission awarded
the California bishops the sum of $904,070.79 in gold.[4]
Mexico paid this amount in thirteen installments by 1890.

This adjudication hardly settled the issue. The agreement
between the two governments covered only the fund's
interest which had accrued for twenty-one years after the
Treaty of Guadalupe-Hildago. Mexico was plainly concerned
over the possibility of being forced to pay an annuity in
perpetuity to the California bishops. Doyle's plan next was to
postpone any further pursuit until after 1890, when Mexico

would have paid all the installments awarded by the commission.

Early in 1890 Doyle and his new partner, William Morris Stewart, a prominent politician who was serving as one of the first two Senators from Nevada, besought the Secretary of State, James G. Blaine, for diplomatic intervention. Stewart communicated with William F. Wharton, Assistant Secretary of State, delivering to him a letter from Doyle and printed materials on the Pious Fund. But the initial fervor quickly cooled when for eleven years no significant action was taken by the State Department. A succession of administrations — Harrison, Cleveland, and McKinley — was besieged with appeals on behalf of the California bishops, at first to no avail.

Riordan had meanwhile left the direction of strategy to Doyle. In 1893, when the Democrats under Cleveland regained federal control, Doyle decided to enlist Senator Stephen Mallory White of California, a Democrat and a Catholic, who lived in Los Angeles. A hardy septuagenarian, Doyle long feared that he would not survive the final settlement of the Pious Fund Case, and he was ever looking for a younger dedicated assistant who would pursue it to its conclusion. The youthful Senator from California momentarily calmed these fears. "Mr. White is only 41 and comes of long lived ancestors," Doyle assured the archbishop.

> He will outlive both of us and see the ending of the Pious Fund Case. . . .And being himself a Catholic *ab ovo*, you cannot employ a better man to succeed me if I am called away before this business is closed.[5]

For the next five years, Senator White unsuccessfully agitated the Cleveland and McKinley administrations on this issue. His colleague from Nevada, William Stewart, had virtually lost all interest in the case, his indifference gravely disappointing Doyle. By 1898 American relations with Spain became so strained over Cuba that the State Department could allow but minimal attention to the Pious Fund Case.

Doyle keenly sensed the stagnation and disappointedly handed over to Riordan Senator White's last report from Washington. Assistant Secretary William Rufus Day, White told Doyle,

> thinks your argument is sound, but he has submitted it to some of his advisers. . . and he told us that the report was on his desk, but he had been unable to take it up, as he was so crowded with business. . . . It is very, very slow, but I do not know of any way of hastening it along. [6]

But White's importance is derived less from his work at the capital than from drawing Riordan into taking stronger leadership in the case. Along with these abortive efforts to commit the State Department, there ran concurrently a conspiracy to change the contract between the Bishops of California and their two chief attorneys. This affair was highly significant not only because it would later draw Riordan into one of the most unfortunate episodes of his public life, but because it also allows a vivid glimpse into the character of the principals involved. It was John Doyle, not Archbishop Riordan, who had first contemplated a modification of the original contract. In 1894, Doyle became so dissatisfied with Senator Stewart, his liaison in Washington, that he secured the additional services of Senator White. White was not admitted as full partner; he would receive a full third of the combined attorneys' fees but was under contract only to Doyle and Stewart for a limited duration. Indeed, Stewart's indifference was so great that it took Doyle two years to affix the Senator's signature to their arrangement with White.[7] Soon White's youth and enthusiasm in pressing the case tempted Doyle to ease out the listless Nevadan from the original partnership, and to substitute White.

Once White has assured the old attorney that he was interested in replacing Stewart in the contract, Doyle decided upon a clever maneuver of indirection. Since neither White nor he was eager to confront the Nevadan, Doyle decided to enlist the cooperation of Patrick Riordan. Apparently, the archbishop had thus far expressed no dissatisfaction with the management, allowing Doyle full control of maneuver. In September, 1897, when progress seemed promising, Doyle acquainted Riordan with his plan and tried to induce him to solicit Stewart's resignation. "I cannot well propose it to him," he said,

> for I am not his client and it is a very ungracious thing to suggest to an associate, and I suggest that you frame a bland diplomatic note to him suggesting that his numerous other occupations. . .prevent his giving to the case the assiduous attention, without which you feel we will not be successful, and asking him to resign.[8]

Riordan favored any plan that would assist the Pious Fund Case, but he shrewdly refused to be the first to confront Stewart in this matter. This was Doyle's responsibility. Aroused, nevertheless, Riordan lost no time in going to Doyle's home in Menlo Park for a personal meeting. As a compromise, he authorized Doyle to inform Stewart of his displeasure.[9]

Meanwhile, Doyle carefully prepared his message to Stewart, a masterpiece of indirection. "The archbishop thinks," reported the old lawyer, "there should be more activity shown, which is perhaps true. He said something about age, and that is a fault I cannot deny, and I fear you, if not equally guilty with myself, could hardly assert your entire innocence of the charge. Between us we could, I imagine, outtop 150 years, and neither of us is as active as at forty years ago." Riordan's impatience, he reasoned, was justified and Doyle adroitly professed to have offered his own resignation.[10] This carefully prepared document, Doyle felt, would infallibly elicit a resignation from Stewart. But as it was "rather a delicate affair," and as he had little confidence in his sense of tact, Doyle first submitted the letter to Riordan for clearance and revision if desired.[11]

While Doyle betrayed an uneasiness about the letter, it was approved by Riordan and directed to Washington. As it proceeded, Doyle was highly optimistic, hoping that during his regular trip to the East, Riordan would collect the resignation. Stewart had, however, no intention of being eased out of the partnership. On conferring with him in Washington, Riordan evidently sensed a conspiracy between Doyle and White. When Riordan returned to San Francisco, he was warmly greeted by Doyle and invited to Doyle's offices in San Francisco on November 15, 1897.[12] The archbishop, however, had elected to take more immediate charge of the case. According to Doyle's several accounts, Riordan and Stewart appeared together, taking him by complete surprise. Together, they announced their agreement to cancel or change the contract. Whatever explanations were made, Riordan took from Doyle the right to select associate counsel, and the three parties agreed to a significant modification in the original contract between the bishops and their attorneys. Accordingly, the attorneys' combined fee remained at twenty-five percent of the amount of money recovered, but it would now be Riordan who would first select the additional attorneys and would secondly apportion their fees out of the twenty-five per cent originally allotted to Doyle and Stewart.[13] If Senator White, or anyone, therefore, were to be added to the counsel, his employment and his fees would be determined by the archbishop alone. This represented an enormous concession that hinged too heavily upon one man's sense of justice.

Significantly, the issue of compensation had transformed Riordan into an active participant in the proceedings. There would be no question that he had at last taken full charge of the case. This last agreement between the archbishop and the attorneys had dealt a severe blow to Doyle. The chief counsel had been deflated and had forever forfeited his premier position. But Riordan's performance was not faultless, only a prelude to future discord. The attorneys' compensation remained a complex and acute problem. In years to come, it would subject the archbishop to many months of the bitterest conflict of his life, and tragically estrange him from perhaps the most prominent layman in California, who had given half a century of his life to the case. In winning this first round, Riordan had overlooked two essential questions: If successful, would the bishops be bound to pay the attorney's percentage perpetually? And who would pay the expenses of the government?

No genuine progress was made on the Pious Fund Case until late 1899. The Department of State had temporarily discontinued negotiations, absorbed in the Spanish-American War and its aftermath. Washington had expected the Bishops of California to exhaust first the lower courts of Mexico before again invoking diplomatic intervention.[14] Even Doyle's close friend, Senator White, had faded from the national scene, having announced in February, 1898, that he would not be a candidate for re-election to the Senate. But with an alarming burst of energy, Senator Stewart had begun to busy himself with the Pious Fund Case. He had already engaged Jackson Harvey Ralston, a young rising attorney of Washington, who was conveniently a cousin of John Hay, the Secretary of State.[15] Doyle was quite irritated at this and frequently protested to the archbishop. Stewart had not consulted Riordan or his partner. Despite Doyle's persistent efforts to remove Ralston, Riordan remained neutral, neither sanctioning nor repudiating Stewart's action.

* * * * *

In any case the team of Stewart and Ralston was able effectively to commit the State Department to the claims of the California bishops against Mexico. Following an interview with them, Secretary Hay, on December 4, 1899, instructed the American Minister to Mexico, Powell Clayton, to re-open negotiation for an adjustment of the Pious Fund claims based upon the principle of *res judicata*.[16] The earlier award in 1875, this central principle contended, had decided the case once and for all. Mexico was therefore obliged to pay the Catholic Church of California an annual interest of

$43,050.99 "for all time," and the bishops of California were the persons properly entitled to this perpetual annuity.

In time Doyle's outlook mellowed. He long resented Ralston's entry into the case although it brough rapid and tangible results. As the case continued to progress promisingly, the aging attorney began to shed his prejudice against Ralston so that by mid-1900 he confessed to Riordan, "I am impressed with the idea that Mr. Ralston is a person of considerable push and activity and he may be, after all, the best man you could engage." [17] This question which tended to divide Riordan's counsel had at length found temporary appeasement when Senator Stewart agreed to pay Ralston's compensation out of his own share of the fee, and Doyle recognized the younger man as an associate on the case. [18]

At the turn of the century, there evolved two advantages that favored the case. By 1900 Mexico had achieved substantial economic stability and was at last, it was felt, able to face its full responsibilities. The State Department was no longer obliged to accept Mexico's pleas of an embarrassed financial condition. The second favorable circumstance to the bishops' case was the person of John Hay, McKinley's third Secretary of State, who was fashioning a dynamic career in foreign affairs. Hay was responding to the imperialist impulses of his generation, having announced an Open-Door policy in the Far East and attempting to settle with Great Britain over the inter-ocean canal in Central America. Riordan's attorneys were highly pleased with Hay's forward-looking attitude toward the Pious Fund Case. He had already accepted the principle of *res judicata* and announced to the senate that it was the objective of his regime "to bring to settlement, in some form, every meritorious claim of an American citizen against a foreign Government, even though it may be one of long standing." [19] There was little cause to doubt Doyle's warm enthusiasm over Hay who, he confided to Riordan, was "by far the best Foreign Secretary we have had within my memory, which goes back freshly to Van Buren's Presidency. . . ." [20]

While Stewart and Ralston were applying continuous pressure in Washington, Stewart felt that the hierarchy might be of assistance. He therefore suggested that Riordan enlist a number of high ecclesiastics in contacting the Secretary of State, particularly Cardinal Gibbons and Archbishop Ireland. Riordan agreed, adding that perhaps pressure might in this way reach the White House and promising to write to Ireland who could use his abilities of persuasion directly on President McKinley.[21] Instead of individual action, there eventually developed a larger plan to compose a letter of petition addressed to the President and endorsed by several bishops. Riordan decided to secure the signatures at the investiture of John J. Keane as Archbishop of Dubuque in April, 1901, a ceremony that would gather the leaders of the American hierarchy.[22] But Riordan's strategy was too ambitious. An appeal to the President, it was felt, might alienate a benevolent Department of State, and the wording was adjusted.[23]

Riordan was unable himself to attend the celebration. The endorsements were secured by Father Daniel Riordan, his brother, who was Pastor of St. Elizabeth's Church in Chicago and who had accompanied Cardinal Gibbons to Dubuque. He managed to get the important signatures, seventeen in all, including those of Gibbons and all the archbishops except Ireland. The Archbishop of St. Paul later signed the petition, taking it himself to Washington and leaving it in the hands of David J. Hill, Assistant Secretary of State, who had direct charge of the Pious Fund Case. Ireland's presentation further impressed the department, and Hill promised him that he would send at once for the Mexican Minister and urge upon him the necessity of a settlement or compromise. The situation was so favorable, Ireland judged, that when Riordan would come in the following autumn to Washington for the meeting of the trustees of the Catholic University of America, "he will be able to give it the final touch."[24] In the month following the Keane celebration, Riordan was able personally to approach McKinley and Hay who were visiting San Francisco. In a

gratifying interview the President and the Secretary revealed
a thorough acquaintance with the case. McKinley even
expressed the hope that he might have news by October
when the archbishop would be in the East.[25]

Parallel to the pressures on Washington were those
applied in Mexico City. Ever since 1891, when the first official
note on the Pious Fund Case was sent, the Foreign
Minister, Ignacio Mariscal, had stubbornly fended off American demands for a satisfactory adjustment. While the State
Department continued to press for settlement, Riordan's
attorneys felt that certain unofficial approaches might
accelerate an understanding between the two governments. In
1901, Riordan planned to visit Mexico as a traveling
companion of Richard C. Kerens, a business and political
leader of St. Louis, Missouri.[26] John Doyle perceived in this a
golden opportunity whereby the archbishop might be able in
person to arrange a settlement. The schedule for the trip was
arranged ideally for a measure of informal diplomacy by
including a certain engagement with the leaders of the
Mexican Government. Kerens, the archbishop's host,
intended to attend the wedding of the daughter of the
Belgian minister and then to spend a month hunting with
General Porfirio Diaz, the President of Mexico. But in the
winter of 1901, as Mexico softened its resistance through
regular diplomatic channels, Riordan was forced to
reconsider the wisdom of his journey. A visit, it was feared,
might suggest an anxiety for a compromise. The excursion
was cancelled when Hay urged that Riordan's trip to Mexico
would "not only be unnecessary, but harmful. . . ."[27] The
Department had by this point taken such command of the
Pious Fund case that such independent help would be
interference.

The Mexican Department of Foreign Affairs could hardly
ignore any longer the American notes on the Pious Fund
claims. In November, 1900, Mariscal broke a year's silence by
issuing a lengthy document that presented the two basic
propositions in his government's argument. The Mixed Claims
Commission that had ruled in the bishops' favor in 1875 had

no valid jurisdiction in the case and was moreover, erroneous in its conclusions.[28] Early the following year, while the two governments stood irreconcilable, there evolved for the first time in the case a strong movement for international arbitration. The United States had long subscribed to the principle of arbitration. Nations engaged in a dispute would accordingly bind themselves to accept the decision rendered by a third party or an impartial body. In the nineteenth century, the growing idealism among nations was making recourse to arbitration a more general practice, and the United States had already provided the world an outstanding example by submitting its *Alabama* claims to arbitration. As the Pious Fund case was developing under the McKinley administration, greater advances for peace and arbitration had been recently made in 1899 as a result of the Hague Conferences, notably in the institution of the Permanent Court of Arbitration.

At this stage of the negotiations, Mexico demanded that the California bishops first exhaust the possibilities in her courts. But Secretary Hay would never allow the claims to be submitted to a Mexican tribunal, convinced that the bishops' case rested soundly on the principle of *res judicata* and was, therefore, one for diplomatic intervention. It was the Solicitor of the State Department, William Lawrence Penfield, who championed arbitration for the Pious Fund case. This blind impasse between Mexico and the United States, Penfield urged, could be best resolved by an international tribunal, impartial and competent, which would be mutually established to review the claims.

Although John Doyle was not at first enthusiastic over this suggestion, Archbishop Riordan and Bishop George Montgomery of Monterey-Los Angeles decided, with certain reservations, to accept Penfield's recommendation. In May, 1901, they authorized the State Department to sound Mexico out.[29] As soon as Hay was able to digest material sent to him from Ralston and Doyle and to recover from a personal tragedy, the death of his son, he directed Powell Clayton to the American Minister in Mexico City, to suggest discreetly to the Mexicans that the controversy be settled by an arbitral tribunal. In this significant message, Hay demanded as a generous compromise that the tribunal be empowered to determine, first, whether the bishops' claim for a perpetual annuity based upon the decision of 1875, falls within the governing principle of *res judicata,* and, if not, whether the entire case should be reopened. The secretary had ingeniously reduced the controversy to two clear issues. As soon as he learned of this new action, John Doyle was ecstatic. Jubilantly he sent a copy of the news to Riordan, who was ailing, as an "excellent prescription for a cold."[30] Clayton immediately delivered Hay's terms, but Mariscal made no reply. After three months of silence, Clayton was granted an interview wherein the foreign minister indirectly consented to arbitration.[31]

It had been ten long and struggling years since the State Department had commenced negotiations in the case. Mexico's vague consent in late 1901 signaled that it had exhausted means of procrastination. Three major decisions faced the archbishop and his advisors before the arbitration could begin. First, no particular tribunal had yet been chosen. Having reviewed the possibility of a Pan-American court, the two governments agreed to negotiate for arbitration at the Hague Tribunal. This institution was a new creation, and no case had yet been submitted to it. In 1899 the first International Peace Conference had convened at The Hague with twenty-six nations attending; but, interestingly, only Mexico and the United States had been represented from the Americas. Although the conference failed in its chief purpose of reducing armaments, it succeeded in founding the Permanent Court of Arbitration, popularly called the Hague Tribunal. The American delegation, which had carried instructions from John Hay, had been notably instrumental in setting up procedures — the only group to arrive with a detailed plan for such a court. [32]

Next, an agreeable protocol between the two governments had to be arranged to define the precise conditions and issues governing the arbitration. Each party

would be solemnly bound by the decision. Framed chiefly by
Ralston, the protocol was signed in Washington in May, 1902,
and quickly submitted to the Mexican Senate. The case, it
provided, would be judged on the two questions of whether
the bishops' claim to the fund had already been perpetually
established by the award in 1875; and, if not, then whether
the case be re-argued completely.[33]

The last step for Riordan and his advisers was the
painstaking selection of the arbitrators. The tribunal provided
for a large list of jurists expert in international law. Both
governments were entitled to select two, and an umpire
would be selected by the arbitrators. This procedure was an
extremely important stage. It required careful inquiries into
the qualifications and attitudes of the candidates -- a
procedure greatly resembling a trial lawyer who scrupulously
examines prospective members of his jury. Detailed histories
were meticulously examined, and American diplomats were
alerted everywhere to secure intelligence. Even to reach
agreement among the American attorneys on this item had
become a cardinal problem. A devoted alumnus of Louvain,
Riordan naturally preferred the Belgians; and Doyle included
also as desirables the English and Austrian jurists. William
Penfield, however, generally favored north European states as
England, Holland, Russia, and the Scandanavian countries.
The Belgians, Riordan and Doyle were to learn, had been
involved in arbitration unfavorable to the United States, the
Germans were strongly affected by religious differences, and
Austria-Hungary was at the moment mildly hostile to this
country.[34]

Despite Penfield's misgivings, Archbishop Riordan along
with his senior attorney, John Doyle, endorsed the Belgians
and the English. Both were ready to conduct their own
reconnaisance. In their view the Belgians were likely to be
Catholics. The English jurists shared with Americans the
heritage of common law, and the California bishops had had
good fortune nearly three decades earlier at the hands of a
British umpire. Concerning the four Belgian members of the
Permanent Court, Riordan consulted his close friend, Canon

Jules De Becker, Rector of the American College at Louvain.
While all were practicing Catholics, only one had a fair skill in
English. This was the Chevalier Descamps, a Belgian Senator
and the Secretary General of the Institute of International
Law.[35] Reviewing the English jurists, Doyle approached
Cardinal Herbert Vaughan, Archbishop of Westminster. With
admirable care, Vaughan assembled an ample report,
recommending Sir Edward Fry as an "excellent lawyer and a
gentleman. He is a Quaker but can be thoroughly trusted."[36]
These independent investigations were of value although
the State Department eventually excluded the Belgian jurists.
By mid-year, 1902, Archbishop Riordan approved the two
arbitrators for the United States, Sir Edward Fry and
Frederick Martens, a Russian.[37]

Mexico's selection was still a dark secret, the protocol
providing each country a full sixty days to make its an-
noucement. As Mexico delayed, deep uneasiness overtook
Doyle and Riordan. Their fears conjured the specter of
French anticlericals or Italian atheists dominating the tribunal.[38] Relief came when Mexico settled upon Jonkheer de
Savornin Lohman and Tobias Asser, both citizens of the
Netherlands and both having been seriously considered as
American choices.[39] A fifth member completed the tribunal
in September when the four arbitrators met at The Hague and
selected as umpire Henning Matzen of Denmark.[40]

This tribunal, it is to be noted, the first to be assembled
and authorized for the Permanent Court of Arbitration, was
composed of impartial and notably distinguished jurists, none
of whom was a Roman Catholic.[41] Ironically, too, it was
commissioned to judge a case in which an openly
Protestant nation was defending the claims of the Catholic
Church against a state allegedly Roman Catholic. These
striking contrasts highlight the extraordinary character of the
Pious Fund case.

The protocol signed and the full tribunal selected, the last
preliminary problem facing Riordan was the question
whether or not he would engage additional counsel.
Compensation and professional relationships remained an

explosive internal issue that plagued the proceedings and aftermath. By the modified agreement of 1897, he possessed the undisputed right to hire more attorneys and to apportion their fees from the twenty-five per cent originally contracted with John Doyle and Senator Stewart alone. Stewart's engagement of Jackson Harvey Ralston, had at first upset Doyle. Eventually Doyle was impressed by the zeal and excellent work of the new attorney and soon transformed his loud protests into approval and enthusiasm. The senior attorney gave an approving nod when Ralston was named agent of the United States who would represent the government at The Hague.[42] Ralston had involved himself deeply in the Pious Fund case, standing ready and eager to expedite the progress. "I take a very hearty interest in the case and no little pride," he assured Doyle.

Riordan seemed stubbornly reluctant to enter further into this knotty problem. He had long declined to authorize Ralston's engagement. Despite Stewart and Doyle's heartiest commendations, he had quietly made an investigation of his own, requesting friends at the Catholic University of America to inquire into Ralston's reputation in Washington. Father Philip J. Garrigan, vice–rector of the university, had reported that he was a "lawyer of poor standing in the city of Washington, and not worthy to be trusted with the care of any heavy interests." Thus advised, Riordan had distrusted Ralston's entry into the case and had himself informed Doyle that he thought it imprudent and inadvisable to engage additional counsel. "The case was undertaken by Senator Stewart and yourself," he insisted, "and I must look to him and you for the management of it." His exclusive prerogative of adding new attorneys, promised Riordan solemnly, "will be used with discretion towards all who have contributed to bring about the desired result, according to their respective deserts."[43] Thus, by the time the protocol was signed and ratified, the archbishop's counsel was quite settled and delighted with the arrangement of fees contracted among themselves: one–eighth of the amount recovered would be divided among Stewart and Ralston and their associates, and

one –eighth of the amount recovered shared by Doyle with
his assistants.

Riordan held himself aloof from further entanglements
and subtleties until April, 1902, five months before the
opening of the litigation. Then both Hay and Penfield,
Riordan told Stewart, "insisted very strongly" on additional
counsel who could be present at The Hague. This earnest
recommendation opened a sore that was not destined to close
until Doyle's death four years later. While Ralston was
certain to be present to argue the government's case, Doyle's
eighty-three years prevented his attendance, and it was very
uncertain whether Stewart would go. Only two months
before the hearing, Riordan appraised the situation and
became so apprehensive that he sternly demanded Stewart's
presence at the tribunal. Doyle, the greatest living authority
on this case, had regrettably to be absent because of age and
health. But his partner had no such excuse. "I hope,"
Riordan told the senator solemnly,

> that your official engagements will be such as to
> permit you to attend at the hearing of the matter. I
> should feel in a sorry plight if a case of this
> magnitude were submitted for decision without the
> presence of either of our attorneys.

The bishops of California, he continued, deserved the
strongest representation at the tribunal, and additional
authorities, warned Riordan, would be needed on canon law
and the history of Church-State relations in Mexico.[44]

The State Department suggested John Bassett Moore,
universally acknowledged as the most widely known
American authority on international law.[45] In Riordan's
eyes, however, Professor Moore would not be the ideal
selection : it may be too difficult and complicated to detach
him from Columbia University, and the Pious Fund case
needed at the Hague Tribunal a " living voice," an advocate
actively practicing law who could best deliver the oral arguments, not a sophisticated and learned authority on inter-

national law. Eventually Riordan assigned to the case Garrett William McEnerney, the attorney for the Archdiocese of San Francisco.[46] A promising young barrister, McEnerney was genuinely beloved by the archbishop. "A man of magnificent abilities," Riordan would describe his friend, "and one of the nicest characters I have ever known: good hearted and genial in every way."[47] Doyle admitted the worth of Riordan's selection, telling Ralston that the new attorney "is of high standing here and of undeniable talents and instruction. . . ."[48]

With all his acknowledged talents, McEnerney could not completely fulfill his role as the "living voice"; for he knew no European languages. For this reason Riordan elected to employ a European publicist who could present the oral arguments in French to the arbitrators unfamiliar with English. The archbishop thus completed his counsel when he engaged the Chevalier Descamps, a noted Belgian Catholic leader.[49]

* * * * *

Once Patrick Riordan had contracted McEnerney in the case, he took on a new confidence and buoyance, proceeding to The Hague in particularly good humor and health. Leaving New York City on August 6 on the *S. S. Celtic,* he visited en route a close friend in Liverpool, Monsignor James Nugent, a leader in the English temperance movement and Catholic Truth Society. The host was delighted in seeing Riordan's good spirits on the eve of the arbitration. "I believe he is full of hope," Nugent reported,

> and already he is thinking of the disposal of the dollars. . . . He is looking so much better than I have seen him for the last ten years. He had so much colour of a healthy character in his cheeks, his eyes were bright and vigorous and altogether he seemed a new man.[50]

In three weeks, he reached the American headquarters at the Hotel des Indes at The Hague. It would be more than two

weeks before the opening of the case, a peaceful interval long
enough to attend to other business. First, a brief visit with
friends at Louvain. Riordan also used the pause to engage
one more member for the delegation — Hilaire Belloc, the distinguished author who supplied books from British libraries.
Riordan finally decided to press the appointment of a coadjutor. Immediately he placed himself in close communication
with the papal charge d'affaires in the Netherlands, Father
Rodolfo Giovannini. Early in 1901 Riordan had been given
permission to secure a coadjutor with the right of succession,
but the eighteen-month silence in Rome had taxed his patience. The lull before the hearing enabled him to invoke
Giovannini's assistance in expediting this matter.

The Pious Fund case opened on September 15, 1902. All
the preliminaries completed, everyone — arbitrators, both
delegations, spectators — sensed the historic character of the
sessions. The American Minister to the Netherlands,
Stanford Newel, delightedly reported the introductory
remark of the umpire, Henning Matzen. This first case before
the court, Matzen said, was due to the "initiative of two
Great Powers of the New World" and might effectively
promote the greater use of arbitral tribunals peacefully to
settle "differences between States on the one solid basis, the
basis of respect for right." [51]

After the introductory ceremonies the litigation began.
So noteworthy were the proceedings that the courtroom
could not accommodate all the diplomats, reporters, and
spectators who sought entrance. The tribunal conducted
sessions for ten days, withdrawing on October 1 for two
weeks of deliberation. By this time Riordan had left the
Netherlands for Rome, planning to meet Father Charles
Ramm in Brussels and together to visit Paris briefly en route.
He had leisurely reached Genoa by October 14 when the
court reconvened in the late afternoon and announced its
unanimous judgment in favor of the United States. The
award in 1875, it adjudged, had rendered Mexico's liability
res judicata. It was obligated to pay the United States, for the
use of the Catholic Church in California, the thirty—three
annuities which had accrued between 1869 and 1902,

amounting in the aggregate to $1,420,682.67. Mexico was further bound to pay "perpetually" in February of each year an interest of $43,050.99. There was one critical concession to Mexico: the payments were to be in Mexican currency, not Mexican gold as the earlier decision had specified.[52]

The case was hailed in many circles as a monumental triumph for the principle of arbitration among sovereign nations. The American press reflected a pride in the fact that two American states had been instrumental in putting the arbitral machinery into operation and demonstrating its efficiency.[53] Americans were now invited to look with great satisfaction upon the republics of the New World as setting an example for the monarchies and reactionary regimes of the Old. In his report to the State Department, Stanford Newel offered several interesting observations. The decision, he recorded, was "generally commended," and the performance of the American delegation had been "notably effective." "It seems to be the general impression," he added, "that our Government has set a good example by the thoroughness with which its case has been presented." His one criticism concerned the selection of the relatively unknown Ralston as agent for the United States. Several diplomats had told Newel that it was "strange that Senator Stewart, Archbishop Riorden [sic] and Judge Penfield should be ranked by a younger and less distinguished man."[54]

The award to the California bishops was not, however, an unconditional victory. "This award in Mexican trash of money," stormed Doyle in California on learning the decision, "is an absolute failure of justice...," and he ordered Ralston to demand a revision. The American attorneys appealed to Hay, and Doyle told Riordan that the award was a "miserable attempt to satisfy both parties by a wretched compromise with their consciences. I shall publish," he vowed, "a history of the thing in one of the legal periodicals." Despite Doyle's constant protests, Hay was determined not to re-open the case. The protocol, replied Hay, allowed the tribunal to fix not only the amount but also the kind of currency in which the award should be paid.[55] And here this matter ended.

Not only had Mexico lost the decision, it also forfeited its
last real opportunity to terminate its obligation perpetually
to pay an annuity and to make a final settlement with
Riordan. During the hearings at The Hague, the Mexican
minister, M. de Zenil, and the agent, Emilio Pardo, remained
in close contact with the papal chargé d'affaires, Father
Giovannini. Frequently, as he later reported to the Holy See,
he had expressed to these two diplomats his astonishment
that in a purely financial case of this kind Mexico has made
no effort to make a settlement with Riordan. Their reply to
him was that "in the heat of discussion the Mexican
government had lost its head: it stood two steps away from
breaking diplomatic relations with Washington." As the
proceedings developed, the Mexican minister welcomed the
idea of a settlement and requested Giovannini to mediate
between his government and the archbishop. The papal
chargé was extemely reluctant. First, this proposal had come
too late, since the debates before the arbitral court had
already begun. Second, however, and more important was the
fact that the Holy See, politically despoiled since 1870, had
been excluded from representation on the Permanent Court
of Arbitration. His position, insisted Giovannini, would be
extremely delicate because any indirect efforts at mediation
would be interpreted in the sense that the Holy See, resentful
of its exclusion, was trying to obstruct the first work of the
arbitral court. The court itself, Zenil had countered, preferred such an informal settlement if it could possibly be
arranged and Pardo assured the chargé that he possessed the
authorization to make the transaction.

With these assurances, Giovannini cautiously approached
Riordan. After some hesitation, he succeeded in making him
accept the "principle" of a settlement and arranged a
personal meeting between the prelate and Pardo.
Unfortunately, the effort collapsed when the latter failed to
see Riordan promptly, losing two precious days in cablegrams
to the Mexican government. When he was at length ready to
confer again with Riordan, the debates had terminated, the
archbishop had left The Hague, and there was no more

opportunity to propose a formal settlement to the arbritral court in session. Even after the decision, the Mexican government was still determined to transact, possibly through Vatican pressures, a settlement that would extinguish American claims to the Pious Fund. Apparently the Mexican hierarchy was encouraged to appeal for papal intervention in favor of a settlement. After consulting with Giovannini, the Vatican notified the bishops that their petition had arrived — one week too late.[56]

By the time Riordan had reached the Eternal City, he had achieved two major successes. The documents naming his coadjutor were safely in his possession, and the twelve-year effort of authenticating the church's claim to the Pious Fund had climaxed in a substantial award to the California bishops. One failure did mark this trip to Europe. He did not succeed in having his colleague, John Lancaster Spalding, named the Archbishop of Chicago—an involved story to be told later. Nevertheless, the disappointment over his friend's promotion failed evidently to dim Riordan's triumphant spirits when he disembarked on November 28 from the *Celtic* at New York City. American newspapers had followed his movements in Europe; and there had evolved some national interest in him. "The eminent prelate looked the picture when he landed," reported the press on his return. "His cheeks were rosy. He walked with a springy step, his shoulders well back. It was plain that his two sea voyages were beneficial." In his first interview with the press after the arbitration, Riordan described the award as an invaluable assist in extending the church's religious and educational work in California and also as an auspicious precedent which showed how minor conflicts among nations could be solved by reason. Even though western civilization was not sufficiently advanced to invoke arbitration in grave international complications, the Hague Tribunal, predicted the archbishop, "will become one of the great and useful institutions of the world." The United States had also earned the distinction of dissolving the doubts of the sceptics when it "broke the ice and gave the tribunal its first case." Riordan referred obliquely to his business in

Rome, alluding to his several audiences with Pope Leo XIII and heartily describing the health and alertness of the ancient pontiff. "He is stronger than I expected to find him," he explained.

> His voice is clear. He can walk without aid, though seldom ventures to, and can read without aid of glasses. At ninety-three Pope Leo XIII is a marvel of strength and mental vigor. His memory is wonderful, as is his knowledge of current events. He knows all that is going on in the world from day to day and keeps himself abreast of the times.[57]

* * * * *

After an imposing welcome in the East, Riordan desired a modest return to his archdiocese, directing his secretary that no public reception take place.[58] There still remained two difficult problems related to the Pious Fund award, a plan of distribution of the money among the eligible parties and the final settlement of the compensation due to the attorneys. Before these problems could be quickly solved, however, Riordan found himself, for over a year, nearly overwhelmed by a score of unexpected obligations. As metropolitan, he had first to attend to the filling of the See of Monterey-Los Angeles left vacant by Bishop Montgomery's appointment as his coadjutor. In this regard he had already assured Cardinal Gibbons and Archbishop Ireland that Bishop Thomas J. Conaty, who was ending his first term as Rector of the Catholic University of America would definitely be named to the diocese.[59] But the appointment of this easterner was not so easily accomplished, and it was only after several months that he was able to secure Conaty's promotion to Los Angeles.[60]

While in Europe, Riordan had also committed himself to raise money for improvements in his beloved alma mater, the American College at Louvain, and on his return he took the lead in inaugurating a national drive for subscriptions among the alumni in the United States.[61] Meanwhile, he was occupied locally in negotiating for the Capuchins to take charge of Mendocino County in the north, in escorting Archbishop Diomede Falconio, the newly appointed apostolic delegate, on his first tour of San Francisco, and in arranging a religious observance of the fiftieth anniversary of the archdiocese.[62] During these hectic months, the archbishop's robust health deteriorated noticeably, and he was soon suffering from what was described as "nervous prostration." On the advice of his physicians, he reduced his activities, declining even to be present at Denis O'Connell's installation as Rector of the Catholic University of America. The only important engagement he undertook was a brief excursion in spring to Chicago to attend the consecration of his brother's church, St. Elizabeth's.[63]

Before the vexing problem of the attorneys' fees was solved, Archbishop Riordan was able to settle the distribution of the Pious Fund award among the eligible religious superiors. A quarter of a century earlier, this had developed into such a serious difficulty for his predecessor that appeal had been sent to the Holy See for a decision. Alemany had contested Amat's persistent claim that a larger portion was due to his diocese because of the numbers and poverty of the Indians. The archbishop wished the monies to be spread more evely throughout the western states and territories, even telling Propaganda in his report that the Chinese in his archdiocese and the Mormons under his care in Utah should now be included within the purposes of the Pious Fund.[64] Certain minor shares would be given to the Franciscans, Jesuits, and the Province of Oregon City. The large remainder of the award should, according to Alemany, be divided into seven equal parts: two portions assigned to the three dioceses in California and one to Utah. Evidently Alemany's argumentation had been lucid and convincing, and in a formal decree of March 4, 1877, Pope Pius IX had accepted his plan of distribution.[65]

Riordan had studied the facts in this rugged conflict between Alemany and Amat. He was now determined, if possible, not to refer the matter of distribution again to the Holy See. While he was in Rome, this question had been raised, and several of the Propaganda cardinals had proposed that the money be divided strictly according to the population and number of missions in each diocese. Cardinal Sebastiano Martinelli, however, a former apostolic delegate to the United States, urged that before this matter be referred to the congregation, the bishops themselves arrive at an understanding. If they reached a satisfactory conclusion independently, he suggested, there would be no need to invoke Rome's assistance.[66] Riordan obviously favored Martinelli's recommendation and strongly wanted to use population figures as the scale, even if this violated Alemany's scheme. But if Rome were encouraged to intervene again, he feared, it would probably apportion the award merely according to poverty and even include the bishops in Arizona and New Mexico. If this happened, he reasoned further, the old rates of distribution would be reversed among the California dioceses, and San Francisco and Monterey-Los Angeles would suffer most. Riordan would have to summon all his resources of diplomacy. It was first important to convince his new suffragan in the south, who would most likely benefit by Rome's intervention of his views. "I am quite positive," Riordan confided to Conaty,

> that the basis of distribution will not be the number of poor missions, but the population and number of parishes and works of charity to be sustained. Sacramento has far more missions than Los Angeles and the number of poor missions than the Bishop of Salt Lake could put on a list, if he were to include all the poor mining camps of Nevada and Utah, would entitle him to the largest share. I have no objection that the whole matter be referred to Rome, but I much prefer, and the Roman authorities much prefer, that we should settle such a difficulty among ourselves.[67]

Conaty owed his diocese to Riordan and could hardly be expected to resist. As the prelate who had successfully conducted the Pious Fund case at the Hague Tribunal, Riordan felt entitled to exert a heavy hand in determining the distribution. In the end the final plan came from his conception. The Jesuit and Franciscan superiors, and the Province of Oregon City were first allotted the same proportions as in the papal decree of 1877. Their sums were already meagre, he judged, and if they were further reduced these parties would write to the Holy See and initiate an "unending wrangle," as he expressed it.[68] The Territory of Utah, furthermore, persisted as a particular problem for the division of the Pious Fund even though Alemany had before managed to secure for it a share of one-seventh. Riordan differed sharply from his predecessor's view of this part of western ecclesiastical history. "Utah was never considered part of California," he correctly told Bishop Lawrence Scanlan, "and from its earliest days belonged Ecclesiastically to Santa Fe." If Alemany had never by chance been assigned its administration, this territory would have received nothing. The Bishop of Salt Lake City offered no loud protest to this stern reasoning and left the matter entirely to the judgment of his metropolitan, who nevertheless promised: "I will see that your interests are well protected."[69]

Riordan had first requested his suffragans to submit in writing frank and full opinions on the distribution. In time he gathered the prelates in a provincial meeting——Scanlan alone being absent——and he was able to have his original plan ratified. According to the papal decree of 1877, each of the California dioceses received equally two shares of the Pious Fund award, but Riordan argued that the apportionment should be revised since San Francisco and Los Angeles had grown into larger dioceses. The money should now be divided into eleven parts, five portions for San Francisco, three for Los Angeles, and the original two and one portions allotted to Sacramento and Salt Lake City respectively. On October 6, 1903, this plan was approved by the bishops of the Province of San Francisco and remained operative while

Mexico continued to pay the annuities. In apportioning the money, Riordan repeatedly urged that accurate and detailed account books be kept, since Mexico as trustee of the Pious Fund had a right to review the figures. He added, however, a curious directive. The dividends, he instructed, were to be invested again and only the interest used.[70] This hypercaution severely and, to all appearances, unnecessarily, limited the value of the fund to western Catholicism.

The distribution of the Pious Fund award was settled relatively simply as compared with the incredibly complicated controversy over the attorneys' fees, a bleak epilogue to the historic undertaking. In his eighty-fourth year, John Doyle was very sensitive to and jealous of the vital role which he had played for over half a century in this case, and he was anxious to have the question of compensation settled immediately. At his advanced age, he was naturally indisposed to tolerate any lengthy delays or to permit an "eleventh hour man" to share substantially in the rewards and credit. Unfortunately Riordan failed to honor the expected impatience on Doyle's part. Instead he allowed less pressing matters to precede payment of the attorneys, exacerbating his chief counsel. "Archbishop Alemany," Doyle confided later to his son Sherman,

> was of course a Spanish (or rather a Catalan) monk with no business talent or knowledge.... Archbishop Riordan, however, is a highly competent business man; his fault is that he takes upon himself more various tasks than he can reach on, and as his ecclesiastical duties claim preference over secular ones, business in his hands suffers from neglect.[71]

The first and most acrid disagreement centered on Riordan's late engagement of the Chevalier Descamps and Garrett McEnerney. Riordan had the two-fold right to hire additional attorneys and to determine their fees which would be drawn from the twenty-five percent of the recovery allotted to Doyle and Stewart. Though Descamps had been attached to Riordan's counsel scarcely two months, his contribution had seemed very worthwhile to some. The papal chargé had been particularly impressed with Descamps' "magisterial" presentation of the principle of *res judicata* and had even dispatched a printed copy of his arguments to the Holy See as a "clear exposition of the whole conflict."[72] Both Riordan and Doyle, however, agreed in not evaluating the Belgian's performance so highly. When he asked $5,000 for his services, Riordan sent the payment to Descamps' colleague, Canon De Becker, but he included the remark: "I must be frank with you in saying that his fee is very large, I must say exorbitant, for the services he rendered, but I cannot afford to dispute it."[73]

While Doyle flatly opposed such a sum for the Belgian jurist, McEnerney's compensation posed a far different question. "If you take," Doyle conceded, "a gentleman of his standing at the bar, ability and large practice away from his home, office, and business, for a considerable time, you must expect to pay him an ample fee." An honorable and honest man, McEnerney would never overcharge his client but, Doyle stressed, his entire fee must not come from the twenty-five percent reserved to Stewart and himself. The presentation that McEnerney had delivered at The Hague, admitted Doyle, "speaks for itself,. . .[and] will do its author no discredit anywhere." But the critical contribution in this historic case had long preceded his involvement.[74]

Eventually, four months after the award, Riordan elaborated his position on the attorneys' fees, the position that he rigidly retained throughout the controversy. "Is this to be wondered at?" Riordan demanded.

> I found that the case was to be tried and argued some thousands of miles from the home of my chief counsel and that he was unable to attend the hearing. I found that his associate, a Senator of the United States, with little acquaintance with the case, had no thought of attending the hearing. In other words, neither of the two men whom I had

employed to take charge of the case had any
intention of going to the place of trial. Do you
suppose that any litigant with a claim of the
magnitude of the Pious Fund Case would have
tolerated the idea that the case should be tried,
argued, and submitted in a tribunal at which
neither of his counsel proposed to attend? And
yet, that was the situation presented to me.

For these reasons, he added, he had decided not to ask
McEnerney to mitigate his fees. The case was not so simple or
virtually won as Doyle contended. Had it been so safe and
elementary, Riordan asked coyly, "why should I, occupying
the position of a trustee, pay twenty-five percent of
$1,420,000 in Mexican silver, as counsel fees in a case which,
according to your letter, had only to be stated to be
won?"[7 5]

Mexico had meanwhile paid to the State Department the
principal award which, once converted to American currency,
amounted to $605,688.65——a lump sum representing the
Thirty-three installments between 1869 and 1902. During
the eighteen months that followed, the tragic
misunderstanding between Riordan and his attorneys
advanced well beyond the point of no return. The archbishop
continually avoided direct, personal confrontation in this
matter, and McEnerney postponed naming his fee. Even a
motion to submit privately to arbitration the amount of
McEnerney's compensation collapsed.[7 6] Personal feelings
were further outraged when Senator Stewart dramatically
directed that his eighth of the award be impounded by the
State Department and a civil suit be initiated in a federal
court in the District of Columbia. Stewart had already agreed
to $10,000 as McEnerney's fee and to paying other legal
expenses: But for several weeks Riordan had appeared to the
Senator to be deliberately obstructing settlement. In
impounding his portion, Stewart dispatched this bitter
telegram to San Francisco: "Your want of frankness is a
disappointment." — an accusation that Riordan was a liar.[7 7]

This charge unnerved and mortally offended the archbishop. "This is the first time during a long public life," he replied hotly,

> that I have ever been accused of a want of frankness in my dealings with people, and I repudiate the accusation as having no foundation in face, and which should not have been made by a gentleman holding your position against one holding mine, until you were sure it could be sustained by the facts.

No further correspondence would be acknowledged from Stewart, he said, until there came an apology for "your unfounded and ungentlemanly action."[78] The senator's insinuations about Riordan's character were not the main source of the latter's irritation: the actual impounding of the money reserved for the counsel by the State Department cast dark suspicions, in Riordan's sensitive judgment, on the honesty of the California hierarchy and on the solvency of the Catholic Church in that state.[79] Jubilantly Doyle welcomed this exchange, characterizing Stewart's action as "the first gun" of a hard struggle ahead and his share too was impounded.[80]

In the year and a half following the historic Hague decision, the Pious Fund case was fast descending into a petty quarrel. Fortunately, Stewart was more eager than his partner to secure his fee as quickly and as quietly as possible. In May, 1904, a compromise was negotiated. The attorneys accepted Riordan's position on compensation, waiving all future rights to annuities to be derived from the Pious Fund, and the archbishop deducted the government's expenses from the total award.[81]

Riordan, assisted by McEnerney, had for several months played an exacting game of matching legal wits and tactics. John Doyle was beyond reconciliation. Though his health was fast declining, he implacably yearned to remain alive long enough to complete an open letter to Riordan. What most

troubled the failing attorney was the haunting stigma upon
his professional reputation, that he had attempted to extort
exorbitant fees from the bishops of California. His last act, he
reasoned, must be to publish and 'Apologia pro vita sua,' a
hopefully irrefutable and meticulously documented exposé
of the duplicity and criminal perfidy of his adversaries. In
February, 1906, he completed in his eighty-seventh year his
letter of vindication and published it with large portions of
his correspondence that rehearsed the provocative details of
the controversy. "I have known several Bishops and two or
three Archbishops in my long life," read a characteristic
passage:

> Bishop Fenwick, Bishop Amat, Bishop Mora,
> Archbishop Eceleston [sic], Archbishop Hughes,
> Archbishop Cardinal McClosky [sic], and
> Archbishop Alemany. I do not believe that any one
> of them would have sanctioned such conduct as
> yours in this case by his example or approval. I
> have known also eminent ecclesiastics of the
> Episcopal church none of whom I am convinced
> would have done so, I do not believe Bishop
> Nichols would approve such action, and I am sure
> Bishop Kipp would not have done so, for he was a
> man of punctilious integrity and honor.[82]

While this booklet was in the hands of the printer, the
secular press rumored that Riordan might be soon raised to
the cardinalate, and Doyle could not wait until publication
before he would deliver his last blow. Writing immediately to
Cardinal Gotti, Doyle promised to send to the Holy Father a
copy of his book that was designed to shed light on Riordan's
"fitness."[83] Within the year the old man was
dead——bequeathing to his son a painful mission of trying to
recover the booklets from circulation.

It is difficult to sort out the subtleties in this last
unfortunate stage of the case to see which position was
justified. In any case, the archbishop's struggle with his

attorneys had made a poor closing to such an historic enterprise and had disappointed several of the other principals. Many years later, Jackson Ralston, then a highly esteemed arbitrator and authority on international law, fondly recalled the experience at The Hague as "one of my most interesting cases." McEnerney, he admitted, had been an indefatigable worker and made an effective presentation before the tribunal, whereas Descamps had been "only window dressing." But the final quarrel about the compensation was most regrettable. "Both were cranky old men," he noted, "and both were wrong. The Archbishop acted badly as to the fees; Doyle should not have published his booklets."[84]

The Mexican Republic continued to honor its obligation to the Catholic Church of California during Riordan's episcopate. Because of internal political convulsions, however, Mexico discontinued its payments after 1914.[85] The case brought with it at the beginning of the twentieth century a bouquet of mixed blessings, bestowing an unparalleled victory upon the bishops of California and upon the growing movement for world peace and arbitration. It provoked at the same time a bitter and unappetizing quarrel among two figures who had contributed most to the outcome.

The Pious Fund had ceased to be only a legend; it was juridically restored by the world's highest tribunal. The Hague Conference, accused by skeptics of having been only an empty spectacle, had, after three years of inaction, been vindicated to a degree by its Permanent Court of Arbitration, proving that it could harmonize the unsteady relationships among nations. But these supreme achievements were distinctly marred in the aftermath when the principal client and his chief counsel died publicly unrepentant and unreconciled.

Ruin and Resurrection

Patrick Riordan's building program continued into the twentieth century and was nowhere more evident than on the parochial level. One of his earliest criticisms of Archbishop Alemany's administration had been that he had built all but three of his parish churches of wood, raising structures which, Riordan lamented, were at best temporary and highly combustible. The Chicago fire of 1871 was an indelible memory. And one of his first experiences in San Franciso was that during a Lenten sermon a fire broke out in the Chinese quarter near the old cathedral. While the congregation, a contemporary recalled, was touched by his eloquence and hesitated to leave during his address, Riordan was able to organize a safe evacuation.[1] Fires were ever a threat. In the years that followed, Riordan urged pastors to use such durable materials as brick, stone, and granite.[2] By 1903, the fiftieth anniversary of the archdiocese, the *Monitor* recorded the results of this new emphasis. In the twenty years since Riordan's arrival, it commented, not only had a number of new parishes been created but old structures had been remodeled or replaced by new ones. "There is hardly a parish existing in 1883," the Catholic weekly observed,

> which has not in the interval since seen some great church building operations. There are to-day thirty-two Catholic churches in the city of San Francisco alone. Of these twenty-one have been built

245

or, at least, rebuilt through the inspiration of
Archbishop Riordan.[3]

In this way, Riordan had spent two-thirds of his episcopate
fortifying the archdiocese against the disastrous fires which
had frequently swept the city, but his ambitions and
well-conceived building program suffered a tragic reversal in
the earthquake of April 18, 1906.

Few citizens anticipated the historic calamity which
struck nearly a death blow to San Francisco. In the previous
year, even Riordan had registered only mild concern over a
series of tremors below the city. "We have been having a
succession of earthquakes here for the past week," he
informed a friend, "which makes living in the city more
severe. Though none of them have been very severe, yet no
one knows when a severe one may come."[4] On Easter
Monday, April 16, 1906, the archbishop departed for the East
with Father Denis O. Crowley, leaving his coadjutor,
Archbishop Montgomery in charge. Riordan's plans included
the archbishops' meeting in Washington, D.C., and in
Connecticut the marriage of a daughter of Adolphus W.
Green, a close friend and benefactor.[5] While he was en route
and visiting in Omaha, the San Andreas Fault, extending
along the Pacific Coast, settled violently on the morning of
April 18, and the greatest earthquake of recorded history
to have struck California shook San Francisco to its
foundations. Its water and gas mains broken, a fire started in
the city, sweeping unchecked for three days through the
central business and residential sections, and mounting into
the most devastating conflagration in the West. The fire
department elected to make its final determined stand along
Van Ness Avenue and specifically at the archbishop's new
cathedral. At this point, the consensus was that if St. Mary's
perished, the western portion of the city was doomed. The
defense of the cathedral area required three days of incessant
labor, but it succeeded. One of the critical moments occurred
when the cathedral's high lantern on the main tower caught
flames. The firemen completely exhausted, a call for

volunteers enlisted two priests of the cathedral — Charles A.
Ramm and Philip O'Ryan — a sailor, and two young boys.
"At the risk of their lives," reported Archbishop
Montgomery, "[they] went up and saved the cathedral and
with it the *rest of the city*."[6] Despite the first highly
exaggerated accounts, the city had suffered a shattering blow.
According to official reports, nearly five square miles,
including most of the commercial district, were destroyed, an
area of 508 blocks and 28,188 buildings; and the total
damage was estimated at a half billion dollars. Casualties
numbered 500 dead or missing; and suddenly homeless and
uprooted was more than half the city's population, some
200,000 persons whose dwellings had been in the Latin,
Chinese, and Irish quarters.[7]

With this abrupt stroke of misfortune, a large and most
important portion of Patrick Riordan's "flourishing"
archdiocese had been devastated. One of the earliest
descriptions of Catholic losses was dispatched to the
archbishop's close friend, Jules Canon De Becker, Rector of
the American College at Louvain. "The first bulletins of the
terrible catastrophe," reported Father Peter Huesges, a curate
at Most Holy Rosary Church in Woodland, California,

> . . . have reached you by this time. Some
> exaggerations may also have crossed the Atlantic.
> Still the whole truth has not been told and never
> will be known. The Cath. Church of our metropolis
> as a body has suffered the greatest loss of all. . . .
> St. Patrick's Seminary, Most Rev. Archbishop
> Riordan's pride and life work is a complete ruin
> (latest: badly damaged), so is a great part of
> Stanford University at Palo Alto. The Jesuits have
> lost more by the earthquake and fire than anybody
> else. But California is full of hope and confidence
> for the future, its people are of the right stuff.[8]

A fortnight later, Huesges detailed for De Becker the ruined
state of the see city itself, prefacing his remarks: "No pen can

describe the real havoc worked by the earthquake and fire in
our beloved metropolis." Surrounding one devastated parish,
he noted,

> most horrible —trolley tracks twisted, streets torn
> and opened where large water mains had burst,
> which lamentable fact caused the ultimate ruin of
> the city, cement and asphalt sidewalks shattered,
> and houses appearing in a state of intoxication,
> some torn from their concrete foundations, others
> sinking one, two stories into the ground.

Huesges further elaborated on the celebrated defense of the
new cathedral. Though located squarely in the path of the
flames, it had been saved through the "heroism" of the two
curates. "They took their lives in their hands," he explained
for his Louvain friend,

> climed [sic] a high ladder held by Rt. Rev.
> Archbishop Montgomery and extinguished with a
> small stream available the fire on top of the
> steeple, saved the cathedral and as all agreed that
> part of the city that is now San Francisco. The
> main altar was badly damaged by the quake. Here's
> to the two cath. priests![9]

News of the catastrophe, as has been noted, reached
Archbishop Riordan in Omaha, where he must certainly have
recalled a similar experience thirty—five years before. Father
Crowley was sent back at once alone, and the archbishop
decided that he could do more by making an appeal in the
East. Riordan's trip with John McMullen in 1871 had
certainly demonstrated to him that appeals outside a stricken
diocese can evoke a generous response. Nevertheless, his
absence was noted, but Montgomery felt that this was
providential. If Riordan had been in San Francisco during the
disaster, he confided to Bishop Conaty, he "would not have
survived," and, further, it was best for the archbishop to have

delayed his return to "the ruins."[10] Conaty agreed: "The sight would have been fatal to him.'"[11] From afar, nonetheless, Patrick Riordan was able to maintain good spirits. During the uncertain early days, a visitor found the archbishop in Chicago fatigued but "full of hope, believing God will enable him to build up what has been destroyed and make still further progress for God and the Church."[12] Learning something of his extensive losses, he immediately telegraphed to each American bishop from Chicago a request for a diocesan collection. "The sad news reached me here on my way to Baltimore," he added. "I return at once to California. The work of fifty years is blotted out. Help us to begin again." [13] This request revealed that the archbishop had not lost his sound judgment, turning disaster into opportunity.

Meanwhile, a number of messages from close friends were directed to Riordan, expressions of sympathy and astonishment. The earliest press releases of the catastrophe had distressed Father Thomas J. Shahan of the Catholic University of America, who immediately wired his condolences. "From this morning's awful dispatches that sound like the reports from the Day of Judgment," he wrote the day following,

> it would seem that very little in the shape of churches or institutions is left to you. . . the only fit commentary must be found in the Lamentations of Jeremiah and the Book of Job: "Quomodo sedet sola civitas plena populo?" . . . I rejoice that our people have a man of your caliber and character at their head in an hour of trial such as perhaps has never before visited any city made by hands.[14]

One of the most touching messages came from a Louvain schoolmate, William Stang, Bishop of Fall River. "The Lord tries you well," he told the archbishop,

> You must be deep into his friendship. . . . How
> strange! I had planned to meet you and to bring
> you to Fall River. . . and to give you a rest in my
> cosy home. God wills otherwise. Fiat![15]

Before Riordan departed from Chicago, Archbishop Keane of
Dubuque begged him not to return at once to the scene of
the disaster. "You could do little or nothing, and the strain
might cost you your life," he counseled. "Come on, all the
same, to Washington and Baltimore, where brotherly love will
surround and comfort you."[16]

Despite Keane's suggestion, Riordan returned within two
weeks to San Francisco, ready to assume control not only of
ecclesiastical affairs but to offer whatever measure of civic
leadership might be expected of him. Reports were
circulating that the city's spirit had been crushed. Already
thousands of refugees had been either evacuated or were
encamped in the parks, and predictions were freely made that
the city would not be rebuilt. While still hurrying westward,
Riordan learned of dispirited encampments, and it was said
that he feared that both health and character would
inevitably deteriorate in the case of "those who are not of
the exceptional stuff of which heroes and pioneers are
made."[17] It was several days before he was able to re-enter
the stricken city where his presence was sorely needed.
Archbishop Montgomery had ably directed operations in the
first days of crisis. "I do not know how I have lived through
[it]," he confided to Conaty only five days after, "but really
I never felt better." Crises pull people together, and
Montgomery cheered the "good humor, the common
interest, and forgetfulness of self that are everywhere."[18]
But time would take its toll and tax his capacity. When one
beleaguered religious superior conferred with him, as it was
later recorded, Montgomery had shown a "kindly interest
and manifested sympathy but had no confidence in the City's
future and said were he not an archbishop he would go away
from it forever." To all appearances, the disaster had "totally
dismayed" him.[19]

After a survey of his see city, Riordan played a conspicuous role in restoring San Francisco. "We shall rebuild," he urged. "We must restore confidence."[20] His most celebrated moment occurred in Franklin Hall, where he attended a meeting of the Citizens' Committee. While many civic leaders were still yet stunned by the enormous loss and the ashes smouldered only eight blocks away, Riordan stood before the gathering without a touch of display and delivered one of the most eloquent and effective addresses of his lifetime, quoting in impressive tones the words of St. Paul. "I am a citizen of no mean city, although it is in ashes," he began.

> Almighty God has fixed this as the location of a great city. The past is gone, and there is no use lamenting or moaning over it. Let us look to the future and without regard to creed or place of birth, work together in harmony for the upbuilding of a greater San Francisco.[21]

Those present who had heard and recalled his words described them as "the most inspiring address heard by the committee," providing the compelling phrase needed to arouse it to a renewal of hope and an effective program of rehabilitation.[22] There were those, too, who felt that these words were more than an expression of a forceful spiritual figure: they had been uttered by one who was thought to be "the greatest single loser of property in San Francisco."[23] Certainly, the archdiocese had been a principal victim; and its leader would have a voice in the material future of San Francisco. Riordan was appointed to the Finance Committee of Relief, which directed the restoration and whose membership included James D. Phelan as chairman and the powerful Edward Henry Harriman of the Southern Pacific Company.[24]

Despite Riordan's encouragement, his archdiocese had suffered a grievous loss estimated initially from two to nearly six million dollars. In the burnt downtown area, twelve

parishes, which included churches, rectories, and schools, had
been virtually destroyed as well as two boys' colleges, four
girls' academies, two hospitals, three day homes, the Home
for the Aged Destitute, and the Youths' Directory. Elsewhere
in San Francisco and beyond the city where the fire had not
reached, four churches still required complete reconstruction,
so severely damaged had they been by the force of the
earthquake.[25] Ironically, the archbishop's twenty-one-year
program of erecting stone and brick buildings had added to
his losses since these heavy structures, unlike the more
flexible frame buildings, were less able to absorb the shock of
the earthquake. Although he first felt that the new cathedral
had been rendered unsafe by the earthquake and might have
to be razed, Riordan was pleased to learn that it was still
sound, only its carrara-marble altar having to be replaced.
"His Grace . . .," Riordan's secretary, Father John Cantwell,
wrote to its builders, "directs me to compliment you on the
manner in which the Cathedral here was built. The recent
earthquake to a great extent [destroyed] the brick buildings
of the city, but the Cathedral itself has suffered very
slightly."[26]

Situated more directly on the San Andreas Fault, the
eight-year-old seminary was not so fortunate. Its senior wing
and chapel were still under construction when the
earthquake struck. The damage in Menlo Park was the one
detail that, it was recalled, Riordan's household feared most
to tell him.[27] The full upper front of the college wing and
the side walls of the chapel had been torn away; and the
tower had collapsed, its stones crushing the granite steps at
the front entrance. No loss among the battered institutions of
the archdiocese, it was true, afflicted Riordan more keenly
than his ruined seminary whose damage was eventually
estimated at $200,000. "As far as I can figure them out," he
told Archbishop Williams of Boston,

> our losses will come very close to six millions of
> dollars .... The principal loss has been our
> magnificent Seminary at Menlo Park which has

been very badly injured. It seems the very center of
the earthquake was in the neighborhood of the
Seminary, and it wrecked almost completely every
building of stone or brick in that locality. . . .[28]

Riordan actively engaged himself in the business of
rebuilding, arranging open-air services for the encampments
and directing his clergy to erect temporary structures. These
improvised chapels, he had decided, would stand for several
years in the devastated areas of the city until it was possible
to judge where the future centers of population would be.[29]
One of his earliest and most magnanimous acts was to find a
residence for the Sisters of the Presentation, who had lost
their mother house on Powell Street and who were
desperately overcrowded,the archbishop learned, in their
convent in Berkeley. "After you left me here today, " he
wrote to the mother superior,

> it occurred to me that I know a house that will suit
> you admirably until the New Convent is built. . .It
> is in the City and will accommodate twenty-five or
> thirty sisters with a large room for a chapel and
> room large enough for a dining room and a room
> fairly large for a community room. It you come
> here Friday morning . . . to my house, I will tell
> you all about it . . . so please do nothing about
> getting a house . . . until you hear about my
> selection,[30]

The sisters were utterly astonished to learn four days later
that he was moving temporarily to San Mateo, a suburb south
of San Francisco, and was assigning the episcopal residence to
them.

The archbishop had meanwhile begun the restoration of
St. Patrick's Seminary, evacuating the institution for a whole
year and leasing an adjacent mansion to accommodate the
faculty and student body. The results of the earthquake had
taught Riordan a lesson in construction, dissuading him from

recommissioning the original architect, Charles Devlin, who had become, in his judgment, "very ordinary" and "too expensive." The stone trimming designed by Devlin had been dislodged and had been a major factor in damaging the new building. "A great deal of our trouble in the Seminary," Riordan wrote years later, "came from heavy blocks of stone put into the tower, they fell inwards on the roof and went through to the lower floor. . . ." Since this was an opportunity to remodel the institution, he selected a new architect, Frank Shea, who removed the fourth story and rebuilt the third with wood and slate, giving the effect of what was described as a "French roof." The arrangement eliminated the heavy stone work,   and the unfinished senior wing, which was eventually opened September, 1911, was reinforced with a steel frame. "If we should have another earthquake here like the one of 1906," observed Riordan smartly, "it would be a great security to have at least part of the building so built that it would not fall down."[31]

The American hierarchy had responded admirably to Riordan's first appeal from Chicago. The majority of the bishops took up diocesan collections and forwarded to San Francisco substantial sums along with messages of sympathy. The clearest expression of the archbishop's appreciation of this interest and generosity, as well as of his hopes and uncertainties, was addressed to Cardinal Gibbons when the former had learned that at their meeting the archbishops had promised financial assistance to their colleague. "I cannot put into words my gratitutde . . . ," he told Gibbons.

> Our priests and people have borne up splendidly under this trying affliction, but we have all set to work as soon as possible. . . . If we suffered only from the fire we would feel the worse was over, but we are visited every day by a slight earthquake and do not know for a moment when another severe one may occur. We have had one just now which interrupted for a moment the writing of this letter, but we must take these things as God sends

them and do our duty bravely to the last. Our
Priests and Sisters are doing splendid work in
relieving the homeless and afflicted, and I think
without boasting that we earned the good will of
all classes in the City irrespective of Creed.[32]

Eventually messages arrived from various parts of the
world. Cardinal Raphael Merry del Val, Secretary of State,
informed Riordan that Pope Pius X had every confidence
that San Francisco would soon regain its spiritual and
material leadership.[33] Archbishop William Walsh of Dublin
told the archbishop that as soon as the news of the disaster
reached his see city a fund of £500 had been promptly
raised, but this sum had been returned to the subscribers,
Riordan learned, because President Theodore Roosevelt had
announced that no such aid would be accepted from
abroad.[34] Sending his sympathies and encouragement from
Sydney, Australia, Cardinal Patrick Moran expressed his
admiration at the "munificent generous aid on the part of the
Sister States and. . .at the indomitable energy on the part
of your Diocese building up anew in still fairer proportions
the many institutions that were overwhelmed in ruin."[35]
Despite his successful appeal and his quiet removal from the
bustle of the city, the task of rebuilding imposed a severe
physical strain upon the archbishop. His secretary, John
Cantwell, noted that soon after Riordan had suffered what he
thought to be a stroke. Like many people so afflicted, the
prelate seemed to become easily emotional, often shedding
tears.[36] At any rate, Riordan admitted to a close friend a
collapse, telling Denis O'Connell eleven weeks after the
earthquake: "I have had a nervous breakdown since my
return and must get strong again before I can do anything
very strenuous."[37]
The work of rehabilitation continued into 1907, when
Riordan received two further blows in succession, the sudden
death of Archbishop Montgomery in January and the Holy
See's evident reluctance to appoint Father Edward J. Hanna

of Rochester as his coadjutor. He was left with no one to help him in his leadership. The restoration of the archdiocese had, nevertheless, progressed so successfully that Riordan judged that he could leave for Rome to press personally for the nomination of a coadjutor and to make at the same time his third *ad limina* report to Propaganda. "The City is beehived with activity," he had told his brother before leaving.

> Buildings are going up on all sides and workingmen are getting the very highest wages. If we can only keep free from strikes during this spring and summer a great many of the business houses will be ready in the fall for business on the old sites, and the City will resume again something of a normal appearance.[38]

Riordan's departure for Rome in October, 1907, marked for him the end of the first stage of rehabilitation. Despite the disaster of April, 1906, his report to the congregation reflected a consistent progress in the archdiocese, its total population having risen to 275,000, a growth of 22 percent since his report eight years earlier. Vocations continued to show promise, the student body at the seminary at Menlo Park having in only nine years increased to seventy-seven with twenty-three major seminarians studying elsewhere for San Francisco. In the past decade, continued Riordan, the archdiocese had nearly trebled its expenditures to $6,924,520, while accumulating a debt of $771,265. In the interval his educational systems had also made singular advances, having more than doubled its investments in the last ten years to $7,660,000 and now comprising 1,182 teachers and 21,969 students of whom 13,980 belonged to his parochial schools. Finally, the archbishop alluded to the earthquake and fire, reporting that from the forty institutions damaged or destroyed, the total financial loss had been scaled at $4,157,000. Within a year and a half, $1,131,000 had already been expended in its restoration.[39]

* * * * *

Two public events in the last years of Riordan's episcopate revealed in a particular way that the archdiocese had, indeed, recovered from the disaster of 1906, his silver jubilee as a bishop and the establishment of Newman Hall at the University of California in Berkeley. On September 16, 1908, the archbishop, now sixty-seven years of age, would reach the twenty-fifth anniversary of his consecration, but he had resolved to scale the commemoration to a modest and strictly religious ceremony, postponing it to October 15. "I have determined to have the celebration as simple as possible," he confided to Archbishop Ireland,

> Pontifical Mass in the forenoon, vespers and benediction with Te Deum in the evening. I have objected to any public reception or banquets, the City is still in ruins on all sides and people only partially recovered from the terrible disaster. It would be unbecoming for me to make merry in the midst of such distress.[40]

Despite his efforts at restraint, Riordan yielded to strong appeals from the clergy and laity and allowed the jubilee to be solemnized. But he adamantly declined a civic reception and insisted that the celebration be confined to the cathedral. The city of San Francisco, as revealed in its daily press, warmly promoted this public tribute. As an archbishop, Riordan had *ex officio* held a distinguished position in the community, but his consistent display of strong civic leadership, particularly after the earthquake and fire, had earned for him admiration from non-Catholics as well. On this occasion, noted the *Jewish Times,* congratulations were due to him, "as a splendid example of manhood, as an utterly good exponent of pure

citizenship."[41] The prelates attending the observance were
Bishops Grace, Glorieux of Boise, Henrique da Silva, a
Portuguese missionary, and Conaty, who preached at the
pontifical Mass and read a benediction from Pope Pius X.
Certainly a highlight of the morning was Conaty's stirring
apostrophe to the jubilarian: "San Francisco in its glory,
San Francisco in its ruins, San Francisco in its resurrection....
Through all these phases he displayed a spirit nothing could
daunt or withstand." At the afternoon luncheon which was
restricted to the clergy, Father Prendergast reviewed the
the archbishop's career, stressing his powers of administration
and recent courage and energy after the earthquake and fire.
In behalf of the priests of the archdiocese he presented a
purse of $15,000 which Riordan promised to use toward the
completion of the seminary.

In the evening at pontifical vespers, a striking ceremony
occurred when Joseph Sadoc Tobin, a prominent banker,
solemnly addressed the archbishop and, representing the laity
of the archdiocese, handed him a check for $35,000. The
prevalent theme running through his twenty-five years as a
bishop, Tobin announced, had been

> that with the humility of all great churchmen you
> disclaim all personal honor, you renounce all
> personal glory. But . . . during the past decade, in
> sorrow and in happiness, in peace and in war, in
> glory and in disaster . . . Your Grace has worthily
> and serenely presented to the eyes of a great state
> the virtue, the power and the majesty of the
> universal and eternal church. Of no man can more
> be said.

The archbishop had reluctantly consented to this collection
from the laity, allowing it only with the provision that he
would apply it to a diocesan project which he particularly
favored. "There are times," he confessed with deep feeling,
"when praise humiliates a man, and this is one of those

occasions. . . ." Ever since his arrival as a zealous young man, he had found the faithful of San Francisco ever eager to support his projects, particularly one ambitious enterprise. "If I have done anything more," concluded Riordan, "I feel proud that I have accomplished the great work of establishing St. Patrick's Seminary at Menlo Park, where young men reared in this state can become servants." The beneficiary of the laity's purse was, the archbishop announced, his last major undertaking, the Newman Hall at the University of California in Berkeley.[42]

The double significance of the Newman Hall was that Archbishop Riordan was both abreast of the advanced thinking of his day and likewise was anxious to spend his last years after the earthquake not merely in reconstructing the archdiocese but in a resumed program of active expansion and innovation. The latter half of the nineteenth century had marked a renaissance in American higher education. As older institutions were remodeled and expanded, over 260 colleges and universities were founded in the United States between 1860 and 1900, and these created a new area of concern for the Catholic hierarchy.[43] An awareness of the needs of Catholic students at secular universities did not crystallize until well into the twentieth century, so preoccupied were the bishops in extending a separate system of education Yet feeble efforts had occurred as early as 1893 when a Catholic Club had been formed at Harvard University and a Newman Club opened at the University of Pennsylvania.[44] Further impetus was given to the movement when in 1895 Pope Leo XIII lifted the ban against Catholic students attending Oxford and Cambridge Universities, provided that the English hierarchy established regular courses for them in philosophy, history, and religion. In 1905 his successor, Pius X, in his encyclical on the importance of teaching Christian doctrine, emphasized the importance of providing for religious instruction where, he said, "there are public academies, colleges, and universities. . .wherein no mention is made of religion."[45]

In the fall of 1898, several students at the University of California made a pioneer attempt to form a Catholic group. But it was not until December 8 in the following year that they succeeded in creating a viable organization which they named after the celebrated English churchman, Cardinal John Henry Newman, and which grew over the next four years to over forty students.[46] Archbishop Riordan would have had no quarrel with the choice of patron for the new organization, for he greatly admired Newman whose spirit and attitudes inspired the movement. Thirteen years later, after reading Wilfred Ward's biography of Newman which, he said, might have omitted two or three letters, he was yet delighted with the work which he had found "most interesting" and "most edifying." Newman "went through a great deal of suffering," the archbishop observed, "owing to the littleness of some people's views, but take him all in all, he was a wonderful man, intellectually and spiritually . . . a great genius, and a most beautiful character." Riordan had warmly approved of Leo XIII's conferral of the cardinalate upon Newman as a gesture which, he said, "gave an imprimatur to his whole life and drew off the barking of men who were much smaller than himself."[47] The archbishop responded favorably, therefore, to the students' initiative, approving their Newman Club and assigning to it as its first chaplain a newly ordained curate of the local parish, Father John J. Cantwell.

Unequipped with quarters of its own, the club under Cantwell was forced to rent halls in the neighborhood. In October, 1900, the members formally adopted a constitution and by-laws providing for the election of officers and for regular meetings to be conducted twice monthly. The club's most ambitious effort in its early history was the commemoration of the centenary of Newman's birth in February, 1901. This occasion attracted the presence of faculty members from the university, including its newly elected president, Benjamin Ide Wheeler. The observance, which was highlighted by Father Peter Yorke's address on "Cardinal Newman as a University Man," had received favorable notices in the college and daily press, encouraging these pioneer members and publicizing the foundation and purposes of the club. [48]

By 1906, there was clear evidence of a growing interest in Catholic students attending secular universities. In February, Father Francis J. Cassilly, S. J., of St. Ignatius College, Chicago, published an article in the *Ecclesiastical Review* that stressed the problems of students on secular campuses and urged as a minimum precaution the appointment of a full-time chaplain.[49] This article prompted a spirited reply in the same journal by the president of the Newman Club at Berkeley. The presence of Catholic students on state campuses was, he argued, no longer an "unmitigated evil" but an opportunity whereby after four years of "this daily clashing of wits" the student had grounded his faith and confidence and had developed a wholesome respect for other positions. There had been at his university no positive attack on Catholic doctrine, only incidental derogatory remarks of various professors that the students had usually dismissed as unfounded. Despite many obstacles and disappointments, his organization had amply demonstrated its value in the university. "The Club has brought the Catholic students together," he concluded,

> and shown them their strength. It has given the weak ones the help that was necessary to keep them from drifting astray. The sight of some fifty to seventy-five Catholics attending communion in a body annually should alone show a sufficient *raison d'etre* for the organization.[50]

Several bishops were by this time willing to take more positive action. In September, 1906, Archbishop Sebastian G. Messmer of Milwaukee appointed a full-time chaplain to the Catholic students of the University of Wisconsin.[51] Meanwhile, Bishop Bernard J. McQuaid of Rochester had long hoped to establish a Catholic college at Cornell University, similar to European colleges affiliated to universities like Oxford. He had sent a letter to the archbishops' meeting of April, 1906, describing his "Cornell Plan and recommending that Catholic colleges be formally attached to secular universities. No action had been taken because of the sharply diverse responses to the proposal among the archbishops, and McQuaid later remarked that "the whole matter was thrown into the wastebasket."[52] It was to this meeting that Patrick Riordan was en route when the earthquake struck San Francisco and forced him to return. As soon as he learned of McQuaid's plan, Riordan sent his hearty approval to Rochester, adding that he had long hoped himself to establish such an institution near the University of California. "No matter what we do or say," Riordan agreed,

> these secular Universitites are going to be frequented by a large number of Catholics, both boys and girls, and unless we provide for their religious necessities such as is done in Oxford and Cambridge these students will drift away from us. When in England some years ago, I visited Oxford ard the system established works very well. I deeply regret that we cannot provide University training for our young men and women, but we have not been able, and are not in any condition to do so just at the present.[53]

After Cantwell's appointment as Riordan's secretary, the responsibility of the Newman Club reverted to the pastor of the local parish of St. Joseph in Berkeley. But the archbishop was determined, even in the immediate aftermath of the earthquake and fire, to secure this enterprise on an independent and more permanent basis with its own chaplain and headquarters. He first inquired whether the project would suit the Paulist Fathers, a favorite community of his, whose founders he had known personally. When he had entrusted to them in 1894 the old cathedral and parish, he had given the Paulists their first establishment outside the Archdiocese of New York, where they had been founded.[54]

Directed by Riordan, Father Henry H. Wyman, C.S.P., the
Paulist superior in San Francisco, presented the proposal to
the superior general, Father George M. Searle, C.S.P., who
granted his approval early in August, 1906, and agreed to
send a young confrere who had returned from Europe, Father
Thomas Verner Moore, C.S.P. This thirty-year-old Paulist
was an eminently qualified scholar, having obtained a doctorate in psychology at the Catholic University of America and
taken further studies in Leipzig under Wilhelm Wundt, although these had been terminated when he contracted pleur-
isy and was forced to return to the United States. As soon as
Moore learned of the Berkeley project, he was highly pleased
and described Riordan's invitation as "providential." "As a
healthy spot for me to be," he told Wyman,

> it could scarcely be surpassed. And then too it
> seems that my university training should count for
> something. If training and good will can do any-
> thing I should be able to do the work required. It
> seems to be just the opening for which I am pre-
> pared. Whether or not I am capable of giving satis-
> faction remains to be seen.

Despite Searle's reservations on the expenses, Moore implored Wyman to "push the matter through a successful
close," and he promised to come as soon as possible.[55]
In October, the superior general formally consented to staff
the Newman Club at Berkeley; and in the following month,
Moore met Riordan in Chicago and accompanied him to San
Francisco.[56]

The next step for Riordan was gradually to introduce
Father Moore to his vision and to secure property for the
club. For the first half year, Moore lived with the Christian
Brothers at St. Mary's College in Oakland, taking courses in
science at the university and continuing psychological
research that he had begun in Leipzig.[57] Since the Newman
Club had originally been a students' enterprise, its executive
committee petitioned in favor of Moore's nomination as
chaplain and spiritual director, and on March 1, 1907, Riordan

made the official appointment. [58] Though the superior general had registered concern over finances, Riordan had assumed personal responsibility, purchasing in April a house selected by Moore and an adjoining lot for the projected chapel and lecture hall, and sending the young Paulist a monthly check for living expenses. Word of the archbishop's activities reached President Wheeler, who characterized the establishment of the Newman Club as a "step taken in wisdom and with righteous regard" for the Catholic students who were coming to the university in increasing numbers. Since his institution, he told Riordan, was unable to provide religious worship and the local parishes were fully preoccupied with their regular routine, he welcomed this specialized mission because it was designed, he said, to "undertake the somewhat distinctive task created by the presence of university students."[59] Heartened by these prosperous beginnings, the archbishop next applied for a second Paulist to assist Moore because, Riordan noted, "there will be ample work for two men if it is done effectively." Searle consented to his recommendation of Father Thomas Lantry O'Neil, C.S.P., of whom, the archbishop had noted, "I have heard so many good things."[60]

The Newman Club was to be ready for the fall semester of 1907, and in August Riordan announced in a pastoral letter its opening, purpose, and needs. Because the club would serve students at a state university, his conception of the work resembled more Archbishop Messmer's effort at the University of Wisconsin than Bishop McQuaid's at Cornell. The mission of the Newman Club was not so much to evolve into an accredited college but simply to minister to the Catholic student on that campus. The multiple duties of the chaplain, therefore, consisted in corresponding with the students' parents, assisting in securing for them proper accommodations, lecturing on ethics and moral theology to law and medical students, and conducting religious services for the students. The one building already operating, the pastoral continued, was not adequate to achieve these objectives. A chapel and lecture hall were planned, at a probable cost of $75,000, as well as an endowment fund. This large expenditure, Riordan admitted, might seem extravagant and inopportune so soon after the disaster of the previous year but, he warned, "if we neglect the Catholic young men at our State Universities, we shall lose many of our educated laymen—either by their falling away from the Church or by having them become indifferent to religion."[61] The pastoral, which in plain and forceful prose presented the problem and Riordan's solution, had its desired effects. The first of many contributions to this new diocesan enterprise was immediately made by the Sisters of Notre Dame de Namur, and Bishop McQuaid found comfort in this new project during the struggle over his Cornell Plan. "With regard to Cornell," he told Father Daniel Hudson, C.S.C., "Archbishop Riordan's outspoken letter, boldly announcing his plan of caring for Catholic students at non-Catholic Colleges, will stay the carping of many who had no fear of me."[62]

While such a promising start had been given to the Newman apostolate at the University of California, there developed an unfortunate clash of personalities between the archbishop and Father Moore, both of whom had fixed ideas on its administration. At the time of the first Mass offered in the clubhouse on August 26, 1907, Moore had announced that these services were exclusively for the students of the university, refusing entrance to all others and obeying, he believed, Riordan's directive not to violate the rights of the local parishes. Evidently, the young priest had conceived too restrictive a policy, and Riordan gently reprimanded him: "You little fool, keep the door open."[63] A second difficulty occurred the following year over the design of the new chapel. Moore had ordered Riordan's architect, Frank Shea, whom the Paulist thought "hopeless," to construct the wooden interior after the fashion of an English Gothic chapel. After a great deal of pressure, Shea consented. Once Riordan learned of this "wild extravagance," he immediately scolded the priest over the telephone and proceeded to eliminate the ornamentation. Years later Moore recalled: "When he came to the beautiful wood ceiling he said

in very emphatic tones, 'plaster it all up.' " For Moore this
stinging rebuke and rejection of the building plans fortified
his resistance to yield to the archbishop as overlord. "Either I
completely misunderstood your conception of the work," he
informed Riordan,

> or your mind has undergone a great change within
> a short time. There will probably be no bitterer
> disappointment in my life than that your mind in
> this matter is so different from my own. . . .
> I sincerely hope that the future plans — with
> which I understand I am to have nothing to do —
> will meet all the requirements of the situation.[64]

With abundant confidence and resourcefulness,
meanwhile, Riordan elected to finance the erection and
endowment of Newman Hall from subscriptions of wealthy
Catholics. The slow recovery from the earthquake and fire
dissuaded him from directing general collections in the
archdiocese and, he reasoned further, a chief beneficiary of
American philanthropy since the Civil War had been
institutions of higher learning. Central to the growth of
American universitites at this time had been the accelerated
development of industry and the emergence of great
fortunes. In the last half century, great new universities had
been built and secured, very often at a single stroke and by a
single millionaire, with sums ranging from Ezra Cornell's
$500,000 and Johns Hopkins' $3,500,000 to the
$20,000,000 which was ultimately derived from the
Stanford estate and John J. Rockefeller's munificent
$30,000,000 for the University of Chicago. Exposed to this
spirit, Riordan was convinced that it had likewise become the
duty of the educated and wealthy Catholic laity to provide
materially for the church's efforts in higher education,
whether they be Catholic colleges or smaller institutions like
the Newman Hall attached to the secular universities. "The
fact is," he wrote to one affluent friend,

> only educated people have an interest in a work of
> this kind. Were it an appeal for charity in aid of

the poor or orphans, all people would understand
it, but for an intellectual charity such as Newman
Hall typifies, few understand its value. I must
necessarily appeal to men of means, of education
and culture. . . . [65]

The first large contribution of $5,000 came in 1908 from
Richard E. Queen, president of the Catholic Settlement and
Humane Society, and toward the end of the year, Riordan
invested a major portion of his silver jubilee gift, amounting
to $40,000. [66] One of the great benefactors of the church in
the Far West had been John William Mackay, an enormously
successful miner and capitalist whose silver mines and Com-
stock interests in Nevada had yielded him a fabulous fortune
and who had later formed the Postal Telegraph-Cable Company. Before Mackay had left California for Europe at the
turn of the century, never to return, his last visit was with
Riordan. When he promised to do something handsome for
the archdiocese after his tour, this pledge hardly satisfied the
archbishop, and Riordan had never forgotten his reply to the
millionaire: "Will you ever return?" [67] As Riordan had
sensed, Mackay died in London in 1902. His son Clarence,
who had succeeded to his interests in communications,
planned in June, 1908, to dedicate a school of mines which
he had given to the University of Nevada in his father's
memory. He requested the archbishop to deliver the baccalaureate sermon because, he told Riordan, "my father had
always been a staunch admirer of yours and your benediction
of the building would be singularly appropriate." [68] When
Riordan declined for reasons of health, Mackay felt that the
church must be represented at this occasion and petitioned
him to send a substitute, "an able and broad gauged priest."
The archbishop selected Father Charles Ramm and instructed
him to acquaint Mackay with the purpose and needs of Newman Hall. At Reno, Ramm accomplished his mission with
great success, delivering a sermon in which he eloquently rehearsed the achievements of John Mackay and the evils of

socialism. "Father Ramm . . . " Mackay reported to Riordan,

> is — and I say it in all sincerity — one of the most
> charming and cultivated men I have ever had the
> pleasure of meeting. I was indeed proud of having
> such a worthy representative of our Faith. He
> made a most favorable impression on everyone, not
> only his scholarly address, but his manner and
> breadth of views.

Both Mackay and his mother responded generously to
Riordan's appeal, pledging $10,000 and $5,000 respectively;
and the industrialist promised a future contribution if
business conditions would improve and William Howard Taft
should be elected in November.[69] When Mackay's draft
reached the archbishop, he told Ramm: "Evidently Mr.
Mackay is a man of his word. . . . Your trip to Reno had been
productive of splendid results. Mr. Mackay writes most
enthusiastically about the good that came of your visit."[70]
Working according to this pattern, Riordan's fund-raising had
become so successful that before the opening of Newman
Hall, he had accumulated over $50,000. "It's rather a big
work to undertake just at the present time," he confided to a
friend,

> but so many people have manifested such an
> interest in it that I do not think that I shall have
> much trouble in getting the required finds [*sic*] and
> I do not think I shall fail now.   [71]

In the meantime, Archbishop Riordan had faced a severe
personal problem when there erupted in mid-1909 an
irremediable quarrel between him and Father Moore that
resulted in the latter's swift removal.[72] In New York, Father
Searle informed Riordan that he could not send an
immediate replacement since his term as superior general had
expired, and he requested the archbishop to wait patiently until
a new chapter meeting would, within a few days, elect his

successor.[73] After the election, Riordan continued to press the new superior general, Father John J. Hughes, C. S. P. After his experience with young Moore, he specified meticulously the characteristics desired of the replacement. Since Newman Hall was scheduled to be opened shortly, the archbishop demanded the prompt appointment of an older and seasoned priest who had high standing in the Paulist community and who could carefully guide the activities of his assistant, Father Thomas O'Neill. The senior chaplain, he said, "is brought into contact day by day with Professors of the University"; and, he continued,

> he must be looked up to by them. No ordinary young Priest will do, a thoroughly settled man of Apostolic zeal will be able to give a Mission of this kind a successful start and I shall not take any other. Father Moore would have done splendid work here in the course of time if he only had a Superior much older than himself to guide him in his work and in his conduct and I felt for a long time that something was going to happen on account of his inexperience more than for any other reason. . . . I feel that this Newman Hall is a great Mission but it cannot be handed over to boys.[74]

Requesting a measure of more patience from Riordan, Hughes promised to devote his fullest attention to the appointment, adding, "We Paulists can never forget that you were the first Prelate to extend our Community beyond N.Y."[75] As the completion of the Newman Hall approached, however, the archbishop emphatically registered his impatience with these delays, insisting on the presence of an older superior well before the dedication. The total investment, he estimated, would be $200,000, divided equally between the new building and the endowment, but, he warned Hughes sternly, "it will all be thrown away, and . . . my hopes will be blasted, unless the Hall and the work be

placed in the charge of a competent head; and I shall consider
it a little short of disastrous to start with a mistake."[76] So
anxious had these appeals been that Hughes appointed to
Newman Hall, George Searle, his seventy-year old predecessor
who, as superior general, had originally accepted this institution
for the Paulists. He was an esteemed astronomer, a former
instructor at the Naval Academy, and professor's assistant at
Harvard University. Archbishop Riordan greeted this
appointment with enthusiasm. He told Hughes that such a
distinguished and holy man "... is just the one to have in
charge of an institution of this kind."[77]

Three months later on March 10, 1910, a portion of
Riordan's dreams was fulfilled when he dedicated the newly
erected Newman Hall to St. Thomas Aquinas, the patron of
Catholic scholars. Adjacent to the university on the gentle
slopes of north Berkeley, the imposing new building
conformed to Riordan's conception of the importance of this
mission, a three-story, half-timber structure of English Gothic
architecture which featured a lecture hall, library, recreation
rooms, and a striking, vaulted chapel.   " The Catholic
students," he commented a year later on the dedication,

> . . .were proud to possess the handsomest students'
> hall in Berkeley, and not a few crypto-Catholics,
> through its agency, have since been brought to an
> open profession and practice of faith, of which the
> building was a visible symbol and a strong expres-
> sion . . . The more I consider this work, the more I
> am impressed by its success and its importance.[78]

* * * * *

Even those who had clashed unpleasantly with Riordan
respected him as a gifted and progressive administrator who
had fruitfully conducted his thirty-year episcopate in
advancing the Archdiocese of San Francisco. To Thomas
Moore he ever remained the "magnificent organizer. . . [who]
had a deep insight into the needs of the Church," and to

Peter Yorke he was the

> man who had seen Chicago grow from a fireswept
> village to become one of the big cities of the world
> and who came to California in the prime of his
> powers and laid his mark deep on the Church in
> this land.[79]

As the archdiocese was growing vigorously under his hand
despite the severe reversal of the earthquake and fire, by 1910
he had personally seen to completion three large projects: the
cathedral, the seminary—"his crowning work"—and the
Newman Hall.

After these substantial successes, the final years of his
administration, as he approached and passed his seventieth
year, were devoted largely to frustrated efforts at securing an
endowment for Newman Hall. The attempt to solicit
contributions from wealthy friends for this project had
failed, and he had discovered that his general faithful, a half
dozen years after the earthquake, were suffering from a mild
depression and were for the first time unable to support his
enterprises as generously as before. "The fact is," he wrote to
a benefactor in 1912,

> we are now suffering more than ever from the
> effects of the earthquake and fire. After the
> catastrophe all of our people had insurance money,
> but now that money is gone, and they are not as
> well able to give anything as they were
> immediately after the disaster came to them.[80]

The hard times had forced Riordan to maintain Newman
Hall, as he said, "from other sources and from little personal
gifts that come to myself."[81] Nonetheless, he never
despaired of the wisdom of the ultimate success of this
operation, establishing in 1913 a second Newman Hall for the
State Normal School in San Jose.[82] In his late
correspondence, he never ceased to boast of efforts for the

students at the University of California. "I look upon our institute at Berkeley," he told his Paulist friend, Walter Elliott, "as one of the most encouraging things of the Pacific Coast, and I am confident that if we get it sufficiently manned it will prove a surprise to you good people of the east."[83] Two years before his death, Riordan made his final and most desperate appeal to Clarence Mackay, who, he said, had been "the first one to take an interest" in the Newman Hall. In his letter the archbishop revealed the sense of achievement and of sacred responsibility which this, his last project, had given him. "It would do your heart good," he told Mackay,

> to see the gatherings we have on Sunday and other times in the chapel of Newman Hall, and in its reading room, and to hear the words of commendation spoken of its influence in University circles, from Mr. Wheeler, the President, down to the youngest professor in the great institution. Newman Hall has made its mark and is recognized as one of the great factors of the University.

* * * * *

> These boys and girls at Berkeley are the children of the poor. They have not means sufficient to procure an education in any of our Catholic colleges. They are obliged, in order to obtain an education, to come to the State University, where the education is gratuitous; many of them work their way through the University years by waiting on tables in hotels and boarding houses, and doing some little odd jobs here and there, in order to procure enough whereby to pay their board and get their clothing. It is my duty as their Supreme Pastor, to put their minds and souls in the great principles of our

religion, teach them to love their country because it is God's will that they should do so, and to keep its laws.[84]

10

"Una Piccola Agitazione"

At the mid-point of his lengthy episcopate, Patrick
Riordan directed serious thought to the selection of a
successor. While this was customarily a fairly prompt and
predictable process, it had occupied his predecessor, Joseph
Alemany, for a weary decade and would likewise develop for
Riordan into a major frustration. Even after the boundary
adjustment with the Diocese of Sacramento, the
metropolitan see retained a considerable territory comprising
twelve counties and portions of three others clustered around
San Francisco. The archbishop, a zealous administrator who
was chronically handicapped with poor health, found it very
difficult to direct its spiritual affairs alone, especially in
visiting remote parishes.

In 1893, Riordan was seriously engaged in tempting
Bishop Mora to hand over the management of his diocese to a
coadjutor. In this effort, at the age of fifty-one and less than
ten years after his consecration, he recorded his first thoughts
of securing assistance. "Even the strongest health is hardly
able to stand the strain of worry and annoyance that presses
on a bishop," he told his senior suffragan.

> Though much younger than you are, I am tired out
> and long for a rest. If I were a little older I would
> certainly ask for a Coadjutor and let him bear some
> of the burden.[1]

275

Nearly seven years later, at the turn of the century, Riordan was in Rome for his second *ad limina* visit, and he secured from Cardinal Ledochowski permission to nominate an auxiliary bishop. Although the archbishop had never submitted a specific name, the San Francisco *Call* would seem to have been alerted by some source about such a negotiation at Propaganda, and after his return it confidently announced without the slightest authority, that George Montgomery, Bishop of Monterey-Los Angeles, had been appointed Riordan's coadjutor.[2] As it happened, the archbishop's secret thoughts, indeed, were running in this direction. After a year of inaction, Riordan told Propaganda that within his archdiocese he had found no priest worthy of the episcopate, except an unnamed pastor whose removal would inflict grave injury to his large parish. A young robust and zealous priest of another diocese assigned to him as a mere auxiliary, Riordan argued, would have at his death no canonical position or prestige in San Francisco. For his welfare and that of the archdiocese, therefore, the man should be given the full rank of coadjutor.[3] Six other metropolitans had auxiliaries at the turn of the century, but the significance of Riordan's request was that though he was still a relatively young archbishop — not quite sixty years — he alone had begun at this early date to arrange his succession. In any case, on March 31, 1901, Pope Leo XIII authorized the presentation of a *terna* for the coadjutorship.[4]

Over the years Patrick Riordan had come to have very decided ideas on candidates for the episcopate. In his first years on the Pacific Coast he had encouraged the promotion of local priests, such as Lawrence Scanlan to Salt Lake City, George Montgomery to Monterey-Los Angeles, and Thomas Grace to Sacramento. A decade's experience as Archbishop of San Francisco, however, had shifted his preference to easterners. Although the seminary had been established to foster native vocations and to relieve the dependence of western dioceses upon foreign priests, the pioneering Far West, Riordan was convinced in his later life, had not yet developed a clergy sophisticated and seasoned enough to produce its own bishops. Likewise, Rome had had a tendency to elevate western priests prematurely, priests who were too young and unripe. ". . . candidates should be taken from some of the Eastern dioceses," he had told a Propaganda official.

> We have no Candidates on this Coast. They should be men from 40 to 50 years of age, tried, and experienced men acquainted with parish work, from actual experience gained in having charge of a parish, and a school, able to direct religious Communities (Sisters). Too many mistakes have been made here by making Bishops of mere boys. Let boys wait until they become men, before the tremendous responsibilities of the Episcopacy are thrust upon them. . . . [5]

It was partly through this conviction that Riordan had attempted in 1896 to disqualify the *terna* for the Diocese of Nesqually which listed three westerners, and also in 1898 to secure the appointment of Archbishop John J. Keane to Oregon City. The great exception to his standard was his former chancellor-secretary, Bishop Montgomery, who had spent his entire priestly life in San Francisco and was less than six years younger than the archbishop.

Riordan had delayed nearly a full year before proceeding to the nomination of a coadjutor, feeling, at first, that his strength was sufficient to govern the archdiocese alone. Finally, on March 14, 1902, his consultors and irremovable pastors drew up a lengthy list, awarding a sizeable majority to Bishop Montgomery and scattering the remaining votes among local and eastern candidates.[6] Within the week the bishops of the province modified the priests' *terna,* naming Montgomery as *dignissimus,* as *dignior* Bishop Thomas Conaty, Rector of the Catholic University of America, and as *dignus* Father James Cleary, pastor of St. Charles Church in Minneapolis.[7] From this investigation, Archbishop Sebastiano Martinelli, the apostolic delegate, reported to the

Holy See that Cleary was ineligible and, more significantly, that the metropolitans had unanimously favored Montgomery as preferable to Conaty who as a New Englander was far less acquainted with conditions in California.[8] While there were at Rome no complications or uncertainties regarding Montgomery's candidacy, the process was delayed in the summer of 1902 by the death of the Prefect of Propaganda. After the summer recess, the congregation recommended promptly on September 1, 1902, Montgomery's appointment as coadjutor with the right of succession, a nomination that was formally sanctioned by the Holy Father four days later.[9]

When George Montgomery returned to San Francisco, it was as no stranger. A native of Kentucky, he had studied for the archdiocese at St. Mary's Seminary, Baltimore, and had been ordained in 1879 by Archbishop James Gibbons. Proceeding then to California for the first time, at the age of thirty-two, he had been appointed by Archbishop Alemany, as he reported to his former superior, Father Magnien, "a kind of Secretary to the Secretary," charged with the finances of the archdiocese.[10] Riordan had retained Montgomery as his secretary and shortly thereafter promoted him to the chancellorship.[11] A conscientious and deeply spiritual man, he had interested himself in social reform, particularly in the temperance movement. In time, Riordan had considered this western priest to be an exception among his clergy.

On February 8, 1903, Riordan formally welcomed his new coadjutor. The approaching autumn, Riordan told the congregation, at the cathedral would mark his own twentieth year in San Francisco. His duties thus multiplying and his health failing, the Holy See indulged him to select a helper and successor and, he continued in a touching passage,

> . . . when I looked about the entire country to see what one in my judgment would be best, I naturally turned towards one who had been associated for

eleven years with me as my secretary and
chancellor and who lived in the intimacy of my
own house, and I may say a personal word, who
knit himself probably more than any other man
ever did into the warmest affections of my heart,
who was ordained for you a priest, who was
consecrated in this sanctuary, who was beloved by
everybody. He comes back to us, not as a stranger
but as a son to his father's house; so we all know
him; we all love him.[12]

Riordan's concern over his successor did not end with this
relatively untroublesome appointment. He was to have the
dubious fortune of surviving his coadjutor. For years,
Montgomery had been under medical treatment for diabetes,
and in 1905 a severe attack of rheumatism had driven him for
a lengthy recuperation to Byron Springs in nearby Contra
Costa County. When he returned to the chancery, Riordan
was not perfectly satisfied with the state of his health. His
presence, nevertheless, offered the older archbishop in the
same year the opportunity to take an eight-month recess from
duties, allowing him to tour the familiar parts of Europe and
to visit, for the first time since his childhood, his birthplace
in Chatham, New Brunswick.[13] In the following year
Montgomery's physical strength had held up well enough
during the earthquake and its aftermath, but the disaster had
depressed him far more greatly than Riordan. A robust
individual who characteristically disliked, as he had confided
to a friend, "being advertised as a sick man,"[14] Montgomery
had not given to others the slightest premonition of
approaching death until the late evening of January 4-5, 1907,
when he was stricken with appendicitis. He rallied after the
operation, but early the following week he suffered a severe
relapse due to his diabetic condition. Archbishop Riordan
was advised to administer the last blessing, and the coadjutor
died on January 10, 1907, one week after his sixtieth
birthday.[15]

Since it occurred so soon after the earthquake,
Montgomery's death evoked another chorus of sympathy
from the American hierarchy. Archbishop Diomede Falconio,
immediately registered his astonishment at the news, entirely
unaware of Montgomery's illness. Recalling Riordan's past
misfortunes within the year, Henry Gabriels, Bishop of
Ogdensburg, comforted him on this second successive blow
to the archdiocese when he said: "It seems that you are a
target for calamities. You will have the reward of your sorrows
hereafter." Another Louvain episcopal alumnus, William Stang,
Bishop of Fall River, directed somewhat the same touching
message to San Francisco: "The Lord must love you, indeed,"
he wrote, "since he sends you so many and such heavy losses.
But this is 'humano modo loquendo'; no sacrifice is loss,—all
is gain 'diligentibus Deum' " The most significant expression
of condolence, however, came from a friend in Rochester,
Bishop Bernard J. McQuaid, who within a few months would
be working very closely with Riordan in arranging a successor
to Montgomery. The eighty-three-year-old prelate could best
comprehend Riordan's grief. He had himself recently selected
his own successor when he consecrated Thomas F. Hickey as
coadjutor in 1905. "With such a grand future before him,"
wrote McQuaid,

> Archbishop Montgomery is suddenly cut short in
> his career, and you are deprived of his help in your
> own declining days, and of the consolation of
> feeling certain that your work would not be
> spoiled after your departure as so often happens.
>   Between the earthquake and this death your
> share of troubles is almost beyond endurance.[16]

Riordan deeply felt the loss of his episcopal partner. As he
faced the prospect of securing another coadjutor, he
lamented how Montgomery had been beloved by all classes
regardless of creed or nationality. "No one feels his loss as I
do," he explained to a friend.

Twenty-three years except when he was in Los
Angeles we worked together in perfect harmony,
and he came nearer to me than almost anybody in
the world. We may get others to succeed him, but
no one will ever take his place in this Diocese.[17]

* * * * *

A month after the obsequies, Riordan rallied from the
heavy blow. This time he was determined not to suffer
another delay as he had in the case of Montgomery's
appointment.[18] In early spring he revealed his careful plans to
Bishop Grace when he asked him to take his confirmation
tour as yet some seven months away. "It is possible and I say
it in strict confidence to you," he wrote confidently,

that I may go as far as Rome and have my
Coadjutor appointed while there. It is the only way
to expedite matters and if I can get my list ready
for the fall it would be better to go over and ask
the Propaganda to make an appointment at once. . .
and then the matter is finished for many years to
come.[19]

Passing over his own clergy, he directed confidential inquiries
to friends about promising young eligibles outside of the
archdiocese, showing at first an interest in Bishop John P.
Carroll of Helena and Father Dennis McMahon, the
supervisor of Catholic Charities in the Archdiocese of New
York.[20] By mid-June the archbishop had made his selection
of three priests, all reportedly not over fifty years old. The
experience of Montgomery's death at the age of sixty had
made that a prime factor in the selection, Riordan insisting
that each candidate be sufficiently young and strong "so
that he may have a long Episcopate before him"[21] In August
the diocesan consultors and bishops of the province, in
separate meetings conducted by Riordan, submitted identical
lists, naming in order Fathers Edward J. Hanna, Richard

Neagle, and John J. Lawler.[22]

The last named, doubtless the nominee of Archbishop Ireland, was the rector of the cathedral in St. Paul; Neagle, who had been recommended first by another former priest of Massachusetts, Bishop Conaty, and strongly endorsed by Archbishop Williams, had been for twelve years the chancellor of the Archdiocese of Boston. Riordan's favorite, however, was Edward Joseph Hanna, the forty-seven-year-old professor of dogmatic theology at St. Bernard's Seminary in Rochester.[23] Endowed with exceptional intellectual gifts, Hanna had prepared for the priesthood in Rome, where he distinguished himself as a superior student in disputations and was personally awarded a doctorate of theology by Leo XIII. After his ordination in 1885, the Rector of the American College, Denis O'Connell, had kept him an additional year as a resident tutor. The Urban College had also appointed the young priest as a professor's assistant to a rising curial figure, Monsignor Francesco Satolli, at the latter's request. O'Connell had tried to keep Hanna in Rome, but in 1887 Bishop McQuaid, then planning a major seminary of his own, ordered him home. In 1893, when St. Bernard's Seminary was opened, Hanna was named its first professor of dogmatic theology, a position that he filled for the remainder of his days in Rochester.

It is unknown when the Archbishop of San Francisco was first attracted to the amiable seminary professor in Rochester, but from the turn of the century there had clearly developed a bond between Riordan and McQuaid. Although the latter had been one of the most conspicuous members of the so-called conservative wing of the hierarchy, he had lately mellowed toward his more progressive colleagues especially after Archbishop Corrigan's death in 1902. In fact, he had even reached an understanding with his chief antagonist and Riordan's close friend, the Archbishop of St. Paul. It would be expected that the old bishop and Riordan would strike an agreeable relationship. Riordan admired McQuaid's dedication to the parochial-school system and to his seminaries, and he had sent a number of his students to St.

Bernard's in its early years, a policy for which McQuaid was ever grateful. By 1903, when McQuaid had publicly refused to implement in his diocese the annual collection for the Catholic University of America, Riordan felt so confident of the bishop's friendship toward him that he assured the rector:

> I am very sorry that my old friend Bishop McQuaide [sic] had declined to take up the collection. I am going to write him today or tomorrow and ask him to have one taken up as soon as possible. I think I can prevail upon him to come into line. [24]

Although Riordan's efforts at persuasion failed to mollify McQuaid's rooted opposition, there had been quite a different reaction three years later after the earthquake in San Francisco. When the archbishop had made his appeal for assistance to the American hierarchy, the bishop responded immediately and most generously. A diocesan collection was ordered for the stricken city, and McQuaid offered to assume the expense of educating Riordan's students at St. Bernard's Seminary. On learning of Riordan's resolve to start anew, he had been personally concerned for the latter's health in this crisis, telling him: "In your physical nervousness so much courage is almost incredible." [25] Archbishop Riordan could hardly be unmoved by this splendid charity from one of the most notable ecclesiastics of his generation. Possibly his truest thoughts of the old bishop were best expressed on the latter's death in 1909 when he told O'Connell, "Our old friend Bishop McQuaide [sic] is gone. He did a great work in his life and with all his peculiarities he was a most Apostolic Bishop." [26]

One last favor which McQuaid would render to the Archdiocese of San Franciscowas to give unstinting assistance, until nearly his death, in the selection of its third coadjutor. Hanna's name having been suggested to Riordan by a friend, the archbishop had sent in April, 1907, confidential inquiries

to McQuaid. In detailing the qualities that he required in a
candidate, Riordan also promised the Bishop of Rochester
that temporal problems were minimal in San Francisco, and a
man of scholarly tastes like Hanna would be given a "free
hand" in the administration. "Financially the Diocese is in
most excellent condition," explained Riordan, "and he will
not have to bother collecting moneys. I wish you would open
your mind fully frankly [to] me as I have great confidence in
your judgment with the experience of a half century."[27]
McQuaid was glowingly enthusiastic. As soon as Riordan
received his letter from Rochester, he announced that Hanna
was his chosen candidate. At the same time, however, he
cautiously sent another secret inquiry to Hanna's close
friend, Denis O'Connell, for corroboration.[28]

In six months Edward Hanna earned excellent
testimonials for promotion to the episcopacy. But before the
apostolic delegate posted his survey to Rome in late
September, 1907, significant events earlier in the month had
delivered an unexpected and shattering blow to the Riordan
request for a successor. On September 8, Pius X issued the
encyclical, *Pascendi dominici gregis,* which climaxed a series of
condemnations of modernism. This was a complex theological
movement within the church whose tendencies toward
agnosticism and relativism menaced the roots of Catholic
faith.[29] Originating in Europe, the movement had little
influence on the church in the United States. Unfortunately, however, Edward Hanna — his promotion virtually
assured — was to become one of the very few Americans
to be accused of this heresy and fall victim to the suspicions
of the Holy See.

In the last stages of investigation Cardinal Girolamo
Maria Gotti, Prefect of Propaganda, received from the United
States a disturbing letter that was outspokenly opposed to
Hanna's nomination. His correspondent was Hanna's colleague at St. Bernard's Seminary, Andrew E. Breen, professor
of Sacred Scripture. In his professional circles, Breen had
been considered rigidly orthodox. His massive study, *A Harmonized Exposition of the Four Gospels* in four volumes,

had been the first American study that received the attention of Marie-Joseph Lagrange, the pioneer Dominican
editor of the *Revue biblique*. In his evaluation Lagrange
had suggested that the only resemblance between Breen's
work and that of other specialists was the organization of
material.Otherwise no recent author had ever betrayed such
naïveté in the biblical sciences as Breen. The Dominican's
salty critique had hardly shaken Breen's confidence. Quietly
he addressed a protest against a promotion to a clerical
friend in Rome, Monsignor Marini, which reached Propaganda through the Secretariate of State. Breen's letter
not only challenged Hanna's orthodoxy, but severely attacked his person, describing him as a "man who covets
his own advancement, and who lacks firmness of character, a courtier, shifting where the wind blows." The scripture scholar alluded also to a series of articles by Hanna,
entitled, "The Human Knowledge of Christ," which, according to Breen, were based on the writings of rationalists and
should be retitled as "The Ignorance of Christ." [30]

The articles in question has been published two years
earlier in the *New York Review* a learned journal edited by
professors of St. Joseph's Seminary in New York. Hanna had
distinguished himself as a gifted theologian and one of the
editors, Father Francis P. Duffy, had urged him to contribute
to its first issue of June, 1905. In explaining its purpose,
Duffy had told Hanna that since scholarly articles were
appearing only in scattered and unprofessional publications,
there was a desperate need for a review in English which, he
said, would be "not a magazine of popular apologetics but a
serious work, and . . . conducted on modern lines." Among
the prospective contributors besides Hanna, added Duffy,
were Baron Friedrich von Hügel, Wilfred Ward, George
Tyrrell, S. J., and Francis Gigot, S. S., of St. Joseph's
Seminary, all of whom would in time be at least suspected of
modernism.[31] Hanna's first controversial articles attempted
to strike a balance within the divine-human composite of
Jesus Christ, and specifically to explore the perilous
theological subject of his human intellect and knowledge.

Claiming that his efforts offered no definitive conclusions,
Hanna suggested in his conclusions possible limitations in
Christ's human intelligence and opened to discussion the then
common teaching of theologians that Christ as man possessed
from birth the beatific vision.[32]

With these disturbing views in hand, Cardinal Gotti
personally drafted an instruction to the apostolic delegate to
investigate Hanna's writings, at the same time forwarding to
Washington a copy of Breen's charges. Gotti took this action
fully aware of its supreme delicacy since Hanna had been
Roman-trained and a protégé of Cardinal Francesco Satolli,
Prefect of the Congregation of Studies.[33] At this point
Hanna's candidacy was further jeopardized. Hardly had
Cardinal Gotti's message to Washington left Rome
when there arrived at Propaganda from the delegate an
unexpected supplementary report on the candidates. While
additional letters from Archbishops Keane, O'Connell,
and Messmer had endorsed Hanna, Archbishop Falconio
mentioned that he had just learned of his articles in
the *New York Review,* a periodical, he added, "which
appears a little suspect of *Modernism.*" The articles, he
continued, were said to have received the attention of
Alexis Henri Lépicier, O.S.M., a Service professor at the
Urban College of Propaganda, who had allegedly refuted
them. Though such writings had passed unnoticed in the
United States, Falconio enclosed a copy of Hanna's articles
in his report for Gotti's judgment.[34] The prefect forwarded
them to Lépicier, who early in December submitted a forceful critique of Hanna's views on the human knowledge of
Christ.[35] Also given to the Servite theologian was an extract
from Hanna's articles on "Absolution," recently published
in the first volume of the *Catholic Encyclopedia.* This too,
Lépicier held, contained fatal errors of modernism.

Riordan, meanwhile, sensed the winds of uncertainty in
Rome. In early October he left San Francisco ostensibly to
arrange some loans in the East and to attend the meeting of
the Board of Trustees of the Catholic University of
America.[37] He was also prepared to continue on to Rome

to present his third *ad limina* report and to make a personal appeal for Hanna. In Washington, the archbishop was distressed to learn of Lépicier's charges, and he promptly expressed his displeasure in strong letters to Cardinals Gotti and Satolli. Though he had not, as he told Gotti, read the incriminating articles, Riordan felt it very strange that suspicion could be cast upon a distinguished former student of Cardinal Satolli. If, however, Rome retained the slightest doubt about his orthodoxy, certainly Hanna could, suggested Riordan, send to Propaganda a full and satisfactory explanation of his writings.[38]

In preparing the next stage in his fight for Hanna's appointment, Riordan enlisted a number of his friends. He first informed McQuaid of Lépicier's opposition, urging that both he and Hanna write. "The Delegate is strongly in favor of Dr. Hanna," he told the bishop, "but is afraid that unless the opposition to him is killed he may not receive the appointment. . . . I may even go to Rome myself if the Delegate thinks that my presence there would be beneficial."[39] He also exploited his presence at the university in extracting a promise from Denis O'Connell to send letters to his highly placed friends in Rome.[40] Riordan had used well this brief interval before his departure from New York on the *Caronia,* and in his last letter to McQuaid he assured the old bishop that the preliminaries had been duly arranged. "The Delegate came to the University yesterday," he wrote confidently, "and told me that he had just mailed a strong letter in favor of Dr. Hanna to Cardinal Gotti. New York has also written. Philadelphia, St. Louis, and St. Paul will write at once. So I think there will be no trouble in getting the appointment made immediately."[41]

There was activity in Rochester as well. For the bishop, this issue embraced not only the reputation of Edward Hanna but also that of his seminary, the supreme achievement of his episcopate. For this reason McQuaid spared no effort in exonerating his professor. Despite his eighty-three years, he offered to go to Rome himself, a suggestion which Riordan mercifully discouraged.[42] While

his   age   handicapped   his   activity,   McQuaid   addressed   a
lengthy defense to Cardinal Raphael Merry del Val, Secretary
of State. "If this charge had any foundation," insisted
McQuaid,

> it would implicate St. Bernard's Seminary and
> myself. I know my professors well, as I am
> constantly with them, and I am sure that there is
> no tinge of unsoundness in their speech and
> thoughts. Nearly all of them have been educated at
> the Propaganda and under Cardinal Satolli himself,
> and if per chance one of them took up a liberal
> tone of speech others would make short work of
> his speculations.

According to these sentiments, McQuaid was yet unaware of
Breen's involvement, suspecting at first that a foreign
theologian like Lépicier had originated the accusations —
someone,   he   told   the   English-born   cardinal,   "not
friendly toward the Doctor, and not master of English [who]
has misunderstood the articles and tried to pick out heresy."
St. Bernard's has struggled, he added, rapidly to become the
foremost seminary in the country. While it could disregard
the "carpings of envious rivals," any rumored weakness in its
faculty or a loss of confidence by the Holy See would
alienate other bishops and crush this promising institution in
its infancy.[43]

The accused professor, however, was reluctant to send
any explanation to Rome as he had been ordered to do so by
Riordan. Hanna feared that by such action he would be
further accused of personal ambition. Apparently he elected
at the start to remain silent. His silence was broken in a
message of congratulations to Denis O'Connell when named
a titular bishop. In Hanna's eyes this was a "day of triumph
and thanksgiving" for the university rector who had long
suffered the misrepresentation and opprobrium that he
experienced at that moment. "While in the joys of your
triumph," he requested O'Connell, "do not forget in your

prayers the poor fellow whose faith in Christ is at this moment under investigation."[44] By mid-December, 1907, however, Hanna was brought round to make his own defense, detailing for Propaganda his unqualified orthodoxy.[45] News of Hanna's predicament had meanwhile enjoyed national circulation, and the third candidate on the *terna,* Father John Lawler, was considering how these developments affected his prospects. Eventually, he confided to Monsignor Jules De Becker, Rector of the American College at Louvain, that Hanna was no longer the strongest candidate. "What my chances may be I do not know," he wrote. "I have no intercessor at Rome — so far as I know. Again I say: *Fiat voluntas Dei.*"[46]

Riordan arrived in Rome early in December, calling immediately on Cardinall Gotti and searching out Cardinal Satolli at the Lateran. At this time, too, strong recommendations of Father Hanna had reached Propaganda from Cardinal Gibbons, Archbishops Ireland, Ryan of Philadelphia, and Glennon of St. Louis.[47] Supported by endorsements of this kind and having received encouragement from certain Roman officials, Riordan gradually yielded to a measure of overconfidence. When he had first confronted Gotti he found him non-committal, though speaking highly of Hanna.[48] The archbishop thereby anticipated no objection to the appointment when the congregation next met after the feast of the Epiphany, and consequently his spirits rose as he approached January. At this time, too, a colleague of Hanna at St. Bernard's Seminary, Father Andrew B. Meehan, professor of canon law and liturgy, was in Rome where he was pursuing a year of study and also detailing developments in this affair in frequent reports to McQuaid. For Meehan as well, the appointment was imminent. "I saw His Grace of San Francisco this morning," he wrote to Rochester. "He is perfectly satisfied that Dr. Hanna will be appointed in the meeting of Propaganda next month. Abbot Gasquet saw Cardinal Gotti Sunday, and said what he could do in favor of Dr. Hanna. He too says that Dr. Hanna's selection is assured."[49]

In the crucial weeks before the Propaganda meeting Riordan's confidence rose to a still higher degree. By the end of
the year he had become so certain that he began remote preparations for Hanna's consecration, suggesting that on his return to the West it would take place in Rochester in mid-
February, 1908. McQuaid, of course, would be the preacher
and he the consecrator.[50]

The congregation was scheduled to make its decision on
January 13, 1908. Shortly before, however, Riordan's dreams
were shattered in an interview with Cardinal Martinelli, the
ponente, or cardinal who presented the official report in this
matter. The archbishop, Meehan reported to McQuaid, had
seen the cardinal's report that included in full the accusations
against Hanna, and in itself the document had seemed
innocuous. In their conversation, however, Martinelli stressed
the danger involved, leaving Riordan with the impression that
there was little chance for the appointment. Bishop Thomas
F. Kennedy, Rector of the American College, later told
Meehan that "there was no hope that knowing the Italians he
was sure from the way they were hedging that they intended
to down Hanna."[51]

But Riordan's foreboding was correct. For when
Propaganda met the case was not even presented, and
Riordan was informed that the next meting would not be
held until March.[52] This tactic had disheartened the
archbishop. In an anxious effort to establish Hanna's
orthodoxy, he immediately instructed McQuaid to have the
professor publish another article in the series in the *New
York Review,* "along the lines that will be indicated by the
Propaganda." Riordan attempted to conceal his frustration
from the bishop, but he added: "I am surely disappointed as
I counted on hav[ing] some one appointed today. But time
has no value for these good people." He further requested
that Hanna be directed to be bound to the greatest secrecy.
"I am afraid," Riordan gently told the old prelate, "that
there are some even in Rochester who would be glad to send
sinister reports about him. So let him be on his guard and
trust very few."[53]

* * * * *

Riordan's last warning pointed to a concurrent issue in this affair, the identity of Hanna's delator. Soon after his arrival at Rome, Riordan had uncovered Breen's involvement but was apparently resolved not to inform McQuaid, fearing that the latter's swift reprisals would serve only to provoke the Holy See.[54] From the start the bishop had never suspected his professor of scripture. But Breen's charges were a poorly kept secret in the Eternal City, his role in Hanna's ordeal gradually unfolding in public view. It must have been a severe shock for McQuaid when he learned from Salvatore M. Brandi, S.J., editor of the *Civiltà Cattolica,* that according to Cardinal Gotti himself the accusation against Hanna had originated in Rochester.[55] McQuaid's own agent in Rome, Andrew Meehan, was himself determined to identify the delator, assuring his bishop: "Everything here ... is known sooner or later"; and by mid-January he reported that both Kennedy and Gasquet had named Breen. "I believe that Dr. B. is honest in the matter from his own viewpoint," observed Meehan further,

> at least to a certain extent. He has always considered Hanna a bluffer and ambitious. As a secondary motive, he may have wished to square himself with Cardinal Merry del Val. I earnestly believe that he thinks it a calamity to give Hanna a mitre.[56]

But this attempt to rationalize Breen's intention fell on deaf ears in Rochester. Even Riordan had correctly anticipated McQuaid's course of action against his professor of Scripture once the bishop learned of his complicity. When the rumor reached him that a teacher at St. Bernard's Seminary had been Hanna's accuser, it seemed "incredible," as he later explained to a friend, and "I refused to believe it." A circular was then presented to the faculty for signatures, stating that each signatory was not responsible for the accusations at the Holy See. Andrew Breen declined to sign, eventually submitting his resignation. This disclosure, recorded McQuaid, had inflicted a deep personal wound, giving

> me a shock from which I did not recover for a couple of days. Not one in the Seminary had received more favors from me than Breen for over 25 years .... His insane jealousy of Hanna, and of everybody more popular than himself was his only excuse. He pleaded conscience but conscience would have been saved had he intimated to me, his Superior, his conscientious scruples and thrown on me the responsibility of Hanna's promotion.[57]

The bishop presented the circular to the local press. Breen countered hotly with a lengthy vindication. He had sent, he claimed, a copy of his charges to San Francisco and insisted that his was not the popular side of the question since, as he put it,

> The people care little for orthodoxy; and they care much for the "glad-hand" and that kindly affability of which the reverend candidate has a goodly store. But I am not pleading for popular favor. I owed it to my honor as a man to declare the facts.[58]

Riordan had secretly dreaded such heavy measures against Breen. Hoping to avert notoriety and further indignation at the Holy See, his aims were never realized. First, Breen promptly reported his condition to Cardinal Gotti, detailing how his bishop had accused him of an enormous offense and discharged him from the seminary. He further described how the student body had turned against him. These heavy penalties, he argued, had been inflicted upon him simply "for having commited *the crime* of advising Rome on the character of Dr. Hanna's writings...."[59] Word had even reached the secular Roman press, and on January 20, 1908, the *Giornale d'Italia* reviewed the affair under the inauspicious title, "Modernism and anti-modernism at Propaganda Fide for the appointment of a coadjutor to S. Francisco."[60]

* * * * *

Despite this unfortunate uproar, Riordan left Rome on January 29, 1908, impatient with Vatican procedures but expectant that his choice would be named in March. Before his departure, so Meehan reported to Rochester, he had been granted a farewell audience with Pius X who alluded to "una piccola agitazione" in the matter of the coadjutorship and, according to McQuaid's agent, advised Riordan that "a little delay would allow the matter to quiet down, that all would end properly." The Holy Father had also promised to confirm the selection were Hanna's name presented to him. Experienced in the ways of Vatican diplomacy, Meehan did not share Riordan's hopefulness. He commented:

> The Archbishop is satisfied *but he is dealing with Italians,* and they may find some excuse for throwing overboard his candidate. Let us hope not! His Grace expressed the hope that nothing radical be done in Dr. Breen's case, till affairs here were settled. I suppose this plan would be the more prudent.[61]

The two prelates in Hanna's favor meanwhile preserved their optimism. On his return in February to the United States, Riordan yielded to public interviews in New York and San Francisco in which he expressed his expectation that the appointment would be made by spring, at the same time cautioning the press that "things move slowly in Rome."[62] His associate in Rochester agreed, telling a friend in the strictest confidence that "in all likelihood Hanna will be consecrated soon after Easter."[63]

Dr. Hanna's partisans thus awaited the Propaganda meeting in March, 1908. To them the situation appeared uncomplicated and hopeful; and Meehan could be counted upon for another analysis. The past meeting of January 13, he confided to McQuaid,

> is as if never held. Very little was said, no vote taken, and they do not consider the matter as having been treated. Cardinal Martinelli seems willing to compromise — and the others also — if Hanna will show in another article that he is sound.[64]

According to Riordan's original instructions, Hanna had begun to draft material on Christ's human knowledge and the Sacrament of Penance, but it was not until late spring that the *New York Review* published two conspicuously orthodox articles. [65] The archbishop was personally anxious for quick action in Rome since the publicity on his relationship with the suspect theologian had embarrassed him at home. Before his departure from Rome Cardinal Gotti had assured him of a prompt settlement, but to his disappointment there was no appointment in March. Riordan sought an explanation for what he conceived as an unreasonable delay. To calm his anxiety McQuaid loaned him the latest reports from Meehan. McQuaid's agent, Riordan learned, foresaw no possibility of Hanna's consecration in April or even before July. "Rome moves slowly," he had warned in March, "and the Propaganda is manifesting no undue haste in this affair." The present was not the prudent moment to press Hanna's orthodoxy, for in this same month the Holy See had betrayed an acute sensitivity to modernism. On March 7, 1908, its most vocal leader, Alfred Loisy, had been ex-communicated *nominatim et personaliter.* [66] Meehan had also seen the knowledgeable Salvatore Brandi. The Jesuit editor believed that Propaganda would allow six months to elapse from the meeting in January before resuming its consideration of the coadjutorship, but, he hoped, Satolli was disposed to introduce it as soon as he judged it opportune.[67] McQuaid forwarded this intelligence to San Francisco, with the assurance that Hanna had kept a discreet silence. And to hearten the archbishop, he inserted his own unalloyed views of Vatican procedures. "What has annoyed me beyond expression," the bishop pointed out,

> is the annoyance and suffering to which Your Grace has been exposed. I had experience with Rome's ways 18 years ago. After having done exactly what the Propaganda told me to do, Rome went back on this action to please others, and without letting me know who the others were. It may have been wise but it is a kind of wisdom whose merit we are unable to appreciate. That you are hampered in your work, and caused much suffering does not concern the good people in Rome. I can only advise the counsel I preach to myself — patienza, santissima patienza![68]

Chafing under these delays, the two prelates were by the early spring resigned to settle down to a policy of watchful waiting. Satolli had reviewed Hanna's freshly written articles in manuscript, Meehan later reported to Rochester. While he refused to bear any responsibility for them, the cardinal urged his former pupil to publish them, adding that the congregation would not act until these articles reached Rome.[69] Meehan's messages were helpful, but no definite word of the Holy See's official position reached the United States until Satolli himself conceived a strategy. Writing personally to his former student, the cardinal first directed that the material be published. Hanna must then send to Propaganda a formal submission to the recent decrees of the Holy See. Satolli further suggested that the entire faculty of St. Bernard's Seminary should subscribe to a similar profession. Once these documents had been sent to Rome, Archbishop Riordan, he concluded, should renew his request for a coadjutor.[70] As soon as word of this plan reached

Rochester, McQuaid notified Riordan. He and his professors, he added, would forward a joint letter of adhesion to the recent encyclical on Modernism, and Riordan should draft a corresponding petition for Cardinal Gotti. "They don't like to be driven." warned the bishop, "so you will have to be cautious in your language."[71] A week later, Hanna posted his second profession of faith and sent to Riordan Satolli's letter with the comment: "I often wonder whether I am really worth all this trouble, all this annoyance. You are the best judge."[72]

These developments gave Riordan a direction in which to proceed. On receiving McQuaid's message, he made a vigorous appeal to the apostolic delegate. Conditions in his battered archdiocese, he argued, were unique, such as confronted no other bishop in this country, and, he added strongly,

> while I am doing the very best I can yet things must necessarily be neglected unless relief comes soon and if it should be delayed too long I shall not be in a condition to profit by it as I am almost on the verge of an utter collapse of physical strength.[73]

Riordan's mind was committed to invoke every means in rekindling interest in the Eternal City, but he elected, he confided to McQuaid, not to enlist Satolli himself. As Prefect of the Congregation of Studies, in Riordan's judgment, the cardinal would not actively intercede for Hanna in Propaganda. "Each one in Rome," he wrote, "seems to be so touchy about the duties of his own office that no one seems inclined to interfere in the slightest."[74] Instead he addressed his appeal directly to Cardinal Gotti, who the previous winter had given him certain assurances. It was a forceful appeal which rehearsed the ravages of the earthquake and urgently repeated the request for a coadjutor, naming Edward Hanna as the preferred candidate.[75]

Riordan perceived at this time other possible complications when according to the apostolic constitution, *Sapienti consilio* of June 29, 1908, the Roman Curia was reorganized. The business of the American Church was now to be transferred from Propaganda to the regular congregations, with the result that such matters as the coadjutorship fell to the Consistorial Congregation.[76] Propaganda would, nevertheless, have its last opportunity to consider Hanna's candidacy in September.

As the important meeting approached, informal reports from Rome were at first encouraging. During his last stay in the Eternal City, Riordan had asked Father Giovanni Genocchi, an intimate friend of Hanna's and a consultor to the Pontifical Commission of Biblical Studies, to intercede directly with the pope. In July the scholar secretly reported the results of a lengthy audience. The Holy Father, he began, was thoroughly acquainted with the case. After the priest vouched for Hanna's orthodoxy and the virtually unanimous endorsement of the American hierarchy, the pontiff, Genocchi recorded meticulously, "finally. . . showed himself 'agreeing in all that,' and 'hoping' for a favorable issue of the next discussion of Propaganda." After a further visit with a number of cardinals at the congregation, "I am now persuaded," he concluded, "that you will soon receive the desired official news. That 'hope,' which I marked above, is to you a hint of much more that I cannot write. And what I wrote is but a confidence to Your Grace."[77] This message served only to raise Riordan's expectations so greatly that in early August he confided to his secretary, John Cantwell, that "everything seems to be going on well although there is no news from the Eternal City. I am looking for it every week."[78]

Regardless of his highly optimistic accounts, Hanna's candidacy continued to remain under a shadow at the Holy See, and chances for his appointment would all but disappear by September. Still suffering from the wounds inflicted in Rochester, Andrew Breen assailed Propaganda with repeated entreaties not to sanction the appointment. The congregation was impressed with his insistence that the promotion of his former colleague would condemn his own pains to preserve the integrity of Catholic doctrine. "My bishop was one of these who opposed the dogma of the infallibility of the

Pope," he reminded Cardinal Gotti further,

> and in the present case prefers to the good of the
> Church, the glory of having elevated a favorite of
> his to the episcopal dignity. The Bishop has pub-
> licly boasted that this delay has been arranged so
> that Your Eminence and others could without too
> much disgrace withdraw from your [original]
> position.[79]

Far more damaging than Breen's recalcitrance, however,
was a six-year-old article of Hanna's which had been
published even before his celebrated series in the *New York
Reiview* and which had lately come to Rome's attention. It
featured a brief survey of literature entitled, "Some Recent
Books on Catholic Theology," and had been published in the
American Journal of Theology, a quarterly originating from
the School of Divinity at University of Chicago.[80] In the
current context of the Church's vigilance against modernism,
Hanna had written it under two severe handicaps: it
described the latest trends among Catholic scholars and was
expressed to make the "new apologetic" intelligible to
non-Catholic readers. It was an article which could be readily
used to impugn Hanna's orthodoxy, and Riordan was aware
of its existence since winter when the author sent him a copy
with a commentary. Again Alexis Lépicier was commissioned
to examine it. In time he presented to Cardinal Gotti
without explanation a number of excerpts that in his view
leaned unquestionably toward modernism. Among them he
cited: Hanna's statement "These formulae [that is, dogmas of
the church] are ever inadequate, and will sometimes appear
inaccurate, if pressed too closely"; and "there is a feeling
that the old concept of doctrinal development was too
narrow, too restricted; that a larger development must be
admitted. . . ."[81] Lépicier felt that he needed to offer
nothing more than such excerpts to conclude that Hanna was
following the lead of two pioneer Catholic biblical scholars,
Franz von Hummelauer, S.J., and Marie-Joseph Lagrange,

O.P., whom the Servite theologian styled as "modernist authors."

Nothing further developed regarding the article until early August when Genocchi caught wind of its impression upon the Holy See and anxiously reported to Riordan:

> A thunderbolt stroke [*sic*] our house! I am informed that another article of Dr. Hanna in an old protestant Review was denounced to the Holy See. I do not know what kind of article it is, but the Card. Secretary of State and the Prefect of Propaganda are now "absolutely" opposed to Dr. Hanna's nomination.

This new discovery had unnerved Hanna's close friend in Rome, taking him completely by surprise and virtually extinguishing all hope of the coadjutorship. "My letter of two or three weeks ago was so different," he lamented, "so joyful! I did not expect a new accusation. . . . What will happen: God knows."[8 2] Following Genocchi's regrets came an equally desperate message from Cardinal Gibbons, whom Riordan had contacted in Rome to plead his cause. The cardinal's first impression was that Hanna's case was "hopeless," and that he should recommend the appointment of another candidate on the *terna*. From the time of his arrival in the Eternal City the Archbishop of Baltimore had spared no effort in Riordan's behalf, visiting the leading cardinals of Propaganda, and from the interviews he concluded that Hanna's appointment was "out of the question." In the next meeting of the congregation, he told Riordan, the historic one in which it would do its last business for the American Church, another candidate would be selected, "most probably Fr. Nagle [*sic*], whom I strongly urged, & from what I hear, you will have reason to rejoice."[8 3]

As the day of this meeting drew closer, hope dimmed in San Francisco and Rochester. Not only did Hanna's promotion seem impossible but it was even uncertain, largely

from Riordan's stubborn support of the theologian, whether
after nineteen months since Archbishop Montgomery's death
he had made any substantial progress in obtaining assistance
from Rome. In late August the archbishop no longer
expected to receive a coadjutor from Propaganda, believing
the frustrating case would be transferred to the Consistorial
Congregation. "I do not know how we are going to fare
with the new Congregation," he told Conaty, "but it cannot
be more dilatory than the old."[84] In these final moments
Genocchi informed Hanna of Rome's reaction to his
contribution in the *American Journal of Theology,* confiding
to him that on its account the situation had become "quasi
desperata." Before the denouement, the beleaguered theologian at last opened his mind to Riordan after such an ordeal, expressing his gratitude to the archbishop for his abiding faith and heroic efforts for the appointment. "I often ask
myself," he wrote,

> am I worth all the pains: You and you only must
> decide that, and the moment your clinging to me
> interferes in the least with the furtherance of your
> great work, I wish you to choose one better than I
> to help you on . . . . Strange it must ever seem
> how blind our fathers in Rome are to the great
> ideals of our age, especially as they are working out
> in our western world. Believe me, I have gotten
> much from our little episode: much wisdom, much
> humility, much strength. . . .[85]

It was thus hardly a surprise when on September 7, 1908,
eight cardinals of Propaganda disqualified the entire *terna*
and recommended a new one, a decision which was
sanctioned by Pius X on September 15.[86] The archbishop
first learned of this action from a press and which to
his chagrin vaguely suggested that one reason for the
rejection of the *terna* was evidence of irregularities in
procedure. Riordan was extremely sensitive to the frequent
insinuations that he had exerted undue pressures for Hanna's
promotion. At the meeting of the consultors and irremovable

pastors, it was true, he had distributed ballots on which were listed suitable candidates, the prelate informing the electors that they were free to choose among these names. Soon after this meeting there had naturally appeared the first charge of pressure, and as a precaution the archbishop had even saved these ballots. One of these electors, he suspected, was the source of this leakage, and unnamed priest of San Francisco who had not voted according to Riordan's list.[87]

He immediately sent a mild protest to Archbishop Falconio. Riordan had heard this charge even in the American College at Rome and had attributed it to "one who has been for many years a mischief maker." The archbishop was resigned to search out three new candidates to be proposed. While he was preparing a new *terna* he told the delegate, he wished to have an auxiliary bishop who would fill the vacuum "for a year or two," especially by administering confirmation in the rural parishes and attending to the convents and schools.[88] Riordan was unfamiliar with the younger clergy in the East and Midwest, and he turned at this time to Archbishop Ireland, asking "for old friendship sake" for the name of a promising priest——a good, active young man, anywhere between forty and fifty years of age with good business sense and a forcible speaker without being eloquent or learned." It would be absolutely useless, he suggested, to recommend one who has "written anything because indications of Modernism will be found probably in the writings by his enemies."[89]

Riordan had been genuinely committed to Hanna and bitterly resentful of the rumors of his alleged intriguing to secure his appointment, and the Holy See learned of his disappointment soon after Propaganda's decision. The chief antagonist to Hanna's nomination, he had been told, was a former apostolic delegate, Cardinal Sebastiano Martinelli, the *ponete*. Even his own secretary, John J. Cantwell, who had been in Rome shortly before the rejection of the *terna* had understood the cardinal to be the "advocatus Diaboli" in the case.[90] Riordan's equilibrium through this ordeal was unduly strained when Ireland sent a clipping from a St. Paul

newspaper which described Martinelli in the meeting of
Propaganda "bitterly assailing" Riordan and Hanna for
"undue pressure" on the Holy See and charged further that
the archbishop's latest conspicuous efforts were, according to
the cardinal, undignified in the extreme."[91]

This indiscreet press account provided Riordan with the
opportunity to release his frustrations. Rome would know his
burning dissatisfaction with its decision. In a moment of
indignation, he dispatched bristling protests to Cardinals
Gotti and Martinelli, sending to both copies of the article
and requesting that the latter make an emphatic denial of this
version.[92] He refused to believe, declared the archbishop,
that the cardinal had made such outrageous statements since,
as he pointed out to Martinelli,

> it is totally at variance with your well known
> character, dignity, reserve and justice, besides
> being wholly contrary to the expressions of esteem
> for Dr. Hanna which I received from your own
> lips in Rome, and to the unvarying courtesy of
> your conduct toward me personally.

Riordan defended in detail the procedure by which the
candidates had been selected and presented to the Holy See,
explaining too his recent conduct in Rome and his
relationship with the *dignissimus.* "Dr. Hanna was not a
personal favorite of my own," he insisted to Martinelli:

> I hardly knew him; I had met him but twice. But I
> placed him at the head of my list because of the
> unusually splendid testimonials from several
> competent sources . . . and Your Eminence knows
> that few candidates for the mitre have come before
> Propaganda with better endorsements from
> Cardinals, archbishops, bishops, and priests than
> Dr. Hanna.

The archbishop next analyzed the character of his

adversaries and traced the origins of this article. The anonymous insinuation of undue pressure, which had first appeared in San Francisco, was forwarded later to Rome and had been published in its enlarged version in St. Paul, said Riordan, so that it would be circulated "over the length and breadth of this whole country. It is difficult to meet such unscrupulous opponents — enemies rather — and such underhand methods." He was himself unafraid of the truth and willing to accept from legitimate superiors any instruction, correction, or rebuke; but, he added, in justice to his reputation, to his forty-three years as a priest, to his twenty-five years as a bishop, and to his historic archdiocese, he could not tolerate these false charges spreading without protest. Regularly, he argued, newspaper items merited no serious attention, and this article less so because it was maliciously designed to inflict great harm on the American Church because of the national interest already aroused over the coadjutorship and the irresponsible comment occasioned through it. "The people of this country in general, and in California in particular," he warned Martinelli gravely,

> will not understand the role in which you are represented in this dispatch, as "attacking" and "bitterly assailing" their Archbishop. More than that, the article is calculated to poison the minds of our Catholic people not only against me but also against Dr. Hanna, an entirely innocent party in this affair, who has no redress, and whom I have innocently led into this trying ordeal.[9 3]

Riordan was not satisfied with angry letters to Rome: he was resolved to get to the source of this article. Archbishop Ireland had deduced that it had been transmitted over the wires of the United Press and suggested to his colleague in San Francisco to engage Salvatore Cortesi, chief of the Associated Press Bureau in Rome, to conduct an investigation. "There are villains in Rome," remarked the Archbishop of St. Paul, whose suspicions fell upon Robert

Seton, Riordan's former classmate at the American College and at present a titular archbishop residing in the Eternal City. Ireland alleged that Seton was probably responsible for mischievous items in the *New York Times* by which he hoped to become a cardinal in curia. "Whether Seton, or some other fool, prompted the correspondent of the United Press—is a question."[94] Riordan authorized Ireland to instruct Cortesi to identify the source, remarking: "It is simply a dreadful thing that we are at the mercy of irresponsible parties in Rome."[95]

Cortesi's secret inquiry failed, however, to uncover the origin of the offensive report — except that the Roman correspondent of the United Press had a history of association with a number of anti-clerical papers in Italy.[96] While this investigation proved inconclusive, Riordan received satisfaction and an explanation from the Holy See. Rarely has any ecclesiastic challenged two high members of the Roman Curia so directly. Cardinal Gotti vehemently denied the published account, empowering the archbishop to denounce it publicly and affirming that no allusion had been made at Propaganda to irregular procedure.[97] In a separate statement Cardinal Martinelli repeated these sentiments. The cardinals he added, had judged Hanna's writings as tending toward modernism and as a compromise had decided to disqualify the entire *terna*, as Riordan learned, "so as not to make it appear that Dr. Hanna was in any sense condemned."[98]

* * * * *

Confronted with the instruction to submit a new list, Archbishop Riordan resumed the familiar task of appealing to his friends east of the Rockies for recommendations. In these weeks of inquiry, he received an unexpected communication from Monsignor Bonaventura Cerretti, auditor of the apostolic delegation in Washington. Riordan was informed in confidence that Bishop O'Connell, Rector of the Catholic University of America, was anxious to leave the institution at the expiration of his term in January, 1909, and had expressed a willingness to the delegation to go to San Francisco as an auxiliary. In two or three years, Riordan understood, O'Connell could be appointed his coadjutor.[99]

The university rector was no stranger to the archbishop who had long regarded himself as one of O'Connell's most devoted friends. Twenty years before, on his first *ad limina* visit, he had expressed his appreciation of O'Connell's invaluable service in Rome where the latter functioned as Rector of the American College and unofficial liaison between many members of the American hierarchy and the Roman Curia. When in 1888 he discovered that O'Connell had been proposed to succeed John Keane as Bishop of Richmond, Riordan had protested vehemently, convinced that his removal from Rome would be "disastrous" to the American Church.[100] Once it became clear that Monsignor O'Connell would remain at his post, Riordan rejoiced, telling Keane that while he realized that Richmond required a strong bishop for the interests of the new university, O'Connell was "so necessary to us" in the Eternal City. "Give him some strong advice about his health," he had added warmly. "I should say command him to take better care of it."[101]

Eleven years later, when the archbishop had concluded his second *ad limina* visit, he had spent his last fortnight in Europe with a mutual acquaintance, Monsignor James Nugent of Liverpool. "He always speaks in the most affectionate and sympathetic terms of you. True friends are rare"[102] Riordan had likewise displayed a personal interest in O'Connell's career as university rector, having been partially responsible for the appointment. In December, 1907, at the time of the announcement of O'Connell's elevation to a titular bishopric, Riordan was in Rome pressing Hanna's appointment as his coadjutor. As soon as he learned the news he cabled his warm congratulations and added significantly in a further letter:

> May you have long to enjoy the new honor and may it be a stepping stone to higher ones. You will

remember that I was the one years ago who asked
for this promotion for you. I am glad that at last it
has been granted.[103]

It remains uncertain why such a major careerist had
revealed to the apostolic delegation his desire to withdraw
from the university, especially since his administration had
successfully coped with several crises and had won the
confidence of the trustees. His decision, however, was not
rash. Riordan himself had been among the first to know
O'Connell's wishes when as early as June, 1907, Cardinal
Gibbons had asked the archbishop to consider him for the
coadjutorship.[104] Riordan had declined then, and some
sixteen months later, when a similar proposal had reached
him unofficially from the delegation, he retained some
uneasiness over O'Connell's fitness for duties in San
Francisco. The sole reason why he had initially dismissed the
rector as a possible coadjutor, he candidly told Monsignor
Michael Lavelle of St. Patrick's Cathedral in New York, was
that he had mistakenly understood O'Connell to be
sixty-two, a little older than even the deceased Montgomery.
This was an age, Riordan was now convinced, that was too
advanced for the rigors and problems of his archdiocese. "I
now learn that he is not more than fifty-seven or fifty-eight
years of age," he wrote, "but still that is too much. He has
already turned the summit of the mountain of life and will
naturally soon reached the period when activity is impossible."[105] Nevertheless, it would soon be two years since
Montgomery's death, and Riordan was acutely conscious at
the rapid passage of time, having just celebrated his silver
jubilee as a bishop. At length he consented to receive the rector as an auxiliary temporarily, until a new *terna* for a coadjutor could be in time submitted to the Holy See, a *terna*
which might conceivably nominate O'Connell. Before he
would make the formal petition, however, he told Cerretti
he demanded positive assurance that O'Connell would
accept this arrangement; for, noted the archbishop, "he
may be looking for something higher."[106]

Throughout his career Riordan had been fastidious regarding episcopal appointments. O'Connell's assignment as his auxiliary, however, was not according to his tastes, possibly because the rector was slightly too old and too sophisticated to function adequately as an assistant in his western diocese. In late October, 1908, when Cardinal Gibbons notified the university's trustees that O'Connell's six-year term was about to expire, they unanimously approved his return for another term of office. Riordan's views were among the most forceful in favoring his remaining at the university. Under O'Connell's administration he argued, its difficulties had largely been solved, and he was himself acquainted with no one capable of replacing him. Well aware of O'Connell's embarrassment, the archbishop strongly objected to what he called that "queer piece of legislation." The university's constitution failed to furnish security or a position for a retiring rector, an unfortunate omission which threatened to discourage the services of able men for the institution. Gibbons' circular stated that the rector's future would be discussed at the next board meeting, but Riordan took sharp issue with the further suggestion that the university had made provisions for O'Connell's two predecessors. "In depriving Monsignore Kane [sic] no provision was made for him as far as I know," he reminded the cardinal.

> He was simply asked to trust to somebody's good will and a promise was made him that something might be done for him. In the case of Monsignore Conaty no provision was made or promised and had I not taken him up for the See of Los Angeles he would have no position whatsoever in the American Church. He has made a splendid Bishop here and I took him for Los Angeles precisely because of no provision had been made for the good man.[108]

While this communication was official, addressed to Gibbons as the university's chancellor, Riordan sent to

Baltimore a second letter, "personal and confidential."
Riordan admitted knowing on "pretty good authority" that
O'Connell might be immediately available for San Francisco.
"I should most willingly receive him as an Auxiliary or even a
Coadjutor," he assured the cardinal. "I have had for a quarter
century the greatest affection for him and I have always
looked upon him as a thoroughly good and loyal man."
Careful not to betray the delegation as the source of his
information, the archbishop requested Gibbons to sound out
their mutual friend regarding his future plans.[108] Riordan's
precise position was this: he preferred for the university's
sake that O'Connell accept a second term as rector; but if, as
it was understood, that he was resolved to resign, the
Archbishop of San Francisco would on this sole condition
receive him as his auxiliary. Riordan's message had solved an
awkward predicament for his friends at the university, and
Gibbons presented the choice to O'Connell. Having
committed the decision entirely to the cardinal, the rector
was counseled to resign and to go to California. "I promptly
advised him to accept your proposal," Gibbons explained to
Riordan.

> I have known Monsignor O'Connell intimately
> since his ordination. He has been as true as gold,
> faithful and reliable. I never found him wanting in
> loyalty in any emergency. He is a man of
> extraordinary intellectual force, of splendid
> judgment and mental poise. He is tender-hearted
> and affectionate; you may rely on his friendship
> and discretion. His presence with you will prolong
> your life by lightening your burden.

Following this enthusiastic endorsement, Gibbons confessed
that he too had considered O'Connell as an auxiliary and
eventual coadjutor, but the fact that he had already been
granted an auxiliary in Baltimore precluded these plans.[109]
    Archbishop Riordan did not attend the meeting of the
university's Board of Trustees, and Gibbons informed him

shortly afterward that John Patrick Carroll, Bishop of Helena, would be recommended to the Holy See as O'Connell's successor. The cardinal felt O'Connell's appointment as "providential" after Montgomery's death and Hanna's rejection, and he gently urged the archbishop to make the formal request to the apostolic delegation.[110] Finally, on Christmas Day, 1908, there reached Archbishop Riordan the announcement of the rector's transfer to the West, and in writing soon after to Gibbons, he said: "I need not tell you how rejoiced I am over the appointment of our dear friend, Bishop O'Connell."[111] Thus had the Archbishop of San Francisco been largely instrumental in determining the later careers of the first three rectors of the Catholic University of America, a story to be finished later.

Bishop O'Connell's ties with the university were formally ended on January 11, 1909, and the sixty-year-old prelate devoted the next three months to the task of moving to the West where he was expected on March 29. This would not be the first instance in which Riordan would welcome him into the archdiocese. In 1895, when O'Connell had been removed from the rectorship of the American College in Rome, the archbishop had urged him to come to the Pacific Coast and remain with him until he felt fit to resume his work. "The climate would suit you admirably," he had written, "and you will be perfectly welcome at my house. You can stay as long as you like, the longer the better. I have a good room, and will take the best care of you."[112] Fourteen years later, Riordan again looked forward to O'Connell's arrival, anxious on this occasion to have him to ease the burden of diocesan administration in his declining years. "At last this long delay is over," he wrote to his brother. "He will have plenty to do when he comes out here, enough to keep him very, very busy, but he is strong and willing."[113] Yet there persisted, significantly, misgivings in Riordan's mind and a certain despondency over having lost his first choice. "I hope that everything has been done for the best," he also told Kennedy of the American College in Rome. "I deeply regret the stain that will always remain on poor Hanna's reputation as a

theologian."[114] Meanwhile, the bishop arrived quietly on
schedule, was greeted simply by a few members of the clergy
and was escorted to the archbishop's residence. On Easter
Sunday, Riordan formally welcomed his new auxiliary in St.
Mary's Cathedral, announcing that it was a double pleasure to
greet one "whom I have known for a quarter of a century,
and for whom for the last twenty years I have had a loving
friendship."[115]

In the two years of their association there were signs that
Archbishop Riordan had from the start conceived the
relationship as only temporary. Bishop O'Connell had not
been his personal choice; and his coming to San Francisco
was an expedient, removing an embarrassment from the
Catholic University and providing a failing archbishop timely
assistance. It is impossible to define Riordan's precise
attitude toward his auxiliary, but it is certain that a personal
friendship of decades would not help determine his choice of
a successor. The courtesies were extended to O'Connell; and
Riordan was particularly delighted when the auxiliary
expressed his preference to live with the archbishop. "Our
house is very large and comfortable," Riordan told him, "and
you will find yourself perfectly at home in it. We have never
had but the happiest kind of a life inside the doors of the
Episcopal residence and I know you will not be a disturbing
element."[116] But there was possibly a secondary purpose
beneath this warm invitation. Evidently Riordan never
entertained the idea that O'Connell would succeed him. For
this reason he would not provide him the opportunity of
sinking deep roots in the West: the auxiliary had come
merely to serve in transient relief.

Without embarrassment Riordan thus assigned to him
virtually no authority in archdiocesan administration. The
younger prelate was appointed neither a pastor nor a
consultor, and was charged simply with the conferral of
confirmation and the affairs of the religious communities.[117]
Nearly a year after his arrival, O'Connell expressed his
irritation over his status in San Francisco, impatient at the

archbishop's continued failure to secure his appointment as coadjutor. Gibbons strongly advised him not to press this ambition. Riordan, he told O'Connell, "is a man of generous impulses, and he may make the desired announcement when you least expect it. A few years more or less will make little difference in your present status."[118] The archbishop, however, seemed to be unaware of O'Connell's secret wish and, apparently, never intended to have him as his coadjutor.

Subject in his late sixties to sudden shifts of mood, Riordan betrayed inconsistencies in his disposition toward O'Connell. Doubtless Riordan appreciated the auxiliary's generous efforts, as well as his geniality as a companion. To their mutual friend, Archbishop Keane, he described O'Connell as "full of activity, and a great comfort to me, as my health is somewhat shattered." Though he felt that his own days of strenuous work were passed and he was able only to superintend, he had found, continued Riordan, "good Bishop O'Connell ready to do anything that he can to help me, and his advice on ecclesiastical matters is most valuable."[119] Despite these glowing professions, however, this arrangement whereby he retained the bulk of administration was no solution for the aging archbishop. "Everything must come to the head if he is present," he confided to his brother, "and although the Auxiliary Bishop is willing to do anything he is asked to do yet I find that he can do very little except give a Confirmation now and then."[120]

Bishop O'Connell had meanwhile lost no interest in the East, and in the early spring of 1911 he took a holiday with Cardinal Gibbons in New Orleans, the latter's family home. In the fall, he again left San Francisco to attend the celebration of the golden jubilee of Gibbons' priesthood and to proceed to the Holy See where he presented Riordan's case in a dispute with the Sisters of the Presentation. A golden opportunity for his return to the Province of Baltimore occurred at this time in the death on October 16 of Bishop Augustine Van de Vyver of Richmond. Bishop O'Connell, as Riordan noted, was in splendid position to promote his candidacy. From the start Riordan anticipated his name on the *terna*. "Richmond, as you know, is his old home," he told his brother, "and while he has never said to me that he would like a place of his own, I feel that his heart is in the East. The Cardinal is very fond of him, and I feel sure that when the Bishops meet his name will be proposed."[121] The archbishop was anxious to learn of O'Connell's chances so as to search out a replacement. In late November Gibbons informed him in confidence that the auxiliary had been named first in both the priests' and bishops' *ternae*, adding that he had no doubt of his appointment to Richmond.[122] Riordan was grateful for this advanced notice. The cardinal was assured that the bishop had been a tower of strength and consolation to him; and in mid-January the Holy See assigned him to the Virginia diocese. Curiously, while the archbishop in successive letters to Baltimore heaped encomia upon his former auxiliary, insisting that his removal would be deeply felt in San Francisco, a significant variation of these sentiments was confided to his brother, a variation of which was probably more genuine in sentiment than those sent to O'Connell's patrons. Bishop O'Connell, observed Riordan candidly,

> will be glad to be back among his own and in his old home. He is too old to transplant or take root here, and he never liked this Western country. He was born in the South, and he has remained a Southern gentleman all through life, with Southern ways. This pushing life of ours is not in keeping with that temperament.[123]

* * * * *

Riordan had, nevertheless, been fond of O'Connell. Their two-year association had been, in his view, a pleasant experience, and his brother later learned that the archbishop had "never known anyone more genial and companionable." But it remains a dark mystery as to why Riordan was willing to accept as his successor a man less personally known to him than Denis O'Connell. Yet as he resumed consideration of a coadjutor, he honestly hoped that whoever replaced him might "be gifted with the same qualities as the good man who is going to Richmond."[124] The archbishop had been confident that O'Connell would not remain long in San Francisco. For that reason, well before the bishop's departure, inquiries on possible coadjutors were sent to friends in the East. Riordan was again searching for a promising young ecclesiastic outside of his own archdiocese, for his experience since 1909 had convinced him of the uselessness of appointing to his see another churchman verging on his sixties.

His first choice fell upon Bishop Dennis J. Dougherty of Jaro in the Philippines. His high reputation Riordan had learned from ecclesiastics passing through San Francisco, and he had been favorably impressed when the bishop visited him en route to his diocese.[125] The name of Edward Hanna was not under consideration in this initial stage of compiling another *terna*. The archbishop so informed the theologian, explaining to him that the Holy See would consider as discourteous the presentation of any of the three candidates who had appeared on the rejected list.[126]

In April, 1912, Riordan's plans received a second unexpected reversal when Cardinal Gaetano De Lai, Prefect of the Consistorial Congregation, judged that his arguments for a coadjutor were not sufficiently convincing. The congregation was willing only to grant him another auxiliary bishop. This instruction placed Riordan in an acute embarrassment. While negotiations for an auxiliary removed the requirement of presenting three candidates, it presented certain handicaps. This arrangement would give the archbishop a helper who would have no assurances of succeeding him. Importantly, too, it virtually eliminated Riordan's chances of securing highly placed ecclesiastics outside the archdiocese. This included Riordan's favorite, Bishop Dougherty, whose appointment as a mere auxiliary would deprive him of a diocese and, in this sense, be regarded as a demotion.

His health failing in the Philippines, the Bishop of Jaro
had expressed his willingness to accept the coadjutorship, and
Riordan appealed to Gibbons to make a special plea to De
Lai.[127] But the cardinal was unmoved by the strong
entreaties from Baltimore and San Francisco, replying that
the congregation desired to retain Dougherty where his
presence was necessary at this moment. Riordan could, he
conceded, recommend a priest outside his archdiocese.[128]
Father Hanna still suited the archbishop's ideal of an
episcopal helper — strong, vigorous and apostolic, fluent in
Italian, and nineteen years his junior. Gradually he became
disposed to submit the theologian's name once more. Five
years earlier, Riordan recalled, Cardinal Gotti had
acknowledged that in his tenure as Prefect of Propaganda no
ecclesiastic had been so highly recommended as Hanna for
the episcopate, until the charges alleged by his colleague,
Father Breen. Even Pius X had personally intimated to the
archbishop that once the excitement passed away he would
approve of Hanna's promotion. Furthermore, it was absurd
to Riordan that there could be opposition on account of doctrine to a priest who had continued to teach dogmatic theology in one of the largest seminaries in the United States.[129]
After forwarding Hanna's name to the apostolic delegate,
Archbishop John Bonzano, he explained to his brother his
thoughts of stoic submission on this occasion:

> I acted very much on the advice of Archbishop
> Ireland, who urged me very strongly to do so. I was
> in the beginning a little reluctant to do it, but
> yielded to what I considered his better informed
> judgment. However, we shall see soon what will
> come of it. If our petition is rejected we shall only
> have to look about and select someone else.[130]

The months of expectation through the summer and
early fall of 1912 were a wearying experience on the
archbishop, who on August 27 reached his seventy-first

birthday. As he told an old friend in Ireland, he found himself busier now than in previous years. Helpers had come and gone, Riordan observed, a coadjutor taken long ago by death and an auxiliary lately promoted to an eastern diocese. "So now," he mused in anticipation, "when I am not as well as some years ago to stand the strain of work, I am left alone, but I have the promise from Rome of some one to come to me before long, and shall then, I hope, have more time to prepare for the greatest event in life — the proper closing of it."[131] His sublime wish was at last filled on October 23 when he received — in mild surprise — Bonzano's announcement of Hanna's appointment. But Rome was sensitive to any possible display of triumph and included also a directive that the consecration be simple and unpretentious.[132] Riordan immediately posted letters to the two men who he felt were most deeply involved in this appointment. To Hanna he sent warmest congratulations, writing: "I cannot tell you how much joy all this has given me — nothing ever gave me greater happiness in my life." He further suggested that the cathedral in Rochester be the site of the consecration, and because of the tedious winter's journey he excused himself from attending, promising, however, to send a representation.[133] And to his close friend, John Ireland, he expressed his profound gratitude. "It was your strong suggestion," he confessed, "that made me think it all possible that I might be able to get him, but I was afraid that he would not receive the appointment after so many years of waiting."[134]

Father Hanna's consecration took place on December 4 in St. Patrick's Cathedral, Rochester. Archbishop Bonzano invested him, assisted by Archbishop James E. Quigley of Chicago, a former Rochesterian, and by Bishop Denis J. O'Connell of Richmond, Hanna's mentor since Roman days and his predecessor in San Francisco. The archdiocese was represented at the solemnities by Fathers John J. Cantwell and Michael D. Connolly; and Father Daniel Riordan also attended, presenting to the newly consecrated a crozier from his brother. At the banquet following the ceremonies in

which Hanna was given a ring left for him by
Bishop McQuaid, Cantwell delivered a formal and eloquent
welcome to his new post in the West, addressing a
distinguished assembly of twenty-one bishops and over 300
priests:

> Bishop Hanna, you are coming to no mean City;
> you enter upon a fair inheritance; your lines have
> fallen in goodly places. . . . In the name of the
> Clergy of San Francisco, we welcome you to a
> land, rich in Catholic traditions and in the
> memories of Spanish Chivalry. You come to us
> with Apostolic Commission, and anyone so
> coming, the Clergy of San Francisco will be there
> with warm hearts and extended arms. You will
> strengthen the arms of the Archbishop and prolong
> the usefullness [*sic*] of a great life.[135]

Unlike the very modest reception which had been extended
to Bishop O'Connell, Riordan was meanwhile preparing an
elaborate welcome which resembled that of Archbishop
Alemany to his young coadjutor from Chicago nearly thirty
years before. Cantwell and Connolly accompanied Bishop
Hanna to California, where on December 31, he was first met
by a delegation at Benecia and then by the archbishop
himself at the terminal in Oakland whence he was escorted to
the city where the younger prelate would make his home for
the next twenty-three years.[136] It was soon evident that
Riordan had chosen the newly arrived churchman as his
successor when he immediately placed him on the
archbishop's council and one week after his arrival named
him vicar general.[137]

The appointment of Bishop Edward J. Hanna represented
one of the greatest joys and personal triumphs of Archbishop
Riordan's life. A full decade had passed since he had first
applied for a successor until one at length arrived in San
Francisco and within three years succeeded to the
metropolitan see. In this struggle to secure the man of his

choice, the archbishop had exhausted every conceivable resource, making the difficult journey to the Holy See, not hesitating to rebuke — indirectly but effectively — two curial cardinals, enlisting churchmen of every rank, and preserving throughout his loyalty and faith in the accused. This extraordinary commitment might partially explain Riordan's enigmatic attitude toward Bishop O'Connell. One irony among many was the fact that Rome's later abrogation of Riordan's long-standing permission for a coadjutor eventually brought Edward Hanna to San Francisco. Together, their administrations would span half a century.

Dr. Hanna was a welcome addition to the Riordan household. In the passage of time, the effort gradually assumed in Riordan's mind the proportions of a prodigious crusade as the aging prelate reflected on the struggle and victory. His unbounded satisfaction was best expressed, with a certain historical license, to the auxiliary's sister, Mother Anne Hanna, R.S.C.J., as he attempted to rehearse the story of her brother's appointment and vindication. "I put his name years ago on the *Terna*, after the most mature deliberation," the archbishop began,

> and having sought the advice of some of the best ecclesiastics in the entire country, and then I went to Rome to urge his nomination, when I heard that there was a probability of his now having been appointed.
>
> When I left Rome to return to this Diocese, I felt that some day or another he would be given, if not to me, to someone else, as a ruler in the Kingdom of our Lord, and I felt also that he would come here. I had a hope, founded on what the Holy Father said to me, that if I would only wait I would get him. When I returned home after my Roman visit, the Rectorship of the University became vacant by the non-election of Bishop O'Connell, and at the request of the Legation in Washington, I consented to receive him until he

would be appointed to some permanent place, which I thought at that time would occur within a few months, or half a year, but it dragged on month after month, until he spent over two years with me. But I never forgot my first choice, and I immediately set to work to secure Dr. Hanna for myself, and at last you know how we were victorious.

I feel he will be perfectly at home here, and we shall take good care of him, to make him comfortable and his life agreeable.[138]

In the papal chambers the Hanna affair had been only "a small agitation." But to an anxious, aging archbishop it lingered as agony and sweet victory.

11

Friends and Foes
in the East

Isolation on the Pacific Coast would remove the Archbishop of San Francisco from the centers of excitement and controversy. In the last years of Joseph Alemany, this factor had dissuaded several outstanding prelates from crossing the Rockies and accepting the post. But seclusion seemed to fit Patrick Riordan's vision and temperament. He was a willing successor to Alemany, at home by the Golden Gate and never to search out a promotion elsewhere. His primary focus remained on the peculiar domestic problems of the West. By nature he was not a controversialist who thrived on national visibility and the mighty struggles within the hierarchy. Perhaps his memories of the Duggan affair during the first five years of his priesthood had tempered an interest in polemics. A supremely sensitive man, he suffered most when principles and personal loyalties clashed as they did with his comrade, John Ircland, over parochial schools.

As a rule, then, Riordan was a satisfied solitary, attentive and well-informed — but unwilling to be drawn intimately into the prolonged disputes in the American church at the turn of the century. For the most part, he remained a vigilant but silent observer of the eastern scene. Nevertheless, there were exceptions. Several friends and projects were especially dear to him, and for these he was disposed to intervene, always unobtrusively and often significantly. One of these projects that early engaged the cautious Archbishop of San Francisco was the Catholic University of America.[1] He had

been one of the few American ecclesiastics of his generation
who had taken a postordination year of study, and his
experience at the Catholic University of Louvain, as well as
his brief professorship at St. Mary of the Lake and his close
association with the intellectual Bishop Spalding, had rooted
in him a respect and genuine solicitude for Catholic higher
education.

In the latter half of the 1880's, the years following the
Third Plenary Council of Baltimore, Riordan had not been
involved in the foundation of the university, being far
removed from Washington, D.C., and having lately succeeded
to the administration of his large archdiocese. But his
instincts certainly supported its earliest champions —
Spalding, Ireland, Keane, and Gibbons. At the plenary
council, Archbishop Alemany had been appointed to a
special university committee which studied and would
eventually implement the establishment of such an
institution. Riordan, however, declined Gibbons' invitation
to join it, telling Keane, the rector, that while he was
committed to the project and believed strongly in its essential
importance, distance precluded his attendance at the
meetings. Despite these handicaps, Keane wanted Riordan on
this committee. As the latter was, in 1888, planning his *ad
limina* journey, the rector asked Gibbons to exploit his
anticipated visit to the East to "insist on his taking the
position. His name and influence will be a power, & he can
give his views in writing when not able to attend the
meetings." Keane would have his own opportunity personally
to confront the reluctant archbishop, for he was due himself
in Rome to secure papal approval of the university's statutes
at the same time as Riordan was going to present his first
diocesan report to Propaganda. No details of this encounter
have been recorded, except that Keane had deliberately
hastened his movements through Europe to rendezvous with
Riordan and had disclosed to him a number of details of his
mission.[2]

Keane's performance must have been persuasive. After his
departure from the Eternal City, Riordan sent Keane from

Paris his New Year's greetings, commending also to divine providence the university which he lavishly characterized as "the most important work of the American Church." Riordan also acknowledged the vital importance of Cardinal Gibbons to the institution at Washington. Keane was, therefore, cautioned that the vacancy in his suffragan See of Richmond must be filled by a first-class prelate sympathetic to it, a possible successor to Baltimore who would see to it that Gibbons' farsighted policies would continue in the province in the event of his death. If the cardinal's replacement "should be a weak man or opposed to the University," read Riordan's earliest thoughts recorded on the subject,

> the great project would languish. It is only a great Bishop in Baltimore who could command the attention of the Bishops of the Country. May the good dear Cardinal live for many years. We all love him.[3]

Though disinclined at first to accept any formal position, Patrick Riordan was enthusiastic over the new university. Wishing always to have his archdiocese represented and to develop his promising young priests, he sent a series of them as soon as it opened in 1889. Father Peter Yorke was his first selection, but an impasse arose over the choice of his successor. As Yorke approached the conclusion of his course, Riordan's commitment to the university became plainly manifest in his efforts to enroll Charles Adolph Ramm, a convert and older student at St. Mary's Seminary, Baltimore, who had been an official at the University of California. But two obstacles hindered the archbishop's plans. In his correspondence with Father Magnien and Bishop Keane, he learned that after only two years of theology, the twenty-seven-year-old Ramm was unqualified to begin the advanced program of study.[4] Though Riordan implored Keane to admit this "model Seminarian and . . . first class student," he capitulated on discovering that Ramm was himself unwilling to go to Washington. He remained, nevertheless, convinced that the young cleric had made a grave mistake in rejecting this invitation. Aside from Ramm's indisposition, Riordan was disturbed at Keane's refusal to accept him because of inadequate training at St. Mary's, and his reply to the rector provided an opportunity for the former Louvain graduate student and professor of dogmatic theology to air his criticism of American seminary training and its relationship to the university. "The University course is none too good for any student," Riordan wrote,

> and any student who is willing to study is all the better for being placed in a first class school from the very beginning of his course. A good student loses his time and weakens his mental health in being obliged to pass three years in pursuing so called preliminary studies, which are as rule of the most elementary character, which consists in giving them a number of facts, instead of giving them the great principles underlying facts. The Baltimore faculty should be equal to the University faculty, and its course of studies for Dogma, Moral, Ch. History, Canon Law, and Sacred Eloquence should not be a whit inferior to the course in the University. In Germany the great faculties are attended by young men who have made no preliminary studies. In Rome and in Louvain, the same. Who ever heard of lawyers and doctors going to a second or third class school of law or medicine to prepare for a first class school.[5]

Finances were a persistent preoccupation in the management of such an ambitious enterprise. Bishop Keane was often forced to appeal to his colleagues for permission to take up a collection in their dioceses. Early in 1890 he approached Riordan, who then recommended a postponement since he had pressed his people in the current cathedral drive. "I am not saying to put you off to some remote future, as trying to escape giving a collection," the archbishop confided to the rector. "My heart is in the great work of which you are the head, and the Church of this country will be forever disgraced should this work fall to the ground. . . through the apathy of the Bishops." Confident after six years of administration that his archdiocese would soon extinguish its debt, he proposed that Keane plan to come in wintertime soon, perhaps between October and May, "the only time," he wrote, "that our people of means are here."

Riordan did not hesitate to make further suggestions for the university's solvency, among them the admittance of pre-ordination students and a rigorous system of collection. A number of eastern bishops whose dioceses were located close to the school, he added, have not supported it materially, not the bishops who had opposed its foundation, but "those who are constantly urging others to give but who do not give themselves." In this class Riordan accused two close friends who also belonged to its board of trustees, Ireland and Spalding. An appeal should be made first to these delinquents since San Francisco had already done its part, having subscribed $50,000 through a benefactor, the Honorable Myles P. O'Connor of San Jose, California. "We are 3000 miles away," Riordan insisted, "our people take no interest in the affairs of the East. We are a people apart, cut off from the rest of the country by two ranges of Mountains."[6] After a lapse of two years, Riordan invited the rector to San Francisco, where he was introduced to the wealthy laity and preached a week's mission at the cathedral which was well-publicized and attended.[7] Keane's abilities of persuasion were again profitably directed to the archbishop at this time who, two months later, indicated his readiness to accept a position on the Board of Trustees.[8]

Since no vacancy had occurred, the appointment was not made until the twenty-first meeting of the Board of Trustees on October 21, 1896, a meeting that was in many ways significant for Patrick Riordan. In the previous month, as a result of factionalism within the American Church, Bishop Keane had been forced to resign, a grave disappointment to

Riordan, who had wished to serve the university under his
rectorship. Soon after being removed by the Holy See,
Keane had decided, in an effort to abandon the scene of so
many trials, to return to friends in California. En route, he
had consulted with Riordan and Ireland in Chicago, both of
whom he told Gibbons were "very gloomy" over the sudden
turn of events.[9] A man of strong liberal convictions, Keane
was also disappointed in Riordan's understanding of the critical
situation in the East.

Once he arrived in San Francisco, he communicated these
impressions to the university's vice rector, describing Riordan
as "hopeless in the extreme, both as to the Univ'y & as to the
general condition now facing the Church in the U.S." Keane
expressly wanted as his successor a nonpartisan who could be
loyal first to the institution and preserve a neutrality in the
face of petty feuds. When he suggested the name of Bishop
George Montgomery of Monterey-Los Angeles, Riordan,
supported by his chancellor and university alumnus, Father
Yorke, had dismissed him as "utterly unfit" for the post.[10]
At the next board meeting, Keane's resignation was formally
read. The trustees drafted a *terna* for his successor, a list of
candidates who were already well-known to Riordan. Named
as *dignior* was the archbishop's own brother Daniel and as
dignissimus Father Thomas Conaty, a pastor of Worcester,
Massachusetts, whom Riordan had already considered worthy
of a western see, having lately recommended him for the
Dioceses of Sacramento and Nesqually. Once this troubled
question of succession had been settled in favor of Conaty,
the board unanimously nominated Patrick Riordan to succeed
Martin Marty, Bishop of St. Cloud, who had served as a
trustee for eleven years prior to his death in the previous
month.[11]

Archbishop Riordan was not actively pulled into the
university's affairs until the appointment of the third rector,
a complex maneuver with which he became associated largely
through coincidence. Conaty's administration had proved less
than successful in restoring the university's prestige after
Keane's publicized departure. There developed within the

Board of Trustees and the faculty a movement to discharge him once his six-year term expired and to nominate in his place Monsignor Denis O'Connell.[12] O'Connell had himself suffered an embarrassment similar to Keane's when he had been removed in 1895 from the rectorship of the American College in Rome. There he continued to live only through the benevolence of Cardinal Gibbons as vicar of his titular church of Santa Maria in Trastevere. But enmity at the Vatican had in the intervening years softened toward O'Connell, who had recovered the favor of Cardinal Satolli, the former apostolic delegate who now as Prefect of the Congregation of Studies had a vital interest in the university. In their conversations, the monsignor learned not only that Satolli was dissatisfied with the Conaty regime, intimating that O'Connell might himself succeed to that position. But also adequate provision for the future must be made for the incumbent rector prior to his departure.[13]

Riordan was introduced to these intricate affairs when he was in Europe in the fall of 1902 pursuing the Pious Fund case at the Hague Tribunal. The major ecclesiastical matters bearing on his mind at first were the nomination of his coadjutor and the appointment of Bishop Spalding to the Archdiocese of Chicago. He was disinclined even to extend his travel to the Eternal City, having, as he told O'Connell, "nothing to do in Rome . . . and most anxious to get back home"[14] Too lengthy a sojourn in Europe might hazard his control over naming the next Bishop of Monterey-Los Angeles. As soon as O'Connell's friends in the United States learned of his restored favor with Satolli, their strategy began to unfold. Elated at this news, Gibbons looked forward to the trustees' meeting in November. It was his innocent hope that Riordan would have concluded his business at The Hague so as to have returned from Europe and be present for the struggle against his friend O'Connell's opponents.[15] But Keane was the first trustee to record the importance of Conaty's graceful withdrawal and of Riordan's role. When reports circulated of Montgomery's promotion to San Francisco, he shrewdly counseled O'Connell: "All will hinge on getting Conaty into

some See — Los Angeles for example. If that can be
accomplished, then we will, I am confident, choose you
Rector. . . ."[16]   It was the perceptive ex-rector, therefore,
who very early connected the naming of Montgomery's
successor with the interests of the university and Denis
O'Connell, giving a key and difficult assignment to Riordan.

Once he was assured at The Hague of Montgomery's
appointment as coadjutor, Riordan was most reluctant to
spend time in Rome, eager to return promptly to California
in order, among other reasons, to preside over the selection
of a successor for the Diocese of Monterey-Los Angeles. In
his frequent correspondence with O'Connell, however, he
never hesitated to profess his admiration and affection for
the fifty-three-year-old monsignor. "You write that the tone
of my letter gives pleasure," he assured O'Connell in a
profuse moment. "If only you knew what I think and feel
about you, the pleasure would be much greater. Would that I
could show my friendship, not in words but in deeds."[17]
Soon after these words were written, Riordan had his
opportunity when he was presented with all the facts by
Father Charles P. Grannan, a professor of Scripture at the
university, who had come to Europe on an energetic
campaign to replace Conaty with his close friend and Roman
classmate, Denis O'Connell. At first, Grannan was hesitant to
call on Riordan, not too well-acquainted with him and
fearing, he told O'Connell, that "he might suspect intrigue,
and react." On reconsideration, however, he searched out the
archbishop at The Hague and disclosed his mission. "I found
him in good humor and left him in better humor," he reported.

> Though the international tribunal was in session
> and his case under discussion, still he had time to
> hear me, at least in outline. That outline contained
> about everything ad rem. I need not rehearse it to
> you.[18]

Woven gradually into the plan and apparently slow to
commit himself, the archbishop consented to pay a short visit

to Rome, principally to urge Spalding's promotion to Chicago. In his communications to O'Connell, he declined to pledge himself to Conaty's candidacy for the Diocese of Monterey-Los Angeles, possibly preferring to have O'Connell himself assigned to southern California. What was uppermost in the archbishop's mind was that Montgomery must not be transferred immediately to San Francisco. Otherwise, the archbishop's absence in Europe would deprive him of a real advantage in naming an easterner as his successor. Because of his unexpected delay in Europe and the importance of this appointment, Riordan, therefore, planned to ask Propaganda to keep Montgomery in control of the suffragan see in the interim. "His presence there as Administrator," he informed O'Connell, "would simplify things very much and the Consultors of the Los Angeles diocese would make a better selection of candidates under his candidacy than under that of another." And again, within the week, Riordan seemed elusive, indicating to O'Connell that he had not decided or that he cared not to commit his decision on paper. "I am anxious," he told O'Connell obliquely," to go back to see that a good man is nominated. . . ."[19] Perhaps Conaty's reputation at the university had tempered Riordan's earlier enthusiasm for him. Perhaps, in Riordan's eye, O'Connell appeared the better prospect as his suffragan. Apparently what had yet to be harmonized were O'Connell's personal goals, the trustees' goals, and Riordan's goals for Los Angeles.

Once in Rome, Riordan judiciously attended to the affairs of the university, telegraphing Gibbons that the Holy Father appeared cooperative and expected a list of candidates. Gibbons interpreted this directive as assuring O'Connell's nomination.[20] As the date for the board meeting in November approached, the monsignor's friends anxiously awaited the return of Archbishop Riordan upon whose voting support they counted. "Abp. Keane & myself are busy in your interest," Ireland told O'Connell tensely. "There will be difficulties: certain directors are adverse to voting for you. We are not, however, discouraged. We need badly Abp.

Riordan's aid. If he is at the meeting, we shall feel comforted
and strengthened."[21] Though Riordan was still in Europe on
a special mission and was unable to be present at the meeting
of November 12, 1902, O'Connell was placed second on the
terna after Conaty and was virtually awarded the
rectorship.[22]

Once O'Connell had the nomination of the university's
trustees, the second, and even more delicate stage — the
graceful replacement of Conaty in favor of O'Connell —
awaited Riordan when he returned to California. The Holy
See's ratification of O'Connell's appointment to the
university would in a measure depend upon some provision
for the former rector. It was at this time that Riordan
engaged in a series of astute, perhaps irregular, maneuvers
that began in Europe and led to Conaty's appointment.
Thirteen years earlier, strong opposition had been
encountered in the Diocese of Monterey-Los Angeles over the
archbishop's control of episcopal candidates. Even stronger
resistance could be expected when Riordan would, for the
first time, propose candidates who belonged not only to
another diocese but to another province as well. This
prospect, he knew, would require his immediate return to
California. Basic to his strategy of making the selection for
the suffragan see was to keep Montgomery in control in
southern California until he returned from Europe and the
succession had been settled. The first task was, therefore, to
secure the official documents naming Montgomery coadjutor.
While at the World Court the archbishop appealed to Rodolfo
Giovannini, the papal chargé d'affaires to Holland, at whose
request the Holy See sent the documents to Riordan at The
Hague.[23] Montgomery's rule in the south would end only
when he would deliver the documents. Next, the most likely
local favorite to succeed Montgomery was Father Patrick
Harnett, his popular vicar general; and it would be his
candidacy among the diocesan clergy that most threatened
Conaty's. At Propaganda Riordan was compelled to name
Harnett. This would have afforded the vicar general an opportunity to strengthen his candidacy, especially while

Riordan was in Europe. But Riordan neutralized this advantage by failing to notify Harnett of the appointment for almost three months, well after the meeting of the diocesan consultors and bishops of the province.[24]

En route to San Francisco, Riordan stopped at Baltimore to tell the cardinal that Conaty would most probably be appointed to Los Angeles, and in Chicago he disclosed his mission to Archbishop Ireland. Riordan "is resolved to put Mgr. Conaty primus on the list for Los Angeles," Ireland reported to O'Connell. "This will be done next week. I now consider your appointment to Washington to be certain."[25] Regardless of Ireland's optimism, Riordan was prepared for another struggle in southern California to secure the appointment of his choice for his suffragan see. In late October, while he was detained in Rome, a movement had developed in the Diocese of Monterey-Los Angeles that favored as the successor to Bishop Montgomery his vicar general, the Very Reverend Patrick Harnett.[26] Ever since the news of Montgomery's promotion, a number of ecclesiastics, the press reported, gloomily expected that "powerful church influences elsewhere" would fill the vacancy with a "church dignity outside the diocese." When it was divulged from Washington that Conaty would be shortly deprived of his rectorship and be recommended for the diocese, a movement of protest was organized among the clergy, circulating a petition in Harnett's favor which was addressed to Cardinal Girolamo Gotti, the new Prefect of Propaganda.[27] Conaty would be the first priest of an Atlantic diocese who was in line for a post in California.

As soon as Riordan reached California in December, he hastened to Los Angeles to convene the diocesan consultors. At their meeting they submitted a *terna* consisting of Harnett in first place, followed by William O'Connor of Stockton and Patrick Cummins of San Francisco. Curiously Bishop Conaty stood in fourth place and was thereby disqualified from the list, perhaps Riordan's effort to show that the rector had some support in the diocese.[28] "The meeting was all fixed before I got there," the archbishop later confided to

O'Connell, "and the Consultors were all pledged to vote a certain ticket. Nothing could change their vote."[29] Within the week, the bishops of the province, Riordan presiding and Montgomery's status technically unclear, unanimously dismissed the *terna* from Los Angeles. Harnett, they explained to Propaganda, had been suffering from poor health since his ordination, making him unfit to govern such a large and rapidly growing diocese. As pastor, he had displayed no administrative ability, sadly neglecting the parochial school adjacent to his rectory. A petition circulated and endorsed by the clergy, the bishops' report warned, was spurious. It had been solicited by two questionable priests from others who were scattered throughout the diocese and unaware of the gravity of the situation. With the remaining two candidates eliminated as well, the bishops proposed instead Conaty in first place, followed by Denis O'Connell and James Cleary of St. Paul.[30]

Subsequent events served to recall the difficulties which Riordan had had in sending Montgomery to Los Angeles, and he was forced again to take a personal hand in this appointment. From Spain Propaganda received a strong commendation of Harnett from Bishop Mora living in retirement in Sarria and from his former vicar general, Monsignor Joachim Adam in nearby Barcelona.[31] The petition had likewise been posted to Rome. The organizer, Father Patrick Hawe, who styled himself the "chairman" of the clergy, cabled Gotti: "Before making appointment to Diocese of Los Angeles, await arrival of petition in favor of Harnett unanimously signed by all the priests. . . ."[32] In the face of these developments Riordan promptly drafted letters to Gotti, to Satolli who was now a consultor of Propaganda, and to Diomede Falconio, the apostolic delegate. In them he explained the new *terna* and denounced the petition as containing a number of untruths and originating from two less than model priests friendly to Harnett who had exploited the absence of a bishop in arranging these signatures. Contrary to its claim, the petition had not the approval of the bishops. Scanlan and Grace had not only refused to endorse it but had personally told its authors that it was an insult to the bishops and the Holy See. Equally false, charged Riordan, was its assertion that a Spanish-speaking ordinary was necessary for the diocese, a requirement that Harnett filled. In the nine-year administration of Bishop Montgomery, the archbishop argued, Harnett had never spoken once in Spanish. Since the composition of the diocese was undergoing rapid transformation through immigration from the East, it was no longer imperative that the bishop be bilingual.[33] Although Riordan was confident that his efforts would succeed, the Holy See delayed its decision as additional appeals reached it from Harnett's partisans. Finally on March 9, 1903, Propaganda awarded to Conaty the appointment to the Diocese of Monterey-Los Angeles, and this was ratified by the Holy Father on March 23.[34] Riordan had achieved the appointment in fulfillment of his promise to Gibbons, Ireland, and other interested trustees of the Catholic University of America.

Riordan's extraordinary efforts to secure Conaty's removal to the West demonstrated his loyalty to the university and his personal feelings for the new rector, Denis O'Connell, and his patrons. Unable to attend the installation in April, 1903, he extended to O'Connell his best wishes for a successful administration. "No one rejoices in your promotion more than I do," the archbishop wrote, "and no one will feel a deeper interest in your welfare than I, who during all these years have ever been a true and loyal friend."[35] Riordan felt a great measure of responsibility in O'Connell's appointment to the university. He was aware, too, that the rector's proclivity to take sides in controversial matters might reassert itself in Washington. The rector might thus arouse his old enemies and suffer the same misfortune as he had at the American College in Rome, an embarrassment to those who had championed his promotion. The archbishop did not, therefore, hesitate to offer shrewd advice at the beginning of O'Connell's regime. "You will be watched very critically for a long time to come," he counseled,

and if I may be permitted, as one who has your
interest deeply at heart, to give advise [sic] it
would be this: First, lose no time in getting down
to vigorous work, and secondly, say very little to
anybody. Words will be repeated and sometimes
wrong meanings attached to them. Work in silence,
should be your motto.[36]

Riordan's confidence in the university, however, was
severely shaken during O'Connell's rectorship by the
financial disaster which resulted from the management of the
treasurer, Thomas E. Waggaman, a Washington lawyer and
real-estate man. The trustees had not pursued a careful policy
of accountability, failing to see that its investments were
properly diversified and entrusting all the sums to one man,
the treasurer, without a systematic accounting. Waggaman
had had virtual control of the university's funds since 1885,
but in 1902 an investigating committee of bishops reported
not only poor business methods but also "an almost culpable
negligence...." It recommended further the creation of a
committee of competent and trustworthy laymen to counsel
the trustees on financial policy.[37] Remote on the Pacific
Coast, Riordan, apparently, was neither fully informed nor
aware of the gravity of this eastern crisis. He not only declined to attend the trustees' meeting in January, 1904, at
which lay committees were created, but also disapproved of
this development if it excluded ecclesiastics, preferring
instead a mixed finance committee. "It will never do that
ecclesiastics be the ones who collect all that money," he
advised O'Connell,

and then turn it over to . . . laymen to invest it
judiciously. You may put my vote as emphatically
opposed to any such exclusion. . . . Any good Priest
could manage the finances of the University just as
well as the. . .layman. . . .[38]

He took an increasingly critical stand as the case became
more entangled and additional investigation uncovered a

thoroughly injudicious handling of the university's funds. During the summer he was in close communication with O'Connell, vacationing in New England at the home of his close friend, Adolphus Green. When he learned from Archbishop John Farley of New York that Waggaman had failed to supply additional security for the funds, the archbishop insisted that the treasurer was "playing for time" and that the university's attorney proceed immediately against him. Riordan was tempted to regard the whole affair as a simple case of embezzlement. Further, he made it emphatically clear that in his judgment the entire Board of Trustees would neither be held culpable for the gross mismanagement — or theft— nor be required to restore the losses. "The Cardinal and the Presidents before you," he told O'Connell sternly, "must be held responsible for the investment of the funds and no one else." [39]

A mild conflict over procedure emerged among the trustees. In an effort to keep the affair private, Gibbons and Ireland favored a more temporizing policy for Waggaman. Riordan, however, disillusioned with the unsound financial history of the institution, urged outright and decisive action by the trustees so as to minimize criticism from other creditors since the collapse would inevitably become public. "We are indeed in a bad bog," he wrote again to the rector,

> and we [are] face to face with a crisis that may wreck the University for our day. Be as hopeful as we may, the shock throughout the land when the affair is made public will be tremendous, and all confidence in the management will be gone. . . . [40]

Riordan was confident of his own administrative abilities and continued to deplore the trustees' "folly" of procrastination. When he eventually suggested that his repeated exhortations had fallen on deaf ears, he threatened to withdraw entirely from the university's affairs. "We are face to face with a great crisis," he firmly warned O'Connell two weeks later,

and the sooner we meet it the better. With full
knowledge of the deplorable condition of things,
we have delayed acting for over a month. . . . Unless
matters are taken up at once in a business way, I
for one shall send in my resignation as one of the
Directors, and cut loose from any connection with
the University.[41]

Cardinal Gibbons had not put much reliance on Riordan's
extreme position, especially after July 13 when Waggaman
privately agreed to provide security for the university's
losses.[42] But the archbishop's early cautions appeared more
enlightened in the following month when involuntary
bankruptcy proceedings were instituted against the treasurer,
making the collapse public and menacing the university with
the prospect of losing all its investments. In a desperate effort
to salvage the school, Gibbons as chancellor approached each
director for a subscription of $50,000 and received a glacial
response from San Francisco. Agreeing that heroic sacrifices
must be made to repair the losses from the "Waggaman
defalcation" — there is no other word for this conduct,
Riordan insisted — the archbishop refused to bind himself
to this sum, neither possessing a "one hundred   part of that
amount" nor able to convince, he continued, his diocesan
council to accept this burden. One discreet measure would be
to win the cooperation of the German Catholics, and, Riordan urged, "the first step to be taken in that direction would
be the appointment of a German Archbishop or Bishop as a
Trustee."[43]

In one of the greatest crises that confronted the
American Church of his generation, Riordan declined to step
forward as a national leader. He was unwilling to be a stoic
supporter of the university in its darkest hour and was
tempted at the same time to wash his hands of the
institution. It had quickly become a liability for which he felt
no responsibility. When he was notified of a trustees' meeting
in November, 1904, Riordan instructed the rector and Bishop
Camillus Maes, secretary, to submit his resignation as director.

The university, he explained, would profit to have in his place an ordinary of a wealthier and closer diocese, and his position in San Francisco precluded any active participation in the business since his health could not sustain the lengthy winter trips to Washington for the meetings.[44] There were other unwritten reasons for this coolness. A critic of the university's program of levying each diocese, he had long advocated a board of collectors who would actively solicit endowments among the educated laity of means.[45] More importantly, he could not forgive the chancellor and the second rector for their responsibility in the Waggaman crisis. "Now, nothing has been done at the University since poor Keane left it," he confided to Ireland nearly seven years later,

> except to lose through the fault of those who were in charge of the moneys which he had collected; and I have always felt that the Cardinal and Doctor Conaty were entirely to blame in this matter which was brought to their attention by you at the meeting at which I was not present, and by myself who remained over and got at the bottom of Waggaman's condition and reported it. Now that is all over of course, and we must accept the present condition of things, but we must not be taxed for what is not our fault.[46]

Despite his acidic criticism that spared no one regardless of rank, the Board of Trustees declined to accept his resignation a striking testimony to his value as a counsel. In its name Maes assured him that "your recent valuable counsel will convince you that your illness will not interfere with your efficiency. . . ."[47]

* * * * *

The religious storms that had raged in the eighties and nineties — such issues as unionism, national churches, the apostolic delegate, parochial schools — had largely calmed by

the turn of the century, and in the latter half of Riordan's
episcopate the American Church entered a welcome period
of harmony and normalcy. As Cardinal Gibbons' vision of
quiet consolidation began to unfold in these years, Riordan
especially followed the later careers of two progressive
colleagues, John J. Keane and John Lancaster Spalding. The
past series of controversies had often forced prelates to take
sides and to choose allies, and in these years Riordan had
developed within the hierarchy a number of close friend-
ships. One ecclesiastic who had been a particular favorite
since their meeting in Rome in 1888 was Bishop Keane,
who had also been one of the most conspicuous victims of
the controversies. An erudite, self-effacing but outspoken
liberal churchman, Keane had generously resigned the Diocese of Richmond to become the first Rector of the Catholic
University of America. During his tenure, unfortunately, his
advanced views and those of members of the faculty whom
he had recruited had alienated a number of bishops, including
the apostolic delegate, Archbishop Satolli, In 1896 he was
removed from the rectorship, receiving in exchange a titular
archbishopric in Damascus and a position in Rome.

So-called conservatives had scored this action as a
triumph, Bishop McQuaid leading the chorus and jubilantly
telling Archbishop Corrigan of New York that Rome's
decision had equally rebuked Gibbons and Ireland.[48] Even
before his resignation had been formally submitted to the
Board of Trustees, Keane had been en route across the
continent to Riordan's country. At the invitation of Judge
Myles P. O'Connor, he planned to retire to San José,
California, determined to remain in the United States and to
withdraw from public life. His associates had different plans
for him; and among them Riordan persuaded him to resume
his active career and to defend himself and his friends even
far from his homeland. "Abp. Riordan has convinced me," he
told a former colleague at the university,

> that it is my duty, for the good of religion, to
> sacrifice my sweet retirement in which I am so con-

tent — go to Rome, and accept the position there
offered me by the Holy Father (and which Car.
Satolli said to Abp. Riordan w'd remain always
open to me), and then demand an investigation of
the charges of heterodoxy made against me by
Car. Satolli, and, thro' me, against so many others.

Riordan had thus assisted his friend to reach a momentous
decision. For the former rector next added: "I feel that this is
the most important step of my life, and I ask the prayers of
all of you in regard to it."[49]

On the strength of this decision, John Keane went to the
Eternal City in 1897, raised to the titular Archbishopric of
Damascus, made a canon of St. John Lateran, and appointed
a member of the Congregations of Propaganda and of Studies. But his sojourn remained an exile and a very unhappy
experience. "He is not the same man he was three years ago,"
one former colleague at the university noted later. "Every
one notices the change. . . . He is a crushed man."[50] Having
pressed his departure for Rome, Riordan certainly felt a responsibility for this deterioration and planned with others to
bring him back to the United States. The first opportunity
occurred in 1897 in New Orleans, following the death of
Archbishop Francis Janssens when the bishops of the province named Keane *dignissimus* to succeed.[51] Despite the
delicacy of the situation and strong opposition from other
quarters, Riordan was the first metropolitan to second this
selection, immediately followed a month later by Archbishop
Ireland.[52] Their initial efforts were abortive since Keane
himself preferred at this time no change of assignment.
Gibbons agreed with Keane's judgment. The cardinal was
pleased that his friend had been chosen first for New Orleans
but felt that the American Church would profit by his
remaining in Rome. Keane had returned to the United States
for the summer, and though he had not been consulted by
the Holy See regarding the appointment, he addressed his
respectful refusal to Propaganda, adding that the French
clergy of the vacant archdiocese would oppose him and that

the prospect of assuming responsibility for a debt of 800,000 francs filled him "with horror."[53] Propaganda complied with these latter suggestions and on November 15, 1897, appointed Placide L. Chapelle Archbishop of New Orleans.[54]

Riordan's second opportunity to lead the campaign in ending Keane's exile occurred one year later at the death of Archbishop Gross of Oregon City; and this time he was disposed to take a more active role. Both the diocesan consultors and the bishops of the province submitted identical lists, choosing as candidates Bishop Alexander Christie of Vancouver, John Brondel of Helena, and Alphonse Glorieux of Boise.[55] A difficulty arose for the Holy See when the apostolic delegate reported a wide diversity of opinion among the American archbishops who had failed to agree on the lists of candidates. Some admittedly were unacquainted with the nominees and, therefore, reluctant to pass judgment, and others disqualified each of the candidates for various reasons.[56]

As the other metropolitan on the Pacific Coast who was best acquainted with conditions and the personnel in the Northwest, Riordan's observations would bear a heavier influence in Rome. Immediately he had strong letters drafted to the delegate and to Propaganda, the only archbishop whose original report excluded the entire *terna* and vigorously recommended the candidacy of Archbishop Keane. Bishop Christie, he urged, has not since his most recent consecration acquired the necessary administrative experience to govern the vacant archdiocese which was sorely crippled by "innumerable financial and spiritual difficulties." The other older candidates whom Riordan had known for nearly thirty-five years were, in his candid judgment, "altogether incompetent" for this critical assignment, endowed with neither the desired intellectual nor business sense. Evidently current on the situation in Oregon, Riordan deprecated the "lamentable" state of this archdiocese with desperately needed, he wrote, "a Prelate of great and mature experience, of fervent apostolic zeal and excellent ability in affairs . . . to inspire confidence in the people, to introduce order into the archdiocese and to pay the debts which are constantly increasing."

While Riordan insisted that he had no personal interest in the Oregon appointment other than the welfare of the church, he respectfully offered the suggestion that John Keane would not only please the laity, non-Catholics and a great majorty of the clergy, but in his judgment he was the only churchman who would best fulfill this assignment.[57] Cardinal Gibbons made an unsuccessful effort to endorse Riordan's proposal. Though he had favored Christie in his first report to the delegate, he eventually recommended Keane to Cardinal Ledochowski in a second letter which arrived too late.[58] Again, Keane was not himself quite ready to leave Rome. On this occasion he had not submitted a refusal and was genuinely grateful to those who had worked, he later told his close friend, Father Magnien, "for my release from a painful situation." But he would not agitate in Rome for his promotion, compelled, as he said, "not [to] desert a post of duty simply because it was disagreeable."[59] His candidacy, in any case, depended solely upon Riordan's strong proposal which carried great authority at Propaganda. Keane's old nemesis, however, Cardinal Satolli, the former apostolic delegate presently attached to the congregation, reminded the other cardinals in his report that the Archbishop of San Francisco had in the previous year made the same proposal regarding the Archdiocese of New Orleans and that both Gibbons and Keane had earlier convinced Propaganda that the latter belonged in Rome in the interests of the American Church.[60] Riordan's case thus collapsed on February 6, 1899, when the congregation named Christie to Oregon City.[61]

At the turn of the century, Riordan's persistent efforts at last scored success although circumstances prevented his resuming the leadership in Keane's behalf. While Riordan vacationed in Europe following his second *ad limina* visit to the Holy See, a third opportunity was created by the death on March 4, 1900, of John Hennessy, Archbishop of Dubuque. Keane had been named second on the priests' *terna,* and the bishops of the province had placed him in first

position, followed by Bishops Thomas O'Gorman of Sioux
Falls and Lawrence Scanlan of Salt Lake.[62] Once these lists
had been distributed to the metropolitans, Keane's friends
urged his nomination, Gibbons taking the lead this time with
a strong letter to Cardinal Rampolla, Secretary of State.
Gibbons' appeal invoked Leo XIII's promise to the deposed
rector of an archiepiscopal appointment in the United States,
and the Holy Father was moved to "second" the cardinal's
request.[63] The only opposition from the United States
arose from Frederick X. Katzer, Archbishop of Milwaukee,
who had a deep interest in this midwestern see. Keane, he
told Propaganda, belonged to the "liberal Americanists" and
was an energetic partisan of Archbishop Ireland, and, if
he were assigned to the Archdiocese of Dubuque, which
bordered on Milwaukee and was adjacent to St. Paul, this
would be hazardous to the interests of his own see. [64]

On a visit to Paris, Riordan had received the *ternae* late,
but he began to exploit immediately his advantageous position in Europe in Keane's behalf. He first dispatched in strict
confidence details of the *ternae* to Denis O'Connell in Rome,
who had already received a brief word from Ireland. The
monsignor was entreated to promote Keane's candidacy,
especially through two amenable cardinals attached to Propaganda, the brothers Serafino and Vincenzo Vannutelli.
"His appointment," Riordan wrote, "would be most acceptable to all the educated Catholics of America, who still feel
bitterly his removal from the University. . . . There is no one
on the list that can be compared to him."[65] The archbishop
pursued his project of recruitment, next seeking out his
friend, Bishop Spalding, who he learned was somewhere in
Paris. As soon as he discovered that Archbishop Kain of
St. Louis, in Riordan's judgment "a true friend of Damascus,"
was bound for Rome, he instructed O'Connell to include
him in the cause. Riordan was willing to spare nothing in
advocating Keane's return. "I thought of writing to Satolli
a frank letter on this subject," he added. "If the Archbp.
is not sent to Dubuque it will be because Satolli opposes
him. What do you advise?"[66] O'Connell's reply has been lost

but in the meantime Riordan had located Spalding and each prelate on May 3, 1900, dispatched his letters in Keane's behalf. Spalding sent his letter to O'Connell, briefly offering to make any personal appeal advisable, and Rioradn wrote directly to the apostolic delegate and to Cardinal Ledochowski. O'Gorman, the archbishop told Propaganda, although able, he earned a reputation of offensive behavior, while Scanlan, whom he knew well as a suffragan, was unsuited for a large diocese, having never received a higher education and having passed his life in a mining area amidst an uncultivated population. "The bishop who is needed for Dubuque," Riordan concluded stoutly,

> must be a man of advanced education, capable in his relations with the higher classes of society of producing favorable impressions by his nobility of conduct and distinction of language. All these qualities are found in the archbishop of Damascus.[67]

The vigorous campaign of three years ended on July 9, 1900, when Propaganda named John J. Keane the second Archbishop of Dubuque.[68]

* * * * *

The second comrade whose career Riordan watched closely was his old schoolmate, John Lancaster Spalding; but the archbishop was less successful in intervening in his behalf. The fall of 1902 had been one of the busiest and most remarkable intervals in Riordan's life. He had spent September at the Hague Tribunal, preparing for and attending the historic sessions of the Pious Fund case. By September 30, he had received the documents naming Montgomery his coadjutor. On the following day, he departed for Rome for what was perceived to be a brief and routine errand. In the Eternal City he would press Conaty's candidacy for Monterey-Los Angeles, O'Connell's for The

Catholic University, and, far more important to him, Spalding's promotion to his home city Chicago. This last mission was personally important to Patrick Riordan. It had been the Bishop of Peoria who had been an ally during the Duggan affair and the key instrument in having had Patrick named to San Francisco. Riordan's admiration for this beloved friend was reflected in the fact that Spalding had preached at the major occasions of the archbishop's life: the dedication of St. James' Church and St. Mary's Cathedral, and at his episcopal ordination. After forty-two years of friendship there was no question that Riordan welcomed the opportunity of championing in Rome Spalding's promotion to Chicago. Ironically, this entangled him in perhaps the saddest and most unexpected experience of his life.

Since the death of Archbishop Patrick Feehan in July, 1902, succession had presented exceptional difficulties because Rome had received conflicting reports and could not focus a clear image of affairs in the troubled archdiocese. Having been himself a priest of Chicago for eighteen years, Riordan was specially equipped to contribute information to the distressed cardinals at Propaganda. He was wholly aware of conditions in the Midwest and was personally acquainted with the leading candidates including Spalding, George Montgomery, his coadjutor-elect, and his own brother Daniel.[69] Not only did he have first-hand data for the congregation, but his opportune presence in Rome at the time lent more authority to his views. He had no business in the Eternal City, Riordan had told Denis O'Connell shortly after his arrival on the continent, except personally "to push the case of my Coadjutor and to press the appointment of Bishop Spalding for Chicago." A genuinely superior man must be appointed to Chicago, he urged, since "affairs there are in the most deplorable condition and I know no one who is able to remedy this except Bishop Spalding."[70] The Pious Fund arbitration had brought the archbishop to Europe; and with the papal documents appointing his coadjutor safely in his hands, he was to concentrate his attention in Rome on having Spalding named the next Archbishop of Chicago.

Riordan himself had been seriously considered a candidate for this important see, even generally believed to be anxious to return to Chicago. He was Spalding's own first choice as he had been for San Francisco almost twenty years earlier.[71] Reportedly, too, members of the older clergy had long favored him as a second choice after Spalding.[72] When the irremovable rectors and archdiocesan consultors had met in July to compose a *terna*, Riordan had polled a strong scattering of votes for second and third places, and as one participating rector noted, "would have more but some of those present feared him as a strict disciplinarian."[73] But Patrick Riordan never pressed his own candidacy. Circumstances nevertheless kept him in the midst of this transition, forcing him into a series of bitter unpleasantries.

First, rumors of recent problems in Chicago were not new to Rome. Less than seven months before his death, Propaganda had seriously considered the unilateral appointment of an administrator to manage the archdiocese for Feehan. This extraordinary intervention was discussed as late as February, 1902, when after a quiet investigation the apostolic delegate, Archbishop Sebastiano Martinelli, advised against it, suggesting that the rumors seemed exaggerated and that an administrator now would further divide and demoralize the archdiocese.[74] After Feehan's death, the congregation's fears were again aroused when several prelates virtually denounced his administration, and these critics included Ireland, Richard Scannell of Omaha, and James McGovern of Alton. At first, Patrick Riordan had not planned to comment on Feehan. Hours before he had left for Europe, he had endorsed Spalding simply by rejecting the other two candidates on the bishops' list, both of whom he knew intimately. Montgomery, he reported, had neither the health to sustain the climate of Chicago nor the experience and firmness to manage so large and "turbulent" archdiocese. Riordan disqualified his own brother in favor of Spalding. Daniel, he reported, had been afflicted with such poor health that he is forced to spend the winter of each year far from home.[75] Many weeks later in Rome, however, he discovered that other candidates still competed with his friend in Peoria, and thus he was forced to comment fully on Chicago as the clinching argument in Spalding's behalf.

With O'Connell's assistance, Riordan drafted for Propaganda two reports highlighting Chicago's desperate situation. The inept administration of Archbishop Feehan, stated Riordan, had for twenty years floundered and blundered, Feehan himself being a weak and incompetent man who had retired from control and lived alone "in his own way, in his own palace, allowing the diocese to shift for itself and adopting with regard to the clergy the norm: 'Live and let live.'" As a consequence of such mismanagement, ecclesiastical discipline has disappeared, and in its place there had emerged dissension and grave scandals of every kind which Riordan vividly described. Today in Chicago, he told Propaganda, it was no longer a credit to be a Catholic. Those who have remained faithful were consumed with shame, the youth having largely deserted the church and the sacraments. Protestants, continued Riordan, regarded the archdiocese as a "bilge of corruption" and accepted the testimony of their ancestors that the Catholic Church was the "whore of Babylon." This extremely strong commentary urging Cardinal Gotti to end the deplorable religious condition in Chicago would, Riordan hoped, assure Spalding's appointment.[76]

Perhaps Riordan's performance was too successful, for a second unpleasantry followed immediately, more undesirable than the first. Propaganda acknowledged Riordan's special qualifications and burning interest, and elected to admit him to its confidence. Rome had long been uncertain of Spalding. A decade earlier, while apostolic delegate, Cardinal Francesco Satolli had taken an enormously critical view of the Bishop of Peoria. In 1892, when Spalding had been considered for the coadjutorship in St. Louis, Satolli had notified Propaganda in the most emphatic accents that Spalding "must not and cannot be selected since he is known to be *fickle*, *haughty*, and scornful of Roman authority." The delegate had gone on to climax his first impressions with a vigorous entreaty—"never can or should he be an archbishop."[77] Nearly two years later, Spalding had further offended Satolli with a hostile article in the *North American Review* that reached the unapproving eyes of Leo XIII and his Secretary of State, Cardinal Mariano Rampolla.[78] The pope had hardly appreciated Spalding's comments on the newly established delegation and ordered Propaganda to remonstrate the bishop.[79] But Spalding had already learned from Washington that his published remarks were, in the view of Rome, "inopportune, harmful, untruthful and . . . absurd."[80]

Now a member of Propaganda who specialized in American affairs, Satolli would in 1902 figure critically in Spalding's future. There was a report conflicting with his own unqualified recommendation, one that tended to disqualify Spalding completely. The Baroness von Zedtwitz, the former Elizabeth Caldwell, a wealthy American heirss who had befriended Spalding in her youth, had advanced the gravest charges against Riordan's friend and threatened a scandal if he were named to Chicago.[81] Having already viewed a variety of accusations against figures involved in this succession, Satolli and the congregation were uncertain as to how serious this woman's charges were to be taken. Riordan was asked in Rome to interview her on his return home. Thus far the baroness had supplied no details, and she and her sister Gwendolyn had had in some circles a reputation of erratic behavior. Riordan was delighted to be given the opportunity to vindicate his friend. Meeting her in Geneva, he was not convinced, finding her charges vague and unsupported and contending that Spalding was a wrongly maligned man.[82] Rome needed more information, and the baroness offered to provide Satolli the needed details and witnesses only at Propaganda and in Spalding's presence.[83]

The congregation was spared this confrontation when Riordan's curiosity prompted him to pursue the investigation a step further. In London, he uncovered that what he judged to be convincing evidence concerning Spalding's intimacy with the baroness' sister. In certainly the most painful

letter he ever wrote, a letter to Satolli that he requested to
be destroyed, he reversed his position of several months and
grimly disqualified the third man on the list, John Lancaster
Spalding.[84] Ironically, blame in America for Spalding's defeated candidacy fell upon Cardinal Satolli, a suspected
irreconcilable who was charged with reporting to the Roman
congregation on the matter. When the appointment of
Bishop James E. Quigley of Buffalo was announced, another
Louvain alumnus, Bishop Camillus Maes of Covington reflected the common assumption, reporting to the college's
rector: *"Satolli haec fecit!"* [85] It was not an enemy who had
cast the vote but the closest of friends.

The year 1902 had given Riordan his share of triumphs.
The first case at the World Court had been settled in his
favor. Montgomery would come to San Francisco as his
coadjutor. Conaty's transfer to Los Angeles and O'Connell's
to the Catholic University looked reasonably assured. But
circumstances had forced him to fail in the project which he
held most dear. Ironically, had not the ill-starred Pious Fund
called Riordan abroad at this time, he would never have been
personally entangled as the central figure in an investigation
which altered the destinies of a singular friend and his home
archdiocese. With a burdened heart he concluded his
fortuitous association with the Chicago succession when he
confided to Denis O'Connell: "The Chicago affair is
settled. . . . He has no chance for promotion. Let him remain
where he is until God calls him."[86]

* * * * *

In these days, too, Patrick Riordan kept close watch
on the first stages of an important transition within the
American Church. A new generation of ecclesiastical
leadership began to surface, an ultramontane leadership
replacing the stalwart Old Guard and one that appeared more
imbued with *Romanità*. When in the conclave of 1902
Cardinal Giuseppe Sarto, Patriarch of Venice, was elected to
succeed Leo XIII and chose the name of Pius X, a number of

American churchmen sensed the winds of change. Several were particularly apprehensive at the new pope's raising the young Spanish Monsignor, Raphael Merry del Val, to the cardinalate and appointing him as Secretary of State. Archbishop Ireland would have preferred Cardinal Mariano Rampolla, Leo's displaced Secretary of State, whose candidacy had been disqualified through the veto of Emperor Francis Joseph of Austria-Hungary. Ireland stoically accepted the result as a *"fait accompli,"* remarking to Denis O'Connell: "Evidently my friends & I do not hold in our hands the threads of destiny."[8 7] While Ireland's views might have expressed a minority opinion, his friend in San Francisco shared from the outset the same foreboding at the transition in Rome. Riordan had been unimpressed with two of the pope's earliest statements, his letter to Cardinal Gibbons endorsing an annual collection for the Catholic University of America and his first encyclical, *E supremi apostolatus*, which presented the orientation of his pontificate. Judging from these initial efforts, the archbishop had grimly predicted to Spalding:

> We shall have a weak and colorless administration and no attempt to settle the great difficulties which beset our progress. The appointment of Merry del Val is to my mind the key-note to the whole administration.

In 1897, Merry del Val had been sent as papal ablegate to Canada to investigate the question of separate schools in Manitoba, and his compromise settlement had prompted Riordan to characterize the new Secretary of State as "essentially a weak man."[8 8]

Soon after, these early misgivings were compounded by the persistent ascendancy of William Henry O'Connell, a rising young bishop of New England whose advance did not conform to the official recommendation of American prelates. He represented a new generation of ecclesiastical leadership and would eventually succeed Gibbons as the dean of the American hierarchy. After six years as Rector of the American College in Rome, O'Connell had begun his episcopal career in 1901 as Bishop of Portland, Maine. During his tenure in Europe, he had become close to Cardinal Francesco Satolli, former Apostolic Delegate to the United States and currently an important figure in the Roman Curia, who had left the New World disillusioned with American Catholic progressivism. Satolli, as one of the consulting cardinals of Propaganda, had been selected to report on the candidates for the See of Portland and had likewise presided at O'Connell's episcopal ordination, assisted by Merry del Val, then Titular Archbishop of Trapezus and Rector of the Academy of Noble Ecclesiastics.[89] His promotion had come as a surprise to some since his name had been proposed by neither the diocesan consultors nor the bishops of the Province of Boston. In Rome even Cardinal Gibbons had urged in the name of the executive board of the American College that O'Connell continue to preside at that institution.[90] But the appointment suited the forty-one-year-old rector, and in an acknowledgement to Propaganda promised "solemnly" to direct all his energies as ordinary in forging a "tighter and stronger link of union and attachment to the Holy See."[91]

Succession to the metropolitan See of Boston three years later became a major concern for a number of American prelates, including Patrick Riordan. As a suffragan, O'Connell was entitled to a voice in the selection of a coadjutor for the failing archbishop, John J. Williams. Constant immigration had swollen the Catholic population of the archdiocese, which in 1903 numbered 560 priests and 700,000 faithful. Williams' auxiliary bishop, John Brady, had long been plagued with poor health. As the archbishop himself entered his eighties, his eyesight began to fail rapidly, and he was convinced that the fiscal administration of his see must soon be entrusted to a younger man.[92] At the head of both the priests' and bishops' *ternae* stood the name of Matthew Harkins, Bishop of Providence, who also received the overwhelming endorsement of the metropolitans. Riordan himself strongly contended that of all the candidates Harkins was the only one worthy and capable of the coadjutorship. In his report to Archbishop Diomede Falconio, the apostolic delegate, Williams likewise signified a preference for him. Complications arose, however, when, as secretary at the meeting of the bishops of the Province of Boston, O'Connell registered strong disapproval of all the candidates, refusing either to speak or to vote for what he obliquely termed as "strong and legitimate reasons."[93]

Invited by the delegate to amplify his views, O'Connell referred to a conspiracy among Boston priests to secure a tractable successor to Williams. More significantly, he charged that none of the nominees on either *terna* was endowed with the qualities necessary for this important promotion and, contrary to the bishops' report, would be acceptable to the clergy of the archdiocese.[94] The Bishop of Portland had additional channels through which to make recourse. From their days together in Rome, a close friendship had been cultivated between Merry del Val and O'Connell. In the present delicate situation the latter had had no hesitation, even before his protest to Falconio, to address a confidential appeal to the papal Secretary of State. "The one frank and avowed motive actuating these men," he claimed in the greatest detail,

> was to keep off the *terna* at all costs any name which stood for Rome, for Roman views and Roman sympathies. This is a well known and well proven fact. Threats, criminal promises, published calumnies—these were the means resorted to for the success of this plot, which in the face of protests of all the good and respected priests of the diocese has thus far succeeded. As God will one day judge me, He knows now that my only thought is to save in this hour of awful peril, the honor of His Church and the very life of that unity with the Apostolic See which again and again is threatened and which at this juncture is in awful

peril here. Boston is at this moment in the balance
between Rome and her enemies.[95]

Having expressed his ultramontanism, the bishop then
pleaded that the Holy See postpone its decision, offering to
come to Rome personally to prove these allegations. The
Secretary of State was alarmed at his description of the
"anti-Roman" maneuvers and forwarded O'Connell's letter to
Cardinal Gotti.

In his own correspondence the Bishop of Portland had
never alluded to his own worthiness for the coadjutorship,
but in this spring of 1904 several of the priests and laity of
the City of Boston sent to the Vatican appeals in favor of his
candidacy. Their choice of arguments was bound to alarm the
Roman authorities. Twenty-one Italian-born laymen
endorsed an emphatic statement that 90,000 of their
countrymen dwelt within the jurisdiction of the archdiocese
and needed greater religious attention that only O'Connell
was equipped and disposed to give. His three years in upper
New England, they explained, had demonstrated his constant
and heartfelt concern for the Italian working class.[96] Father
Patrick J. Daly, pastor of St. Francis de Sales Church in
Boston, referred to an episcopal intrigue among the Boston
suffragans to prevent O'Connell's promotion. What these
bishops wanted, reported Daly, was " 'home rule' and not
'Rome rule' this time."[97] A curate and alumnus of the
American College, Father Patrick Supple of St. Peter's
Church, Cambridge, developed much the same theme. It was
"jansenistic Americanism" which had inspired the opposition
to O'Connell and which had already infected the first-named
candidate for Boston, Bishop Harkins.[98] Another irate
Boston priest, Father John F. Cummins of Sacred Heart
Parish, accused Riordan's friend, Archbishop Ireland, of
being an active accomplice in subverting O'Connell's career.
"In God's name . . .," exclaimed Cummins,

have we two Popes, one in Rome, and one here
who pretends to [have] more power than our Holy

Father. The Archbishop of St. Paul does what even
our Holy Father himself does not do. He interferes
in every selection of a Bishop. . . .[99]

The Holy See could hardly act decisively in the face of
these communications, particularly as it studied O'Connell's
offer to present additional information either by letter or in
person. On August 22, 1904, Propaganda decided to defer
the appointment to Boston.[100] As the official word was
delayed, probably mislaid in the mails, rumors began to
circulate within ecclesiastical circles, while interested parties
carefully watched the movements of Cardinal Satolli during
his visit to the United States in the summer, including his
special trip to Portland, and those of Bishop O'Connell, who
quietly sailed to Rome in the late autumn.[101] Although no
appointment of a coadjutor was forthcoming in 1905, an
important development occurred soon after O'Connell's
return from Europe when he was selected as a papal envoy on
a temporary mission to Japan. In October, Archbishop
Riordan offered hospitality to him and his companion,
Father Supple, when they stopped briefly in San Francisco
en route to the Orient.[102] By the middle of January, 1906,
the Bishop of Portland returned with his report to Rome,
approximately a week before the cardinals of Propaganda
were to meet on the question of the Boston coadjutorship.
On the other edge of the continent, Patrick Riordan
had a keen interest in this appointment. John J. Williams,
first Archbishop of Boston, had stood high in Riordan's
estimation—a respected octogenarian who had governed the
see for over three decades and whose devoted service,
Riordan felt, merited a successor of his choice. During the
national controversies of the 1880's and 1890's, Williams,
like his colleage in San Francisco, had held himself aloof,
though showing liberal tendencies and soundly supporting
Archbishop Ireland on the Faribault-Stillwater issue.[103] So
highly did Riordan regard this "venerable" churchman that
on his authority he would shortly name the chancellor of
Boston, Richard Neagle, *dignior* on the *terna* for his own

coadjutor.[104] Furthermore, although there was no recorded association between Riordan and Bishop Harkins, both were close friends of another Boston suffragan, William Stang, Bishop of Fall River. Also an alumnus of Louvain's American College who had remained for a time on its staff as the first vice-rector, Stang had co-operated with Riordan in periodic efforts to raise money for the college. Closely attached to Harkins as well, this German-born ecclesiastic had belonged to the Diocese of Providence. When it was divided and the new See of Fall River created, Stang was named its first bishop.[105] He was the most active among Harkins' partisans, and it was largely through him that Riordan kept in close contact with the Boston succession.

Riordan had no right to intercede directly for Harkins, but it was through his advice that, with O'Connell absent in the Orient, Archbishop Williams and his suffragans had in December, 1905, besought Propaganda to name a coadjutor as soon as possible. For the past year, the bishops urged, they had been awaiting day by day an announcement from the Holy See, and the appointment was imperative since Williams, at eight-four years of age, had recently undergone a second operation on his eyes.[106] Rome remained unmoved into the new year, and the word of these last developments was relayed to San Francisco when, on the very day that Propaganda reached its decision, Stang wrote anxiously from Fall River:

> The "Boston affair" is still unsettled; things are growing desperate. We have sent the document as suggested by you (through Archp. Ireland & Bp. McQuaide) [sic], but Rome remains silent. "Quare fremuerunt gentes?" Bp. Harkins is the ideal of a Catholic Bishop. God grant us patience![107]

Fresh from his mission to Japan, Bishop O'Connell was in the Eternal City on January 22, 1906, when eleven cardinals of Propaganda elected to advance him from Portland to Boston as Williams' coadjutor with the right of succession,

another unexpected promotion that was sanctioned by Pius
X on February 1.[108] News of this appointment created a
sensation in Boston and took a number of ecclesiastics by
surprise since O'Connell's candidacy had not been presented
on either *terna*. Riordan himself was shocked; and to
Monsignor William Byrne, Boston's vicar general, whom
O'Connell had named as the leader of the priests' conspiracy,
he confessed that it was difficult to phrase his reaction. "I do
not hesitate to say to you," he remarked tartly,

> that such an appointment is a national scandal. I
> do not see any use in holding meetings and sending
> money across the Atlantic when no attention is
> paid to the proceedings of the Bishops and the
> Archbishops.

A movement was soon afoot to petition the American
archbishops to protest to the Holy See what the bishops of
the Province of Boston viewed as an arbitrary
appointment without appropriate consultation. But this was
an extreme step which Riordan discouraged, telling Byrne
candidly: "It is a loss of time in my opinion to do anything.
Nobody knows what may follow this and your fears may be
realized." Redress seemed impossible at this moment. During
his last trip to Rome, Riordan confided to Byrne, Pius X had
given him the distinct impression that O'Connell would not
be nominated, and from the lips of Cardinal Gotti he had
learned that once Archbishop Williams renewed his request
for a coadjutor the appointment would be promptly made.
The prefect had intimated further that Propaganda's choice
would fall on the Bishop of Providence. "Even Cardinal
Merry del Val assured me," he added, "that Portland was
never mentioned in connection with Boston."[109] The same
strong sentiments were communicated to Harkins' most
ardent enthusiast, Bishop Stang, who found it well nigh
impossible to reconcile himself to Rome's decision. In a
confidential comment to San Francisco, he revealed both his
indignation and appreciation of Riordan's efforts in behalf of

the Province of Boston. "You have been the cause of our last petition to the Holy See, requesting an early appointment," he told Riordan.

> The answer to it is known & terrific. He who was "dignissimus" in the conscientious opinion of Bishops and priests is pushed aside. . . . We now feel that the Archbishops at their next meeting should take a firm stand, & respectfully protest against the complete ignoring of the "terna" & the intrusion of a man who is not wanted, because not "idoneus."
>
> The Suffragans (with the exception of Manchester) will advise the venerable Archbishop of Boston to head such a protest.
>
> Things have come to such a state that American Bishops are treated like a lot of unreliable schoolboys. The nefarious influence of Cardinal Satolli who is despised by Catholics & non-Catholics throughout the land should come to a speedy end.[110]

The alert apostolic delegate sensed this rampant indignation. The American hierarchy, Archbishop Falconio reported to Rome, apparently felt that it had been "humiliated and stung sharply"; and the Holy Father would most likely be deluged with protests and petitions. Archbishop-elect O'Connell, he warned solemnly, must be told to use the greatest prudence when returning to America; otherwise, he would arouse the most distressing complications.[111]

The rise of William O'Connell, among many things, had a telling impact on the American hierarchy. As his confidential statements to Rome have indicated, he represented an intense form of ultramontanism and irritated his colleagues by his ascendancy through independent channels. He had not once secured an episcopal appointment through a regular nomination on a *terna*. His promotions to Portland and

Boston had originated in Rome, not from the recommendations formulated in the United States. Furthermore, the protestations of his fidelity to the papacy implied a treacherous indifference among the elder prelates who had resisted his advance. Riordan, for one, resented this. In the years that followed O'Connell's succession to the See of Boston on the death of Archbishop Williams, Riordan's attention continued to span the continent towards New England, reflecting largely the reaction of the Old Guard and carefully noting his movements with express disapproval. In late 1909, when after a delay of nearly two years John J. Nilan was appointed to the Diocese of Hartford, Riordan regarded this as a defeat for O'Connell who, Riordan was informed, had himself dismissed the original *terna* and proposed a candidate of his own. "The Delegate [Diomede Falconio] took up the cause of the 'Terna,'" he commented to Father Dan, "and made it, I understand, a personal fight and won out. From all accounts the Archbishop of Boston has lost, or nearly lost, all the favor he enjoyed in Rome."[1 1 2]

Riordan was further alienated in the spring of 1911 by O'Connell's most celebrated decision since assuming control of the archdiocese when he displaced the Sulpician Fathers from his seminary, St. John's in Brighton, and staffed it entirely with diocesan clergy. Riordan had himself seen copies of the documents that had been exchanged between Boston and Paris. While he never questioned O'Connell's right to act, he deplored the means used and the demoralizing effect upon the society. "The Superior General called on him," Riordan recorded confidentially for his brother,

> and he then gave him formal notice in the presence of the officials of the diocese to go two years from this coming July. Twenty days afterwards he rescinded this two years delay, and ordered them to go at the end of this year.

In Riordan's judgment the decision was almost an irreparable blow to the Sulpicians, who had recently withdrawn from St.

Joseph's Seminary in New York as well as having been expelled by the government from their institutions in France. At the moment their very existence appeared to be jeopardized with these losses and all too few replacements of the older members. "It is a great pity," added Riordan, "because they have done in their way wonderfully good work, and they have kept before the young seminarians the highest ideals of the priesthood."[113]

While Archbishop O'Connell's ascendancy continued during the pontificate of Pius X, Riordan remained genuinely devoted to John Ireland, judging him to be the leading member of the American hierarchy and hoping, with scores of others, that this might be sanctioned through the conferral of the cardinalate on the Archbishop of St. Paul. The American church had had meager representation in the Sacred College of Cardinals. Until the turn of the century only two Americans had been chosen to receive the red hat, John McCloskey of New York, who died in 1885, and James Gibbons of Baltimore. As Catholicism grew stronger in the United States, however, and had been elevated in 1908 from the status of a missionary church, it was expected that this honor would be extended to more Americans. Even as early as the 1890's, there had evolved several movements among Ireland's admirers to have him made a cardinal, and the honor had also been rumored for other heads of large dioceses in the East and Middle West. These rumors had grown more insistent toward the end of 1911 since the pope had held no consistory for nearly four years.

Riordan was convinced that his friend in St. Paul had earned the hat, but unable to sense Rome's direction in the matter, he was keenly sensitive to the stirrings in the press. In 1909 he had sighted a notice announcing the appointment soon of a new American cardinal who was described evasively as a distinguished citizen of the United States, who had already voted thrice for presidential candidates and was thoroughly conversant with the history of this country. Riordan anticipated that Rome's preferences had accordingly fallen either on Archbishop Falconio, who was a naturalized

citizen, or on Archbishop Farley because of the prestige of
New York. "It would not surprise me if this were done," he
told Ireland bitterly.

> It would be an Italian way of solving what they
> consider now a difficulty, but it would be a
> solution of the most ridiculous character, and
> would provoke laughter instead of praise; but
> anything may be expected these days.[114]

As it turned out, Riordan's instincts proved to be nearly
perfect. Yet he was stunned two years later when on
October 28, 1911, the Holy See announced that among the
new cardinals to be created at the next consistory were three
residents in this country, namely, Falconio, Farley, and
William O'Connell. To Riordan, the first two selections were
welcomed with universal favor, while the third, as he
confided to Denis O'Connell, "with just the
opposite—universal disfavor."[115] The severest blow,
however, was the conspicuous disregard of Ireland.
Feeling as he did, Riordan had not the heart even to send his
sympathy to St. Paul, having believed so confidently that if
more than one American was named, his friend would be
among them.

"Evidently his day is past, he will receive no
recognition," Riordan commented privately.

> He is certainly the most prominent and greatest of
> all the Heads of the Hierarchy, and an honor would
> have been conferred on the entire country if the
> promotion had been given to him. Catholics and
> non-Catholics alike would have rejoiced, and now
> there is resentment and bitterness which are not
> pleasant indications of public feeling.[116]

To the Archbishop of San Francisco, the reason why
O'Connell had been honored instead of Ireland remained a

mystery. The oversight, he judged, was an affront to a noble
and zealous churchman who of all the ecclesiastics in the
American church had most merited an acknowledgement
from his superiors in Rome; and his friends must bear their
disappointment with resignation.[117] Even sturdy Archbishop
Ireland was yielding to the wear of old age, about to reach at
this time his fiftieth year in the priesthood; and a month
after the consistory when Riordan received a letter from St.
Paul, he told his brother that he noticed for the first time a
distinct tremor in Ireland's script. "Everybody who comes
from the East wonders that he was not appointed," he added,
"and wonders still more that the promotion should have been
given to Boston."[118] This last decision in Rome had
convinced Riordan that his colleague's chances had already
been extinguished at the end of Leo XIII's regime in 1903.
From hindsight, the archbishop regretted that Ireland's
patron, Cardinal Rampolla, had not secured the distinction
for him years ago when he was enormously influential as Leo
XIII's Secretary of State. "He may have been a friend,"
lamented Riordan acidly, "but he lacked the loyalty which I
have always associated with true friendship. I suppose the
quality of friendship is determined by race, and the Italians
are satisfied with surface friendship."[119]

It was the "changing of the guard." Riordan's closest
friends were fixed in their current assignments: Spalding in
Peoria, Keane in Dubuque, and Ireland in St. Paul—none of
them to receive additional honors or to exert the same
authority as they had in the past. For Riordan, the rise of
William O'Connell from his rectorship of the American
College in Rome to the cardinal's hat in Boston indicated
that the American Church was reaching a new stage. The
spirit of stout independence which had marked his
ecclesiastical generation in the controversies and their
dealings with Rome was rapidly fading. American churchmen
seemed to be settling into an interval of serenity among
themselves and of unquestioned public fidelity to the papacy.
Perhaps Patrick Riordan could sense that succeeding to the
position of national leadership in the American church was a

man not of the spirit and choice of his generation, William
Cardinal O'Connell. It would be O'Connell who at Gibbons'
death in 1921 would begin a twenty-three-year reign as dean
of the American hierarchy. But Patrick would be long gone
before that grim day.

PORTFOLIO 3

Desolation up Nob Hill past Old St. Mary's

The Jesuit Church Afire in 1906
Courtesy of California Historical Society

Breadlines around the Cathedral
Devastation halted across the Avenue
Courtesy of California Historical Society

Newman Hall, Berkeley

Earthquake Wreckage at the Seminary

Bishop Bernard McQuaid with the Faculty at
St. Bernard's Seminary, Rochester: Edward Hanna,
third from left in back row; Andrew Breen, first from
left in front row; Andrew Meehan on far right in front row
(following two pages)

Monsignor John J. Prendergast
d. 1913

Alexis-Marie Lépicier,
later as Cardinal
1863 - 1936

Father Charles A. Ramm
sketch, 1940; d. 1951

Denis J. O'Connell
Auxiliary Bishop
1908 - 1912

Cardinal Francesco Satolli
1839 - 1910

Reverend M. D. Connolly
Rector, St. Paul's Church

Cardinal Rafael Merry del Val
1865 - 1930

Courtesy of Diocese of Portland, Maine

Bishop William H. O'Connell in 1901
1859 - 1944

The Successor:

Bishop Edward J. Hanna

The Archbishop and Father Ramm relaxing with the
Tobin Family; Joseph Sadoc Tobin is seated second
from left.

Courtesy of Cyril Richard Tobin

A Last Portrait 1912

12

"Very Few Left"

The twilight years are precious in any man's life, particularly for one who had lived such a rich and varied life as Patrick Riordan. He had built and rebuilt an archdiocese. He had faced controversy from within and without. As he entered upon his seventies he approached the completion of three decades later as a leader of a great western community. Once he had secured the auxiliary of his choice, he was able to embark upon his last years in peace and tranquility. Since the earthquake and fire, the round of duties had so multiplied and his health so failed that he contemplated retirement. On the eve of his seventieth birthday, eighteen months before the coming of Bishop Hanna, he candidly told his brother that he would gladly resign and pass the few remaining years in preparation for eternity if, he added, "I had several things fixed up, or in the hands of some one who would attend to them."[1] Hanna's arrival late in 1912, however, heartened the old archbishop immeasurably, enabling him to face the inevitable with confidence and ease. Riordan often recorded his secret thoughts on death without trace of fear or remorse, and exactly one year before the end he shared them with an old friend of Belgian days. "I have felt more than ever," he confided,

> that the infirmities of old age are coming on, and
> that I am not able to do what I did twenty-five or
> thirty years ago. This is the [toll] that advancing

361

years place on us, and we are reminded by our
infirmities that the end is not far away. A most
beautiful disposition of Divine Providence, this
constant reminder that we are here to prepare for
another world.[2]

Sensitive to his own physical decline, Riordan attentively
and regretfully observed a parallel among his closest friends
in the hierarchy. His Louvain collegemate in Peoria had been
the first to betray signs of collapse when in January, 1905, he
suffered a stroke of paralysis. Riordan had two years earlier
prevented the appointment of Bishop John Lancaster
Spalding to the Archdiocese of Chicago, and it was
understood among his confidants, including Archbishop
Ireland and Bishop Denis O'Connell, that no public issue
would be made of the matter as long as Spalding was not
promoted.[3] This investigation had been perhaps the most
difficult trial for Riordan. Soon after his return from Europe,
he had ordered O'Connell to destroy all relevant
correspondence, adding: "I wish to blot the whole of that
thing out of my memory and it is better that no record of it
remain."[4] Yet there had lingered through the years certain
threats to destroy Spalding's reputation, and it had been with
mixed feelings that Riordan learned of the bishop's stroke
and partial paralysis. On telegraphing Peoria for details, he
had discovered that the bishop's condition was not so serious
as had been reported in the press. No matter, however, how
successful his recovery might be, the archbishop was
convinced that Spalding's days of active usefulness had
passed. "He has done good work during all the days of his
ministry," Riordan had told his own brother who was
Spalding's closest friend, "and more than any other Bishop of
the Country, he is listened to by the intelligent and cultured
outside our religion."[5] But Spalding's partial paralysis had
the welcome effect of lessening the menace of scandal. To
Denis O'Connell, Riordan confessed a measure of relief
when he observed shortly after: "His days for active work
are over, and of course this will preclude any possible

promotion so much dreaded by certain parties."[6] The university rector had long been in Riordan's confidence. He likewise perceived the broader significance in Spalding's collapse, acknowledging that the stroke had probably ended what he called "the war" and that it had been "a wretched feeling of always apprehending an outbreak."[7]

Spalding's closest friends at length prevailed on him to resign his see. This was accomplished in September, 1908, largely through Riordan's strong urging by mail and Ireland's visit to Peoria. When Riordan read in the paper the unofficial notice of his friend's retirement, he lamented to Ireland that this action sealed the closure of what had promised to be one of the brightest and most glorious episcopates in the United States. "The ending of it is unexpressibly sad," he commented,

> and the causes which lead to ending are still more so. I cannot bring myself to write at length about it. We have been friends for eight and forty years when I met him first in Louvain and I was always deeply and most affectionately attached to him.[8]

Five years later Riordan was genuinely disappointed at being unable to attend the celebration of Spalding's golden jubilee in the priesthood in November, 1913, an anniversary which Riordan himself was never to reach. By this time his own health had been seriously impaired, and he dreaded the tedious journey to the Middle West. In framing his message of congratulations from a sick bed, he warmly recalled his own presence at Spalding's ordination in Mechlin, and he added emphatically:

> Your priesthood has been one of the great factors in making our Church well thought of, not only by those within its fold, but by those outside as well; your name will be associated with some of its greatest works, disinterested and intelligent in the highest degree.[9]

Father Dan Riordan planned to attend the solemnities where
he could represent his brother as well, and to him too the
archbishop revealed his admiration and affection for the
Bishop of Peoria, professing that from the day of the latter's
ordination a half century ago to the present they had
remained faithful and intimate friends. "There are very few
left who were alive then," wrote Riordan solemnly, "and I
feel that it would not only be my duty but the very acme of
pleasure to be with him and to talk over the past."[10]

Another beloved colleague was at this time suffering the
wearing effects of old age as conspicuously as Spalding,
Archbishop John J. Keane of Dubuque. His health breaking
as he neared seventy, Keane petitioned Rome in mid-1909
for a coadjutor with the right of succession. After several
attempts, however, the Holy See declined his request and
instructed that no new nominations be forwarded, intimating
that his resignation would be in order. Riordan was, as
before, concerned with Keane's future, and he regarded it an
unmerited humiliation for Rome to refuse a coadjutor for
Dubuque and not allow the archbishop in this way to remain
in his see. As soon as he was informed that Keane had
decided to resign and to retire to Washington, D.C., Riordan
sent a pressing invitation for him to spend his last days as his
guest in California. He planned to place at Keane's disposal a
new residence built on the campus of the seminary at Menlo
Park, a gift of his benefactor, Michael Cudahy. This house
was complete in every detail and designed ideally for an
ecclesiastic. Nothing, according to Riordan's offer, would
be omitted to make the archbishop welcome and
comfortable. While located near the seminary building, it was
still shielded from its "noise and bustle" and was kept by the
sisters who were charged with the seminary's domestic
service. "All that is needed to make it complete for you,"
urged Riordan,

> would be the hiring of a man for a valet. This I will
> attend to if you will accept my offer. As you
> know, the grounds are beautiful about the

Seminary. The climate is perfect, and every want
of yours will be attended to. You will have the
ease, quiet, and comfort which a sick man needs,
and if I should go down to spend two or three days
with you there is plenty of room for me. You will
be your own master in it, and have your own
servants, and I should be glad to know that your
declining days were made happy.[11]

But Archbishop Keane declined this generous invitation.
He had meanwhile applied for an auxiliary and had been
given convincing assurances that this request would be
granted. Riordan was pleased with this news, noting for his
brother that this last letter from Dubuque was "written in
his usual firm hand, and it reads as if it came from in his palmiest
days." From this evidence the archbishop judged that despite
contrary reports, Keane's mental powers had remained strong
and intact, adding that it would be an injustice for Rome to
force him to withdraw from his see.[12] Riordan's affection
for Keane was so genuine and zealous that in promoting this
petition for an auxiliary for Keane, he offered, in a message
to Ireland, to do everything possible, even to make a direct
appeal to the Holy See for one whom he characterized as
"our dear friend in Dubuque." Rome would grant Keane's
request, Riordan was convinced, only if Cardinal Gibbons
earnestly endorsed it, and the Archbishop of San Francisco
feared, as he told his friend in St. Paul, that if Gibbons
"merely writes a weak letter to those who have charge of
these matters in Rome, it may be put aside and nothing come
out of it." There was not within the American hierarchy,
insisted Riordan, "a nobler or better man, and the greatest
kindness should be shown him by the authorities in
Rome."[13] Riordan was at first dissatisfied with the
announcement in early May, 1911, of Keane's resignation; he
would have preferred that he be left at least as nominal head
of the see in his last days. Some months later, however, he
acknowledged the wisdom of the Vatican's decision. "The
old archbishop, I have heard lately, is not well," he told his

brother Dan. "He is gradually sinking away, and will need for now constant care and nursing. His memory is entirely gone, so I am informed, and it was the very best thing to do to insist on his resignation."[14]

Keane's was the second resignation to which Riordan gave halting approval. Fortunately, his own poor health never crippled his ability to govern, nor would it ever force him to abdicate. Ironically, however, his two old comrades in Peoria and Dubuque, impaired as they were, would survive their friend in San Francisco.

* * * * *

To the end, politics struck a special nerve in Patrick Riordan. Midway through his episcopate, he had displayed a disposition for political engagement when in 1900 he helped direct a successful campaign in revising the state constitution and exempting church property and buildings from taxation. In his last years, however, two principles seemed to guide his views on public issues. On national topics, first, he was a self-styled conservative, reflecting little sympathy for the rise of progressivism in American political life. He watched the multiple efforts in the state to destroy machine politics by introducing mechanisms that progressives claimed would restore popular control of government. Such mechanisms in California included the initiative, referendum, and recall. But the Archbishop of San Francisco greeted these reforms with no enthusiasm or understanding. They threatened, he was convinced, stable and representative government, transferring too much power from the elected legislature to the state bureaucracy. "I am afraid," he told his brother, "we are drifting into troubled waters in the near future."[15]

The presidential election of 1912, the last in which he would vote, prompted Riordan to make private comments on several of the most significant personalities of his time. Critical of the tumultuous conventions in Chicago and Baltimore, Riordan was pleased that Theodore Roosevelt had failed to win the Republican nomination. "He is a boisterous man," he noted, "a disturber of the peace." The less familiar figure of Woodrow Wilson failed to attract the archbishop who acknowledged his inclination of dismissing this candidate simply as a "theorist." The progressive Governor of New Jersey was, in Riordan's estimate, too intimately associated with "these new fangled notions of government, such as 'initiative,' 'recall,' and elements of the like." The archbishop's favorite was William Howard Taft—"a good man and safe man."[16] Riordan knew the President personally, having once vacationed with him and recommended several names for federal posts. "Mr. Taft will be a most excellent President," Riordan told Gibbons, "wise, conservative and without bigotry, and I hope and pray that he will be elected."[17] As it turned out, Riordan's markedly conservative views were in the minority, supporting the only President in American history who ran third in a presidential contest. To his death, Riordan acidly reproached the Wilson government, especially in its policy toward Mexico. The New Freedom diplomacy had at first favored the Constitutionalist revolution under Venustiano Carranza and his general, Francisco Villa, but the movement had inevitably dissolved into a civil war. Refugees from Mexico had brought to Riordan reports of atrocities and anticlerical oppression. In his last letter, he coldly characterized Carranza and Villa as "simply brutes." Though a man with many defects in character, Roosevelt, in Riordan's judgment, could provide "the strength and bravery to take charge of our affairs." Wilson had so far displayed only weakness and indignity "so that we are the laughing stock of the nations."[18]

Riordan's second principle was that his clergy must not become involved in political debate, even remotely. While he professed strong personal preferences, the archbishop did not hesitate from censuring priests who violated this principle of strict non-engagement. In 1911, Father Joseph Gleason, the unofficial chronicler of the archdiocese, had undertaken a speaking tour in favor of women's suffrage and was ordered to cancel the commitment.[19] A month later, the San Francisco newspapers reported the public association of

Father Denis O. Crowley, the Director of the Youths'
Directory and a friend of Riordan, with James Rolph, Jr., a
mayoral candidate. Riordan instantly sent a severe
reprimand, warning against any further activity that might be
construed as "political partisanship."[20] The most celebrated
priest who challenged this principle of non-engagement,
however, was the gifted polemicist, Peter Yorke.

After his resignation as chancellor in 1898, Father Yorke
still managed to remain active in public affairs—lecturing
frequently and working on his textbooks of religion,
promoting the Gaelic Union and arranging a successful Irish
Fair. He had participated prominently in the Teamsters'
Strike of 1901 and in the following year inaugurated the
publication of the *Leader*, a weekly devoted to Irish and
labor interests.[21] But his behavior had extinguished any
possibility of ecclesiastical advancement under Archbishop
Riordan, and the estrangement between the two churchmen
was never fully healed. In spite of his activities, Yorke had
received since his resignation no official appointment from
the archbishop. He accepted the invitation of Father
Peter Casey to assist him at St. Peter's Parish, San Francisco.
In December, 1901, there occurred a vacancy in the Diocese
of Cheyenne when Bishop Thomas M. Lenihan died
unexpectedly. The diocesan consultors drew up a *terna* for a
successor and nominated Yorke in third place, but the
bishops of the Province of Dubuque rejected the entire list in
favor of three new candidates. In their report to the Holy
See, the bishops, whose metropolitan was Archbishop John J.
Keane, Riordan's close friend as well as Yorke's former
superior as Rector of the Catholic University, offered a brief
reason why the latter's candidacy could not be considered.
"Although brilliant and eloquent," the report read, "he is so
offensive to his Ordinary, the Most Reverend Archbishop of
San Francisco, that he cannot be proposed by us."[22]

Beginning in 1902, Yorke's access to the pages of the
Leader led him again into the role of controversialist. His first
target was his alma mater, the Catholic University, to which
the Ancient Order of Hibernians had donated $50,000 for a

chair of Gaelic studies. When a professor of Yorke's choice had been dismissed, the weekly denounced the decision, even suggesting that the trustees had managed the endowment dishonestly. "So far as the church and education are concerned," charged a bristling editorial, "the function of the Irish is to put up or shut up."[2][3] Such a fulmination was bound to reach the archbishop. Immediately he sent word back to Washington, D.C., suggesting that the university refute the attack publicly and "offset these lying insinuations." "It is deplorable," Riordan added, "how many priests are willing to do the Devil's work."[2][4] The archbishop was shortly given the opportunity to communicate his bitterness to Rome during the negotiations for his coadjutor.

As soon as he learned that his petition to select a coadjutor with the right of succession had been granted, he convened the consultors and irremovable rectors to draft a list. George Montgomery, Bishop of Monterey-Los Angeles, was awarded the largest number of votes, but behind him was Peter Yorke, who received three votes and was placed in a tie with Bishop Thomas Grace of Sacramento and Father James Cleary of St. Paul. An embarrassment occurred at the subsequent provincial meeting. On reviewing the consultors' list, the bishops readily nominated Montgomery as *dignissimus* and Cleary as *dignus* but an unexpected difficulty arose when Grace excluded himself from the *terna*. In place of replacing the vacancy with Yorke, the bishops named as *dignior*, Bishop Thomas Conaty, Rector of the Catholic University of America, who had originally polled only two votes from Riordan's consultors.

The explanation for the final list sent to Propaganda elaborated on Yorke's unfitness for the episcopate. First, he was too young, merely a curate in a parish, one who has had no administrative experience. More importantly, the bishops' report continued, his constant entanglement in politics had made him "obnoxious to the larger and more sensible segment of the people." To the detriment of the priestly dignity, he had quarreled constantly with political factions and leaders, so much so that his archbishop had been forced to dismiss him from the office of chancellor and to deflate him to the less responsible position of curate. His behavior, the bishops noted, had been repugnant to both the sound members of the clergy and to the laity. The report also referred to the recent articles in the *Leader* on the Gaelic chair at the Catholic University. Charges were repeated that the trustees — who included Cardinal Gibbons — had deliberately misapplied the endowment, an obviously overstated argument. For all these reasons the unanimous recommendation regarding Yorke was that "the Holy See never promote him to so great a dignity."[25] This devastating commentary finished whatever chance Yorke may have had to advance to the episcopacy as long as Riordan was alive. Thus when the Diocese of Monterey-Los Angeles became vacant in 1903 with Montgomery's transfer to San Francisco as Riordan's coadjutor, the diocesan consultors met to suggest a successor and nominated two priests of San Francisco, William O'Connor and Patrick Cummins. It was significant that Peter Yorke with whom they were better acquainted as an editor and lecturer was not considered.[26]

In 1903 Yorke was given his first official appointment in nearly five years when he was named pastor of St. Anthony's Church, Oakland.[27] Even with the San Francisco Bay dividing him and the archbishop, the strain continued. In 1906 a substantial portion of Yorke's parish was assigned to neighboring St. Elizabeth's, a German national parish that had now been given territorial boundaries. Yorke protested the division of his parish and appealed to the apostolic delegate, Archbishop Falconio.[28] On his part, Riordan charged that Yorke's appeal was "full of misrepresentations and glaring untruths," and he asked the delegate for permission to arbitrate a settlement. Otherwise, as he told a friend, the result would be the infinite complication of dividing parishes as well as a "triumph given to intrigue and mendacity."[29] At the delegate's order, a neutral board was named; and the outcome was what Riordan had initially prescribed, the creation of St. Elizabeth's as a territorial parish with its boundaries as originally proposed.[30]

Yorke's continued work through the *Leader*, meanwhile, kept him in Riordan's view. In 1906 the weekly took up a spirited defense of Abe Ruef and Eugene Schmitz, Mayor of San Francisco, both of whom the grand jury had indicted on counts of graft. Riordan deplored this new crusade. "This man Yorke," he told Keane, "is engaged in politics of the dirtiest kind. . . .He is never at home in his parish. He is in his newspaper office doing politics and making money out of them."[31] But the archbishop was acquainted with the power of political priests, especially the lessons learned in New York during the turbulent term of Archbishop Michael A. Corrigan. He was still reluctant to bridle Yorke punitively. "I am powerless to stop him," he confided to O'Connell. "If I did, we would have a worse trouble on our hands than McGlynn caused in New York."[32]

Only three years later the apostolic delegate made inquiries concerning the *Leader* and Father Yorke's relationship, and Riordan decided to move, though quietly and indirectly. In 1909 he assured Falconio that Yorke had been alerted to the general regulations governing the editing of newspapers and periodicals. Riordan even acknowledged his temptation to use the penalty of suspension of any priest, including Yorke, for such activity; but there appeared no genuinely effective means of control.[33] The archbishop had long nursed the notion that newspaper work, even in Catholic publications, regularly played a curiously distorting effect on priests. They were constantly subject, Riordan would tell a confidant, to losing "their heads because their little articles are read outside of their own small circle."[34] Despite his quandary regarding Yorke, Riordan began at once on the draft of a public letter to the clergy. After months of meticulous preparation, the document was published on October 12, 1909.[35] Its argument scrupulously based on irreproachable papal sources, it strictly forbade the clergy from participating in "public discussions and newspaper controversies of a political character." Though Yorke's name was never invoked, Riordan's strategy succeeded. For the

second time within a decade, Yorke displayed the capacity to
submit to the discipline of his superior. Three days after the
publication of the letter, he formally resigned from the
Leader. It was his candid fear, he told the weekly's manager,
that "unscrupulous and designing persons" would exploit
Riordan's poor health to precipitate a scandalous public
argument between them. He promised to publish only an
occasional article in the weekly with his by-line.[36] This
remarkable self-restraint may have signaled the first thawing
between Yorke and the archbishop.

Through the years, Peter Yorke had accumulated a
considerable number of enemies, some condemning political
entanglements of any Catholic priest, and others violently
clashing with him over specific issues. In 1911 two petty
crises arose, both of which erupted beyond Yorke's apparent
control and could have destroyed the harmony. In private
correspondence, Father Joseph M. Gleason had recalled
Yorke's past activities in a notably unfriendly tone. "I am
familiar with the history of this Archdiocese," Gleason had
written.

> I wrote the official account published on the oc-
> casion of the fiftieth anniversary of its foundation,
> and I have been assigned also the article on this
> subject in the Catholic Encyclopedia. Now, in the
> history of this archdiocese there has [sic] been two
> priests only, who could be called priest-policitians.
> One is dead, the living one is Father York [sic].[37]

Yorke had intercepted this letter and forwarded it to
Riordan, contending that Gleason's statements alleged
political activities explicitly forbidden in the archdiocese. "If
I am [guilty]," urged Yorke, "then Your Grace is remiss in
your duty in not proceeding against me. If I am not, then the
Rev. Joseph M. Gleason is a common slanderer."[38] The
archbishop, however, refused to be trapped in this dilemma
and thereby encourage a quarrel. Evidently, Riordan

was satisfied that Yorke had kept his pledge and quietly
dismissed Gleason's complaint.[39]

A bizarre and more serious emergency arose shortly after
when Joseph T. Harrington, manager of the *Leader*,
published a "Detective Report" in pamphlet form which he
circulated in the "strictest confidence." Years before, Father
Yorke had been engaged in a lively newspaper war with the
San Francisco *Star* which was edited by his former colleague
during the Great Controversy, James H. Barry. During their
conflict, the *Leader* had employed an undercover agent
whose extensive reports were published unvarnished.   He
allegedly uncovered a conspiracy against Yorke which
included Archbishop Riordan and a number of notables
among the clergy and laity. A copy of the pamphlet, Riordan
learned, had reached the new apostolic delegate, Archbishop
John Bonzano, and had made "the worst possible impression
upon him." The latter was thoroughly provoked at this odd
publication and had stated that he had absolutely no patience
with such underground methods.[40] Mildly alarmed at this
latest development, Riordan was still confident meanwhile,
of Yorke's fidelity and elected to investigate some others
involved. He was particularly interested in the authenticity of
a particular passage wherein Father Robert E. Kenna, S.J.,
former president of Santa Clara College, had been reportedly
distressed that the archbishop had broken his agreement with
the conspirators in failing to "side with us and come out
openly and crush" Yorke. "But, for some unaccountable
reason," Kenna was quoted to have told the agent, "he failed
to respond. But you know you never have the Archbishop for
a minute. He is peculiar."[41]

In explaining this statement, Kenna indignantly denied
any complicity in the intrigue and characterized the brief
description of Riordan attributed to him as "false as hell."
Ever since his first appointment to the college in 1883, the
Jesuit educator had long been an alert witness to
ecclesiastical developments in California. Despite sharp
differences of opinion, he had made a conscious effort to
pronounce a careful and impartial judgment on Peter Yorke,

ever regarding him as a splendidly talented priest whom he would have rejoiced to have seen promoted to a high position. In his elaboration to Riordan, he offered a curious assessment of Yorke's character and career. "I have always admired Father Yorke," commented Kenna, "but I am not one of his followers." He then continued:

> He has wondrous gifts and glorious qualities; but there are lacking in his character certain qualities essential in a great and safe man. Had he a wise mentor, a true friend who could advise him and whom he would follow he would have been one of the greatest glories of the Church in America. This is the simple truth. I should have said, if he had the humility to follow the advice of such a friend, he would have been a glory and a bulwark of the Church in America, for he had such a great and wise friend who was his father and who would have guided him safely, surely, wisely in his work. That mentor, God-given to him, was his Archbishop, whom he deserted and in an evil moment disobeyed and became his own guide. Pride, self-confidence and intense malevolence in his animosities and other kindred passions that ruled him drove Father Yorke to many things that are hard to explain in a Christian Priest and were the cause of many miscarriages and failures that brought sorrow to the hearts of thousands, and I think it none more than the great, good Father and Archbishop to whom he was an ingrate.[42]

The history of the relationship between Archbishop Riordan and Father Yorke presents a stormy record of high hopes and grave disappointments, but before the end there had come an open reconciliation.

In his last years Patrick Riordan never yielded to a petty vindictiveness toward Yorke, never failing to acknowledge his splendid attributes and zeal; and apparently

Yorke never broke the covenant with Riordan. Past
wounds hindered these two churchmen from restoring
the original bond between them, but the archbishop
professed an enduring affection for his former chancellor.
Riordan was present in December, 1912, when Yorke
commemorated his silver anniversary in the priesthood.
The festive celebration proceeded customarily until the
conclusion of the solemn Mass when Riordan delivered a
most feeling and personal tribute to the celebrant. When he
had received the invitation to attend, he began, he had
marveled at the quick passage of these twenty-five years, it
seeming "only a few days ago that he came from Baltimore
to begin here his work in the ministry and afterwards under
my own roof." In a particularly moving passage, the prelate,
who by this time was feeling the burden of his seventy-one
years, joyously recalled the past quarter century, especially
the historic days of the Great Controversy. "Looking back
over all these years," he said, addressing his clergy and
Yorke's parishioners,

> I can only say in all truth that, although my life,
> now necessarily coming to a close, has been in
> many ways cast in pleasant places, the most
> pleasant years of my ministry among you are those
> that I spent when Father Yorke lived with me,
> when as a young man he was set apart to carry out
> a vocation which I saw in him, the defense of
> religion and the providing of things necessary for
> the mental sustenance of our people.
>
> When. . . we were attacked on all sides, I set
> Father Yorke to combat our enemies: and I need
> not tell you that he has won a debt of gratitude for
> that work which can never be sufficiently repaid.
> And as I sit down some times in moments of lei-
> sure, though they be few — and the moments of
> a man coming to the close of life are generally
> full of reminiscences, living more in the past days
> of my episcopal ministry, days of conflict and of

strife, but days of victory — days that under my
roof, the one who is now your pastor spent in the
service of religion and in the building up of the
Kingdom of God.

I am glad that we have lived to see this day. I
am glad that so many priests of the Archdiocese
have assembled around him to hear these words of
praise. But the younger members of the clergy can
never know what debt of gratitude and of gratifi-
cation we who are older must cherish in ourselves
until the day of our death for him who in the days
of strife led the hosts of our Holy Church into
battle and always came out victorious.

You cannot feel this probably as I do, you
young men, for you have only heard of his achievements, but we older ones have lived with him and
seen him face to face. . . .It was a great pleasure to
be present, when these great things were done, and
in those moments of our lives, when we are not
busy with other things, we sit down and are happy
in the thought of them.[43]

Perhaps these sentiments, as touching as they were, were
meant as much for Yorke's critics as for the jubilarian.

Riordan's recovery of affection for Yorke was last
revealed a year later when he brought the priest back to San
Francisco and awarded him St. Peter's Parish, a large and
important parish where Yorke had worked for four years as a
curate. Yorke himself acknowledged the "princely spirit" in
which the appointment was made.[44] Not all were pleased.
Francis J. Sullivan, brother-in-law of James Phelan, expressed
his annoyance over the promotion, recalling the "feud"
between the archbishop and the priest. In response, Riordan
denied any "feud," shrewdly adding that such advancements
were governed by canonical procedures.[45]

* * * * *

One secret of Patrick Riordan's strength was his capacity
to follow up large commitments, such as the new cathedral,
seminary, the Pious Fund, and Newman Hall. Death,
however, prevented him from seeing two important projects
to completion. The first disappointment concerned unhappy
conditions in the Diocese of Salt Lake. Lawrence Scanlan
was, in the judgment of most who knew him, an ideal
churchman. In his tour of 1900, Father Walter McDonald had
included a two-day visit to Salt Lake City. "A model bishop
if ever there was one," recalled the seminary professor. "He
worked and looked like any Irish curate." To McDonald's
astonishment, Scanlan seemed to be one of the few Catholics
who had achieved a working accommodation with the
Mormon majority. Unlike other Christians in the area, the
bishop refrained from publicly denouncing polygamy. This
practice, Scanlan explained to the visitor, outright as it was
among the Mormons, was "not a whit worse—but better, if
anything" than some of the clandestine habits of their most
righteous critics.[46]

Riordan shared McDonald's admiration for his pioneer
prelate. He had promoted his appointments as vicar apostolic
and ordinary and then spared no effort in keeping Scanlan in
this unique western post. After nearly forty years of
exemplary and heroic work in Utah, Riordan was nonetheless
forced to alert his suffragan to repeated complaints related to
his diocese. In late 1912, Archbishop John Bonzano, the
apostolic delegate, sounded out Riordan regarding certain
unnamed reports alleging deplorable conditions into which
Scanlan's diocese had fallen. Diocesan institutions and
interests were neglected, it was charged. The quality of the
clergy was low; Catholic education was not promoted; and
the bishop seemed to be controlled by a malevolent vicar
general.[47] This news came as a severe shock to Riordan.
There was perhaps no more "apostolic" priest whom Riordan
knew than Lawrence Scanlan. This Irish-born missionary had
lived in the greatest poverty and never abandoned this most
trying assignment. The old bishop, Riordan would confess,
was not erudite, his life spent in going from one mining camp

and railroad town to another; but he had a store of practical wisdom and good sense. Largely through appeals to European mission-aid societies, he was able to finance awesome enterprises—a cathedral, hospitals, an orphanage, and several schools—all of which had earned the metropolitan's respect. Alongside of Scanlan through this long struggle stood his stalwart vicar general, Father Dennis Kiely.

In framing his report to the delegate, Riordan launched into a spirited defense of his suffragan and the vicar general. There was no question that Catholic education and interests have been supported as much as possible in Utah. As long, however, as Scanlan was forced to accept unattached priests into the diocese, Riordan acknowledged, he was compelled to take risks in personnel. Perhaps, Riordan hoped, this problem would be solved when native vocations in the diocese would develop and be trained at St. Patrick's Seminary. Father Kiely, continued the archbishop, was the busiest man he had ever known, having served the diocese for nearly forty years and established a solid newspaper that managed to survive in such a sparse population. Years ago, Kiely had requested permission to return to San Francisco, his original diocese; but the citizens of Salt Lake City, Catholics and non-Catholics as well, anxiously sought the archbishop to keep Kiely with them. Such local admiration seemed to deflate the charges that Kiely had abused his office. Riordan suspected that the source of the complaint was the Marist Fathers. This community managed All Hallows College in Salt Lake City and were in conflict with Scanlan over the question whether their school chapel may have open services. Though the delegate had not indicated any sources, Riordan volunteered Scanlan's position regarding this quarrel. The bishop, it was argued, has had to oppose the Marists because their competition in public services violated the contract with the diocese and would destroy the cathedral parish. While able yet to govern the territory, Scanlan was painfully crippled with rheumatism, and the prospects of an auxiliary seemed agreeable to him. When he might become disposed to request one, the bishop would need the soundest counsel; otherwise,

Riordan cautioned, he would likely make a great error in judgment.[48]

True to his nature, however, the archbishop chose to pursue the issue on his own authority. In such a sensitive matter, however, Riordan overestimated Scanlan's confidence in him; and in his further efforts to assist his accused friend, his intentions were misinterpreted as an attempt to interfere. Alluding obliquely to the delegate, Riordan confidentially relayed the charges to Scanlan and inquired whether Kiely was feuding with the Marists, refusing to advertise their school in his newspaper. This letter evoked a heartily indignant reply from Scanlan. The Marists, Riordan learned, had never offered to pay for any advertisements in Kiely's paper and had never even taken a subscription. Scanlan severely scolded the archbishop for having quoted anonymous charges—attributed to "this mysterious 'some one'"—and threatened to write directly to the delegate about the accusations and sources. No one was needed to defend Salt Lake, warned Scanlan, including the metropolitan: "All I wish is the facts and name or names of the miscreants and I will defend myself."[49]

Riordan had inadvertently placed himself in an awkward position, and the delegate's next communiqué did not relieve the discomfort. Archbishop Bonzano declined to implicate the Marists or to identify his sources of information, except to say that they were "various and reliable." The metropolitan was then directed to persuade his suffragan, now aroused and angry, to petition in favor of a coadjutor or auxiliary.[50] But Riordan knew that at the moment he could ask nothing of Scanlan. Though he was the bishop's most loyal friend, Scanlan ironically suspected that Riordan was the origin of these nameless accusations. Nevertheless, Riordan favored the appointment of a coadjutor and began to consider candidates—"a good man about forty or forty-two years of age," he felt, "level headed, with a gift of ready speech—he need not be an orator—and with good business capacity."[51]

To evaluate the charges himself, Riordan sought out Thomas Kearns, a former United States Senator. Scanlan's rheumatism, it was learned, had forced him to spend several months annually at a sanitarium in Arizona, and Kiely was fast losing his sight if he was not already totally blind. "There seems to be no head," Kearns sadly commented and urged Riordan to conduct a visitation.[52] With this information, Riordan casually passed through Salt Lake City on a spring holiday trip to Chicago but failed to convince his suffragan of the need for a coadjutor with the right of succession. The bishop would, however, accept only an auxiliary proposed by Scanlan alone. For the first time in thirty years, there might be named in this province a bishop regarding whose nomination Riordan would have no final word, and the delegate consented to this arrangement.[53] The last months of the archbishop's life were spent in searching out prospects for Scanlan's list. There were handicaps. The office of auxiliary bishop, Riordan had long argued, offered no canonical security and would not interest the superior kind of priest needed to assist Scanlan. The search was in vain. Scanlan's own list of candidates was discarded by Rome, and within his last week alive, Riordan was asked to compile a new list of his own, an assignment to which he was not allowed to attend.[54]

The second major frustration encountered in these last days was Riordan's near success of partially restoring the classical curriculum for the Christian Brothers. For the archbishop, the historic "Latin Question" commenced in 1897 when in Paris the general chapter of the brothers forbade the teaching of Latin and Greek in their American schools. The study of the classics, it was argued, was contrary to the rule of the Institute and would divide the congregation into "patrician" brothers who taught these subjects in the exclusive academics and the "plebeian" brothers who served basic programs in elementary schools. This decision profoundly affected one of the major teaching orders in the United States. Before the turn of the century, the study of the classical tongues had served as a basis for a liberal

education, and Latin had been therefore required in several
states for a teacher's certificate. The classics were also an
essential part of professional education, such as law,
medicine, and theology.[55] Hence, several prelates were ready
to protest the decision as forcefully as possible, among them
Patrick Riordan in whose archdiocese the brothers operated
Sacred Heart College in San Francisco and St. Mary's College
in Oakland. The removal of the classics from the instructional
program, in Riordan's view, would be "disastrous."[56]

Within two years consensus had been reached among the
archbishops that the classics be restored as soon as possible.
Otherwise, the brothers' schools in America would lose their
enrollment to the public systems. By 1899, the archbishops
were ready to appeal to Rome, appointing Bishop Thomas S.
Byrne of Nashville to present Propaganda with their petition
in favor of annulling the prohibition of the classics. But after
a stay of over six months in the Eternal City, he was unable
to win a decision. Impatient with delays, the archbishops
then commissioned Riordan in Washington to present their
appeal again when he was to be in Rome shortly on his
second *ad limina* journey.[57] Riordan would be a devoted
advocate. In the previous year, nine students from Sacred
Heart College had entered the new St. Patrick's Seminary.
The prohibition of the classical curriculum would virtually
eliminate this source of vocations and pre-seminary training.
If the American brothers, he had already concluded himself,
were still forbidden to teach the classics, the Holy See should
grant their autonomy from the French Institute.[58] During
his visit in Rome, Propaganda ruled against the archbishop's
petition, upholding the policy prohibiting the study of the
classics. When this decision was announced, Riordan, it was
noted, exhibited neither surprise nor sorrow. But he
communicated the outcome to Bishop Byrne, then in Cairo,
with the words: "We are irrevocably condemned."[59]

The chief impetus for repeal would have to come from
the hierarchy. The American brothers who had opposed the
prohibition had received severe reprisals from their superiors,
and they could hardly be expected to work alone for a

revocation of policy. "Our Bros.," Denis O'Connell was told, "are afraid to open their mouths about it. The Sups. would certainly punish."[60] Riordan was not himself reconciled to Propaganda's decision. From a long correspondence with Brother Justin McMahon, founder of the California province, he was encouraged to support such compromise solutions as having lay instructors teach the classics in the brothers' schools—an arrangement which would conform literally to the prohibition and satisfy the educational needs of the archdiocese. Consequently, Riordan was instrumental in having the archbishops in 1906 direct another petition to Pope Pius X.[61] Though he assisted in the early drafts of the document, the San Francisco earthquake denied him a more active role, and the effort dissolved without conclusion. A year later, nevertheless, he made inquiries regarding the petition, ready to take up the cause again at Propaganda during his third *ad limina* pilgrimage to Rome.[62]

Only in the last year of his life was Riordan able to make some progress against the resistance to the classics, and, significantly, it was an individual effort. In late 1913, he offered an unusual compromise to Cardinal Gaetano De Lai, Secretary of the Congregation of the Consistory. After the disaster of 1906, De Lai was told, the archbishop had been forced to relocate the brothers' high school near the cathedral, having invested well over a million *lire* for the property and buildings. In the new school, which belonged to the archdiocese, a special room was reserved wherein a diocesan priest would teach the classical languages. Unfortunately, Riordan continued, since the brothers' superiors seemed unwilling to accept even this arrangement, he was compelled to appeal directly to the Vatican to endorse an accommodation which did not violate Propaganda's ruling of 1899. At the moment of his writing, Riordan warned, Sacred Heart College was the only fully operative Catholic high school in his see city, the Jesuit academy yet having limited facilities. A city as large as San Francisco would be deprived if its only restored Catholic high school failed to offer a classical curriculum.[63]

The archbishop's persuasive efforts almost succeeded
until a strange sequence of events intervened. In early 1914,
the Congregation of Religious granted an indult authorizing
Riordan's plan: Latin could be taught in Sacred Heart
College by an instructor who did not belong to the Institute.
But the Institute's authorities in Rome would not yield to
this exception, and their vigorous insistence forced the
congregation to suspend the execution of the indult.
Scheduled to visit Rome in the summer, Bishop Hanna
planned to settle this awkward matter. The auxiliary
bishop appealed directly to Pope Pius X, who ordered the
indult to be executed as planned. Unfortunately, Hanna's
tactic met with two reversals. The Holy Father, first, failed to
commit his concession to writing before his death in August,
1914; and the congregation and Institute were both
embarrassed because of his negotiations beyond them. The
election of a new pope and the outbreak of World War I
beclouded the issue with more confusion. It was soon
rumored that in October Benedict XV had confirmed what
his predecessor had granted, and the Institute's Procurator
General in Rome gravely feared that San Francisco would
have its exception. The congregation, however, refused to
execute the indult until it received a written papal rescript. It
likewise encouraged the Institute itself to confront the pope
in this matter and wondered in the meantime what Riordan
would do in San Francisco. Would he immediately implement
the verbal concession of a deceased pope or first request an
official confirmation from the congregation?[64] On the edge
of success, however, Patrick Riordan died before he made his
choice.

* * * * *

To nearly the end of his seventy-three years of life,
Patrick Riordan remained in full command of his powers,
alert to the great issues of the day, although there appeared
frequent symptoms of melancholy and depression. In his last
year, 1914, he often deplored the unpromising conditions in

San Francisco, where the city was filling up with hundreds of
unemployed and where it was nearly impossible to secure
loans from the banks. For that reason he eagerly looked
forward to the Panama-Pacific Exposition in the following
year to relieve the financial constriction. A chronic critic of
the administration of Woodrow Wilson, he studied the results
of the congressional elections of 1914, interpreting them as
evidence of the President's lack of popularity and
anticipating a restoration of a Republican regime in 1916.
The outbreak of World War I had a pronounced effect upon
the old archbishop who had spent a large portion of his life in
Europe. Day by day he followed the scattered press reports
on the German devastation of his beloved Belgium,
desperately seeking information about the American College
at Louvain and its rector, Monsignor Jules De Becker. In
October, the second full month of hostilities, Riordan
painfully lamented what he conceived to be the fate of the
Belgian Church and its ancient university, and he told his
brother:

> The dreadful war still goes on, and although the
> papers seem to hint at the success of the Allies, I
> am inclined to think that Germany is getting the
> best of it so far. Poor Belgium is now declared to
> be a German province, and of course we know
> what that means, if the Germans succeed in coming
> out of this war victoriously, then the Religious will
> have to go; the Jesuit Fathers will have to go; the
> University will have to go; and all the schools will
> become State schools. It is a dreadful thing to
> contemplate. But we cannot tell what yet may
> occur.[65]

While he was not especially saturnine in temperament,
Riordan's private correspondence reflected concern over his
approaching end when in 1911 Patrick J. Ryan died, the
Archbishop of Philadelphia who had been appointed in 1884,
the same year in which Riordan had succeeded to the See of

San Francisco. In Riordan's ingenuous judgment, Ryan had been an impeccable ecclesiastic whose advancement had come unsought, having, as he said, "no one engineering a way and devising plans to bring honors to him."[66] Riordan had known Ryan well in these latter days. His passing prompted the Archbishop of San Francisco to reflect soberly: "One by one the older men are dropping out. I am now, and have been for some years, the senior Archbishop of the entire country with the exception of the Cardinal. It is a fact which makes one think and be ready."[67] Subsequent accounts of the elaborate obsequies in Philadelphia for Ryan distressed Riordan, whose simple inclinations preferred quiet, unadorned observances to the lavish spectacle described in the press. He was firmly opposed to such shows, he commented to his brother. He believed it far more appropriate to have confined the funeral to the cathedral and placed the remains in the vault immediately after the services. "It was against good taste, I think, to take the remains around the block, and expose it to the gaze of an irreverent and thoughtless crowd."[68]

Ever since he had been forced a half century earlier to discontinue his priestly studies at the American College in Rome, Riordan had accumulated a history of chronically poor health. Even with the relaxation of duties after Bishop Hanna's coming to San Francisco, his health steadily deteriorated. He had long been troubled with a bladder condition which had made impossible his attendance at long ceremonies. In late 1913 an infection set in, provoking painful skin eruptions on his lower limbs and temporarily confining him to the hospital. "I am confined to my bed a prisoner," he told Spalding, "and a prisoner suffering a great more than I can put into words. However, these are the miseries that advancing years bring to most people, and I have only to be resigned to the will of Almighty God."[69] Dr. John B. Murphy of Chicago, a close friend and one of the outstanding surgeons in the United States, had intimated to him that he would be compelled soon to face an operation, at first offering to perform it himself if Riordan would come to

Illinois. Upon closer study of the patient's strength and age, however, Murphy expressed a doubt whether he should submit to surgery. The archbishop thereby postponed the operation and was able after several weeks to leave the hospital and to find a large measure of relief from his frequent visits to the seminary. "Now I am much better but the cause of the whole trouble remains," he reported during these fatiguing days, "and I never know when an attack may come, so I am a very uncertain quantity as to work. The only thing to do is to be fully prepared when the time comes to be taken away from this life."[70]

The final important function performed by the aging prelate was to preside at the funeral of Monsignor John Prendergast, who died on January 19, 1914. His vicar general had been for over half a century an outstanding priest and one of the last clerical pioneers in California. For five years Riordan had sadly noted his visible decline ever since Prendergast's golden jubilee in the priesthood in 1909. On the eve of the funeral, Riordan described for Father Dan how the old priest had gradually faded away, suffering no pain and passing into eternity "as a child goes to sleep." For the fifty-four years of his priesthood, Prendergast had been a true and noble churchman, added the archbishop, a model to the clergy and laity of San Francisco, but, he mused further: "There is hardly anybody left now who met me and greeted me thirty years ago; they have gone, and their children take their places. . . ."[71]

His own end was not distant. Toward the close of the year he often complained of the strain and fatigue at the chancery, commenting that his work had seemingly increased a hundred-fold in the past six years. As the feast of Christmas approached, there was not the least concern over his health, as he spent the previous week dedicating a new chapel and attending the funeral of an old friend. On December 23, however, he caught cold, his throat became congested and made swallowing difficult. As a fever rose, nurses were sent to the archbishop's residence and additional physicians were called into consultation. Although his household was

alarmed, the archbishop's condition was far from critical.
Nevertheless, as his temperature continued to rise, Dr. J.
Wilson Shiels advised the administration of the last rites
which Riordan received fully conscious and making the
responses in a firm, clear voice. He appeared soon after to
regain his strength and to rest quietly with the result that
friends again became hopeful of his recovery. On December
27, 1914, shortly before dawn, however, the housekeeper
looked in on the patient, and finding him breathing
irregularly she aroused the others in the house. Patrick
Riordan was dying, his respiration growing fainter and
fainter, until it ceased entirely at 4:04 A.M., one day short
of three full decades as Archbishop of San Francisco.[72]

As soon as word of his death circulated through the
country, a flood of messages streamed into San Francisco,
expressing condolences and tributes to his memory. His
trusted associate in St. Paul, John Ireland, was stricken by
the news, telegramming: "The Church has lost a valiant
soldier, the American Hierarchy one of its most brilliant
members, myself the truest of friends. Deep is my grief."
Among the other messages, Archbishop John B. Pitaval of
Santa Fe lamented the loss of "one of the greatest pioneers
of the far west," and Father Edward Dyer, S.S., the
American superior of the Sulpician Fathers, wired: "A great
leader has been taken from us and the Church of America
mourns."[73] The man whose destinies had been altered by the
deceased and who would soon be commissioned to carry on
his work, Edward J. Hanna, in an eloquent statement
described his patron as a "noble man, a loyal friend, a
faithful priest, a mighty ruler of the flock of Christ." His
achievements in California, he proclaimed, compared
favorably with those of the most distinguished members of
the hierarchy, leaving to his successor "a united, loyal,
faithful people, a cultured clergy, a wealth of magnificent
institutions."[74]

The funeral took place on the last day of 1914, preceded
by a vigil at the cathedral where the body had lain in state for
three days. Six western prelates came to San Francisco for

the obsequies—Archbishop Alexander Christie of Portland, Oregon, Bishops John P. Carroll of Helena, Charles J. O'Reilly of Baker, Oregon, and Edward J. O'Dea of Seattle, and two suffragans, Bishops Conaty and Grace. The latter celebrated the pontifical requiem Mass, and Bishop Hanna preached the eulogy. After the absolutions before the altar, an elaborate procession escorted the coffin to Holy Cross Cemetery, where Hanna pronounced the final prayers. The remains of Patrick Riordan were then sealed within the crypt.[75]

* * * * * *

The career of Patrick Riordan had embraced a manifold variety of experiences and achievements, and a rehearsal of its highlights would point to the extraordinary executive abilities of a patrician churchman. What may be overlooked, however, is that beneath this strength of character lay the flesh and blood of a man who formed the deepest and most abiding of loyalties and who was tender and gentle to those whom he loved. His aristocratic and highly efficient manner must not obscure the warm humanity which had given to his person another rich dimension. It was he who could, as an illustration, include within his numerous interests the spiritual welfare of Mrs. Leland Stanford, sending her religious books and visiting her often in Palo Alto. In 1904, when she was touring the world, the archbishop had requested acquaintances in Italy to prepare for her arrival and extend their hospitality, remarking: "A little kindness might be all that is needed to bring her into the fold of the Church."[76] His efforts had failed to win her conversion, but when her unexpected death in the following year ended a fifteen-year friendship, he acknowledged, perhaps with no exaggeration, to her niece, Jennie Lathrop, that nothing since his arrival in California had ever moved him so deeply as the passing of this "great and good woman."[77]

His own spirituality had been simple, genuine, and thoroughly masculine. The Mass had remained central to this priest, and in his thirty-one years in San Francisco, he had never accepted an offering, desiring to leave himself free for his own intentions and the requests of friends. "I have always kept the Sacrifice of the Mass free from anything like money or personal favors," he told a close lay friend. "It is too transcendent a thing in my judgment... to connect it with money or temporal things." Throughout his episcopate he had invariably offered Mass on each Saturday for his living friends and benefactors and on each Monday for deceased ones.[78]

Seldom have men who have been characterized as financial wizards displayed the sensitivity and personal generosity of Patrick Riordan. Perhaps this characteristic was the secret as to how he was able to persuade the wealthy laity to endow his projects. "Generosity is contagious," he had often been heard to say, "the generous man can always awaken the spirit in his fellows." Members of his household knew of his private benefactions, on such occasions as when on ship he had once organized an appeal among the passengers for the family of a Neapolitan seaman who had fallen from the rigging to his death, or when a few days before his own death his magnanimity rescued a stranger from prison and public disgrace. Never known to miss an appointment, his efficient manner reflected a thoughtfulness. If expected at an assembly, he was punctual to the instant; he would tolerate in himself not even a delay of five minutes. Whenever possible, he answered his letters, even a child's, on the day of its receipt.[79]

Patrick Riordan was able to harmonize dignity with genuine simplicity. Peter Yorke recalled two characteristics of his work: "Whatever he did, he did in princely fashion, and he did it without display...."[80] While he lived at his first residence at 1122 Eddy Street, students from nearby Sacred Heart College warmly recalled the archbishop's regular stroll to Frank's barber shop on Larkin Street. There, it was remembered, "he would wait his turn like any other man in the shop, regardless of the fuss 'Frank' made over him and the flurry into which His Grace's entrance threw things generally."[81] This lack of pretension survived his major successes. After the settlement of the classic Pious Fund litigation at the World Court, the archbishop never used the historic case to enlarge his reputation at home, wiring to his secretary that upon his return no reception would take place.[82] Years later, Riordan and William Nichols, the Episcopal Bishop of California, had been elected honorary members of the Pacific Union Club in San Francisco. For many, it was a coveted honor to be cited by one of the most exclusive organizations in the world as one of the "distinguished citizens of the United States."[83] Though he moved easily with men of means and power, the archbishop betrayed no interest in belonging to their clubs. When Bishop Nichols suggested a public dinner in celebration of the award, Riordan gracefully declined, commenting further: "Its publicity would be strangely interpreted by a good many people, especially the poor."[84]

At intervals, of course, difficulties arose in dealing with this prelate. Occasionally it was troublesome for subordinates to detect a consistency in him, a predicament noted during the negotiations of a theology faculty at Menlo Park. "Though one is never absolutely sure with his Grace that he will not modify his statements later, however emphatic he appears to be," the rector desperately confided to his superior, "yet I think that in the present we have his last word."[85] His first director of Newman Hall in Berkeley never forgot Riordan's inclination to become a bit angry without much provocation. During the building of the Hall, Father Thomas Verner Moore had requested sturdy oak floors. When he suggested to the archbishop that the architect's choice of pine would quickly deteriorate under the heavy shoes of the students, Riordan thundered: "Nonsense!" Pique could rapidly evolve into full fury, as Moore soon discovered, when he was shortly banished from California.[86] Little wonder that in 1902 during the negotiations for a successor to Archbishop Feehan some clergy of Chicago eyed Riordan as a "disciplinarian."[87]

These flares of harshness, however, could not suppress the tender spirit beneath. Riordan was perhaps the most concerned confrère who had long watched the decline of the venerable John Prendergast, pastor of the cathedral for forty-three years. On the occasion of Prendergast's golden jubilee in the priesthood, Riordan had thoughtfully arranged through Cardinal Merry del Val the conferral of a domestic prelacy, with the title of "monsignor." In his last days, when the vicar general was confined largely to his apartment, Riordan transferred in the most graceful fashion the administration of the cathedral to Father Charles Ramm. To his death, Prendergast remained the pastor, and Ramm had been told simply to "take hold of things."[88] Another object of the archbishop's affectionate solicitude was Peter Yorke. In 1913 the priest had published a collection of sermons under the title *Altar and Priest*. The volume contained a notable eulogy delivered over his benefactor, Peter Casey, who had taken the ex-chancellor as curate at St. Peter's when Riordan had left no assignment. The nostalgic sermon ended with a stinging sentence that referred to this unpleasantry of thirteen years earlier. "At a time when I sorely needed a friend," Yorke had preached, "he was a good friend to me."[89] Nevertheless, Riordan took no offense at the remark and was pleased to receive the volume. "It is hard to put down, once it is taken up, without finishing it," commented Riordan to the author. "Though I listened to some of the sermons as they were preached, yet they seemed even more beautiful when I read them yesterday."[90]

There was no question that throughout the years Riordan spared nothing on behalf of those whom he admired. There was always a fear that Riordan's later reservations about the Catholic University might complicate his relationship with its foremost champion, Cardinal Gibbons. In 1911 Gibbons estimated that the annual collection for the support of the institution might not be taken up in San Francisco after the ten-year pledge had expired. Riordan strongly assured the cardinal of his personal support. "I have known you and loved you too many years," was his word to Baltimore, "not to be always ready to give you whatever assistance it may be in my power to render whenever you ask it."[9][1] Gibbons was so touched by his profession that he sent an extraordinary reply to San Francisco. Every sentence of the archbishop's message was a delight, the cardinal said, adding almost rhapsodically:

> ...I literally kissed the paper on which it was written, and I had to say to myself, "that man has his heart in the right place; he is a man of generous impulses."[9][2]

But Riordan's personal commitments were not limited to the safe and approved figures of his time. They included those accused and even condemned on charges of heterodoxy or a fatal indiscretion. This sense of fidelity had been evident as an unflinching loyalty to the four John's—McMullen, Spalding, Ireland, and Keane—all of whom had their long moments of controversy and disfavor. Another less known indication of Riordan's capacity for personal loyalty in the midst of trial was his friendship with George Tyrrell, perhaps the most tragic figure among that noted group of liberal Catholic thinkers known as modernists. A thoroughly orthodox prelate who had duly commanded his clergy to subscribe to the oath against modernism, Riordan was no alarmist in the face of this heresy, and he had early even manifested an admiration for Tyrrell. In 1904 the archbishop had chanced upon *The Soul's Orbit*, a book which contained Tyrrell's notes on the *Spiritual Exercises* of Ignatius of Loyola. Riordan privately wondered why such a valuable and suggestive book had not been made available to the general public. In the following years, Tyrrell was confronted with the prospect of expulsion from the Society of Jesus and, without success, he applied for incardination to the Archbishops of Westminster and Dublin. Evidently, Riordan had made him some confidential offer to bring him to his archdiocese. In reply, he explained to the archbishop that the Jesuit General had made it fairly clear that I am to be secularized under somewhat onerous & vexatious conditions & that as soon as my disgrace can no longer compromise the Society I am to be the object of some sort of ecclesiastical censure. Unless I can get some very solid assurance against this menace I will certainly not risk bringing myself into possibly embarrassing relations with one so kind as Your Grace had proved. In that case, they must dismiss me on their initiative; & either provide me with a bishop or leave me in a state of suspension. I will not mention Your Grace's offer to them. Should I obtain a guarantee of peaceful intentions I may turn to you again; but assurances from diplomats are not easy to trust.[93]

Riordan's relationship with Tyrrell endured even the latter's excommunication in 1907. In one of his last requests before he died two years later, Tyrrell appealed to Riordan to accept into the archdiocese a young German priest, hoping, as he said, that in this request the archbishop "will forget the Modernist & remember the man."[94] Exhibiting a remarkable tolerance, Riordan was at first favorable to this proposal and added in reference to Tyrrell himself: ". . .there is a place for him and plenty of work for him to do in the great Church of Christ."[95]

Thus did Patrick William Riordan lead his full and purposeful life, so quietly and unobtrusively that it had never attracted attention or serious study of any kind since the writing of his obituary. Regardless of this neglect, he possessed the substance of great citizens and churchmen. Only poor health and geographic insulation had prevented him from becoming a more visible leader. A less complicated individual than Ireland or Spalding, his ultimate characteristic was personal fidelity to his colleagues, except on those few occasions when they conflicted with what he had judged as the pressing interests of religion. Few knew him better than John Lancaster Spalding who in his condolences to

Father Dan on the archbishop's death had best epitomized,
without a false sentiment, the essence that was Patrick
Riordan:

> I have loved him ever since I first met him in
> Louvain more than fifty years ago, a long span of
> life which has now shrunk to a point.
>
> He was one of the best and noblest men I have
> ever known.[96]

The Sources

This study has been based chiefly on unpublished sources. Despite Archbishop Riordan's importance, there is known to this writer neither a single monograph nor special study devoted to him, except virtual reprints of an obituary.[1] For this reason the writer used almost exclusively manuscript sources both in Europe and in the United States. A number of pertinent printed sources and newspapers were consulted to place the archbishop in his proper milieu. These secondary materials, which were indispensable to certain aspects of this study, have been explained and evaluated in the footnotes. The following survey of the writer's experiences in various depositories may be of value to the reader, while at the same time it will serve to indicate the base on which this biography depends.

The most important manuscript collection was the archives of the Sacred Congregation "de Propaganda Fide" in Rome, without which this study would have been impossible. This congregation transacted the Roman aspect of the business of the Church in the United States from its foundation to the year 1908 when jurisdiction was transferred to the Consistorial Congregation. The Propaganda archives contain a massive store of materials bearing on the most important phases of American Catholicism, and it was the writer's good fortune to be able to work directly with these materials. Regularly, the congregations of the Roman Curia commit their records every twenty-five years to the

Vatican Archives, which has thus far refused to allow consultation of items less than a century old. Propaganda is an exception, maintaining its own staff and archives[2] ; and through the intercession of the Most Reverend Leo T. Maher, Bishop of San Diego, California, the late Prefect of Propaganda, Cardinal Gregory Agagianian, permitted the examination of all pertinent American materials. The documents consulted ranged forty years, from the dispute over the Chicago succession (1868) to Archbishop Riordan's first failure to secure Edward Hanna as a coadjutor (1908). In his research efforts, the writer was constantly aided by the late Father Nicolas Kovalsky, O.M.I., the archivist, and Mr. Anthony Debevec, a research worker in the employ of the Academy of American Franciscan History.

Up to the year 1892 inclusive, the materials have been largely indexed, calendared, and divided into five series.[3] In the first collection, "Scritture originali riferite nei congressi," fifty-seven volumes are devoted to affairs in the United States and Mexico, or "America Centrale" (abbreviated as *Congressi, A.C.*), and comprise letters directed to Propaganda on various minor questions. This large series is neither indexed nor calendared but bound into large volumes chronologically. Normally, the nature of the matters related herein required the attention only of a *congresso* which is a restricted committee of Propaganda officers consisting of the prefect, the secretary, and a lower official, or *minutante* who had special competence for the United States. The second collection, "Lettere di Propaganda Fide" (abbreviated as *Lettere*) is fully calendared, comprising handwritten copies of decrees and letters of the prefect and secretary to correspondents in the United States.

The most important of the Propaganda series are the "Scritture originali riferite nelle congregazioni generali" (abbreviated *Cong. Gen.*) which contain the documents related to the formal decisions of the cardinals of the congregation. Such include the erection of dioceses, appointments of bishops, questions of ecclesiastical discipline, acts and decrees of diocesan, provincial, or national councils. Originals of the relevant incoming correspondence and documents are contained in this series, having been given to one of the cardinals, the *ponente*, who was assigned to study the question and present a report, or *ponenza*. Generally in the nineteenth century, this *ponenza* was printed, along with the more important documents, and was presented in a full session of the cardinals of Propaganda, called "general congregation." At the end of the *ponenza* the findings were summarized in the form of one or more questions, or *dubbia*, which were submitted to a vote; and the decisions of these general congregations were then submitted to the pope for sanction.

The "Acta di Sacra Congregazione" (abbreviated as *Acta*) contain simply the *ponenza* and the decisions of the congregation; and the pope and of the latter two series only the *Acta* has been indexed. The fifth series, "Udienze di Nostro Signore" (abbreviated as *Udienze*) refer to "audiences," or official meetings, between the pope and the prefect of the congregation, and record the Holy Father's granting of ecclesiastical faculties, privileges, indulgences, and other favors. This collection, too, has been indexed. Each of the five series is bound in large volumes which contain from 600 to over 1,000 folios which are numbered on their *recto* side either by hand or by stamp. Individual items dated after 1892 have not been catalogued — this is one of the good reasons why there is a reluctance to release them — and are contained loosely in folders according to topic. The writer's experience at the archives of Propaganda was one of the most rewarding and satisfying of his time spent on this study. There he noted no effort of any kind to conceal any document which he requested, nor was there any restriction beyond the dictate of fairness, in his use of controversial materials.

Examination of several diocesan archives had been of inestimable assistance in documentating Patrick Riordan's episcopate. Second in importance to Propaganda were the archives of the Archdiocese of San Francisco, housed at the chancery (445 Church Street) and consisting of a mass of

materials which had not been calendared.[4] This depository
enjoys a somewhat unique position among the original materials for Catholicism in the Far West since it contains the
papers of the earliest archbishops whose jurisdiction as
metropolitans embraced California, Nevada, and Utah. The
writer made full use of Riordan's correspondence although he
found it incomplete. Part of the story was doubtless reflected in the archbishop's remark to his brother when he
said "I am very particular in writing and you need not be
afraid that any of your letters ever remain unguarded, especially if they contain anything private."[5] Official records
cover his entire episcopate, but the vast majority of letters
incoming and outgoing date from the turn of the twentieth
century and are loosely sorted in a number of large file cases
and in fifty-six letterbooks. Unfortunately, Riordan's important correspondence with his brother, Father Daniel Riordan,
pastor of St. Elizabeth's Church in Chicago, and with Archbishop Ireland is missing, except for what appears in the
letterbooks.

Among the other metropolitan sees of the country, the
archives of the Archdiocese of Baltimore, Los Angeles, and
St. Paul yielded fruitful returns. In the chancery in Baltimore
(320 North Charles Street), the papers of Archbishop Martin
J. Spalding provided insight into the dispute on the Chicago
succession of 1868 since it was he who was appointed by the
Holy See to make a thorough investigation.[6] The papers of
Cardinal James Gibbons comprise one of the richest manuscript sources for Riordan's generation, ranging from Archbishop Alemany's search for a coadjutor to his successor's
involvement in national issues. The writer was unable to visit
Los Angeles in person, but he was supplied by the archdiocesan archivist, Monsignor Francis J. Weber, with a score
of photostated items of significance. In September, 1961,
the writer visited the Archdiocese of St. Paul, where the Ireland Papers were housed and in the process of being calendared in the St. Paul Seminary. Evidently Ireland obeyed
Riordan's frequent reminders to destroy his letters, for only
one has survived there. The late custodian of these papers,

the Reverend Patrick H. Ahern, graciously furnished photostats of this and related items.

Two diocesan archives were of maximum importance, those belonging to the Dioceses of Richmond and of Rochester. The correspondence of Denis J. O'Connell, Bishop of Richmond, has been microfilmed and is also available at both The Catholic University of America and the University of Notre Dame. Pertinent to this study was a number of letters to O'Connell, who, in the last years of the nineteenth century and into the twentieth, functioned as the Rome liaison between the Holy See and several American prelates. The Archbishop of San Francisco and Bishop Patrick Manogue trusted him in this capacity, their correspondence not only reflecting the former's position on a number of national issues but also illuminating his stormy relationship with the pioneer Bishop of Sacramento. The writer was likewise unable personally to visit Rochester, but he was given every cooperation from the diocesan archivist, the Reverend Robert F. McNamara. The McQuaid Papers include an abundance of material on Father Edward J. Hanna's early Roman years as well as Riordan's unsuccessful efforts to secure his appointment as coadjutor in 1907. These documents were photographed and promptly dispatched on request. It should be added that inquiry was made personally in Sacramento and Salt Lake City, but in the case of both these suffragan sees of San Francisco, the result was meager, though Father John J. Hedderman, Chancellor in Utah, provided a set of superb photographs.

Apart from diocesan archives, a number of institutional depositories consulted by the writer proved to be rewarding sources. One of the great libraries of the western hemisphere is the Bancroft Library on the campus of the University of California at Berkeley. This special library is devoted to collecting and servicing source materials related to the history of western North America. Although it long ago ceased to be a private collection and has become a part of the general library of the university, it maintains an independent program, with its own budget and staff. A thorough examination

of the thirty-four letterpress copy books in the papers of
John Thomas Doyle was indispensable to the treatment of
the Pious Fund Case and the subsequent dispute over the attorneys' fees, as well as other minor legal matters. While the
massive papers of James Duval Phelan yielded but a few incidental letters from Riordan on civic affairs, the Bancroft
Library has preserved rare and irreplaceable printed matter —
books, tracts, and newspapers — which offered a helpful
background for the analysis of nativism in California. The
papers of another principal in the Pious Fund Case, Jackson
Harvey Ralston, had not been indexed, but related materials
are presently available for consultation.

Another major depository was the manuscript collections
at the University of Notre Dame, splendidly arranged and
calendared under the direction of the late archivist, the Rev-
erent Thomas T. McAvoy, C.S.C., and located in ample quarters in the new Memorial Library. Various collections were
examined, such as the papers of leading Catholic laymen like
James A. McMaster, James F. Edwards, and William Onahan,
which shed considerable light on certain phases of Riordan's
career and personality. The early papers of the Archdiocese
of Cincinnati, chiefly letters to the first archbishop, John B.
Purcell, revealed new dimensions on the issue of the Chicago
succession of 1868. Since Riordan considered himself an
alumnus of this institution, a few choice items were likewise
found in his correspondence with Edward Sorin, C.S.C.,
Superior General of the Congregation of Holy Cross, and
Daniel E. Hudson, C.S.C., editor for many years of *Ave
Maria*. Of some value were the microfilmed papers of the
Society for the Propagation of the Faith at Lyons and
Fribourg which contained little directly related to the second
Archbishop of San Francisco but whose reports from pioneer
bishops and priests in the West painted a rich, though extrav-
agant, picture of early Catholicism in Riordan's province.
An attempt was made to consult the archives of the Sisters
of the Congregation of Holy Cross for material on their work
in Utah, whose depository is located nearby at St. Mary's
College, Notre Dame, Indiana. Unfortunately, a week before

the writer's arrival, a water main had burst in the archives, soaking the documents and making them unfit for use for an indefinite length of time. The Archives of the Archdiocese of Portland, Oregon, have preserved nothing relevant from the episcopate of William Gross, and his successor, Alexander Christie, was notoriously unconcerned about preserving records.

The Richard A. Gleeson Library at the University of San Francisco houses the small but significant Ralph A. Hunt Collection on Father Peter C. Yorke. An investigation yielded nothing from his correspondence since the letters preserved date from 1917. But very helpful for the discussion on nativism and Riordan's relations with Yorke were the scrapbooks, notebooks, copies of lectures, and particularly the unfinished manuscript on Yorke's life by Father John Hunt. This library also contains a rather full file of Yorke's weekly, the *Leader*, and it has lately acquired the San Francisco *Star*, the important weekly edited by James H. Barry. The California Room at the San Francisco College for Women has preserved a number of printed items of John Thomas Doyle which were pertinent to the history of the Pious Fund. The papers of Monsignor Joseph M. Gleason, once the unofficial historian of the Archdiocese of San Francisco, included nothing of interest to this biography.

The National Archives in Washington, D.C., contain the official documents related to the litigation before The Hague Tribunal in 1902 and the history of subsequent payments by Mexico to the bishops of California. The student of this case may still be disappointed at the availability of these documents since the Department of State had, at this writing, impounded the later ones and has them in its custody. An examination of the presidential papers in the manuscript collection at the Library of Congress yielded next to nothing, the McKinley, Theodore Roosevelt, Taft, and Wilson materials containing few items of immediate interest. The papers of John M. Hay in the same institution revealed nothing essential to the Pious Fund Case. A number of important items relating to the early negotiations in this case were

discovered in the papers of Stephen Mallory White, United
States Senator from California and a Catholic, which form
part of the Borel Collection in the Division of Special Collections at Stanford University. His colleague, Senator William
Morris Stewart, pursued the case to its conclusion, and typescript copies of pertinent documents were sent to the writer
by Mrs. Clara S. Beatty, Director of the Nevada State Historical Society in Reno. Before Stewart, John T. Doyle had
vainly attempted to interest Samuel L.M. Barlow, the powerful New York attorney; and his voluminous papers at the
Huntington Library, San Marino, California, contain several
interesting items from Doyle and one unexpected letter from
Riordan.

An examination of the archives of the Dominican Sisters
the the Dominican College in San Rafael, California, uncovered few significant items, but another pioneer sisterhood
in the Archdiocese of San Francisco, the Sisters of the Presentation, proved to be an abundant source for this study.
Mother Mary Ursula Lowe, P.B.V.M., generously allowed the
writer to consult documents and the handwritten "Annals"
which recorded the amalgamation of the community by
Riordan, the earthquake and fire, and a property dispute
with the archbishop. An inquiry directed to the Paulist
Fathers in New York brought the reply from Father Vincent
F. Holden, C.S.P., the late archivist, that their archives had
preserved only two inconsequential letters from Riordan.
The writer had the same disappointing experience at Newman Hall in Berkeley, where only a scrapbook had been
preserved. The same was true at St. Patrick's Seminary in
Menlo Park, California, where nothing was extant except a
diary of Father Henry Ayrinhac, S.S., and a splendid manuscript history of the seminary by John McDonough, S.S.

Two very important institutional depositories in the East
were those of the Catholic University of America and St.
Mary's Seminary in Baltimore. The administrative records
of the former and the papers of its first four rectors disclosed
Riordan's activity as a trustee and, incidentally, his involvement in several national controversies, as well as Father Peter

Yorke's erratic, earlier association with the university. The
Magnien Papers at St. Mary's Seminary at Roland Park,
Baltimore, contain a number of letters from Riordan and
George Montgomery on various questions. Most revealing
were the scattered, handwritten notes of Francis P. Havey,
S.S., an ardent student of history who recorded many inter-
views with Riordan's contemporaries. Though this source
has preserved the correspondence of the original faculty at
St. Patrick's Seminary, there are extant few letters written to
or by its long-termed superior, Father Ayrinhac. In the Santa
Barbara Mission Archives, Maynard Geiger, O.F.M., unearthed the once confidential materials related to Father
Yorke's conflict with the Franciscans over the division of
his parish.

Archbishop Riordan spent a great deal of his early life
abroad, and throughout his career he maintained connections
with several European educational institutions and religious
communities. Of primary importance were the archives of
the American College of the Immaculate Conception at the
Catholic University of Louvain, Riordan's alma mater, which
managed through two world wars to safeguard its precious
collection of records and correspondence. Half of the papers
of the college have been admirably catalogued by Father
John D. Sauter as part of his doctoral program at the University of Louvain, but the papers dated after 1898 await
sorting. Riordan's school records are intact as well as a number of his letters to various rectors. Here the papers of Monsignor Jules De Becker are as yet a valuable and untouched
source, including correspondence from missionaries in the
West and from Bishops Camillus Maes and William Stang
which related Riordan's career and loyalty to the college. Far
less success was encountered at the North American College
in Rome, where Riordan had spent one year of study, and
the same was true of several missionary colleges in Ireland.
From a personal inquiry at the American College, Rome, it
was learned that the papers and records of the archbishop's
generation had been destroyed, probably during a hasty
evacuation in World War II. The writer toured certain Irish

seminaries where priests were trained for the Archdiocese of
San Francisco and to which, possibly, the young missionaries
reported impressions and conditions in the West. Despite a
gracious reception by the superiors, there were no pertinent
records extant at St. Patrick's College, Maynooth; St. Patrick's College, Carlow; St. Kieran's College, Kilkenny; St.
John's College, Waterford; and St. Patrick's College, Thurles.
All Hallows College in Dublin proved the exception, for there
ample correspondence from Archbishop Alemany, Bishop
Eugene O'Connell, Father John Prendergast and others was
found. This material, gathered in fifteen packets for San
Francisco and five packets for Marysville, provided superb
background for Catholicism of the American West. Unfortunately for this study, however, its substance thinned considerably after the year 1880.

Other European centers of material were the archives of
selected religious communities. The archives of the Marist
Fathers in Rome are a model in every respect, well-indexed
and neatly arranged in filing cabinets. Here the writer received every courtesy and cooperation from Father James
Lambert, S.M., secretary general and archivist, and his two
assistants, Fathers Gaston Lessard, S.M., and Jean Coste,
S.M. This depository comprised rich material on Riordan's
efforts to establish a successful seminary in the West and a
French parish in his see city, as well as the early fortunes of
the society in Salt Lake City. A tour of the archives at
the generalate of the Dominican Fathers at the Convent of
Santa Sabina in Rome brought the writer into contact with
material for the period of Archbishop Alemany, who had
sent a number of reports to the master general. The general
archives of the Franciscan Fathers in Rome yielded virtually
nothing. Father Robert F. Elliott, C.Ss.R., consultor general
to the rector major, graciously introduced the writer to the
general archivist of the Redemptorist Fathers, André M.H.H.
Sampers, C.Ss.R., who produced an unexpected wealth of
material on the Redemptorists' abortive and forgotten work
among the Germans in San Francisco.

At the Generalate of the Brothers of the Christian Schools, Rome, Brother Charles Henry, F.S.C., generously uncovered a variety of documents recording Riordan's seventeen-year association with the "Latin Question." Unsuccessful efforts were made to consult the archives at the generalates of the Jesuit and Capuchin Fathers. The writer was prevented access to the former by the imposition of the hundred-year rule and was discouraged from the latter after several personal visits. Riordan had been the first prelate to bring the Salesian Fathers to the United States to work among immigrant Italians, and the Central Salesian Archives in Turin contain some correspondence and printed items which record simultaneous negotiations from New York and San Francisco, as well as the pioneer days in the latter city. While Father Irénée Noye, P.S.S., was most helpful and generous with his time, the writer was disappointed with the lack of material in the Archives of the Company of the Priests of Saint Sulpice in Paris. It would appear that the correspondence from Rome and San Francisco has been lost, and all that remains regarding the establishment of St. Patrick's Seminary are the entries recorded in the "Assemblées Générales des Assistants de la Compagnie de St.-Sulpice" and "Assemblées des Consulteurs." While a firmly orthodox prelate, Riordan had a relationship of genuine friendship with the Jesuit modernist, George Tyrrell, a relationship which seemed untempered by the proscriptions of Rome. The papers of the latter's literary executrix, Maude Petre, at the British Museum in London, fleshed out the background and purpose of his remarkable letters to San Francisco.

References

PREFACE

1 San Francisco *Call*, December 29, 1914, p. 8.

2 John B. McGloin, S.J., *California's First Archbishop* (New York, 1966).

3 It might be noted that efforts had been made to correct the default. Joseph M. Gleason spent years in gathering documents for a history of the Archdiocese of San Francisco and regarded his collection as "outside the Bancroft Library one of the best private collections of materials on California history in this state." (Archives of the Archdiocese of San Francisco, hereafter cited as AASF, Gleason to Riordan, Tomales, California, July 29, 1909.) An extremely sensitive man, however, his project failed largely through lack of positive encouragement from his superiors. His papers are housed at Lone Mountain College, San Francisco. Further, one of the first acts of John J. Mitty upon his arrival in San Francisco in 1932 as coadjutor archbishop was to develop a questionnaire to record the essential past of each parish and institution. This instrument, he felt, "might be of use for the future historian." (AASF, Mitty to Peter Guilday, San Francisco, July 19, 1933, copy.)

CHAPTER ONE

1 Baptismal and marriage records, certified on April 22, 1964, by the Reverend B. M. Broderick, P.P., St. Patrick's Church, South Nelson, New Brunswick. In this marriage record, the bride is registered as "Molly Dunne," and according to an investigation of the civil record,

"neither Mary Dunne nor Eliza Dunne were able to sign — their mark only is given."(Broderick to the writer, South Nelson, N.B., April 22, 1964.)

2 Archives of the American College, University of Louvain. *Americanum Collegium, Liber C,* Number 35. A record of Riordan's birth is not preserved in the Department of Health for the Province of New Brunswick since civil registration of births did not begin in that Province until 1888. (A.E. Wilby, the Registral General, to the writer, Fredericton, New Brunswick, April 2, 1964.) The baptismal records of St. Michael's Church date from 1837 but have no entry which registers Patrick William's, only that of a younger sister, Catherine. Rev. A.L. McFadden, pastor of St. Michael's, to the same, Chatham, April 22, 1964.

3 Edward MacLysaght, *Irish Families: Their Names, Arms and Origins* 1957), pp. 257-58.

4 This grant is registered to Patrick Riordan and is on file in the Provincial Department of Lands and Mines, Fredericton, New Brunswick.

5 Guy F. H. Riordan to the writer, Riordan, Gloucester County, New Brunswick, July 19, 1965.

6 Before Irish independence County Leix was known as "Queens County." Mary Dunne's agrarian background has been questioned, but later Archbishop Riordan's secretary, Father John J. Cantwell, once alluded to his superior's affection "for the old homestead where his mother was born" — an expression which most likely refers to a small farm. (Archives of the Archdiocese of San Francisco, Letterbook number 25, folio 91 [hereafter cited as AASF, LB-25(91)], Cantwell to M.J. Murray [San Francisco], December 26, 1907, copy.) It is definite, furthermore, that Mary's brother Dennis was born at Stradbally. (Archives of the Seminary of Quebec, "Acte d'ordination de Denis Dunn," copied for the writer by the Right Reverend Arthur Maneux.) The writer is very grateful to three priest members of the Dunne family who researched meticulously into the family history and supplied these details: Fathers Michael J. Dunne of the Archdiocese of Los Angeles, William P. Dunne of the Archdiocese of Chicago, and George H. Dunne, S.J.

7 This grant for a tract of land in the "Parish of Chatham" is registered in the Provincial Department of Lands and Mines, Fredericton, New Brunswick. The names of Mary's brothers were Dennis, Peter, Edward, William, Michael, and Patrick. Her relationship to Eliza Dunne, the witness at her wedding, is uncertain, but her

parents, it is known, were Patrick W. Dunne and Amelia Marcella Malone, who brought their large family to New Brunswick. (Michael J. Dunne to the writer, Pasadena, California, May 17, 1964; William P. Dunne to the same, Chicago [July 10, 1964].) Mary's brother Peter, it is interesting to note, was the father of Peter Finley (later Finley Peter) Dunne, the creator of "Mr. Dooley," who was himself baptized on July 19, 1867, in St. Patrick's Church by his own cousin, Father Patrick Riordan, and whose godmother was the minister's own mother, Mary (Dunne) Riordan. (Copy of entry in the baptismal register of St. Patrick's Church, Chicago, certified by the pastor, the Reverend Stephen J. O'Donnell.)

8 For details and an excellent analysis of Ireland's inner discontent, cf. John E. Pomfret, *The Struggle for Land in Ireland, 1800-1932* (Princeton, 1930), chap. I, "The Irish Peasants 1800-1850"; William Forbes Adams, *Ireland and Irish Emigration to the New World from 1815 to the Famine* (New Haven, 1932), chaps. I-III, P.S. O'Hegarty, *A History of Ireland Under the Union, 1801 to 1922* (London, 1952), chap. V, "Ireland Under the Union"; R.B. McDowell, *Public Opinion and Government Policy in Ireland, 1801-1846* (London, 1952), esp. chap. I, "Ireland in the Early Nineteenth Century"; R.D. Collison Black, *Economic Thought and the Irish Question, 1817-1870* (Cambridge, 1960).

9 Guy F. H. Riordan to the writer, Riordan, January 3, 1966. William R. Godfrey, *History of Chatham* (Chatham, New Brunswick, 1962). James Hannay, *New Brunswick: Its Resources and Advantages* (Fredericton, New Brunswick: Crown Land Department, 1902).

10 Baptismal Register, St. Michael's Church, Chatham, New Brunswick. This is the only recorded reference to Riordan's younger sister Catherine who was baptized on March 22, 1844, by the Reverend John Shanahan.

11 Arthur Canon Stritch, pastor of the Parish of Kinsale, to the writer, Kinsale, April 20, 1964. The sponsors for Daniel Riordan were Daniel McCarthy and Margaret Aherne. Canon Stritch searched for the origins of Matthew Riordan and failed to find any evidence in the parish registers which begin in 1815.

12 Many accounts have appeared on the Great Famine. Among the most authoritative are R. Dudley Edwards and T. Desmond Fitzgerald (eds.), *The Great Famine: Studies in Irish History, 1845-1852* (New York, 1957); Cecil Woodham-Smith, *The Great Hunger: Ireland, 1845-1849* (New York and Evanston, 1962).

13 AASF, LB-17(265-66), Riordan to R. C. O'Connor [San Francisco], January 18, 1906, copy.

14 Oliver MacDonagh, "Irish Emigration to the United States of America and the British Colonies during the Famine," in Edwards and Williams, *op.cit*. p. 366.

15 *Ibid.*, pp. 374-76.

16 Michael J. Dunne to the writer, Pasadena, April 16, 1964; William P. Dunne to the same, Chicago [July 10, 1964] ; *New World* (Chicago), April 4, 1900, p. 45. Born in Ireland in 1824, Dennis Dunne was ordained in 1848 for the Diocese of Chicago by Bishop Peter P. Lefebvre in Detroit. After a brief professorship at the University of St. Mary of the Lake, he was appointed to care for the missions along the Illinois-Michigan Canal, his headquarters located at Ottawa, Illinois. In 1854 he was transferred to Chicago where he became pastor of St. Patrick's Parish. (A.T. Andreas, *History of Chicago: From the Earliest Period to the Present Times* [Chicago, 1885] , II, 404-405.)

17 For details on this history in every phase, see the exemplary history of the city by Bessie Louise Pierce, *A History of Chicago*, 3 vols. (New York, 1937, 1940 and 1957).

18 An excellent article suggestive of this theme is Arthur C. Cole, "The Passing of the Frontier," *Mississippi Valley Historical Review*, V (December, 1918), 288-312.

19 Teresa S. Miller, "A Tribute to the Memory of Archbishop Riordan," *Notre Dame Quarterly* (San Jose, California), VII (March, 1915), p. 70. Another boyhood memory was Riordan's attendance at a speech delivered by Stephen A. Douglas. AASF, LBR(3a), 367-69, Riordan to Mrs. Roger D. Williams [San Francisco] , February 15, 1912, copy.

20 Robert Frederick Trisco, *The Holy See and the Nascent Church in the Middle Western United States, 1826-1850* (Rome, 1962), pp. 93-96, 146-48.

21 The writer wishes to acknowledge his debt to Sister Hortence Marie Brennan, D.C., who provided a great deal of research information and who located the record of the deed at the Chicago Title and Trust Company. (Sister Hortence Marie Brennan, D.C., to the writer, Chicago, August 17, 1966.) The reference to the location of the convent is from AASF, LB-30(88), Charles A. Ramm to Sister Frances, D.C., San Francisco, July 9, 1909, copy.

22 *Catholic Almanac. . .1855* (Baltimore, n.d.), p. 167; *Catholic Almanac. . .1856*(Baltimore, n.d.), p. 90. See also *New World* (Chicago, April 14, 1900), p. 35; [James J. McGovern] *Souvenir of the Silver*

Jubilee in the Episcopacy of His Grace the Most Rev. Patrick Augustine Feehan, Archbishop of Chicago ([Chicago, 1891]), pp. 161-62; hereafter cited as *Souvenir*; [Joseph J. Thompson] *The Archdiocese of Chicago: Antecedents and Developments* (Des Plaines, Illinois, 1920), p. 23.

23 AASF, LBR(1a), 500, Riordan to Mrs. J. M. Doyle [San Francisco], December 10, 1909, copy.

24 "Archbishop Riordan," begins an account probably written or inspired by his brother Daniel, "upon his arrival here became a student at the University of St. Mary of the Lake in this city." (*New World* [Chicago, January 2, 1915], p. 1.)

25 A splendid history of this institution is Harry C. Koenig's unpublished manuscript, "University and Seminary of St. Mary of the Lake. " Monsignor Koenig graciously allowed the writer to consult his material.

26 Daniel J. Riordan, "University of St. Mary of the Lake," *Illinois Catholic Historical Review*, II (October, 1919), p. 141. When Monsignor Daniel Riordan died in 1922, he was known as "the last priest-alumnus of the old University of St. Mary of the Lake, which he attended from 1859-1863," Francis J. Epstein, *Decet Meminisse Fratrum: A Necrology of the Diocesan Priests of the Chicago Archdiocese, 1844-1935* (Chicago, 1937), p. 29.

27 *Catholic Almanac. . .1854* (Baltimore, n.d.), p. 127; *Catholic Almanac. . .1856* (Baltimore, n.d.), p. 185

28 *Notre Dame Scholastic*, XLVIII (January 9, 1915), p. 225.

29 See William Alan Moloney, "Notre Dame du Lac," *Catholic Encyclopedia* (New York, 1911), XI, 132-33. AASF, LBR(3a), 274-75, Riordan to the Right Reverend Monsignor Denis O'Haran [San Francisco], December 18, 1911, copy. O'Haran was the dean of St. Mary's Cathedral, Sydney, Australia.

30 M. D. Connolly, "Personal Recollections of the Late Most Reverend Archbishop Riordan," *Monitor* (San Francisco), Christmas, 1915, p. 6.

31 James J. McGovern, *The Life and Writings of the Right Reverend John McMullen, D.D., First Bishop of Davenport, Iowa* (Chicago and Milwaukee, 1888), pp. 104-105; hereafter cited as *McMullen*.

32 AASF, LB-8(124), Riordan to Joseph Chartrand [San Francisco, April 6, 1903].

33 AASF, LBR(3a), 274-75, Riordan to O'Haran [San Francisco], December 18, 1911, copy. Cardinal Patrick Moran (1830-1911), one of

the greatest leaders of the Australian hierarchy, became Bishop of Ossory in 1872 and in 1884 succeeded to the Archbishopric of Sydney.

34 An article by Francis J. Pabisch, in the *Catholic Telegraph and Advocate* (Cincinnati), January 14, 1860, p. 4.

35 *Pilot* (Boston), January 28, 1860, p. 2. No exact transcript was taken recording Barnabò's exact words; these are the words from a summary signed by "Alumno di Propaganda." For a detailed description of the institution's beginnings, see Robert F. McNamara, *The American College in Rome, 1855-1955* (Rochester, 1956), chap. III, "Grand Opening."

36 Henry A. Brann, *History of the American College of the Roman Catholic Church in the United States* (New York and Cincinnati, 1910), p. 57. These "Notes" (pp. 56-59) are attributed "probably" to Riordan although no name had been appended to them.

37 *Tablet* (London), December 24, 1859, p. 819.

38 See Robert Seton, *Memories of Many Years (1839-1922)* (London, 1923), pp. 197, 225; and John Tracy Ellis, *The Life of James Cardinal Gibbons* (Milwaukee, 1952), I, 228; II, 422-23.

39 AASF, LBR(4a), 197-99, Riordan to Margaret Casserly [San Francisco], December 18, 1912, copy.

40 ACUA, Riordan to John J. Keane, San Francisco, January 24, 1887.

41 *Tablet* (London), *loc. cit.*

42 *Voice* IX (January, 1932), 6; Archives of the Séminaire du Saint-Esprit, "Nomenclature, Statistiques des Elèves, 1846-1900," p. 75. Accordingly, Riordan left this seminary on August 6, 1861; and there is no further note recorded of him for this year except tthat he had not received ordination to tonsure or minor orders at this institution. Bernard-Nöel, C.S.Sp., Archiviste Général du Congregation du Saint-Esprit, to the writer, Paris, May 4, 1964, and September 1, 1965. See also Reuben J. Parsons, "Early Days of the American College," and the "List of Students," in Henry A. Brann, *op. cit*, pp. 464-547.

43 AACL, *Collegium Americanum, Liber C*, No. 35.

44 Roger Aubert, *Le Pontificat de Pie IX (1846-1878)* (Paris, 1952), pp. 163-71, 217-18, 250-52. See also Alois J.V. Simon, *Le Cardinal Sterckx et son temps (1792-1867)*, 2 vols. (Wetteren, 1950).

45 AASF, LB-12(154-155), Riordan to Thomas J. Carr, Archbishop of Melbourne [San Francisco], September 19, 1904, copy.

46 AACL, "Collegium Americanum Immaculatae Conceptionis Beatae Mariae Virginis...Prospectus," No. III, Lovanii, in festo S.

Josephi, 1899, handwritten by Jules De Becker and endorsed by Camillus Paul Maes.

47 John De Nève, the second Rector of the American College, had been in the United States three years as a priest of the Diocese of Detroit. He began his first administration of the college in January, 1860, and remained until 1871; after an interval of a decade, he was reappointed rector, serving during the years 1881-1891.

48 AACL, "Collegium Americanum. . . Prospectus," No. II.

49 John D. Sauter, *The American College of Louvain (1857-1898)* (Louvain, 1959), p. 113. In these ten years there were also a few students from Canada and one from Hungary.

50 M.D. Connolly, "Personal Recollections of the Late Most Reverend Archbishop Riordan," *Monitor*, Christmas, 1915, pp. 6-8.

51 AACL, F-6-16, The Missionary I (January 19, 1862), 1-2. Thirteen issues are preserved in these archives, the last issue dated May 11, 1862; and there is no evidence that further editions had appeared.

52 AACL, *The Missionary*, No. 2, p. 6, quoted in the *American College Bulletin*, I (January, 1905), 20.

53 AACL, F-6-16, *Thee Missionary*, I (May 11, 1862), 1-2. This article most probably refers to Riordan since the other student for the Diocese of Chicago, John A. Fanning, was Irish-born; moreover, the internal evidence points to Riordan, particularly the allegations of his eloquence and a reference to a companion described as "one of his own countrymen," who had a certain relationship with the "Louisville Evening Journal." This latter was possibly Riordan's good friend, John Lancaster Spalding.

An educated guess as to why Riordan would be called the "nephew of Douglas" might have been an association with Stephen A. Douglas of Illinois, the "Little Giant" whose wife was a devout Catholic, and who, in 1861, according to the testimony of William J. Onahan, was received on his death bed into the Catholic Church by Bishop James Duggan. For an interesting and exhaustive discussion of Douglas' death, see Sister M. Sevina Pahorezki, O.S.F., *The Social and Political Activities of William James Onahan* (Washington, 1942), pp. 13-14, n. 38.

54 *Monitor* (San Francisco), September 26, 1883, p. 1.

55 AACL, *Collegium Americanum, Liber C*, no. 76.

56 AASF, Dunne to Riordan, Chicago, July 31, 1909; no close relation to Riordan.

57 AASF, LBR(6a), 196-70 and 217-18, Riordan to Maes [San Francisco], November 13 and December 10, 1914.

CHAPTER TWO

1 Wyatt Wilson Belcher, *The Economic Rivalry Between St. Louis and Chicago, 1850-1880* (New York, 1947), p. 156. For details in addition to Belcher's superior dissertation, see Pierce, *op. cit.*, III.

2 *Ibid.*, III, 5, n. 1. This phenomenal growth of Chicago was distinctly characterized by a continued immigration of *families* which accelerated the rate. At the beginning of 1854, continues Pierce, the population was 298,977 with 59,497 families. In these sixteen years the population nearly quintupled, but the number of families increased more than six-fold. *Ibid.*, III, 5, n. 4.

3 Dunne and Butler's appointments were recorded in the *Catholic Almanac. . .1860* (Baltimore, n. d.), p. 185 and McMullen's in the *Catholic Almanacc. . .1861* (Baltimore n. d.), p. 163.

4 E. Colbert, *Chicago: Historical and Statistical Sketch of the Garden City. . .* (Chicago, 1868), p. 114; quoted in Pierce, *op. cit.*, III, p. 363.

5 James J. McGovern, *The Life and Writings of the Right Reverend John McMullen, D.D., First Bishop of Davenport, Iowa* (Chicago and Milwaukee, 1888), p. 144; hereafter cited as McMullen. For an extensive account of St. Mary's early days, one should consult Harry C. Koenig, "University and Seminary of St. Mary of the Lake," pp. 27-41.

6 Riordan, *art. cit.*, p. 150.

7 John Lancaster Spalding, "Introduction," in McGovern, *McMullen*, pp. xxii-xxiii.

8 McGovern, *McMullen*, p. 159.

9 [James J. McGovern] *Souvenir*, p. 201.

10 *Idem.* Only Fischer's appointment is recorded in *Sadliers' Catholic Directory. . .1868* (New York, 1868), p. 135. Halligan's appointment was temporary, dependent upon the return of the bishop.

11 AAB, 39A-U-1, Report of Joseph P. Roles to Martin J. Spalding [Chicago], October 14, 1868, p. 1; hereafter cited as "Roles' Report."

12 *Sadliers' Catholic Directory. . .1868 (New York, 1868)*, p.136. A fifth member of this governing board was Thaddeus Butler, the bishop's secretary, who evidently did not actively support the actions of his four colleagues.

13 AACL, Den. I, ST, R, 16, Patrick Riordan to De Nève [Chicago, January or February] 9, 1867. Sauter incorrectly attributes this letter to Daniel Riordan (Sauter, *op. cit.*, p. 258.)

14 The "Duggan Affair" has been extensively treated in the writer's "Patterns of Ecclesiastical Authority: The Problems of the Chicago Succession, 1865-1881," *Church History*, XXXXII (June, 1973). For another perspective, see Thomas Spalding's fine *Martin John Spalding: American Churchman* (Washington, D.C., 1973).

15 APF, *Cong. Gen.*, vol. 996 (1869), foglii 1492-1497, Kenrick to Barnabò, Chicago, August 10, 1868. Although the four did not appear in person in their defense, McMullen and Roles presented themselves before Kenrick, and written statements were submitted to Rome. McGovern was reportedly away on vacation, and Dunne was himself mortally ill. AAB, "Roles' Report," pp. 5-6.

16 APF, *Lettere*, vol. 360 (1868), fog. 1020v-1022rv, Barnabò to Kenrick, Rome, September 9, 1868; all *Lettere* are copies.

17 *Cong. Gen.*, vol. 996 (1869), Fog. 1387r, *Ponenza* of Cardinal Camillo Di Pietro, "Sui Provvedimenti da prendersi nelle attuali esigenze della Diocesi di Chicago negli Stati-Uniti di America," September, 1869, *con secreto pontificio*; hereafter cited as Di Pietro, *Ponenza*.

18 McMullen to McGovern, Rome, November 19, 1868; reprinted in McGovern, *McMullen*, pp. 177-78.

19 Di Pietro, *Ponenza*, fog. 1390r.

20 *Congressi A. C.*, vol. 22, fog. 607rv-608r, Riordan to McMullen, Joliet, Illinois, December 8 [1868]; fog. 606r, McMullen's translation into Italian of the portion from Riordan's letter which testified to the origins of the article published and a four-line postscript by McMullen.

21 *Cong. Gen.* vol. 996 (1869), fog. 1468ar, clipping.

22 AAB, 36-A-N-20, McGovern to Spalding, Chicago, March 10, 1869.

23 Copies of Duggan's printed circular to his clergy may be found in AAB, 38-E-1, and in UND, MC, Purcell Papers, III-2-1. The newspaper account is found in the Chicago *Tribune*, October 12, 1868, p. 4.

24 New York *Tribune*, October 23, 1860, p. 2. The unidentified author is known only as "an occasional correspondent," but one New York priest very close to McMullen, who could have inspired the article, was Edward McGlynn. Both had been contemporaries at the Urban College; it would be McGlynn who would preach at McMullen's consecration; and it would be McMullen who would recommend his New York friend in 1882 for the vacant See of Charleston.

25 AAB, 35-F-15, McCloskey to Spalding, New York, October 24, 1868.

26 UND, MC, Purcell Papers, II-5-d, Spalding to Purcell, Baltimore, October 15, 1868.

27 *Cong. Gen.*, *loc. cit.*, fog. 1447rv-1448r, McMullen to Barnabò [Rome], n.d. Unfortunately, McMullen failed to date this important communication and thereby to leave evidence of its influence on Propaganda. It most probably was submitted before November 19, 1868, the day on which the congregation agreed to investigate McMullen's claims and informed Kenrick that it was not content with his assurances regarding Chicago. (*Lettere*, vol. 360 [1868], fog. 1253rv-1254v, Barnabò to Kenrick, Rome, November 19, 1868.) McMullen further cheered his friend McGovern, reporting that Barnabò "had consulted with the Holy Father and read to him a letter of mine explaining the difficulty and then read a translation of the Bishop's letter. The Cardinal seems to understand matters very well and will insist on our rights — time will tell." (McMullen to McGovern, Rome, November 19, 1868, reprinted in McGovern, *McMullen*, pp. 177-78.)

28 Di Pietro, *Ponenza*, fog. 1387v. In his report Kenrick attributed the imprudent publication to McMullen, an opinion noted by Propaganda. *Cong. Gen.*, *loc. cit.*, fog. 1502rv-1503rv, Kenrick to Barnabò, St. Louis, December 11, 1868.

29 The major religious communities — Jesuits, Redemptorists, and Benedictines — seemed to be bitterly indignant at the four accusers. The majority of the diocesan clergy, while expressing respect and good will for their good qualities, evidnetly agreed that two of them were wretched mismanagers of their own financial affairs.

30 *Cong. Gen.*, *loc. cit.* fog. 1461rv-1463r, Laitner to Barnabò, Dixon, Illinois, January, 1869. Evidently, McGovern personally witnessed this scene and was able to add a number of details for Propaganda's benefit. It was McGovern and Roles who counseled Dunne, who was "expelled from the Diocese and died in an alien house like a missionary priest," to send for Duggan and arrange a reconciliation. Seven times the bishop demanded a retraction and left very displeased. "Many other particulars," noted McGovern, "I omit because it would appear incredible to Your Eminence, but I have narrated them for Father McMullen." *Congressi. A.C.*, vol. 22 (1868-69), fog. 644rv-645v, McGovern to Barnabò, Chicago, December 30, 1868. In their accounts published later, McGovern and Daniel Riordan, who depended heavily on McGovern, presented an entirely different version which pointed to final and tender reconciliation between Duggan and Dunne. See McGovern, *McMullen*, pp. 178-79; D. J. Riordan, *art. cit.*, p. 154.

31 *Congressi, A.C.*, vol. 22 (1868-69), fog. 384r-385r, a clipping sent by McGovern, identified only as "Chicago, Sunday, December 17, 1868."

32 *Cong. Gen., loc. cit.*, fog. 1461rv-1463r, Laitner to Barnabò, Dixon, Illinois, January, 1869. The funeral cortege included the Irish Legion and a number of Catholic societies. A full description may be found in the Chicago *Tribune*, December 28, 1868, p. 4.

33 *Congressi, A.C., loc. cit.*, fog. 644rv-645v, McGovern to Barnabò, Chicago, December 30, 1868.

34 *Lettere*, vol. 361 (1869), fog. 82rv-83v, Barnabò to Duggan, Rome, January 22, 1869; *ibid.* fog. 390rv-393r, same to same, Rome, April 6, 1869.

35 AAB, 36A-L-9, Kenrick to Spalding, St. Louis, April 18, 1869.

36 UND, MC, Purcell Papers, II-5-d, McCloskey to Purcell, Louisville, May 12, 1869.

37 AAB, 36A-L-7, Kenrick to Spalding, St. Louis, May 13, 1869.

38 AAB, 36A-L-8, Kenrick to Spalding, St. Louis, April 15, 1869.

39 *Congressi, A.C.*, vol. 22 (1868-69), fog. 961rv-962rv, McMullen to Barnabò, Chicago, May 15, 1869.

40 *Ibid.* fog. 709r-720r, Laitner, Riordan, McGovern, and Thomas Burke [pastor of St. Columbkill's] to baBarnabò, [Chicago], n.d.; the entire letter is in Riordan's script. *Ibid.*, fog. 984r-985v; this list, too, is in Riordan's script. In his won letter, Laitner supported Riordan's explanation as to why the lengthy list recommending McMullen could not contain authentic signatures: "...the distances and lack of time." *Ibid.*, fog. 1076rv-1079r, Laitner to Barnabò, Chicago, July 10, 1869. Riordan's *completed* list is found in *Cong. Gen.*, vol. 996 (1869), fog. 1528Ar-1528Br.

41 *Ibid.*, fog. 1528r.

42 AAB, 38-E-4, Kenrick to Spalding, St. Louis, July 7, 1869.

43 *Ibid.*, 38-E-7, Luers to Spalding, Chicago, July 20, 1869.

44 *Lettere*, vol. 362 (1869), fog. 865rv, Barnabò to Arnold Damen, S.J., Rome, August 2, 1869.

45 Di Pietro, *Ponenza*, fog. 1391rv.

46 *Lettere*, vol. 362 (1869), fog. 679rv-680rv, Barnabò to Spalding, Rome, June 16, 1869.

47 APF, *Acta*, vol. 235 (1869), foglii 721rv-723r, Spalding to Barnabò, Chicago, July 22, 1869, printed copy. An incomplete draft of the report and a Latin transcript of the interviews may be found in AAB, 38-E-8 and -9.

48 *Cong. Gen.*, vol. 996 (1869), fog. 1393r. The appointment was determined by Propaganda on September 27 and was formally confirmed by Pius IX on October 3.

49 AAB, 76-B-2, Elder to Gibbons, Cincinnati, August 8, 1881.

50 AACL, *Collegium Americanum, Liber C*, No. 76; *New World* (Chicago), April 14, 1900, pp. 45-46. Daniel Riordan did not return to Chicago until October, 1870. His first pastorate, it is noteworthy, was St. Rose of Lima Church in Wilmington, Illinois, where he succeeded John McMullen before being appointed as Foley's secretary and chancellor. *Sadliers' Catholic Directory. . .1872* (New York, 1872), p. 149.

51 UND, MC, Clarke Papers, I-2-n, Riordan to Richard Henry Clarke, Chicago, March 11, 1885.

52 AAB, Letterbook, p. 436, Spalding to McCloskey, Baltimore, February 8, 1869, copy.

CHAPTER THREE

1 UND, MC, Clarke Papers, I-2-n, Riordan to Clarke, Chicago, March 11, 1885.

2 McGovern, *McMullen*, p. 194. *Sadliers' Catholic Directory. . .1871* (New York, 1871), pp. 145, 147; *Sadliers' Catholic Directory. . .1872* (New York, 1872), p. 146. In the later years of Foley's episcopate, the restoration of the three priests was completed. McMullen succeeded in 1877 as vicar general and was named to the bishop's council, and later Roles received the historic parish of St. Mary's in Chicago, the mother church of the diocese, and McGovern was named to St. Patrick's in nearby Lake Forest. These moves were judiciously effected before the division of the diocese in which the new See of Peoria acquired Bloomington in 1876 and Rock Island in 1880. *Sadliers' Catholic Directory. . .1879* (New York, 1878), pp. 205-06.

3 *New World* (Chicago), April 14, 1900, p. 38, *Sadliers' Catholic Directory. . .1872* (New York, 1872), p. 147.

4 AAB, 34-A-5, Foley to Spalding, Chicago, June 1, 1871.

5 An excellent brief account of the disaster may be found in Pierce, *op. cit.*, III, 3-19.

6 McMullen to Eliza A. Starr [Chicago], October 14, 1871; reprinted in McGovern, *McMullen*, p. 199.

7 At the age of seventy-one, Riordan recalled this experience of collecting money in Halifax. During a return trip in 1905, and a brief visit to a local academy, he reminisced, "I met one of the sisters who remembered me when I was in Halifax forty years ago, just after the

Chicago fire, collecting some money to repair our losses." AASF, LBR(4a), 141-42, Riordan to Winifred McAvoy [San Francisco], November 25, 1912, copy. In his account McGovern implies that the tour possibly ended at Halifax because McMullen had learned there of his father's death. McGovern, *loc. cit.*

8 *Western Catholic*, January 9, 1873; quoted in *New World* (Chicago), April 14, 1900, p. 36.

9 Chicago *Tribune*, May 24, 1880, p. 3.

10 *Monitor*, September 26, 1883, p. 1.

11 *Reverend Hugh McGuire: A Memorial* ([Chicago, 1911]), unpaginated.

12 AASF, LBR(2a), 324-25, Riordan to Daniel Riordan [San Francisco], February 20, 1911, copy.

13 AASF, LBR(3a),114-15, Riordan to Conaty [San Francisco], August 22, 1911.

14 AASF, LBR(3a), 197-98, Riordan to Dunne [San Francisco], October 6, 1911, copy.

15 Peter C. Yorke, "Essentially a Churchman," *Leader* (San Francisco), January 2, 1915, p. 4.

16 *New World* (Chicago), October 7, 1899, p. 16.

17 AASF, LBR(3a), 178, Riordan to Francis W. Kunkel, S.S. [San Francisco], September 23, 1911, copy.

18 AASF, LBR(4a), 261-62, Riordan to Mrs. Margaret Guerin [San Francisco], January 7, 1913, copy. See also his sentiments expressed to Guerin's daughter; *ibid.*, 259-60, Riordan to Mother M. Guerin, R.C.S.J. [San Francisco], January 7, 1913, copy.

19 AASF, LBR(2a), 149-50, Riordan to Mrs. Michael Cudahy [San Francisco], November 29, 1910 copy.

20 AASF, LBR(2a), 166-67, Riordan to Mrs. Mary A. Lilly [San Francisco], December 2, 1910, copy.

21 AASF, LBR(3a), 347, Riordan to Mrs. Nellie Donohue [San Francisco], February 2, 1912, copy.

22 APF, *Acta*, vol. 243 (1875), fog. 14rv, Kenrick *et al.* to Cardinal Alessandro Franchi, Prefect of Propaganda, St. Louis, March 11, 1874, printed copy.

23 *Acta*, vol. 243 (1875), fog. 19v-20rv, Foley to Franchi, Chicago, May 22, 1874, copy.

24 Propaganda had officially approved of the new see in its conference of January 11, 1875, but complications arose when its original appointee, Michael Hurley, declined the bishopric in April. The refusal was delivered to Pius IX, who suspected that excessive humility

might have motivated Hurley, and before accepting the resignation he ordered a full investigation. It was not until April 23, 1876, that the pope acknowledged Hurley's refusal and allowed a second *terna* to be considered and an intensive investigation begun on Spalding's candidacy. The appointment was made eventually on November 27, 1876, by the cardinals of Propaganda and confirmed on December 3, 1876, by Pius IX. *Acta*, vol. 244 [1876], fog. 295v-298r, *Realzione* of Cardinal Alessandro Franchi, "Sulla scelta. . .del Vescovo di Peoria: Articolo Secundo," May, 1876; *ibid.*, fog. 368rv-369r, "Appendice alla Relazione del Maggio 1876," November 1876.

25 *Freeman's Journal* (New York), May 12, 1877; cited in Davic. Sweeney, O.F.M., "Life of John Lancaster Spalding, First Bishop of Peoria, 1840-1916," unpublished doctoral dissertation, The Catholic University of America, Washington, D.C., 1963, p. 122. This detail was omitted in Sweeney's published biography.

26 AASF, LBR(5a), 397-98, Riordan to Riordan [San Francisco], May 1, 1914, copy.

27 McGovern, *McMullen*, p. 224. A *terna* is a list of three candidates who are recommended for the episcopacy.

28 *Acta*, vol. 248 (1880), fog. 269rv, Kenrick *et al.* to Simeoni, St. Louis, April 16, 1879, copy. James O'Connor, Vicar Apostolic of Nebraska, who attended the provincial meeting, reported that none of the bishops at St. Louis seemed to know much about Daniel Riordan, "except Bishop Spalding through whose position and urgent recommendation his name came to be accepted." (*Ibid.*, fog. 275v, O'Connor to Simeoni, Omaha, December 27, 1879, copy.)

29 *Acta*, vol. 248 (1880), fog. 269rv, Kenrick, *et al.* to Simeoni, St. Louis, April 16, 1879, printed copy. The original documents on the appointment of Feehan in 1880 are missing in the Propaganda archives; only the printed *Acta* are available.

30 *Acta*, vol. 248 (1880), fog. 265rv-266r.

31 *Congressi, A.C.*, vol. 35 (1881), fog. 147rv-148rv, "Several priests of Chicago" to Simeoni, Chicago, January 12, 1881.

32 *Congressi, A.C.*, vol. 35 (1881), fog. 177rv-178r, "Many Priests of Chicago" to Simeoni, Chicago, February 1, 1881. Attached was a financial statement of the archdiocese for the year ending November 30, 1880. This report indicated that McMullen, rector of the cathedral, had failed to pay the orphans' tax assessed at $900, the seminary tax at $400 and the cathedraticum. Roles, as pastor of St. Mary's, according to this statement compiled by Daniel Riordan, likewise failed to pay these same taxes which had been assessed at a lower rate.

And Patrick Riordan at St. James, although he had fulfilled most of his obligations, still owed $400 on the orphans' tax. See *ibid.*, fog. 176rv.

33 *Lettere*, vol. 377 (1881), fog. 96r-97r, Simeoni to Feehan, Rome, February 19, 1881. Simeoni may have been referring to the list of the diocesan consultors and pastors which had named Riordan *dignior* for Chicago in 1879; or he may have confused Patrick's name with that of his brother Daniel, who had been, in the previous year, the first choice for Council Bluffs, Iowa, a proposed see to be separated from Dubuque.

34 This appointment was confirmed by Leo XIII on May 8, 1881. *Cong. Gen.*, vol. 1031 (1881), fog. 817rv, report of the general congregation of May 2, 1881. The decree of erection is dated May 25, 1881. *Lettere*, vol. 377 (1881), fog. 298rv.

35 McGovern, *McMullen*, p. 232. A full description of the ceremonies may be found in the Chicago *Morning News*, July 28, 1881, p. 4.

36 UND, MC, Clarke Papers, I-2-n, Riordan to Clarke, Chicago, March 11, 1885.

37 A recent biography of Alemany providing the early details is John B. McGloin, S.J., *California's First Archbishop: The Life of Joseph Sadoc Alemany, O.P., 1814-1888* (New York, 1966).

38 Donald C. Shearer, *Pontificia Americana. . .* (Washington, 1933), pp. 288-89.

39 Shearer, *op. cit.*, pp. 320-21; UND, MC, Purcell Papers, II-4-0, Alemany to Purcell, San Francisco, May 25, 1859.

40 AAB, 33-A-9, Alemany to Martin J. Spalding, San Francisco, October 15, 1868; UND, MC, Purcell Papers, II-5-4, Alemany to Purcell, San Francisco, October 15, 1868.

41 *Acta*, vol. 250 (1882), fog. 208r, report of the general congregation of July 4, 1882. This decision was ratified by Leo XIII on July 9, 1882.

42 *Cong. Gen.*, vol. 1017 (1883), fog. 189r, report of Elder, *et al.*, Cincinnati, July 27, 1881; *ibid.*, fog. 191rv-192v, "Notale. . .Revdus, Patricius W. Riordan, Dignior. . .," written in Elder's script but gathered by Bishop Joseph Dwenger of Fort Wayne.

43 *Ibid.*, fog. 193rv-194rv, Elder to Simeoni, Cincinnati, August 12, 1881.

44 *Ibid.*, fog. 176r, Cardinal Gaetano Alimonda, *Ristretto con sommario*, "Circa la scelta di un Vescovo per la diocesi di Nashville negli Stati Uniti di America," January 1883.

45 It may be noted that at the provincial meeting, the senior suffragan and secretary, Thomas A. Becker of Wilmington, championed the candidacy of Bishop Henry A. Northrop, Vicar Apostolic of North Carolina. The bishops, however, preferred to retain him in his difficult post and kept him off the Charleston *terna*. At this point there occurred a strange maneuver. As secretary, Becker drafted the report of the meeting for the Holy See but, quite unauthorized, he gave Propaganda the impression that it might appoint one of these three candidates — William Wayrich, C.S.S.R., a pastor in New York City, Riordan, or Daniel Quigley, vicar general and present administrator of Charleston — either directly to Charleston or to North Carolina if Northrop were given the former see. Technically, therefore, Riordan could have received the Vicariate of North Carolina. (AAB, 76-0-7, Northrop's record of the provincial meeting, Baltimore, March 22, 1882; *Cong. Gen.*, vol. 1017 [1883], fog. 131rv, Cardinal Camillo Di Pietro, *Ristretto con sommario*, "Circa l'elezione del Vescovo di Charleston," January, 1883; *ibid.*, fog. 137r-138r, Becker to Simeoni, Wilmington, March 23, 1882.)

46 AAB, 76-0-6, McMullen to Gibbons, Davenport, March 16, 1882. The only reasonable estimate is that McMullen had by now learned of Spalding's newly conceived campaign to free Riordan from Charleston for the appointment to San Francisco. Spalding would launch it in less than five months. It is true that in early 1883 McMullen spent time in Los Angeles and San Francisco, seeking relief from abdominal cancer. He may have, at this time, become convinced firsthand that prospects in the West were more promising than what eastern ecclesiastics were willing to concede. (AALA, Mora to Alemany, January 27, 1883.)

47 *Cong. Gen.*, vol. 1017 (1883), fog. 141rv-142rv, Gibbons to Simeoni, Baltimore, April 17, 1882.

48 *Lettere*, vol. 378 (1882), fog. 388rv, Simeoni to Spalding, Rome, July 21, 1882.

49 AAB, 76-C-9, Spalding to Gibbons, Peoria, August 30, 1882.

50 *Congressi, A.C.*, vol. 37 (1882), fog. 138rv, Spalding to Simeoni, Peoria, August 31, 1882.

51 *Gen. Cong.*, vol. 1017 (1883), fog. 261rv-262r, McQuaid to Simeoni, Rochester, August 5, 1882; fog. 253r, Cardinal Pier Francesco Meglia, *Ristretto con sommario*, January, 1883.

52 *Ibid.*, fog. 139rv, Gibbons to Simeoni, Baltimore, September 9, 1882. See AAB, Gibbons' Diary, September 9, 1882, p. 163.

53 *Acta*, vol. 251 (1883), fog. 55rv, report of Propaganda's meeting of January 11, 1883. Thirteen cardinals voted to name Riordan to North Carolina, and seven preferred to have Northrop administer it from Charleston.

54 *Ibid.*, fog. 54r, "In Congne Generali....Pro nunc committatur R.P.D. Northrop administratio Vicariatus Apostolici Carolinae Septentrionalis...."; fog. 74r, "In Congregatione Generali...Dilata et exquirantur informationes juxta mentem panditam a R.P.D. Archiespiscopo di San Francisci super D.D. Riordan et Chatard." *Lettere*, vol. 379 (1883), fog. 33rv, Simeoni to Alemany, Rome, January 24, 1883.

55 AASP, Spalding to Ireland, Rome, January 21, 1883.

56 *Cong. Gen.*, vol. 1017A (1883), fog. 1026rv-1027v, Alemany to Simeoni, San Francisco, March 15, 1883.

57 *Acta*, vol. 251 (1883), fog. 504r, report of the sacred congregation of June 18, 1883. *Lettere*, vol. 379 (1883), fog. 356rv, Simeoni to Alemany, Rome, June 30, 1883.

58 AAB, 77-H-8, Keane to Gibbons, Rome, June 25, 1883.

59 *Monitor*, July 14, 1883, p. 4.

60 AUND, Sorin Papers, Riordan to Sorin, Chicago, July 17, 1883.

61 *Lettere*, vol. 379 (1883), fog. 356rv, Simeoni to Alemany, June 30, 1883. *Monitor*, July 25, 1883, p. 5.

62 *Ibid.*, September 19, 1883, p. 4.

63 *Lettere*, vol. 379 (1883), fog. 393r, Simeoni to Riordan and to Feehan, Rome, July 13, 1883. *Congressi, A.C.*, vol. 39 (1883), fog. 36r, Riordan to Simeoni, Chicago, August 8, 1883.

64 *Lettere*, vol. 379 (1883), fog. 417rv, Simeoni to Riordan, Rome, July 30, 1883.

65 AASF, Riordan's Last Will and Testament, instructions to Edward J. Hanna, Charles A. Ramm, and John J. Cantwell, executors, San Francisco, December 7, 1912.

66 *Monitor*, September 26, 1883, p. 1.

67 AASF, Riordan's Last Will and Testament.

68 Chicago *Tribune*, October 1, 1883, p. 3.

69 *Ibid.*, October 30, 1883, p. 8; *Monitor*, October 31, 1883, p. 5.

70 Charles A. Ramm, interview, April 8, 1942; quoted in Sister Gertrude Mary Gray, "A Preliminary Survey of the Life of the Most Reverend Joseph Sadoc Alemany, O.P., First Archbishop of San Francisco," unpublished master's thesis, The Catholic University of America, Pacific Coast Branch, San Rafael, California, 1942, p. 79.

71 *Monitor*, November 7, 1883, p. 4.

72 *Ibid.*, November 14, 1883, p. 4.

73 Dunne to Charlotte Dunne, December 1, 1901; cited in Elmer Ellis, *Mr. Dooley's America: A Life of Finley Peter Dunne* (New York, 1941), p. 262. Dunne eventually reversed his two first names from Peter Finley to Finley Peter.

CHAPTER FOUR

1 Harold E. Collins to the writer, San Francisco, June 20, 1964.

2 *Congressi, A.C.*, vol. 41 (1884), fog. 206rv-207r, Riordan to Simeoni, San Francisco, January 31, 1884.

3 *Cong. Gen.*, vol. 996 (1869), fog. 1528r-1529v. Propaganda had no reason to suspect that Riordan was engaged in a personal vendetta. The congregation had received from an independent source a printed notice which acknowledged both Conway and Riordan as members of a clergy committee in Chicago in 1877 organized to gather a donation for Bishop Foley as an expression of esteem. *Congressi, A.C.*, vol. 28 (1877), fog. 733r. It might be noted, too, that Conway attended the dedication of St. James' Church. Chicago *Tribune*, May 24, 1880, p. 3.

4 *Ibid.*, fog. 210r-211r, Riordan to Simeoni, San Francisco, May 24, 1884.

5 *Ibid.*, fog. 212r-213r, Spalding to Simeoni, Peoria, May 30, 1884.

6 *Congressi, A.C.*, vol. 39 (1883), fog. 317r, Alemany to Simeoni, San Francisco, October 18, 1883.

7 Archives of the Order of Preachers, Casa Generalizia, Santa Sabina, Rome, Alemany to José Maria Larroca, San Francisco, January 7, 1884; hereafter cited as AOPR.

8 *Lettere*, vol. 379 (1883), fog. 654v-655r, Simeoni to Alemany, Rome, December 13, 1883.

9 *Lettere*, vol. 380 (1884), fog. 347v, Simeoni to Riordan, Rome, July 3, 1884.

10 *Congressi, A.C.*, vol. 41 (1884), fog. 8rv, Alemany to Leo XIII, San Francisco, July 10, 1884.

11 *Ibid.*, fog. 72r-77r, Riordan to Simeoni, San Francisco, July 24, 1884.

12 *Ibid.*, fog. 6r, Alemany to Simeoni, San Francisco, July 10, 1884; fog. 582v, Riordan to Simeoni, Chicago, October 29, 1884.

13 See John Tracy Ellis, *The Life of James Cardinal Gibbons* (Milwaukee, 1952), I, 203-51.

14 AAB, 77-U-6, Alemany to Gibbons, San Francisco, April 14, 1884.

15 *Ibid.*, 78-A-11, Riordan to Foley, San Francisco, May 3, 1884.

16 Baltimore *Sun*, December 8, 1884, p. 1.

17 *Lettere*, vol. 380 (1884), fog. 661rv, Simeoni to Alemany, Rome, December 31, 1884. "Udienze di Nostro Signore" (hereafter cited as *Udienze*), vol. 210 (1884), foglii 2543v, 2545r, report of the papal audience of December 28, 1884.

18 AASF, LBR(4a), 228-29, Riordan to Riordan [San Francisco], December 27, 1912, copy.

19 AOPR, Alemany to Larroca, San Francisco, January 26, 1885; Archives of the Order of Preachers, Province of the Holy Name, San Francisco, Alemany to Larroca, San Francisco, January 26, 1885; *Congressi, A.C.*, vol. 42 (1885), fog. 166r, Alemany to Simeoni, San Francisco, February 10, 1885. *Monitor*, February 4, 1885, p.4.

20 *Congressi, A.C.*, vol. 42 (1885), fog. 192rv, Riordan to Simeoni, San Francisco, February 16, 1885; *Lettere*, vol. 381 (1885), fog. 141rv, Simeoni to Riordan, Rome, March 9, 1885.

21 *Lettere*, vol. 381 (1885), fog. 180v, Simeoni to Mgr. Boccali, Rome, March 14, 1885; fog. 205v, Simeoni to Alemany, Rome, April 16, 1885. *Congressi, A.C.*, vol. 43 (1885), fog. 133r, Alemany to Simeoni, Rome, July 24, 1885.

22 *Monitor*, February 25, 1885, p. 1.

23 P.W. Riordan, "Joseph Sadoc Alemany," *Catholic Encyclopedia* (New York, 1907), I, 282-83. Alemany's most recent biographer considers this article as yet the best of the standard sketches which have appeared in various encyclopedias. (John B. McGloin, S.J., *California's First Archbishop: The Life of Joseph Sadoc Alemany, O.P., 1814-1888* [New York, 1966], p. 373.)

24 AAB, 79-M-5, Riordan to Gibbons, San Francisco, June 5, 1885.

25 Ellis, *op. cit*, I, 300-301, 325-326.

26 *Monitor*, September 23, 1885, p. 5.

27 UND, MC, Onahan Papers, IX-1-a, Riordan to Onahan, Santa Clara, California, February 7, 1885. A friend also of Ireland and Spalding, Onahan was the secretary of the Irish Catholic Colonization Association and would serve as secretary of the American Catholic Congress which was held during the Chicago World Fair in 1893.

28 The boundaries of the archdiocese at this time were set according to latitudes, extending between 37° 5' and 40° N. latitude. It comprised the following counties: San Francisco, Mendocino, Lake, Sonoma, Napa, Marin, Solano, Contra Costa, San Mateo, Alameda, San Joaquin, Stanislaus, and portions of Santa Cruz, Santa Clara, and Merced north of 37° 5' N. latitude.

29 *Congressi, A.C.*, vol. 49 (1888), fog. 1437rv-1443rv, report by Riordan, Rome, November 21, 1888; fog. 1436rv, observations by Fiocchimo Ma. Corrado (?) [Rome], July 11, 1889. See also *Lettere*, vol. 385 (1889), fog. 574rv, Simeoni to Riordan, Rome, August 7, 1889

30 Herbert Vaughan, "California and the Church," *Dublin Review*, LVIII (January,1866), 30-31.

31 Benjamin E. Lloyd, *Lights and Shades in San Francisco* (San Francisco, 1876), pp. 86-87.

32 *Congressi, A.C.*, vol. 35 (1881), fog. 216r, report of Joseph Sadoc Alemany [San Francisco, November 3, 1880].

33 *Monitor*, May 16, 1883, supplement. A careful historical account of the cathedral, probably composed by its long-term rector, Charles A. Ramm, records that in March, 1882, this property was deeded to Archbishop Alemany. AASF, Parish Files, History of St. Mary's Cathedral.

34 *Monitor*, December 16, 1885, unpaginated; December 24, p. 4. The ground was broken for the cathedral in December 1885.

35 *Ibid.*, November 9, 1887, p. 4.

36 *Ibid.*, May 4, 1887, pp. 1, 4; January 14, 1891, pp. 1, 4. The figures on the excavation originate from Charles A. Ramm and John M. Byrne. (Harold E. Collins to the writer, San Francisco, June 20, 1964.)

37 AASF, LB-14(79-80), Riordan to Conaty [San Francisco], March 6, 1905, copy.

38 *Congressi, A.C.*, vol. 35 (1881), fog. 214r.

39 *Ibid.*, fog. 219r, observations by Vittorio Piazresi (?), Rome, March 5, 1881.

40 *Metropolitan Catholic Almanac. . .1854* (Baltimore, n.d.), p. 202; John J. Prendergast, "The First Seminary of San Francisco," in the *Monitor*, September 17, 1898, unpaginated. Zephyrin Englehardt, *Mission Santa Inés, Virgen y Martir, and Its Ecclesiastical Seminary* (Santa Barbara, 1932), p. 97. Apparently, the parish responsibilities provided too many distractions for the smooth administration of the seminary. Its extensive cemetery, Prendergast often remarked in later years, "took more of my time than the Seminary." But contemporaries

disputed his contention. "The Mission Dolores," ran one testimony, "was not a large parish; — but the remains of the old Spanish settlement, with a limited. . .population, a half hour by horse-cars over sand hills from the city." The seminary rector was responsible for only two Masses on Sunday and had a curate to assist him. (Archives of St. Mary's Seminary, Baltimore, Maryland, Timothy Callaghan, Pastor of St. Matthew's Parish, San Mateo, California, in an interview with Francis P. Havey, S.S., on July 24, 1927, preserved in Havey's Notes.)

41 *Lettere*, vol. 374 (1878), fog. 539v-540r, Simeoni to Alemany, Rome, November 4, 1878. *Congressi, A.C.*, vol. 30 (1879), fog. 342r, Alemany to Simeoni, San Francisco, March 2, 1879. When Alemany failed to secure the Sulpicians, his secretary, George Montgomery, was disheartened and told his former superior at St. Mary's Seminary in Baltimore that his community had "lost the golden opportunity for gaining a foothold in this western paradise where was situated the Garden of Eden. . . ."(ASMS, Magnien Papers, Montgomery to Alphonse Magnien, S.S., San Francisco, April 26, 1880.) An excellent narrative on Alemany's second seminary which is based on the correspondence in the Archives of the Society of Mary in Rome is Leon L. Dubois, S.M., "St. Thomas Seminary at San Jose, California," *Acta Societatis Mariae*, No. 17 (August 15, 1955), pp. 373-82.

42 This tax was derived from payments to the bishops of California by the Mexican government. In February, 1881, Alemany had proposed to apply the whole income from the Santa Inés Ranch for a provincial seminary, but Mora refused to accept his plan, denying the Diocese of Grass Valley any rights to the ranch and keeping a half share for his own see. Alemany was thereupon forced to use the income from the Pious Fund paid by Mexico, and he assessed the sums of $16,000 due to the Diocese of Grass Valley. See pp. 112-13.

43 Archives of the Society of Mary, Pestre to Julicn Favre, S.M., Superior General, San Jose, California, January 26, 1883; hereafter cited as ASM. See also Charles E. O'Neile, "St. Thomas' Seminary," in the *Monitor*, September 17, 1898, unpaginated.

44 Pestre to Favre, San Jose, March 28, 1883.

45 ASM, Pestre to Favre, San Jose, December 21, 1883.

46 Pestre to Favre, San Jose, February 3, 1884.

47 *Congressi, A.C.*, vol. 40 (1884), fog. 779r, Alemany to Simeoni, San Francisco, May 7, 1884.

48 ASMS, statement of Jean-Baptiste Vuibert, S.S., n.p., n.d., in Havey's Notes.

49 ASM, Riordan to Pestre, San Francisco, April 2, 1885, copied in Pestre to [Favre], Dublin, April 9, 1885.

50 *Ibid.*, "Procès Verbaux du Conseil (1879-1887)," entries for June 17, September 11, and December 12, 1885; APF, *Udienze*, vol. 223 (1887), fog. 1704v, 1731r.

51 *Voice* (St. Mary's Seminary, Baltimore), IX (January, 1932), p. 6. In ASMS, an anonymous manuscript, "Le Seminaire de St. Patrice á Menlo Park, California," describes the first meeting between Leo XIII and Riordan. When the pope asked if his archdiocese had a seminary, Riordan was reported to have replied: "No, Most Holy Father, but I desire with all my heart to establish one. Only I have no one to whom I can entrust it; on my way in Paris I asked the Sulpicians, but Father Icard would not listen to me." The pope promised in return to intercede for him, declaring: "You shall have the Sulpicians." Unfortunately this document has been mislaid. The account is contained in John McDonough, S.S., "St. Patrick's Seminary, Menlo Park, California, 1898-1948," an unpublished manuscript in the archives of St. Patrick's Seminary.

52 *Lettere*, vol. 384 (1888), fog. 611v-612r, Simeoni to Icard, Rome, November 17, 1888.

53 *Congressi, A.C.*, vol. 29 (1878), fog. 793rv, Icard to Simeoni, Paris, September 23, 1878.

54 Archives de la Compagnie des Prêtres de Saint-Sulpice (hereafter cited as ASS), "51ème Assemblée Générale des Assistants de la Compagnie de St.-Sulpice," Fourth Register, folios 326-328, sixteenth session, August 24, 1879. The most recent history of the Sulpicians incorrectly applies this reference to Riordan's later appeal through Simeoni. See M. Boisard, *La Compagnie de Saint-Sulpice . . . : Trois Siecles d'Histoire*, n.p., n.d., II, 611, 625, n. 166.

55 Boisard, II, 605, 608; *Congressi, A.C.*, vol. 50 (1889), fog. 370r, Icard to [John J. Keane], Paris, December 5, 1888. *Ibid.*, vol. 46 (1887), fog. 526r-527rv, Corrigan to Simeoni, New York, March 27, 1887.

56 There is no record in ASS of this agreement; and in ASMS, only informal accounts of Riordan's testimony. According to one account, the archbishop arrived at Paris in time to participate in the celebration of Icard's sixty-second anniversary in the priesthood. Studying the octogenarian superior, Riordan is recorded to have said that in view of his advanced age a foundation in California would be most likely the last in his lifetime. "It should be done; otherwise I despair of your salvation." After consultation the eighty-three-year-old superior informed Riordan that the Sulpicians would staff his projected seminary. "Good," the archbishop told Icard, "now I no longer have apprehension for your salvation." (McDonough, *op. cit.*, I, pp. 115-16.)

57 ASS, "51ème Assemblée Générale . . . ," Fifth Register, folio 27, tenth session, July 21, 1890.

58 ASMS, Riordan to Magnien, San Francisco, July 11, 1891.

59 ASMS, Riordan to Magnien, San Francisco, July 30, 1891.

60 ASS, "Assemblée des Consulteurs," meeting of October 26, 1896, tome IV, folio 155.

61 Doyle to Riordan, n.p., December 18, 1890, and January 8, 1891, copies; the papers of John T. Doyle, Bancroft Library, University of California, Berkeley; hereafter cited as DP. Permission to quote from these papers has been kindly given by George P. Hammond, former Director of the Bancroft Library.

62 These "Founders" of the seminary who contributed $50,000 each were the following: Mr. and Mrs. F. S. Wensinger, the MacDonough Estate, Judge Myles P. O'Connor, Joseph A. Donohoe, Mrs. Peter Donahue, and an anonymous benefactor. Riordan had estimated $500,000 as the endowment fund for the seminary. Three of these above donations had already been paid by the seminary dedication in 1898, and the fourth was due shortly. *Monitor*, September 17, 1898, pp. 2, 3.

63 ASMS, Riordan to Magnien, San Francisco, July 11, 1891.

64 DP, Doyle to Riordan, n.p., April 23, 1891, copy.

65 This description of the site is found in DP, a contract between Riordan and Mrs. Jane L. Stanford, December, 1901, copy.

66 DP, Doyle to Riordan, n.p., July 18, 1891, copy.

67 DP, Doyle to Riordan, n.p. [July 24, 1891], copy.

68 DP, Doyle to Mrs. Kate Johnson, San Francisco, July 24, 1891, copy.

69 *Monitor*, January 8, 1898, p. 1.

70 ASMS, Havey's Notes.

71 Peter C. Yorke, "Essentially a Churchman," *Leader* (San Francisco), January 2, 1915, p. 4.

72 ASMS, Riordan to Magnien, San Francisco, November 25, 1890.

73 *Monitor*, September 17, 1898 [p. 30]; September 24, p. 17.

74 *Ibid.*, August 27, 1898, p. 9. AASF, LBR(1a), 253-56, Riordan to Archbishop Alexander Christie [San Francisco], August 4, 1909, copy.

75 Orrin Leslie Elliott, *Stanford University: The First Twenty-Five Years* (Stanford, California and London, 1937), pp. 137-41, 453-55.

76 DP, Doyle to Riordan, n.p., November 28, 1901; and an Agreement between Patrick W. Riordan and Jane L. Stanford, December, 1901, copies.

77 *Monitor*, August 20, 1904, p. 11.

78 ASMS, Riordan to Vuibert, San Francisco, June 1, 1898.

79 ASMS, Havey's Notes.

80 ASMS, Riordan to Magnien, San Francisco, May 24, 1899.

81 ASMS, Vuibert to Dyer, Menlo Park, August 24, and 31, 1903; Riordan to A. Captier, P.S.S., Menlo Park, September 4, 1903, copy.

82 ASS, "Assemblée des Consulteurs," meetings of December 28, 1903, May 2 and June 6, 1904, tome IV, folios 213, 219, and 221.

83 AASF, LB-8(236), Riordan to Royal B. Webster [San Francisco, June 4 or 5, 1903], copy.

84 ASMS, Havey's Notes.

85 *Ibid.*, statement of the Reverend Daniel O'Sullivan, Pastor of All Hallows Parish, San Francisco, Havey's Notes.

86 AASF, LB-28(185-86), John J. Cantwell to John Foley [San Francisco], December 26, 1908; LB-30(266), Charles A. Ramm to Foley [San Francisco], August 4, 1908, copies. At this time, it must be noted, Riordan did preserve cordial relations with St. Patrick's College in Thurles, Tipperary.

87 *Monitor* July 4, 1908, pp. 1, 4.

88 AASF, LBR(3a), 645-46, Riordan to Riordan [San Francisco], September 13, 1912, copy. For the same sentiments expressed three months before his death, see *ibid.*, LBR(6a), 45-47, Riordan to Riordan [San Francisco], September 29, 1914, copy.

89 APF, Protocol Number (hereafter cited as P.N.) 99/36791, Report of Riordan [Rome, December 18, 1899], signed copy. After 1892, the Propaganda archives are not divided and classified according to the customary series, and for this reason the more recent material is identified simply by the protocol number.

90 Walter McDonald, *Reminiscences of a Maynooth Professor*, ed. Denis Gwynn (London, 1925), p. 217. McDonald's brother James was pastor of St. Charles' Parish, San Francisco.

91 *Monitor*, September 26, 1883, p. 1.

92 Peter C. Yorke, "Essentially a Churchman," *Leader* (San Francisco), January 2, 1915, p. 4.

93 *Idem.*

94 *New World* (Chicago), October 7, 1899, p. 16.

CHAPTER FIVE

1 An Irish-born immigrant who had come to the United States in
1848, Patrick Manogue (1831-95) had taken his junior course at the
University of St. Mary of the Lake, Riordan's *alma mater* in Chicago
and, after graduation two years later, had come to California where he
was for some time in Moore's Flat, Nevada County. Eventually, he
disposed of his interests and sailed for Europe where he prepared for
the priesthood at St.-Sulpice, Paris, and was ordained in 1861. (ASS,
"Noms des Elèves entres au Seminaire de Saint-Sulpice de Paris, depuis
le 11 Octobre 1847," folio 192r.) In the following year, he was
appointed pastor of St. Mary's Church in Virginia City with jurisdiction
over almost the entire country which now forms the State of Nevada,
and through his long pastorate, he acquired great influence among the
miners of the region and also among the Piute Indians, many of whom
he converted. A hardy and forceful individual, Manogue had long been
the outstanding ecclesiastic of this area, serving as one of Bishop
Eugene O'Connell's vicars general and mentioned often as his successor.
There is no question of Manogue's attractiveness even to the
non-Catholic community. Arthur McEwen, an independent and
influential journalist, was a genuine admirer of Manogue who, he said,
had been in Virginia City a man "imbued with the hearty, masculine
spirit of the place, and his sturdy, kindly spirit was too broad for
church lines when need appealed to his sympathy." At the bishop's
death, McEwen lauded his achievements as a pioneer priest, noting in an
extraordinary tribute: "There are more polished, more scholarly priests
in the Catholic community on the Pacific Coast but none more godly,
more manly than was Patrick Manogue." *Arthur McEwen's Letter* (San
Francisco), March 2, 1895, p. 3; in the Bancroft Library. When
O'Connell was negotiating for a coadjutor, the leading priests of the
diocese recommended Manogue as the only man who could rectify the
mishaps attributed to the bishop. Manogue "is a child of the diocese,"
they informed Propaganda, "knows all its wants and necessities, is a
man of the most practical sound sense, good judgment, and has more
influence than any priest or bishop in the diocese, and he is the choice
of the priests of the diocese." *Congressi, A.C.*, vol. 28 (1877), fog.
660r-668r, Thomas J. Dalton, V.G., Charles M. Lynch, Daniel Meagher,
Matthew Coleman to Cardinal Alessandro Franchi, n.p. [November 23,
1877]. On July 5, 1880, he was selected by the congregation as
O'Connell's coadjutor with the right of succession and was consecrated
on January 16, 1881, as titular Bishop of Geremos. *Lettere*, vol. 376

(1880), fog. 382v, Cardinal Giovanni Simeoni to O'Connell, Rome, July 22, 1880; *ibid.*, fog. 717r, "Decretum," July 20, 1880. In 1884, when Pope Leo XIII accepted O'Connell's resignation from the see, Manogue succeeded as Bishop of Grass Valley, beginning an eleven-year reign which would end in his death in 1895. *Ibid.*, vol. 380 (1884), fog. 101v-102r, Simeoni to O'Connell, Rome, February 23, 1884. The only work which approximates a biography of Manogue is Clarence Roy Kline, "Patrick Manogue; Miner, Priest, Pastor, Bishop 1831-1895," an unpublished master's thesis, University of California, Berkeley, 1960. A good précis may be found in John B. McGloin, S.J., "Some Letters of Patrick Manogue, Gold Miner and Bishop of Nevada and California," *Records* of the American Catholic Historical Society of Philadelphia, LXXI (March, June 1960), 3-4.

2 AASF, Bull erecting the Vicariate of Marysville, Rome, September 28, 1860; Bull erecting the Diocese of Grass Valley, Rome, March 3, 1868.

3 UND, MC, Society for the Propagation of the Faith (Paris), Grass Valley, F-62a, fol. 3753, Manogue to the Directors, Virginia City, Nevada, February 12, 1868, microfilm copy.

4 *Cong. Gen.*, vol. 1024 (1885), fog. 702rv, Alemany, O'Connell, Mora, and Manogue to Simeoni, San Francisco, February 24, 1881.

5 *Cong. Gen.*, vol. 1024 (1885), fog. 740rv-741rv, Manogue to Schulte, Virginia City, July 29, 1884, copy and translation.

6 *Lettere*, vol. 381 (1885), fog. 146v-147r, Simeoni to Manogue, Rome, March 14, 1885.

7 *Cong. Gen.*, loc. cit., fog. 747rv-748rv. Manogue to August J. Schulte, Grass Valley, April 23, 1885. Father Schulte was a staff member of the American College in Rome.

8 *Ibid.*, fog. 749rv-750r, Manogue to Schulte, Marysville, April 30, 1885, copy and translation.

9 The ten counties proposed to be detached from the Archdiocese of San Francisco were the following: Sacramento, Yolo, Placer, El Dorado, Amador, Calaveras, Tuolumne, Alpine, Mariposa, and Mono. In a series of further observations, Riordan suggested that parts of Fresno, Inyo, and Sutter Counties be apportioned to Grass Valley, (*Ibid.*, fog. 704r-709r, Riordan and Manogue to Simeoni, San Francisco, June 12, 1885; fog. 710r-715r, Riordan to Simeoni, San Francisco, July 1, 1885.)

10 *Ibid.*, fog. 767rv-768rv, Alemany to Simeoni, Rome, August 3, 1885.

11 *Ibid.*, fog. 716r-718r, Riordan to Simeoni, San Francisco, September 2, 1885.

12 *Acta*, vol. 254 (1885), fog. 562E, report of the general congregation of December 10, 1885; *Lettere*, vol. 381 (1885), fog. 648v-649r, Simeoni to Manogue, Rome, December 31, 1885; *ibid.* vol. 382 (1886), Simeoni to Riordan, Rome, January 18, 1886; fog. 335v-336rv, "Decretum," May 16, 1886. According to the final decree, detached from San Francisco were the following counties: Sacramento, Yolo, El Dorado, Tuolumne, Calaveras, Alpine, Amador, Mono, and Mariposa, and portions of Fresno, Inyo, Sutter, Placer, Yuba, and Colusa Counties.

13 *Congressi, A.C.*, vol. 55 (1891), fog. 94rv-97rv, "The Santa Inés Ranch," a summary of its early canonical history. For a fuller description of its history, see Zephyrin Engelhardt, *Mission Santa Inés, Virgen y Martir, and Its Ecclesiastical Seminary* (Santa Barbara, 1932); and William E. North, *Catholic Education in Southern California* (Washington, D.C., 1936), pp. 80-101.

14 *Congressi, A.C.*, vol. 55 (1891), fog. 66rv-67rv, Manogue to Denis J. O'Connell, Sacramento, September 11, 1888, copy; fog. 68rv-71r, Manogue's Memorial, n.p. [October, 1888].

15 *Ibid.*, fog. 83rv-84rv, "Observations" of Riordan, Rome, October, 1888.

16 *Lettere*, vol. 384 (1884), fog. 618Arv-618Br, Simeoni to Manogue, Rome, November 23, 1888, ms.

17 ADR, Riordan to O'Connell, San Francisco, April 16, 1889. *Udienze*, vol. 233 (1889), fog. 1486rv, same to same, San Francisco, June 11,1889.

18 *Cong. Gen.*, vol. 1039, (1891), 87rv-92r, Manogue's report to Simeoni, Rome, June 26, 1890.

19 *Lettere*, vol. 386 (1890), fog. 559v-560r, Simeoni to Riordan, Rome, August 12, 1890.

20 *Cong. Gen.*, vol. 1039 (1891), fog. 98r-111r, Riordan to Simeoni, San Francisco, October 31, 1890.

21 *Lettere*, vol. 387 (1891), fog. 7rv-8r, Simeoni to Manogue, January 9, 1891.

22 *Cong. Gen.*, vol. 1039 (1891), fog. 115rv-116rv, Manogue to Jacobini, Grass Valley, February 7, 1891. For the formal closing of the question, see *Lettere*, vol. 387 (1891), fog. 192rv-193r, Simeoni to Manogue, March 16, 1891.

23 APF, P.N. 95/11398, Manogue to Satolli, Sacremento, January 8, 1895.

24 P.N. 95/11397, Riordan to Ledochowski, San Francisco, January 8, 1895. See also Ledochowski to Satolli, Rome, February 5, 1885, copy.

25 P.N. 95/11825, Riordan to Ledochowski, San Francisco, February 28, 1895, telegram.

26 P.N. 95/11889, Riordan to Ledochowski, San Francisco, March 2, 1895, telegram. *Monitor*, March 9, 1895, p. 9.

27 P.N. 95/12317, report to Ledochowski endorsed by Riordan, San Francisco, March 12, 1895.

28 P.N. 95/12877, Riordan *et al.* to Ledochowski [San Francisco, April 18, 1895].

29 P.N. 95/13266, Satolli to Ledochowski, Washington, D.C., May 24, 1895.

30 P.N. 95/14656, Charles Lynch, Matthew Coleman, Lawrence Kennedy, and John Blynes to Ledochowski, n.p., August 15, 1895. See also P.N. 95/14252, Grace to Ledochowski, Sacremento, July 25, 1895; Agostino Ciasca, Secretary of Propaganda, to Grace, August 13, 1895, copy.

31 P.N. 96/16753, "Decree," Rome, February 24, 1896, copy. *Monitor*, June 20, 1896, pp. 8-9.

32 For details on the history of Utah, see Hubert H. Bancroft, *History of Utah, 1540-1887* (San Francisco, 1891); Rupert Norval Richardson and Carl Coke Rister, *The Greater Southwest* . . . (Glendale, California, 1934); Robert J. Dwyer, *The Gentile Comes to Utah: A Study in Religious and Social Conflict, 1862-1890* (Washington, 1941); Nels Anderson, *Desert Saints: The Mormon Frontier in Utah* (Chicago, 1942); Fawn Brodie, *No Man Knows My History: The Life of Joseph Smith, the Mormon Prophet* (New York, 1945); Ray Benedict West, *Kingdom of the Saints: The Story of Brigham Young and the Mormons* (New York, 1957); Milton R. Hunter, *The Utah Story* (Salt Lake City, 1960).

33 *Acta*, vol. 255 (1866), fog. 542r, Cardinal Lorenzo Randi, *Ristretto con sommario*, "Erezione del Vicariato di Utah, e nomina del Vicario Apostolica," September, 1886; hereafter cited as Randi, *Ristretto*. See also Donald C. Shearer, *Pontificia Americana* . . . (Washington, 1933), pp. 336-37. For a helpful survey of the ecclesiastical beginnings of Utah, see Robert J. Dwyer, "Pioneer Bishop: Lawrence Scanlan, 1843-1915," *Utah Historical Quarterly*, XX (April, 1952), 135-58; and for the pre-Scanlan days see Jerome Stoffel, "The Hesitant Beginnings of the Catholic Church in Utah," *Utah Historical Quarterly*, XXVI (Winter, 1968), 42-62.

34 *Congressi, A.C.*, vol. 22 (1868-69), fog. 833rv-836r, Machebeuf to Barnabò, Denver, March 15, 1869. For a resumé of Machebeuf's tour and the mission of Father Edward Kelly of Marysville, see W. R. Harris,

The Catholic Church in Utah (Salt Lake City, 1900), pp. 281-86; and W. J. Howlett, *Life of Right Reverend Joseph P. Machebuef, D.D.* (Pueblo, Colorado, 1908), pp. 349-51.

35 Randi, *Ristretto* fog. 542r.

36 Lawrence Scanlan (1843-1915), born in Ireland, received his seminary training at All Hallows College, Dublin, and in 1868 was ordained for the Archdiocese of San Francisco. His earliest pastorates included Woodland, California; Poiche, Nevada; and Petaluma, California; and in June, 1873, he was named pastor of the whole Territory of Utah. *Annals of All Hallows College for the Year 1896* (Dublin, 1896), pp. 58-60.

37 UND, MC, Papers of the Society for the Propagation of the Faith (Paris), Salt Lake City, F-139, fol. 7242, Scanlan to A. Guasco, Salt Lake City, August 24, 1892.

38 AASF, LBR(3a), 100-10, Riordan to the Most Reverend John Bonzano, apostolic delegate [San Francisco], November 13, 1912, copy.

39 Landi, *Ristretto* fog. 542.

40 *Acta*, vol. 255 (1886), fog. 546v-548rv, Riordan to Simeoni, San Francisco, April 17, 1886.

41 *Ibid.*, fog. 544r, report of the general congregation September 6, 1886. *Lettere*, vol. 382 (1886), fog. 669, "Decree," November 22, 1886. The six counties of Nevada included within the vicariate were Elko, Lander, Eureka, White Pine, Nye, and Lincoln — an area slightly more than half of the state.

42 AASF, LBR(3a), 100-10, Riordan to Bonzano [San Francisco], November 13, 1912, copy.

43 *Lettere*, vol. 382 (1886), fog. 226rv, "Decretum," April 29, 1887. See also *Udienze*, vol. 228 (1887), fog. 2830r, Gibbons to Simeoni, Rome, March 5, 1887. On March 20, 1887, Leo XIII formally committed the Vicariate Apostolic of Utah to the Province of San Francisco.

44 *Cong. Gen.*, vol. 1035 (1890), fog. 331rv-333rv, Burke to Simeoni [Rome], n.d., registered at Propaganda on December 30, 1889.

45 *Ibid.*, fog. 336r, Scanlan to Simeoni, Salt Lake City, February 12, 1890; fog. 337r-340r, same to same, Salt Lake City, February 12, 1890.

46 *Ibid.*, fog. 324v-325rv, Cardinal Tommaso Maria Zigliara. *Relazione con sommario*, "Sopra le dimissioni di Monsig. Vescovo di Chejenne, l'erezione in Diocesi del Vicariato di Utah, l'elezione . . . del Vescovo di Omaha," June, 1890.

47 *Sadliers' Catholic Directory* ... *1876* (New York, 1876), p. 333; *Sadliers' Catholic Directory*...*1879* (New York, 1879), p. 209.

48 *Cong. Gen.*, vol. 1035 (1890), fog. 335r, Riordan to Farrelly, San Francisco, February 3, 1890, copy and translation.

49 *Ibid.*, fog. 458rv-459rv, Riordan to [O'Connell], San Francisco, April 15, 1890, copy and translation.

50 *Acta*, vol. 260 (1889), fog. 124r, report of the general congregation of June 15, 1890. The Diocese of "Salt Lake" was renamed the Diocese of "Salt Lake City" in 1951.

51 *Lettere*, vol. 386 (1890), fog. 458v, Simeoni to Riordan, Rome, July 7, 1890.

52 *Cong. Gen.*, vol. 1037 (1890), fog. 684r, Riordan to Simeoni, San Francisco, August 28, 1890.

53 *Ibid.*, fog. 657rv, Cardinal Tommaso Maria Zigliara, *Relazione con sommario*, "Sopra . . .," December, 1890.

54 *Acta*, vol. 260 (1890), fog. 324r, report of the general congregation of December 16, 1890. This recommendation was formally sanctioned by Leo XIII on December 17, 1890. See also *Lettere*, vol. 387 (1891), fog. 93r, "Decree," Rome, January 12, 1891.

55 George W. Bemis, "Sectionialism and Representation in the California State Legislature, 1911-1913," unpublished doctoral dissertation, University of California, Berkeley, 1933, p. 19, *et passim*, and charts. See also *Cong. Gen.*, vol. 1037 (1890), fog. 54r-58r, Riordan to Simeoni, San Francisco, September 28, 1889.

56 Cuthbert Butler, *The Vatican Council* (London, 1930), II, 113. See also Francis J. Weber, *California's Reluctant Prelate: The Life and Times of Right Reverend Thaddeus Amat, C.M. (1811-1878)* (Los Angeles, 1964).

57 *Congressi*, A.C., vol. 35 (1881), fog. 359rv-363r, Mora's report on the Diocese of Monterey-Los Angeles [May, 1881]; *ibid.*, fog. 364rv-365rv, observations by an official of Propaganda, Rome, December 10, 1881. Francis Mora (1827-1905), a native of Catalonia, Spain, had come to America as a student with Amat. He was ordained in 1856 and succeeded Amat as bishop in 1878. Francis J. Weber, *Francis Mora, Last of the Catalans* (Los Angeles, 1967).

58 AALA, Mora to Simeoni, Los Angeles, January 11, 1889; Simeoni to Mora, Rome, February 16, 1889; Mora to Simeoni, Los Angeles, March 24, 1889. *Cong. Gen.*, vol. 1037 (1890), fog. 1rv, Cardinal Serafino Vannutelli, *Relazione con sommario*, "Sopra l'elezione del Coadiutore del Vescovo di Monterey e Los Angeles, e sul progetto della divisione di Monterey," September, 1890; hereafter cited as Vannutelli, *Relazione (1890)*.

59 *Lettere*, vol. 385 (1889), fog. 296v-297r, Simeoni to Riordan, Rome, May 4, 1889.

60 *Cong. Gen.*, vol. 1037 (1890), fog. 36r-41r, Riordan to Simeoni, n.p., June 1, 1889.

61 *Ibid.*, fog. 42rv-43r, Riordan to O'Connell, San Francisco, June 2, 1889, copy and translation. Also, *Udienze*, vol. 233 (1889), fog. 1486rv, same to same, San Francisco, June 11, 1889, copy and translation.

62 *Cong. Gen.*, vol. 1037 (1890), fog. 3r, Vannutelli, *Relazione (1890)*; *Lettere*, vol. 385 (1889), fog. 476r, Simeoni to Riordan, Rome, July 8, 1889; fog. 477v, Simeoni to Mora, Rome, July 8, 1889.

63 *Cong. Gen.*, vol. 1037 (1890), fog. 11r-14r, Riordan, Mora, Manogue, and Scanlan to Simeoni, San Francisco, September 18, 1889. Dunne died as Bishop of Dallas.

64 *Ibid.*, fog. 19r-21r, Riordan, Manogue, and Scanlan to Simeoni, San Francisco, September 18, 1889.

65 *Sadliers' Catholic Directory . . . 1890* (New York, 1890), p. 302.

66 *Acta*, vol. 261 (1891), fog. 50r, report of the general congregation of February 23, 1891. *Lettere*, vol. 387 (1891), fog. 204rv, Simeoni to Mora, Rome, March 21, 1891; fog. 209v, Simeoni to Riordan, Rome, March 31, 1891.

67 *Lettere*, vol. 387 (1891), fog. 271v-272r, Simeoni to Verdaguer, Rome, April 14, 1891.

68 *Acta*, vol. 261 (1892), fog. 307rv, Cardinal Achille Apolloni, *Relazione*, "Sul divieto fatto a Monsig. Mora Vescovo di Monterey e Los Angeles di alienare o contrarre debiti sui beni della Diocesi," August, 1891. *Ibid.*, fog. 308r, report of the general congregation of August 17, 1891. *Lettere*, *loc. cit.*, fog. 645v-646r, Simeoni to Mora, Rome, August 29, 1891.

69 P.N. 93/626, Mora to Ledochowski, Los Angeles [January, 1893]; P.N. 93/669, Riordan to Ledochowski, San Francisco, January 20, 1893.

70 P.N. 93/626, 669, Ledochowski to Mora, Rome, March 8, 1893; P.N. 93/669, Ledochowski to Riordan, Rome, March 13, 1893, copies.

71 P.N. 93/1966, Mora to Ledochowski, Los Angeles, April 11, 1893.

72 AALA, Riordan to Mora, San Francisco, January 21 and March 31, 1893.

73 P.N. 93/3753, report of Consultors' Meeting by Polydore Stockman, Los Angeles, August 7, 1893; P.N. 93/3692, Mora to Ledochowski, Los Angeles [August] 9, 1893.

74 P.N. 93/3975, Riordan to Ledochowski, San Francisco [August 30, 1893].

75 P.N. 93/4674, Riordan to Satolli, San Francisco, October 20, 1893.

76 ADR, Riordan to O'Connell, San Francisco, October 20, 1893.

77 P.N. 94/5185, "Decree," Rome, January 11, 1894, copy. The news of the appointment first appeared in the *Monitor*, January 20, 1894, p. 4. It was on April 8, 1894, that Riordan consecrated Montgomery as titular Bishop of Tumi. *Ibid.*, April 14, 1894, pp. 8-9, 12.

78 ADR, Riordan to O'Connell, San Francisco, January 11, 1894.

CHAPTER SIX

1 On the definition of nativism, see John Higham, *Strangers in the Land: Patterns of American Nativism, 1860-1925* (New Brunswick, 1955), and "Another Look at Nativism," *Catholic Historical Review*, XXXXIV (July, 1958), 147-48. Also relevant is Donald L. Kinzer, *An Episode in Anti-Catholicism: The American Protective Association* (Seattle, 1964).

2 U. S. Bureau of Census, *Bulletin 103*, "Special Report, Religious Bodies" (Washington, 1910), 43; quoted in Gilman Marston Ostrander, "The Prohibition Movement in California, 1848-1933," an unpublished doctoral dissertation, University of California, Berkeley, 1954, p. 123.

3 *Compendium of the 11th Census, 1890*, Part II, United States Department of the Interior, Census Bureau (Washington, D.C., 1894), pp. 604-607.

4 *Arthur McEwen's Letter* (San Francisco), March 24, 1894, p. 1; available at the Bancroft Library, University of California, Berkeley.

5 See John Higham, "The American Party, 1886-1891," *Pacific Historical Review*, XIX (February, 1950), 37-46.

6 Charles F. Lummis, "A Jason of the Coast," in *The Land of Sunshine*, III (June-November, 1895), 237; quoted James Richard Wotherspoon, "The San Francisco *Argonaut*, 1877-1907," an unpublished doctoral dissertation, University of California, Berkeley, 1962, p. 23.

No biography has yet appeared on Frank Morrison Pixley, a figure who had left a deep impression on the development of California. Born in 1825 in upstate New York, he first studied law, passing the bar examinations, but came to California in 1849. His failures in prospecting revived his interest in law, but at this time he had too involved himself in various economic and political ventures. In March, 1877, he joined with Fred Somers in founding the *Argonaut* and fashioned it into a polished weekly. After a stormy career, Pixley relinquished his editorial writing in 1893 and died on August 11, 1895. His death removed from the western scene one of the most powerful personalities of the day and one of the most admired journalists in the country. (Wotherspoon, pp. 3-23.)

7 *Argonaut*, XIX (December 4, 1886), p. 3.

8 *Congressi, A.C.*, vol. 49 (1888), fog. 1439r, report of Patrick Riordan, Rome, November 21, 1888.

9 *Arthur McEwen's Letter* (San Francisco), March 2, 1894, p. 2.

10 Kinzer, *op. cit.*, chaps. II and III; and John Higham, "The Mind of a Nativist: Henry E. Bowers and the A.P.A.," *American Quarterly*, IV (Spring, 1952), 16-24.

11 *Monitor* April 18, 1893, p. 3; April 22, p. 2, July 22, p. 5.

12 San Francisco *Examiner*, February 6, 1894, p. 12.

13 David Joseph Herlihy, "Battle Against Bigotry: Father Peter C. Yorke and the American Protective Association in San Francisco, 1893-1897," *Records* of the American Catholic Historical Society of Philadelphia, LXII (June, 1951), 97. See also Joseph S. Brusher, S.J., "Peter C. Yorke and the A.P.A. in San Francisco," *Catholic Historical Review*, XXXVII (July, 1951), 129-50.

14 P.V.N. Myers, *Outlines of Medieval and Modern History. A Textbook for High Schools, Seminaries, and Colleges* (Boston, 1888).

15 San Francisco *Examiner*, February 16, 1894, p. 12. There is some testimony that many passages in the *Outlines* were hostile to the Catholic Church. Frederic A. Hyde, president of the Board of Education, was quoted as having confessed: "I have never read the work, but if those quotations are correct it will undoubtedly be dropped." John Swett, the former State Superintendent of Public Instruction, admitted substantially the same.

16 Riordan's elaborate list of objections was given in the San Francisco *Examiner*, March 15, 1894, p. 16. For an account of the origin of the archbishop's complaint, see the *Monitor*, October 27, 1894, pp. 4-5.

17 J.Q.A. Henry, *Rome's Hand in Our Public Schools, A Protest!* (San Francisco, 1894); available in the Bancroft Library.

18 San Francisco *Examiner*, March 19, 1894, p. 3.

19 San Francisco *Call*, April 12, 1894, p. 3. The voting of the board was rather close, seven to four. An alternative motion presented by Director Charles L. Clinton was defeated, that the book was sectarian within the concept of the state law and should, therefore, be dropped. At the same time the board resolved significantly that the last Friday of each month be reserved for patriotic exercises, songs, and "instructions by teachers in the principles of government and the duties of American citizenship."

20 AASF, LB-22(153-154), Riordan to James J. Keough [San Francisco], March 13, 1907, copy.

21 Riordan, "The Apostolate of the Press" in the *Monitor*, July 16, 1910, p. 61.

22 A helpful guide based on obituaries and other published articles is Evelyn G. Varnier, "A History of the Monitor" (San Francisco, 1945), an unpublished typescript in the Bancroft Library. Alemany, it should be noted, did in 1877 make the weekly the official organ of the Archdiocese.

23 AASF, Monitor File, "Articles of Copartnership made and entered into, the 12th day of Oct., A.D. 1880." Also, George R. B. Hayes to Riordan, San Francisco, September 17, 1891.

24 AASF, Monitor File, Manogue to Grey, Sacramento, January 23, 1892.

25 AASF, Monitor File, Manogue to Montgomery, Sacramento, February 14, 1892.

26 The new joint-stock company was organized on February 1, 1892, and its certificates of incorporation were filed with the government of the State of California on February 10. The new corporation, as a final action, adopted its by-laws on February 20.

27 *Catholic Review* (New York), quoted in the *Monitor*, June 8, 1896.

28 AASF, LB-22(153-154), Riordan to Keough [San Francisco], March 13, 1907, copy.

29 AASF, Monitor File, Manogue to Montgomery, Grass Valley, September 29, 1892.

30 AASF, Monitor File, report of the Finance Committee of the Monitor Publishing Company, San Francisco, January 13, 1893; McGuire to Riordan, San Francisco, February 24 and March 24, 1893. Eventually McGuire left the *Monitor* for employment on a secular daily in San Francisco and may have been instrumental in securing the *Call's* interest in the later religious controversy. See Charles Shortridge's "Open Letter" to Yorke, San Francisco *Call*, August 11, 1896.

31 AASF, Monitor File, Flanagan to Riordan, San Francisco, May 26, 1894.

32 AASF, Monitor File, Quinn to Riordan *et al.*, San Francisco, December 15, 1894.

33 ASMS, "Register," Vol. II, 35, No. 1265; and a birth certificate registered by the County of Yorke's early life may be found in Bernard C. Cronin, *Father Yorke and the Labor Movement* (Washington, D.C., 1943), pp. 22-28; Richard J. Purcell, "Peter Christopher Yorke," in the *Dictionary of American Biography*, edited by Dumas Malone (New York, 1936), XX, 614-15; and a lengthy obituary in the *Leader* (San Francisco), April 11, 1925, p. 5; Manuscript Collection at the University of San Francisco, hereafter cited as USF, MC. The writer is grateful to have consulted in its pre-published state the late Joseph Brusher's biography, *Consecrated Thunderbolt: Father Yorke of San Francisco* (Hawthorn, New Jersey, 1973).

34 Archives of St. Patrick's College, Maynooth, *Calendarium Collegii Sti. Patritii apud Maynooth* (Dublin, 1884-1886).

35 AASF, H6, "Seminarians, 1886... ," handwritten entry under "Maynooth," dated May, 1886, unpaginated.

36 ASMS, "Register," Vol. II, 35, No. 1265.

37 ASMS, Montgomery to Magnien, San Francisco, January 31, 1890, *confidential*.

38 ACUA, Keane Papers, Riordan to Keane, San Francisco, March 21, 1891.

39 *Third Annual Report of the Rector of the Catholic University of America*, April, 1892 (Washington, D.C., 1892), p. 7.

40 ACUA, Keane Papers, Riordan to Keane, San Francisco, March 21, 1891.

41 ACUA, Riordan to Keane, San Francisco, June 13, 1891.

42 San Francisco *Chronicle*, March 19, 1894, p. 3.

43 *Arthur McEwen Answered* was issued as a weekly between March 10 and April 21, 1894, by A. F. Chapman and R. B. Avery, and in the issue of April 21 Chapman withdrew. Copies are preserved in the Bancroft Library.

44 See Yorke's "Valedictory," in the *Monitor*, October 15, 1898, p. 1.

45 It is impossible to determine the precise date when Yorke took charge of the *Monitor*, but it is most likely that he directed operations against the A.P.A. during most of 1894. Quinn continued to publish his name as editor until the very last issue of 1894. See *Monitor*, December 29, 1894, p. 4. In later correspondence, Riordan recalled that in his

appointment as chancellor, Yorke had become editor of the diocesan weekly. (APF, P.N. 96/18621, Riordan to Cardinal Camillo Mazzella, San Francisco, May 20, 1896.) Possibly this reference coincided with the autumn appointment of Father Patrick E. Mulligan as secretary to relieve Yorke of some of his duties and to allow him thereby to devote more time to the paper.(November 10, 1894, p. 10.) Even the nativist press assigned to Yorke the responsibility of the *Monitor's* strong reactions to the American Protective Association during 1894. In early 1895, the *American Patriot* described Yorke as the "scurrile editor of the Romish organ, the *Monitor*, who for the past year has made it the channel for pouring the vilest billingsgate concerning everybody and everything in any way inimical to the papist cause." (*American Patriot*, March 30, 1895, p. 1.)

46 *Monitor*, August 25, November 3, 1894.

47 *Monitor*, November 10, 1894, p. 5. See also the San Francisco *Call*, November 8, 1894, p. 8.

48 See Priscilla F. Knuth, "Nativism in California, 1886-1897," an unpublished master's thesis, University of California, Berkeley, pp. 157-173.

49 San Francisco *Chronicle*, November 25, 1895, p. 11.

50 San Francisco *Examiner*, November 28, 1895, p. 12.

51 San Francisco *Examiner*, January 6, 1896, p. 12.

52 San Francisco *Chronicle*, January 14, 1896, p. 9.

53 This is the written testimony of Father Ralph Hunt, a confidant of Yorke who succeeded him as pastor of St. Peter's Church, San Francisco. In his statement of the situation, he elaborated on Riordan's position regarding the protest of some stockholders. "At a public meeting some years after [1894], the Archbishop, alluding to his and similar protests from certain Catholics, took upon himself the whole responsibility for the style of language used in the campaign. The Catholic Clergy, as a body, were in thorough agreement with the policy adopted by Father Yorke." (Ralph Hunt to Priscilla F. Knuth, San Francisco, March 3, 1947; quoted in Knuth, *op. cit.*, p. 155, n. 147.)

54 P.N. 96/16279, [John B.] Brondel [to Ledochowski], Vancouver, Washington, January 2, 1896. Junger was the second Bishop of Nesqually, succeeding Augustine N. A. Blanchet in 1879. In 1907 the see was transferred to Seattle, Washington.

55 P.N. 96/18484, Cardinal Vincenzo Vannutelli, *Relazione con sommario*, "Sulla elezione del nuovo Vescovo di Nesqually . . .," May, 1896, p. 3, n. 6; AAB, 94-G-9, Riordan to Gibbons, San Francisco January 13, 1896.

56 P.N. 96/17421, William H. Gross, John B. Brondel, and Alphonse J. Glorieux to Ledochowski, Portland, Oregon, February 28, 1896.

57 *Idem.* The *terna* incorrectly informed Propaganda that Peter Yorke was aged thirty-five years and was a native American, one of the features desired in the nominees. Yorke, it was further remarked, took graduate courses "con grandissimo profitto" at the Catholic University of America and was at this moment fulfilling his office as chancellor with great success.

58 P.N. 96/17421, Ledochowski to Satolli, Rome, March 23, 1896, copy.

59 P.N. 96/18418, Satolli to Ledochowski, Washington, D.C., May 5, 1896.

60 P.N. 96/18418, Imoda to Satolli, San Francisco, April 18, 1896; a report attached, seven pages, handwritten, unsigned and unpaginated.

61 It is difficult to identify the author of this report, but when the *Examiner* had three months earlier asked Imoda to comment publicly on Yorke's campaigns, the Jesuit superior was reported to have been "in full accord with all that Father Yorke has done through the controversy," and had his representative, Father Henry Woods, S.J., the prefect of studies of St. Ignatius College, elaborate his views for the press. According to Woods, Imoda admired and fully supported Yorke's behavior, saying: "That gentleman has routed the enemy and driven them from the field." In the same interview, however, an important distinction was introduced regarding the quality and purpose of Yorke's later expositions. "Father Yorke," said Woods, "is now writing on the doctrines of the church. He is no longer dealing in polemics . . . . His letters upon the doctrines of the church explain themselves." Hence, according to these two Jesuits, the controversy had in mid-January, 1896, been virtually concluded, the enemy having been "pushed to the wall." This achieved, the triumphant Yorke was no longer involved in the mere argumentative exchange between controversialists, but was "now engaged in simply stating the principles of the church." (San Francisco *Examiner*, January 8, 1896, p. 8.)

62 P.N. 96/18418, Satolli to Ledochowski, Washington, D.C., May 5, 1896.

63 AAB, 94-G-9, Riordan to Gibbons, San Francisco, January 13, 1896.

64 P.N. 96/18822, Satolli to Ledochowski, Washington, D.C., June 2, 1896.

65 P.N. 96/18621, Riordan to Mazzella, San Francisco, May 13, 1896.

66 P.N. 96/18695, Riordan to Ledochowski, San Francisco, May 20, 1896; P.N. 96/18822, Satolli to Ledochowski, Washington, D.C., June 2, 1896; a typescript copy of Riordan's "Relazione," [San Francisco, May, 1896], unsigned. Both Conaty and Cleary had already been mentioned for Sioux Falls, and Riordan expressly disfavored O'Dea. (P.N. 96/19035, Riordan to Ledochowski, San Francisco, June 9, 1896.)

67 P.N. 96/18695, Ledochowski to Riordan, Rome, June 10, 1896, copy.

68 *Monitor*, June 13, 20, and 27, 1896.

69 UND, MC, Yorke to Mulligan, San Francisco, November 5, 1896, telegram.

70 See *Monitor*, December 12, 1896 - March 13, 1897.

71 This lengthy series continued without interruption from May 8, 1897, through May 7, 1898.

72 *Monitor*, May 22, 1897, p. 12.

73 *Monitor*, October 9, 1897, p. 1; October 15, pp. 5, 9.

74 The lectures were entitled as follows: "Ghosts in General," October 18, 1897; "The Gunpowder Plot," October 25; "The Tall Bully Ghost" [The Popish Plot], November 1; "Gordon Ghost," November 8; "Ghost of a Name" [Restoration of the English Hierarchy and the Ecclesiastical Titles Bill], November 15; "Our Own Ghosts," November 22.

Each lecture was reprinted in the *Monitor*, October 23 through November 27, and was distributed in a slightly fuller edition, first by the Catholic Truth Society in pamphlet form. The original plates were destroyed in the fire of 1906, but the lectures were later published in book form under the new title, *The Ghosts of Bigotry* (San Francisco, 1913).

75 *Monitor*, December 4, 1897, pp. 10-11.

76 *Ibid.*, May 2, 1898, p. 5; see also August 27, p. 1.

77 *Ibid.*, May 21, 1898, p. 1.

78 AASF, Yorke to Riordan, San Francisco, July 11, 1898. This letter strongly suggests a long progressively mounting strain between Riordan and Yorke.

79 AASF, same to same, San Francisco, July 13, 1898.

80 Elizabeth Moore to Sister Catherine Julie Cunningham, S.N.D., San Francisco, August 2, 1951. Mrs. Moore's aunt, Mrs. R. J. Byrne, had assisted Yorke in establishing the Catholic Truth Society at the Presidio in San Francisco during the Spanish-American War; and her husband had served as Yorke's secretary an officer in the *Monitor*. The writer is grateful to Sister Catherine Julie for this reference.

81 James G. Maguire, *Ireland and the Pope, A Brief History of Papal Intrigues Against Irish Liberty From Adrian IV to Leo XIII* (San Francisco, 1888). The editor of the *Monitor*, Stephen J. McCormick, had published weekly articles which refuted Maguire's position in great detail and which were gathered into *The Pope and Ireland* (New York and Cincinnati, 1889).

82 *Monitor*, August 27, 1898, p. 1.

83 AASF, Monitor File, Charles J. O'Malley to Daniel Riordan, Louisville, August 16, 1898. Through his brother, Father Daniel Riordan, the archbishop had invited O'Malley, editor of the *Midland Review*, to assume the editorship of the *Monitor*. When O'Malley respectfully declined his offer, Riordan continued to make inquiries and eventually became interested in Thomas A. Connelly, editor of the Cleveland *Universe*. (AASF, Alphonse Magnien, S.S., to Riordan, Baltimore, October 31, 1898.)

84 Father James Long, an admirer of Yorke, believed that Riordan had at the time expected a substantial gift from Phelan for the newly constructed St. Patrick's Seminary and that Yorke's pronouncements were endangering this hope. (Memorandum in the Library of the San Francisco College for Women, interview with the Reverend James Long, conducted by Florence Bourret, R.C.S.H., December 21, 1956.) This much is certain, that after the election the family of James D. Phelan donated $25,000 to the endowment fund of the seminary. (AASF, LB-[406-407], Mulligan to Phelan, San Francisco, August 17, 1899, copy.) Yorke's partisans have preserved the account that during the last days of the campaign Yorke had seen, from a balcony in Riordan's home, Phelan talking with the archbishop and that after this conversation the archbishop's attitude toward him and his work had altered. T. J. Mellott, interview with Sister Catherine Julie Cunningham, S.N.D., San Francisco, June 30, 1951. Mr. Mellott was, with Yorke, a co-founder of the *Leader*, a San Francisco weekly which began publishing in 1902 and specialized in labor issues, religion, Catholic education and Irish causes. None of this, of course, demonstrates a bargain between the mayor and the archbishop; it only suggests the way whereby Phelan communicated his grievance.

85 Vernier, *op. cit.*, p. 16.

86 *Monitor*, October 15, 1898, p. 1.

87 Interview with the Reverend James Kiely, Petaluma, California, January 10, 1964. On October 26, a group of laity presented Father Yorke with a check for $3,000 for his extended trip. In his acknowledgement he referred to the "censure" he had received for his vigorous stand and concluded significantly: "God knows that I am not

sorry to cease work for a while, for while some may have thought that I was possessed of a perverse delight in making trouble, what I did was from a sense of duty to combat the wrong to the utmost of my power and ability." *Monitor*, October 29, 1898, p. 9.

88 San Francisco *Call*, November 1, 1898, p. 14. This speech was published and distributed as a political circular, "Father Yorke to Mayor Phelan" and "Father Yorke to Mr. Maguire," copies of which have been preserved in both the AASF and the Bancroft Library.

89 San Francisco *Bulletin*, November 1, 1898, p. 1.

90 San Francisco *Bulletin*, November 2, 1898, p. 1.

91 San Francissco *Chronicle*, November 2, 1898, p. 9; *Examiner*, November 2, p. 12; *Call*, November 2, p. 14.

92 AASF, McClatchey to Riordan, Sacramento, November 1, 1898, telegram.

93 San Francisco *Bulletin*, November 2, 1898, p. 1.

94 San Francisco *Examiner*, November 3, 1898, p. 3.

95 AASF, LB-1(391), Riordan to Yorke [San Francisco], November 7, 1898, copy.

96 Walter McDonald, *Reminiscences of a Maynooth Professor*, edited by Denis Gwynn (London, 1925), pp. 217-18.

97 *Monitor*, November 18, 1899, p. 136.

98 Elizabeth Moore to Sister Catherine Julie Cunningham, S.N.D., San Francisco, August 2, 1951.

CHAPTER SEVEN

1 Roger Aubert, *Le Pontificat de Pie IX ((1846-1878)* (Paris, 1952), p. 225; emphasis mine. The most detailed description of the conservative-liberal division of the American Church in this period may be found in Robert D. Cross, *The Emergence of Liberal Catholicism in America* (Cambridge, Massachusetts, 1958). Briefer statements are found in Ellis, *op. cit.*, II, 1-2; Patrick Henry Ahern, *The Life of John J. Keane: Educator and Archbishop* (Milwaukee, 1954), pp. 89-90; Colman J. Barry, O.S.B., *The Catholic Church and German Americans* (Milwaukee, 1953), pp. 183-84; Thomas T. McAvoy, C.S.C., *The Great Crisis in American Catholic History* (Chicago, 1957), pp. 42-93.

2 It is of the greatest interest to note that Rome had become alarmed over the division. In a draft of the instructions to the newly named Apostolic Delegate to the United States, the *first* order of business was to settle the discord among the American bishops. This

confidential document cited the polarization, noting within the hierarchy "two diferent tendencies . . . . Some are perhaps too conciliatory toward the State, others more rigid." (APF, file on the establishment of the Apostolic Delegation, 1893).

3 In the Archives of the Archdiocese of San Francisco there have been preserved very few letters between Ireland and Riordan either in the letter-files and the letterpress copy books. Among the Ireland Papers in the Archives of the Archdiocese of St. Paul there is but one letter from Riordan to Ireland dated December 17, 1913. (Patrick H. Ahern to the writer, St. Paul, July 4, 1963.) Apparently, too, Daniel Riordan destroyed all his brother's letters, but the "Archbishop's letterbooks" in the AASF contain his own letters to his brother from 1909 until his death.

4 A helpful contemporary account of this phenomenon is W. S. Harwood, "Secret Societies in America," *North American Review*, CLIV (May, 1897), 617-24. Arthur M. Schlesinger has also treated this subject in *The Rise of the City, 1878-1898* (New York, 1933), pp. 289-90; and "Biography of a Nation of Joiners," *American Historical Review*, L (October, 1944), 1-25. For a thorough treatment of the church's problem with secret societies until 1897, see Fergus Macdonald, *The Catholic Church and Secret Societies in the United States* (New York, 1946).

5 *Collectanea Sacrae Congregationis de Propaganda Fide* (Rome, 1907), II, 198-200, no. 1615, Decree of May 10, 1884; *Lettere*, vol. 385 (1889), fog. 466v-467r, Simeoni to Chatard, Rome, July 3, 1889. Riordan once quoted this latter decision of the Holy Office: "Juxta exposita non esse tolerandum." *Congressi, A.C.*, vol. 49 (1889), Riordan to Jacobini [Rome, November 22, 1888].

6 The minutes of the sessions of this council are contained in *Acta et decreta concilii plenarii Baltimorensis tertii* (private edition), pp. lxxv-lxxviii.

7 *Acta et decreta concilii plenarii Baltimorensis tertii* (Baltimore, 1886), pp. 143-44.

8 Archives of the Archdiocese of New York (hereafter cited as AANY), E-T, Riordan to Corrigan, San Francisco, May 3, 1886; reprinted in Macdonald, *op. cit.*, pp. 138-39.

9 *Congressi, A.C.*, vol. 49 (1889), fog. 1503rv, Riordan to Jacobini [Rome], November 22, 1888. The Minutes of the Archbishops' Meeting held in Baltimore on October 28, 1886, are silent on their recommendation regarding the A.O.H. (AAB, 82-D-8); but according to Riordan's account: "nel mese di Ottobre di quell'anno gli archivescovi Americani dopo matura consultazione, misero a Roma un

voto raccomandando che i membri di quest'ordine non fossero molestati."

10 *Lettere*, vol. 384 (1888), fog. 714r, Jacobini to D. Annibale, Assessor of Holy Office, Rome, December 5, 1888; *ibid.*, vol. 385 (1889), fog. 466v-467r, Simeoni to Chatard, Rome, July 3, 1889; *Congressi, A.C.*, vol. 51 (1889), fog. 12rv-17r, Chatard to Simeoni, Indianapolis, July 3, 1889.

11 AAB, 90-Q-3, Minutes of the Meeting of the Archbishops, New York, November 16-19, 1892; 91-V-1/1, Minutes . . . , Chicago, September 12-13, 1893.

12 AAB, 93-L-1, Riordan to Gibbons, San Francisco, October 2, 1894.

13 AAB, 93-L-4, Minutes of the Meeting of the Archbishops, Philadelphia, October 10, 1894.

14 AAB, 93-N-3, Ireland to Gibbons, St. Paul, December 7, 1894.

15 AAB, 93-N-7, Riordan to Gibbons, San Francisco, December 17, 1894.

16 AAB, 93-N-10, same to same, San Francisco, December 29, 1894.

17 Ellis, *op. cit.*, I, 471.

18 AAB, 93-R-9, Riordan to Gibbons, San Francisco, February 20, 1895.

19 AASF, Riordan to his clergy, San Francisco, February 28, 1896, a printed circular which contained the decree of the Holy Office of January 18, 1896, and Satolli's letter of February 13, 1896.

20 AASF, handwritten first draft of a letter to his clergy, n.d. In 1907 Riordan, along with the other metropolitans, was queried by Diomede Falconio, the apostolic delegate, regarding three other societies, the Modern Woodman, the Knights of the Maccabees, and the Improved Order of Red Men. Riordan strongly opposed their condemnation since his investigation had revealed that they were strictly benevolent societies in no way hostile to the interests of religion. (*Ibid.*, LB-21 [387-388], Riordan to Falconio [San Francisco], February 7, 1907, copy.)

21 For a complete treatment of this issue, see Henry J. Browne, *The Catholic Church and the Knights of Labor* (Washington, 1949), and Ellis, *op. cit.*, chap. XII, "The Knights of Labor," pp. 486-546.

22 Ira B. Cross, *A History of the Labor Movement in California* (Berkeley, 1935), chap. IX, "The Knights of Labor," I, 151-55.

23 Brown, *op. cit.*, p. 212.

24 The leading passages of this pastoral may be found in Frederick J. Zwierlein, *The Life and Letters of Bishop McQuaid* (Rochester,

1927), III, 7-11. Although no definitive study has yet appeared on this conflict, the most judicious account is Ellis, *op. cit.*, chap. XIII, "The Case of Henry George and Dr. McGlynn," I, 547-94. Partisan studies include Zwierlein, *op. cit.*, III, 1-82; Stephen Bell, *Rebel, Priest and Prophet: A Biography of Dr. Edward McGlynn* (New York, 1937). A standard biography on George which deals with the controversy in some detail is Charles Albro Barker, *Henry George* (New York, 1955), *passim.*

25 ACUA, Keane's Papers, Riordan to Keane, San Francisco, January 24, 1887.

26 AASF, LBR(2a), 280, Riordan to Riordan [San Francisco], January 20 [1911], copy.

27 An excellent treatment of this problem is Colman J. Barry, O.S.B., *The Catholic Church and German Americans* (Milwaukee, 1952).

28 *Congressi, A.C.*, vol. 31 (1879), fog. 403r, Alemany to Simeoni, San Francisco, November 12, 1879.

29 *Monitor*, June 24, 1893, p. 1; *Congressi, A.C.*, vol. 41 (1884), fog. 72r-77r, Riordan to Simeoni, San Francisco, July 24, 1884.

30 GARF, Vol. II, fasicle 4-d/, Louis Koch [Cook], C.Ss.R., to Michael Ulrich, C.Ss.R., New Orleans, January 18, 1887; hereafter cited as GARF. The briefest mention of this forgotten episode is alluded to in Peter Geiermann, C.Ss.R., *Annals of the St. Louis Province of the Congregation of the Most Holy Redeemer* (privately published, 1924), I, 168.

31 *Udienze*, vol. 213 (1885), fog. 138ir, Riordan to Simeoni, San Francisco, April 16, 1885; GARF, Pr. S.L., vol. II, fasc. 4-b/, Riordan to [Nicolas Mauron, C.Ss.R.], San Francisco, April 16, 1885.

32 GARF, fasc. 4-b/, report of the general congregation of June 21, 1885; copy.

33 GARF, fasc. 4-c/, Loewekamp to Riordan, St. Louis, March 5, 1886, copy.

34 GARF, fasc. 4-c/, Riordan to Loewekamp, San Francisco, May 16, 1886, copy; fasc. 4-d/, Koch to Ulrich, New Orleans, January 18, 1887.

35 GARF, fasc. 4-c/, John B. Neu, C.Ss.R., to [Loewekamp, San Francisco], May 12, 1886, copy; Aegidius Smulders, C.Ss.R., to [Loewekamp, San Francisco], May 26, 1886, copy. On another occasion Smulders described Riordan's part in a celebration on the feast of St. Boniface. "The German Catholic Congregation assembled in a Public Hall," he began.

The Archb. presided & a dozen of priests were on the platform & F. Neu gave a real good lecture on the Church to between 1200 and 1300 German Catholics. Before the lecture they sang some beautiful German pieces . . . with a volume of voices & enthusiasm as I heard it 40 years ago in St. Alphonsus, Baltimore. In a short address the Archb. showed his pastoral love for the Cath. Germans & his great esteem & gratitude for the C.Ss.R. He received a thunder of applause.

Ibid., Smulders to [Loewekamp, San Francisco] , June 8, 1886, copy.)

36 GARF, fasc. 4-c/, Mauron to Riordan, Contamine, July 9, 1886; fasc. 4-d/, "Contractus," St. Louis, August 6, 1886, signed only by Loewekamp.

37 GARF, fasc. 4-d/, Koch to Ulrich, New Orleans, January 18, 1887.

38 GARF, fasc. 4-d/, Riordan to Koch, San Francisco, January 14, 1887.

39 GARF, fasc. 4-d/, Riordan to Loewekamp, San Francisco, January 30, 1887, copy.

40 Quoted in Marion A. Habig, O.F.M. (ed.), *Heralds of the King: The Franciscans of the St. Louis-Chicago Province, 1858-1958* (Chicago, 1958), p. 227.

41 *Congressi, A.D.*, vol. 46 (1887), fog. 177rv-178rv, Reidhaar to Simeoni, San Francisco, February 2, 1887.

42 *Lettere*, vol. 383 (1887), fog. 132r, Simeoni to Riordan, Rome, March 8, 1887.

43 *Congressi, A.C.*, *loc. cit.*, fog., 286r, Reidhaar to Simeoni, San Francisco, February 16, 1887; fog. 552r-555r, Riordan to Simeoni, San Francisco, April 5, 1887.

44 *Udienze*, vol. 229 (1888), fog. 2431rv-2431Ar, Riordan to Simeoni [Rome, November, 1888] ; fog. 2432r, Raphael of Aurilaco, O.F.M., to Leo XIII Rome, November 11, 1888; fog. 2433rv, Riordan to Ferdinand Bregmeyer, O.F.M., Minister Provincial of the Province of the Sacred Heart (St. Louis, Missouri) [Rome, November, 1888] ; fog. 2374r, no. 44, 2377r, report of the general congregation of November 18, 1888.

45 ACUA, Keane Papers, Riordan to Keane, San Francisco, January 24, 1887. For details on this episode, see Barry, *op. cit.*, pp. 64-69.

46 ADR, Ireland to O'Connell, St. Paul, September 13, 1887.

47 ADR, same to same, St. Paul, December 3, 1897. For details on the Schroeder case, see Barry, *op. cit.*, pp. 230-34, and Peter E. Hogan, *The Catholic University of America, 1896-1903: The Rectorship of Thomas J. Conaty* (Washington, 1949), pp. 148-58.

48 For background on the school question, see Daniel F. Reilly, *The School Controversy (1891-1893)* (Washington, 1943), pp. 1-38. This monograph is, to date, the most complete study of the controversy although he used as his manuscript sources only the Archives of the Archdiocese of Baltimore and thereby highlights the activities and views of the progressives.

49 *Congressi, A.C.*, vol. 41 (1884), Riordan to Simeoni, San Francisco, July 24, 1884.

50 GARF, Pr. S.L., Vol. II, fasc. 4-d/, Koch [Cook] to Ulrich, New Orleans, January 18, 1887.

51 *Congressi, A.C.*, vol. 49 (1888), fog. 1437rv-1443rv, Riordan to Simeoni [Rome, November 21, 1888]; *Monitor*, January 23, 1904, p. 27.

52 See John Ireland, *The Church and Modern Society* (Chicago, 1897), I, 217-32.

53 *Congressi, A.C.*, vol. 53 (1890), fog. 288rv-290rv, Melchers to Simeoni, Frascati in Rufinella, August 19, 1890. Melchers had been the medium through whom most of the complaints on the German question had been channeled to Propaganda. See Ellis, *op. cit.*, I, 361; and Barry, *op. cit.*, *passim*.

54 Reilly, *op. cit.* pp. 78-82.

55 Minutes of the Archbishops' Meeting at St. Louis, November 29, 1891. (AAB, 89-D-5/1), recorded by Ireland as secretary, made no allusion to the subject. In his report to the Holy See, Gibbons described this phase without mentioning names, except that of Archbishop Williams of Boston, who enthusiastically congratulated Ireland. (*Acta*, vol. 262 [1892], fog. 133v-135rv, Gibbons to Leo XIII, Baltimore, March 1, 1892, printed copy.)

56 *Acta*, vol. 262 (1892), fog. 98rv-102rv, Cardinal Serafino Vannutelli, *Relazione con sommario*, "Sopra la cessione di due Scuole Parrocchiali dell'Archidiocesi di S. Paolo alla Commissione Scolastica governativa," April, 1892, *riservatissima*. The prelates who had reported "decidedly" unfavorably to Ireland were Archbishops Frederick X. Katzer of Milwaukee, Michael A. Corrigan of New York, Patrick J. Ryan of Philadelphia; and Bishops Bernard J. McQuaid of Rochester, Winand M. Wigger of Newark, and Francis Silas Chatard of Vincennes. Bishop Louis De Goesbriand of Burlington, Vermont, declined to offer an opinion since, he felt, his see was too distant from Minnesota.

57 *Civiltà Cattolica*, Series XV, vol. I (1892), 755-61. The letter was dated December 18, 1891.

58 *Congressi, A.C.*, vol. 58 (1892), fog. 404r-407r, Corrigan (New York), Feehan (Chicago), Elder (Cincinnati), Ryan (Philadelphia), Gross (Oregon City), Janssens (New Orleans), and Katzer (Milwaukee) to [Salvatore M. Brandi, S.J., editor of *Civiltà Cattolica*], New York, April 16, 1892, copy.

59 Recorded in AAB, 89-U-9, Riordan to Magnien, San Francisco, April 23, 1892, copy.

60 *Idem*. While rumors circulated that Riordan had signed the memorial, Magnien sent on to Denis O'Connell a copy of this letter which, Magnien added, "makes me believe that New York did not dare to reckon him on his side." (ADR, Magnien to O'Connell, Baltimore, May 31, 1892.)

61 *Congressi, A.C.*, *loc. cit.* Also *ibid.*, fog. 403r, 408r, Corrigan to Ledochowski, New York, April 15, 1892. It was not clear at this time to Ireland's partisans in the United States how Propaganda learned of this memorial. "I understand," Magnien told O'Connell,

> that the protest was, at least by some, signed not for the
> Holy See, but simply to be sent to the Civilta Catolica [*sic*]
> and only for the needs of the controversy; how is it that it
> was sent directly to the Propaganda?

(ADR, Magnien to O'Connell, Baltimore, May 31, 1892.)

62 *Acta*, vol. 262 (1892), fog. 104rv, report of the special congregation of April 21, 1892. The pertinent words of the decision are, "Firmis in suo robore manentibus Decretis Conciliorum Baltimoriensium super scholas parochiales, conventio inita a R. P. Ireland relate ad scholas de Faribault et Stillwater, perpensis omnibus circumstantiis, tolerari potest."

63 New York *Herald*, May 7, 1892, p. 8.

64 Ellis, *op. cit.* pp. 680-82.

65 ADR, Magnien to O'Connell, Baltimore, May 31, 1892.

66 AAB, 89-W-4, Riordan to Gibbons, San Francisco, May 29, 1892. A copy in Magnien's hand was forwarded to O'Connell and may be found in ADR.

67 ADR, Riordan to O'Connell, San Francisco, March 15, 1892.

68 ADR, Ireland to Keane, "The Ocean," July 3, 1892.

69 Quoted in AAB, 89-W-7, Riordan to Gibbons, San Francisco, June 4, 1892.

70 ADR, Riordan to O'Connell, San Francisco, June 4, 1892.

71 AAB, 89-W-7, Riordan to Gibbons, San Francisco, June 4, 1892. Copies of the two letters to Gibbons on this matter (May 29, 1892, and June 4, 1892) are available in AASP. (Patrick Ahern to the writer, St. Paul, July 4, 1963.)

72 ADR, Riordan to O'Connell, San Francisco, July 9, 1892. For an announcement of Magnien's arrival, see the *Monitor*, July 9, 1892, p. 5.

73 The complex story of the establishment of the apostolic delegation is best found in Ellis, *op. cit.*, chap. XIV, "The Apostolic Delegation," I, 595-652. While Satolli's mission was ostensibly to bring as papal ablegate a number of valuable maps and charts for exhibition at the World's Columbian Exposition in Chicago to be held in 1893, he was sent, it was known, on a "special mission." the chief purpose of which was possibly to reconcile conflicts between bishops and priests and specifically to rehabilitate Edward McGlynn. The latter had for many years advocated a permanent papal representative in the United States and had in July, 1892, expressed to Ledochowski a willingness to be reconciled. (*Lettere*, vol. 388 [1892], fog. 641r, Ledochowski to Satolli, Rome, November 14, 1892; fog. 686r, "Decree," November, 1892.)

74 AAB, 90-D-4, Riordan to Gibbons, San Francisco, August 30, 1892. He vigorously repeated his sentiments in *ibid.*, 90-E-8, same to same, San Francisco, September 12, 1892.

75 An official Latin version of Satolli's proposition is found in the appendix to the *Relazione con appendice* of Cardinal Ignazio Persico, "Sulla questione scolastica negli Stati Uniti di America," May, 1893, Prot. No. 93/2916, *Con Segreto Pontificio*; hereafter cited as Persico, *Relazione*. A translation is available in Reilly, *op. cit.*, pp. 271-76.

76 Persico, *Relazione* pp. 2-3. In addition to the ordinaries of dioceses, the Holy See consulted John Keane who, as Rector of the Catholic University of America, was a titular bishop.

77 *Congressi, A.C.*, vol. 36 (1882), fog. 194-217, "Report on the present state of the Catholic Church in the United States of America," n.p., n.d. Conroy's report of 1878 has long been lost in the Propaganda archives, having been misfiled under the wrong year. Cf. Ellis, *op. cit.* I, p. 195, n. 120.

78 APF, file on the establishment of the Apostolic Delegation, no protocol number, "Instructions given in 1893 to the visiting Ap. Del. of the United States," *riservata*.

79 AAB, 91-C-2, Riordan to Gibbons, San Francisco, January 18, 1893, telegram.

80 Persico, *Relazione*, p. 3. Fourteen bishops declined to offer an opinion.

81 APF, no Prot. No., in file entitled "School Question," Riordan to Leo XIII [San Francisco, January (?), 1893].

82 For details see John Tracy Ellis, *John Lancaster Spalding: First Bishop of Peoria, American Educator* (Milwaukee, 1961), pp. 61-70; and David F. Sweeney, O.F.M., *The Life of John Lancaster Spalding: First Bishop of Peoria, 1840-1916* (New York, 1965), pp. 202-19, especially p. 210.

83 APF, *ibid.*, no Prot. No., Spalding to Leo XIII, Peoria, January 11, 1893. In the passage quoted, written in French, Spalding uses the word "coterie" which has been translated as "clique." Later in this letter in which he recorded his displeasure at the recent establishment of the apostolic delegation, he referred to the same, in French, as "clique," a term very familiar among Corrigan's partisans.

84 AAB, 89-W-7, Riordan to Gibbons, San Francisco, June 4, 1892.

85 UND, MC, Onahan Papers, IX-1-d, Riordan to Onahan, San Francisco, January 12, 1893.

86 *Ibid.*, same to same, San Francisco, February 1, 1893.

87 APF, P.N. 93/3047, Leo XIII to Gibbons, Rome, May 31, 1893, copy; a translation may be found in Reilly, *op. cit.*, pp. 226-30.

88 *Monitor*, October 28, 1893, p. 4; December 2, p. 8. The essence of Riordan's views may be found in a summary of his address at Santa Clara College, reported in the *Monitor*, December 2, 1893, p. 8.

89 ACUA, O'Connell Papers, Riordan to O'Connell, San Francisco, December 28, 1903.

CHAPTER EIGHT

1 *New World* (Chicago), October 18, 1902, p. 13.

2 No single publication provides a complete detailed review of the three-century history of the Pious Fund. Until this appears, the reader may be wee served by Kenneth M. JJohnson, *The Pious Fund* (Los Angeles, 1963). An attorney with an acute historical sense, this author conducted many years of archival research and interviews; but in rendering many of his judgments he has heavily relied upon printed materials and too uncritically upon thewritings of John Thomas Doyle. The most recent study is Francis J. Weber, *The United States Versus Mexico: The Final Settlement of the Pious Fund* (Los Angeles, 1969).

3 John Thomas Doyle (1819-1906), a native of New York City and a graduate of Georgetown College, had first practiced law in New York City and had in 1851 become deeply involved in a project of constructing an inter-oceanic canal across Nicaragua. After two years in Central America where he engrossed himself in the study of Spanish colonial policy, he proceeded in 1853 to San Francisco where he opened a law office. An expert in Hispanic colonial history, he had been retained by Archbishop Alemany and succeeded in obtaining a ratification of the original title of the Catholic Church and missions to much of the land which the church had controlled in California under Spanish and Mexican rule. For this reason Doyle was the best qualified attorney to pursue the Pious Fund Case and devoted to it half a century of effort. Aside from his association with this celebrated cause, he was a distinguished figure in early California, having frequently raised his voice on political matters, especially on railroad abuses. Despite his prominence, however, he consistently declined to be a candidate for public office. For an appreciative biography, see Oscar Shuck, *Bench and Bar in California: History, Anecdotes, Reminiscences* (San Francisco, 1888); and the *Monitor*, January 27, 1912, pp. 1-3.

4 In the course of the litigation, it must be noted, Caleb Cushing, the eminent American diplomat who represented Mexico, had in 1871 filed a motion to dismiss the claim insofar as this particular Commission had no jurisdiction over such claims preceding the Treaty of Guadalupe-Hildago and insofar as these American bishops of California were not the legal successors of Bishop Garcia Diego. This very important motion was considered thoroughly and denied. On November 29, 1875, Thornton awarded $904,700.79 to be divided equally between Lower and Upper California; and on October 24, 1876 this sum was correctly adjusted to $904,070.79. This decision, based on an inventory of 1842, also fixed the capitalized value of the Pious Fund at $1,436,033, and ruled that for twenty-one years, the years between the Treaty of Guadalupe-Hidalgo (1848) and the establishment of the Claims Commission (1869), Mexico owed to the bishops of Upper California one-half of the annual six per cent interest on the capitalized value of the fund, or twenty-one installments of $43,050.99, or an aggregate of $904,070.79 in Mexican gold.

5 AASF, Pious Fund Scrapbook, III, 729, Doyle to Riordan, San Francisco, December 10, 1894. White was no stranger to Archbishop Riordan, who had invited him to deliver the principal address at the Columbus celebration, October 12, 1892. When White was elected United States Senator, Riordan sent him these warmest

congratulations: "Your election is a matter of pride to all decent men irrespective of party. We all feel that at last a man goes to the Senate whose hands are free from corruption and on whose character there is not a stain. As a Bishop of the Church, I am overjoyed that one of her sons can challenge by the purity of his own life and the splendid abilities of his professional career the criticism of her enemies and force them to admit that a most worthy choice has been made." (WP, Riordan to White, San Francisco, August 12, 1892, and January 21, 1893.) It is to be noted, lastly, that White's first contract in the Pious Fund Case was valid only during the remainder of his term in the Senate and would terminate on March 5, 1897. (DP, Doyle and Stewart to White, Washington, D.C., December 24, 1894.)

6 AASF, Pious Fund Scrapbook, III, 746, White to Doyle, Washington, D.C., February 15, 1898, copy.

7 DP, Stewart and Doyle to White, Washington, D.C., December 24, 1894; Doyle to White, n.p., November 24, 1896. AASF, Pious Fund III, 729, Doyle to Riordan, San Francisco, December 10, 1894.

8 DP, Doyle to Riordan, n.p., September 14, 1897. Doyle had also attached a form of resignation which Riordan could present to Stewart.

9 DP, Doyle to White, Menlo Park, September 17, 1897.

10 AASF, Pious Fund Scrapbook, III, 735, Doyle to Stewart, Menlo Park, September 7, 1894, copy.

11 AASF, *Ibid.*, 737, Doyle to Riordan, Menlo Park, September 17, 1897.

12 *Ibid.*, Doyle to Riordan, n.p., November 10, 1897.

13 AASF, Pious Fund Scrapbook, IV, a statement in the form of a letter: Doyle and Stewart to Riordan, San Francisco, November 15, 1897, manuscript signed by Doyle and Stewart.

14 *Foreign Relations of the United States, 1902: United States Versus Mexico* (Washington, D.C., 1903), p. 747; hereafter cited as *Foreign Relations;* Day to Powell Clayton, the American Minister to Mexico, Washington, D.C., March 10, 1898.

15 Jackson Harvey Ralston (1857-1945), born in Sacramento, had graduated like Doyle from Georgetown University and had established a practice of law in Washington, D.C. During his distinguished career, Ralston became an authority on three areas of law. Prominent first in tax legislation, he had been the president of the Board of Commissioners of Hyattsville, Maryland, when in 1892 it became the first American city to adopt Henry George's single tax for local revenue purposes. He was also acknowledged as expert on constitutional labor

law, serving as the attorney for the American Federation of Labor from 1897 to his retirement in 1924. His participation in the Pious Fund Case before the Hague Tribunal helped make him a world-renowned authority on international law. Immediately after this success, the United State named him umpire in the Italian-Venezuelan Claims Commission. An author of many studies on taxation and arbitration, he spent several years of his retirement as a lecturer in international law at Stanford University.

16 AASF, Pious Fund Scrapbook, III, 761, Hay to Clayton, Washington, D.C., December 4, 1899, copy; also in *Foreign Relations*, pp. 751-53.

17 AASF, Pious Fund Scrapbook, III, 775, Doyle to Riordan, Menlo Park, May 16, 1900.

18 *Ibid.*, 786, Doyle to Riordan, San Francisco, November 12, 1900. See also SP, Stewart to Doyle [Washington, D.C.], November 2, 1901, copy. In fairness, Doyle planned to compensate Stephen White out of his own share.

19 AASF, Pious Fund Scrapbook, III, 776, Doyle to Riordan, Menlo Park, June 6, 1900.

20 *Ibid.*, 786, Doyle to Riordan, San Francisco, November 12, 1900.

21 *Ibid.*, 776, Stewart to Doyle, n.p., n.d., quoted in Doyle to Riordan, Menlo Park, June 6, 1900; DP, Doyle to Stewart, Menlo Park, November 27, 1900.

22 Riordan likewise demanded that Doyle and Senator Stewart arrange a similar letter to the President or the secretary of state endorsed by the senators whose states would benefit by the Pious Fund, i.e., California, Nevada, Oregon, Washington, Utah, Idaho, and Montana. The two California Senators, George C. Perkins and Thomas C. Bard, declined to sign such a petition. (DP, Doyle to Ralston, Menlo Park, February 2,   and March 12, 1901; AASF, Pious Fund III, 806, Doyle to Riordan, Menlo Park, March 7, 1901.)

23 AASF, Pious Fund Scrapbook, III, 796, Ralston to Doyle, Washington, D.C., March 25, 1901, copy; 798, *ibid.*, Doyle to Riordan, Menlo Park, March 31, 1901; DP, Doyle to Ralston, Menlo Park, April 4, 1901.

24 Ibid., 828, Ireland to Daniel Riordan, St. Paul, May 13, 1901.

25 Library of Congress, McKinley Papers, Series 3, Riordan to George B. Cortelyou, San Francisco, May 17 and 21, 1901; Series 2, Cortelyou to Riordan, San Francisco, May 19, 1901, copy.

26 Richard C. Kerens (1842-1916) was a wealthy railroad builder and politician who had reputedly controlled Republican politics in Missouri for forty years. He commanded a position of influence in Mexico after having served on the Continental Railway Commission and helping to build a railroad through fifteen South American republics. A mighty figure in the G.O.P., he had served three consecutive terms as national committeeman (1884-1900); and McKinley had unsuccessfully offered him any diplomatic post except London, Berlin, and Paris. A notable Catholic layman as well, Kerens was in 1904 awarded the Laetare Medal.

27 AASF, Pious Fund Scrapbook, III, 833, Doyle to Riordan, Menlo Park, July 29, 1901; 855, Ralston to Doyle, Washington, D.C., December 28, 1901, copy. DP, Doyle to Ralston, Menlo Park, August 31, September 20, October 23, and December 19, 1901; Doyle to Riordan, Menlo Park, September 17, and December 1, 1901; Doyle to Stewart, Menlo Park, December 20, 1901. SP, Stewart to Doyle [Washington, D.C.], November 2, 1901, copy.

28 AASF, Pious Fund Scrapbook, III, 795, Mariscal to Powell, Mexico City, November 28, 1900, copy; reprinted also in *Foreign Relations*, pp. 768-75.

29 DP, Doyle to Ralston, Menlo Park, May 10 and 11, 1901.

30 AASF, Pious Fund Scrapbook, III, 833, Doyle to Riordan, Menlo Park, July 29, 1901.

31 AASF, Pious Fund Scrapbook, III, 848, Clayton to Hay, Mexico City, November 13, 1901, copy; also *Foreign Relations*, p. 777. Clayton's original message was dated August 21, and his meeting with Mariscal took place on November 8. This document does not record the foreign minister's actual consent, but judging from his attitude and the circumstances, Clayton wrote that "we shall be able to arrive at an understanding in conformity with the views of the Department to submit the matter to arbitration."

32 Andrew D. White, *Autobiography* (New York, 1905), pp. 253-55.

33 AASF, Pious Fund Scrapbook, III, 903, Stewart to Riordan, Washington, D.C., May 22, 1902, telegram.

34 DP, Doyle to Ralston, Menlo Park, December 19, 1901; AASF, Pious Fund III, 857, Ralston to Doyle [Washington, D.C.], January 3, 1902, copy. Also, NA, Department of State, Miscellaneous Letters, Ralston and Siddons to Hay, Washington, D.C., February 11, 1902. A list of the members of the Permanent Court of Arbitration sent by Ralston is found in AASF, Pious Fund Scrapbook, III, 859, typed copy.

35 AASF, Pious Fund Scrapbook, III, 873 and 898, De Becker to Riordan, Louvain, January 28, and April 26, 1902. AACL, Riordan to De Becker, Washington, D.C., April 12, 1902; Ralston to De Becker, Washington, D.C., May 9, 1902.

36 DP, Doyle to Vaughan, Menlo Park, March 11, May 6, July 5, 1902; AASF, Pious Fund Scrapbook, III, 913, Vaughan to Doyle, London [April 21, 1902], copy. The personal choices by Riordan for the tribunal reveal the influence of the letters from Cardinal Vaughan and Canon De Becker, for he chose as arbitrators Sir Edward Fry and Sir Edward Baldwin Malet, both Privy Councilors in Great Britain. (DP, Doyle to Ralston, May 20, 24, and 29, 1902; AASF, Pious Fund Scrapbook, III, 904, [Riordan and Montgomery] to Hay, San Francisco, May 24, 1902, copy.)

37 Sir Edward Fry (1827-1918) was a renowned British barrister, having been made in 1877 a judge of the high court of justice and having served (1883-1892) as Lord Justice of the Court of Appeals. Frederick Martens, or Feodor Feodorovich Martens (1845-1909), a Russian publicist and possibly the most famous international lawyer of his generation, had already been instrumental in laying the foundations for the two Hague Conferences. Permanently attached to the Russian foreign ministry, he had successfully participated in many arbitrations, earning the informal title of Chief Justice of Christendom. The official announcement of this selection and of other principals was made to the International Bureau of the Hague Tribunal in early August. (NA, dispatch No. 520, John W. Garrett, Chargè d'Affaires *ad interim*, to Hay, The Hague, August 11, 1902.)

38 DP, Doyle to Ralston, Menlo Park, June 19 and 29, 1902; see also Doyle to Vaughan, Menlo Park, July 5, 1902.

39 Jonkheer A.F. de Savornin Lohman, a distinguished Dutch jurist, had been for a long time a professor at the Free University of Amsterdam. For more than two decades he had served in both chambers of the States General of the Netherlands, a term broken only by two years as the Minister of the Interior. Mexico had originally selected an Italian member of the Permanent Court, Jean Baptiste Pagano Guarnaschelli, First President of the Court of Cassation and a Senator who had been a notorious anti-papal leader. Since a death in his family intervened, his place was filled by Tobias Michael Carel Asser (1838-1913), another eminent Dutch statesman. A specialist on international law, with many publications to his credit, Asser had attended many international conferences, including the Hague Conference in 1899, and had been the founder and the president of the Institute of International Law. Through his life he championed

international arbitration and in 1911 shared the Nobel Peace Prize. (NA, dispatches 506 and 509, Stanford Newel, United States Minister to the Netherlands, The Hague, June 17 and 23, 1902; Garrett to Hay, The Hague, August 24, 1902, telegram.)

40 Henning Matzen was the only Danish publicist accredited to the Hague Tribunal. At this time he was Counsellor-Extraordinary for the Danish Supreme Court and the President of the Chamber of Deputies, or the *Landsthing*.

41 Sir Edward Fry was a Quaker; Frederick de Martens, a Russian Orthodox; Jonkheer de Savornin Lohman, a Calvinist; Tobias Asser, a Jew; and Henning Matzen, a Lutheran. (William T. Stead, "The United States and Mexico at the Opening of the Hague Court," *Review of Reviews*, XXVI [October, 1902], 423-24.)

42 DP, Doyle to Ralston, Menlo Park, May 29 [1902].

43 AASF, Pious Fund Scrapbook, III, 785, Garrigan to Riordan, Washington, D.C., October 18, 1900; *ibid.*, 788, Riordan to Doyle, San Francisco, November 23, 1900, copy signed by Riordan.

44 AASF, Pious Fund Scrapbook, III, 911, and LB-7(58-59), Riordan to Stewart, San Francisco, June 25, 1902, copy. Only in July, it should be noted, did Stewart announce his plans to go to The Hague. (*Ibid.*, unnumbered, Stewart to Riordan, Washington, D.C., July 10, 1902, telegram.)

45 John Bassett Moore (1860-1947) was at this time at the beginning of a notably distinguished career in diplomacy and international arbitration. After serving as a law clerk and third assistant secretary in the Department of State, Moore had resigned in 1891 to take the newly created chair of international law and diplomacy at Columbia University. This position granted him the first full professorship in this subject in the United States. In his later career he represented the United States on numerous important international commissions and in inter-American conferences. In 1912, he became a member of the Permanent Court of Arbitration at The Hague, and in 1921 was appointed one of the first judges of the newly organized Permanent Court of International Justice, or the World Court. His major published works include *A Digest of International Law* (8 vol., 1906), *Principles of American Democracy* (1918), and *International Adjudications, Ancient and Modern* (8 vol., 1929-1936.)

46 Garrett William McEnerney (1865-1942) was a successful attorney who since 1895 had practiced independently in San Francisco. Prior to the Pious Fund Case, he had participated in no distinguished litigation and was at this time defending the archdiocese in this same

case against the claims of Nathaniel Wilson and Philip Phillips, whom Eugene Casserly had retained in the proceedings before the Mixed Commission. (AASF, Pious Fund Scrapbook, III, 882, Doyle to Riordan, Menlo Park, February 16, 1902.) The Pious Fund Case was a great blessing to his career, and after the San Francisco earthquake and fire of 1906, he drafted the famous "McEnerney Act" which permitted owners of real property to restore their record titles lost through the destruction of public records. This important legislation he promoted in the state legislature and defended its constitutionality in the California courts. From 1901 until his death he served actively on the Board of Regents of the University of California, and in 1915, the Catholic University of America conferred on him the honorary doctorate in canon law.

47 LBR(2a), 427, Riordan to Daniel J. Riordan [San Francisco], April 12, 1911, copy.

48 DP, Doyle to Ralston, Menlo Park, June 29, 1902. In inviting McEnerney down to Menlo Park to receive the pertinent materials, Doyle wrote to him that "no associate could be personally more agreeable to me . . . ." (DP, Doyle to McEnerney, Menlo Park, June 29, 1902.)

49 The Chevalier Descamps was a Belgian senator and the Secretary General of the Institute of International Law. During the first Hague Conference he had played a very active and prominent role, displaying a great measure of eloquence. At this historic gathering, too, he championed the protest against the exclusion of Pope Leo XIII whose de jure sovereignty over a temporal state was in doubt.

50 AASF, James Nugent to Patrick E. Mulligan, Liverpool, August 30, 1902.

51 NA, dispatch No. 542, Newel to Hay, The Hague, September 26, 1902; quotations are Newel's.

52 NA, dispatch 550, Newel to Hay, The Hague, October 20, 1902.

53 See Washington Evening Star, October 15, 1902, pp. 4, 6; New York Times, October 16, 1902, p. 8. Ever since the institution of the Permanent Court in 1899, many nations had been reluctant in submitting disputes, evidently skeptical of the efficiency and justice of such a unique tribunal. Great Britain had been mercilessly castigated when it refused to submit to the Hague Tribunal its violent dispute with the Boer Republic in South Africa. (Stead, art. cit., p. 419.) But the smooth settlement of the Pious Fund Case immeasurably enhanced the reputation of the tribunal and immediately after its conclusion six nations announced their willingness to present cases. (Outlook, LXXII [October 25, 1902], 441-42.)

54 NA, dispatch No. 550, Newel to Hay, The Hague, October 20, 1902.

55 DP, Doyle to Ralston, Menlo Park, October 15, 1902; Doyle to Hay, Menlo Park, October 17, 1902; Doyle to Riordan, Menlo Park, October 22, 1902.

56 APF, Folder on the Pious Fund settlement, P.N. 02/52516, Giovannini to Gotti, The Hague, November 25, 1902. This sixteen-page report on the history and the arbitration of the fund is the principal source describing the Holy See's activities during the litigation.

57 *Monitor*, December 6, 1902, p. 9.

58 AASF, Riordan to Mulligan, Paris, November 9, 1902, telegram.

59 ADR, Gibbons to O'Connell, Baltimore, November 29, 1902; Ireland to O'Connell, New York, December 7, 1902. See also *ibid.*, Riordan to O'Connell, San Francisco, December 30 [1902].

60 APF, Folder entitled, "Monterey e Los Angeles... Elezione del Vescovo," *Acta*, P.N. 03/54025, Cardinal Francesco Satolli, *Relazione con sommario*, "Sulla elezione del nuovo Vescovo di Monterey e Los Angeles," March, 1903; *ibid.*, report of the general congregation of March 9, 1903.

61 AASF, LB-7(390-391), Riordan to Spalding [San Francisco], January 13, 1903; LB-7(426), Riordan's circular to the alumni of the American College, Louvain, n.p., n.d.; copies.

62 *Ibid.*, LB-8(422), Riordan to Bernard of Andermatt, Minister General, Order of Capuchins (San Francisco, *circa* July 31, 1903), copy. *Monitor*, May 9, 16, and 23, 1903; and November 7, 1903.

63 AASF, LB-8(123), Riordan to Conaty [San Francisco, April 6, 1903]; LB-8(78), Riordan to James E. Quigley [San Francisco, *ca.* March 20, 1903]; LB-8(138), Riordan to O'Connell [San Francisco, *ca.* April 8, 1903]; copies. *New World* (Chicago), May 16, 1903, p. 26. His brother Daniel had just spent many months in San Antonio, Texas, recuperating from a severe illness, and the archbishop was genuinely concerned and had resolved to use the occasion of the consecration of his church in noting the exact state of his health.

64 APF, Folder entitled, "California... denaro dato dal Governo Messicano" [1902], no protocol number, Alemany to Franchi, San Francisco, January 25, 1877.

65 *Ibid.*, report of the papal audience dated March 4, 1877, unsigned copy.

66 AASF, Pious Fund Scrapbook, IV, Riordan [to suffragan bishops], San Francisco, n.d., a rough draft written by Riordan.

67 AASF, LB-9(52-54), Riordan to Conaty [San Francisco], September 10, 1903, copy.

68 *Idem.*

69 *Ibid.*, LB-9(54,80-81), Riordan to Scanlan [San Francisco, September 10 and] September 17, 1903, copies; Scanlan to Riordan, Salt Lake City, September 14, 1903.

70 AASF, Pious Fund Scrapbook, IV, Riordan [to suffragan bishops], San Francisco, n.d.; "Memorandum of Agreement covering the Distribution of Moneys Collected and to be Collected upon Account of the Pious Fund," dated October 5, 1903, signed ms.

71 DP, Doyle to Sherman Doyle, Menlo Park, May 19, 1903.

72 APF, Folder on the Pious Fund settlement, P.N. 02/52516, Giovannini to Gotti, The Hague, November 25, 1902.

73 AASF, Pious Fund Scrapbook, III, unnumbered, Descamps to Riordan, Louvain, November 14, 1902; LB-9(64), Riordan to De Becker [San Francisco], September 15, 1903; see also LB-9(259), same to same [San Francisco], November 11, 1903, copies.

74 DP, Doyle to Sherman Doyle, Menlo Park, January 31, 1903; Doyle to Ralston, Menlo Park, April 6, 1903.

75 *Ibid.*, same to same, San Francisco, February 14, 1903, copy.

76 The suggestion that Judge James M. Seawell and the State Department arbitrate fell through when Doyle wished Seawell to fix the amount between $5,000 and $10,000 and McEnerney felt that $10,000 would be his minimum. See the Doyle Papers of June, 1903, particularly Doyle's summation of the "friendly controversy" attached to Doyle to Riordan, Menlo Park, June 9, 1903. This stage of the conflict ended when Doyle telegrammed Stewart: "I abandon all hope of arbitration at present believing they having been amusing me to gain time and collect money. I will now accuse them and perhaps learn something." (DP, Doyle to Stewart, Menlo Park, June 20, 1903.) For Riordan's views, see AASF, LB-9(74-78), Riordan to Doyle [San Francisco], September 16, 1903, copy.

77 AASF, Stewart to Riordan, Washington, D.C., July 29, 1903, telegram. NA, Bureau of Accounts, Entry 286, E. H. Thomas, counsel for Stewart and Doyle, to Hay, Washington, D.C., July 31, 1903; and supplemental brief.

78 AASF, LB-8(431-432), Riordan to Stewart [San Francisco], August 3, 1903, copy.

79 AASF, LB-9(133), Riordan to Doyle [San Francisco], October 12, 1903, copy.

80 DP, Doyle to Charles Siddons, Menlo Park, July 28, 29, and 30, 1903; Doyle to Stewart, Menlo Park, July 29 and 30, 1903, telegrams copied; NA, Bureau of Accounts, Entry 286, E. H. Thomas to Hay,

Washington, D. C., July 31, 1903; and supplemental brief.

81 AASF, Pious Fund Scrapbook, IV, William M. Stewart, Charles J. Kappler, Jackson H. Ralston, Frederick L. Siddons, and Ralston and Siddons to The Roman Catholic Archbishop of San Francisco, a corporation sole, *et al.*, "Receipt for $62,853.62 in full payment of all claims under contracts for counsel fees made December 24,1889, and November 15, 1897, and release in full of all demands to date, and transfer of all future rights under contracts," dated May 13, 1904, ms.

82 John T. Doyle, *In the International Arbitral Court of The Hague: The Case of the Pious Fund of California* (San Francisco, 1906), I, 95. The volume contains in two sections edited versions of Doyle's correspondence between December, 1902, and June, 1904. His open letter to Riordan is dated February 12, 1906, and is found on pages 85-104.

83 APF, P.N. 06/70736, Doyle to Gotti, Menlo Park, February 22, 1906.

84 Kenneth M. Johnson, *The Pious Fund* (Los Angeles, 1963), p. 65.

85 Evidently only ten installments actually reached California. Payments for 1913 and 1914 were held, at Riordan's directive, in a border bank in Mexico in the hopes of a better exchange. (NA, Edward J. Hanna to Robert Lansing [San Francisco], October 1, 1917). In 1967 the governments of the United States and Mexico settled the Pious Fund claim, ending a dispute which had ranged another half century. Accordingly, Mexico paid a lump sum of $719,546 — a sum almost all of which was given to Montezuma Seminary in Mexico. (AASF, Joseph T. McGucken to Cardinal John Cody, San Francisco, September 20 and November 27, 1967.)

CHAPTER NINE

1 M. D. Connolly, "Personal Recollections of the Late Most Reverend Archbishop Riordan," *Monitor*, Christmas, 1915, p. 6.

2 *Congressi, A.C.*, vol. 41 (1884), fog. 73r, Riordan to Simeoni, San Francisco, July 24, 1884.

3 [Joseph Gleason] in the *Monitor*, January 23, 1904 [p. 15].

4 AASF, LB-13(313), Riordan to Gertrude O'Brien [San Francisco], January 13, 1905, copy.

5 *Ibid.*, LB-18(229-230), Riordan to Conaty, [San Francisco], April 7, 1906, copy.

6 AALA, Montgomery to Conaty, San Francisco, April 23, 1906; emphasis is Montgomery's.

7 *San Francisco Relief Survey: The Organization and Methods of Relief Used After the Earthquake and Fire of April 18, 1906* (New York, 1913), pp. 3-8; hereafter cited as *Survey*.

8 AACL, Huesges to De Becker, Woodland, California, May 12, 1906.

9 *Ibid.*, Huesges to De Becker, Woodland, May 30, 1906.

10 AALA, Montgomery to Conaty, San Francisco, April 23, 1906.

11 *Ibid.*, Conaty to Montgomery, Los Angeles, April 26, 1906, copy.

12 ACUA, O'Connell Papers, Brother Justin, F.S.C., to Denis O'Connell, St. Louis, April 21, 1906, *private*. Brother Justin, a pioneer educator in California who had served as the first provincial in California, was at this time the Director of the Christian Brothers' College at St. Louis, Missouri.

13 AASF, "Earthquake Letters" (hereafter cited as E.L.), reprinted in several circulars.

14 *Ibid.*, Shahan to Riordan, Washington, D.C., April 20, 1906.

15 *Ibid.*, Stang to Riordan, Fall River, April 21, 1906.

16 *Ibid.*, Keane to Riordan, Dubuque, April 19, 1906.

17 Quoted in *Survey*, p. 78.

18 AALA, Montgomery to Conaty, San Francisco, April 23 and 24, 1906.

19 Archives of the Sisters of the Presentation, Annals, pp. 124, 142; hereafter cited as ASP.

20 ASMS, Havey's Notes.

21 San Francisco *Call*, April 28, 1906, p. 1.

22 *Ibid.*, December 29, 1914, p. 8.

23 ASMS, Havey's Notes.

24 *Survey*, p. 15.

25 AASF, LB-19(340-41), Montgomery to James H. Williams [San Francisco], August 11, 1906, copy.

26 *Ibid.*, LB-18(326), Cantwell to Egan and Prenderville [San Francisco], May 10, 1906, copy. See also *ibid.*, Frances O'Connor to Riordan, Paris, May 25, 1906.

27 Peter C. Yorke, "Essentially a Churchman," *Leader*, January 2, 1915, p. 4.

28 AASF, LB-19(53-54), Riordan to Williams [San Francisco], June 23, 1906, copy. The first estimate of the damages of the seminary sent to Propaganda was fixed at $350,000; but after the restoration

Riordan reported $200,000. *Ibid.*, LBR(1a), 253-56, Riordan to Alexander Christie, Archbishop of Portland, Oregon [San Francisco], August 4, 1909, copy.

29 *Ibid.*, LB-20(407-408), Cantwell to Herman J. Heuser [San Francisco], November 15, 1906, copy.

30 ASP, "Annals," pp. 137-38, Riordan to Mother M. Josephine [San Francisco], June 4, 1906, copy.

31 AASF, LBR(2a), 326-28, 331, Riordan to M. Gorman, R.C.S.J. [San Francisco], February 20 and 21, 1911; LBR(3a), 417-19, Riordan to Jane Fox, R.C.S.J. [San Francisco], March 19, 1912, copies.

32 AAB-103-M-5, Riordan to Gibbons, San Francisco, May 5, 1906.

33 AASF, P.N. 06/18114, Merry del Val to Riordan, Rome, June 10, 1906.

34 E.L., Walsh to Riordan, Dublin, June 8, 1906.

35 E.L., Moran to Riordan, Sydney, August 4, 1906.

36 Interview with Cardinal Timothy J. Manning, Rome, September 30, 1963. Cardinal Manning had been Archbishop Cantwell's secretary, and it was from him that he learned this.

37 ACUA, O'Connell Papers, Riordan to O'Connell, San Francisco, July 14, 1906.

38 AASF, LB-22(106-111), Riordan to Riordan [San Francisco], March 8, 1907, copy.

39 P.N. 07/79494, Report of Riordan [November or December], 1907.

40 AASF, LB-27(173-74), Riordan to Ireland [San Francisco], September 11, 1908, copy.

41 *Jewish Times*, October 16, 1908.

42 *Monitor*, October 17, 1908, Jubilee Issue. See also San Francisco *Call*, October 15, 1908, p. 16; October 16, pp. 1-4; *Bulletin*, October 15, pp. 1-2; *Examiner*, October 16, pp. 1-3; *Chronicle*, October 16, pp. 1-2.

43 Arthur Meier Schlesinger, *Political and Social Growth of the American People, 1865-1940*, 3d ed. (New York, 1941), p. 201.

44 *Monitor*, June 10, 1893, p. 5. See also Sister M. Alexander Gray, O.S.F., "Development of the Newman Club Movement, 1893-1961," *Records* of the American Catholic Historical Society of Philadelphia, LXXIV (June, 1963), 71-79.

45 *Acta Sanctae Sedis*, XXXVIII (1905), 623; quoted from the encyclical, *Acerbo nimis*, dated April 15, 1905.

46 Ester M. Phillips, "The Newman Club of the University of California," *Newman Hall Review*, n.d., pp. 6-7; copy in files of the

National Newman Club Federation, Washington,D.C. An edited version of this article appeared in the *Monitor*, September 17, 1927. Another early history may be found in A. G. Eccles, "A Successful Catholic Hall at an American State University," *Ecclesiastical Review*, XLIX (August, 1913), 207-13. The fullest history may be found in J. Whitney Evans, "The Newman Movement: A Social and Intellectual History of Roman Catholics in American Higher Education, 1884-1969," an unpublished Ph.D. dissertation at the University of Minnesota (Minneapolis, 1970).

47 AASF, LBR(3a), 393-94, Riordan to Daniel Riordan [San Francisco], March 7, 1912, copy.

48 Phillips, *loc. cit.*

49 Francis B. Cassilly, "Catholic Students at State Universities: A Growing Educational Problem," *Ecclesiastical Review*, XXXIV (February, 1906), 113-20.

50 Robert L. McWilliams, "The Presence of Catholic Students at our State Universities," *ibid.*, XXXV (August, 1906), 197-200.

51 AASF, "Newman Club" File (hereafter cited as NC), "Prospectus of the Proposed St. Paul's University Chapel at the University of Wisconsin, Madison" [Madison, n.d.], p. 14.

52 AASF, Minutes of the Archbishops' Meetings, Washington, D.C., April 26, 1906, article xiii. Rochester *Democrat and Chronicle*, April 16, 1906; quoted in Michael J. Murphy, "The Cornell Plan of Bishop Bernard J. McQuaid," *St. Meinrad Essays*, XII (May, 1959), 70.

53 AASF, LB-19(184-185), Riordan to McQuaid [San Francisco], July 24, 1906, copy.

54 *Ibid.*, LBR(3a), 570-71, Riordan to John J. Hughes, C.S.P. [San Francisco], August 5, 1912, copy.

55 NC, Moore to Wyman, Caldwell, New York, August 4, 1906. Pablo Maria [Thomas Verner] Moore, O. Cart., "The Beginnings of Newman Hall at the University of California and the Personality of Archbishop Riordan," a handwritten manuscript, Burgos, Spain, May 25, 1963, p. 1; hereafter cited as "Beginnings." The writer also had the good fortune of having had Father Moore comment on this section before his death in 1969. A helpful summary of Father Moore's rich life is found in the *New Catholic Encyclopedia*, *XVI*, Supplement 1967-1974 (Washington, D.C. and New York, 1974), pp. 300-1.

56 AASF, NC, Searle to Riordan, New York, October 22, 1906.

57 Moore, "Beginnings," p. 2. At this time Moore gave a very lengthy description of his experiments on hypnosis to Denis O'Connell, Rector of the Catholic University of America. ACUA, O'Connell Papers, Moore to O'Connell, Berkeley, March 16, 1908.

58 NC, Martin A. Centner, *et al.*, to Riordan, Berkeley, February 21, 1907; AASF, LB-22(54), Cantwell to Moore [San Francisco], March 1, 1907, copy.

59 AASF, Wheeler to Riordan, Berkeley, May 7, 1907.

60 *Ibid.*, LB-23(242), Riordan to Searle [San Francisco], June 28, 1907, copy; NC, Searle to Riordan, New York, July 17, 1907.

61 NC, Riordan, "The Catholic Chapel and Lecture Hall at the University of California," brochure, n.d.; see also *Monitor*, August 24, 1907, p. 1

62 AASF, LB-24(64), Cantwell to Mother Bernadine, S.N.D. [San Francisco], August 28, 1907; UND, MC, Hudson Papers, X-4-f, McQuaid to Hudson, Rochester, September 3, 1907.

63 Moore, "Beginnings," p. 2; NC, Moore to Cantwell, Berkeley, August 27, 1907; Moore to Riordan, Berkeley, September 3, 1907. Moore places a measure of blame upon his own temperament at the time. "My personality matured slowly," he noted, "and though about 30 years old at the time, I was something of a wild and reckless adolescent." Moore, "Beginnings," *loc. cit.*

64 NC, Moore to Riordan, Berkeley, December 17, 1908. Years later, Moore recalls that in Riordan's absence from San Francisco he had persuaded lumbermen to donate the heavy lumber and fine wood for the ceiling. "So when the Archbishop came back," he remarked, "I was able to explain things in a way that he scolded Shea for the changes [in design] he had ordered, saying that he never meant any such thing." Moore, "Beginnings," p. 4.

65 AASF, LBR(4a), 173-77, Riordan to Clarence H. Mackay [San Francisco], December 12, 1912, copy.

66 NC, Queen to Riordan, San Francisco, April 16, 1908.

67 AASF, LBR(4a), 173-77, Riordan to Clarence H. Mackay [San Francisco], December 12, 1912, copy.

68 *Ibid.*, Mackay to Riordan, New York, March 24, 1908.

69 *Monitor*, June 13, 1908, pp. 7, 8. AASF, LB-26(384-385), Riordan to Clarence Mackay [San Francisco], June 23, 1908; LB-26(386-387), Riordan to Mrs. Marie Louis Mackay [San Francisco], July 23, 1908, copies. NC, Mackay to Riordan, New York, July 3 and 20, 1908. Two years later, Mrs. Mackay donated another $5,000. *Ibid.*, Riordan to Cantwell, New York, April 12, 1910.

70 *Ibid.*, Riordan to Ramm, Santa Clara, July 8, 1908. In the last five years of his life, Riordan continued with less success to solicit substantial contributions to the Newman Hall. From 1909 through 1913, the donations were $10,000 from the estate of Michael Cudahy;

$5,000 each from Mrs. Bertha Welch and James L. Flood; $2,000 from Adolphus W. Green; $1,000 each from the estate of Mrs. Teresa Casserly, Garrett W. McEnerney, and Joseph S. Tobin; and $500 from Frank G. Drum. *Ibid.,* "Donations: Newman Hall, Berkeley."

71 AASF, LBR(1a), 139-40, Riordan to Madame O'Meara, R.C.S.J. [San Francisco], June 8, 1909, copy.

72 From the priests of Old St. Mary's Church, Moore had learned of a conspicuous name-plate fastened on the pulpit inscribed with the names of benefactors and bearing among them that of Eugene Schmitz, the former Mayor of San Francisco, who had been prosecuted on charges of graft. In the absence of the superior, Father Wyman, Moore on his own authority had removed the plate and deposited it in San Francisco Bay on his return to Berkeley. Shortly thereafter, he was interviewed by the Sacramento *Bee* which was preparing an attack on Wyman that as chaplain of the State Senate in Sacramento, he had never once used the name of Christ. In an effort to prevent this, Moore recounted the incident of the name-plate which the *Bee* published on June 20, 1909. Moore had given this story in order to spare Wyman unmerited embarrassment.

As soon as Moore told Wyman of the interview, the latter accused him of conspiring to have the article written against him, and the incident was reported to the archbishop. Wyman's explanation had so infuriated Riordan that he refused to see Moore on this matter and demanded that the superior general, George Searle, C.S.P., remove the young Paulist, charging that this evident interference in local politics has become a "grave scandal." Searle learned further that Riordan had for some months intended to request his withdrawal since Moore was given more to "visionary theories," and after this incident, the archbishop, on Wyman's request, insisted on his removal not only from the Newman Club but also from the archdiocese. This must be done quietly, Riordan advised, possibly through a simple letter of transfer to New York, but if action was postponed, he threatened to take matters into his own hands. "This whole affair is very distressing," Riordan concluded,

> and has almost broken the heart of poor Father Wyman. Father Moore had ability, but in my judgment he lacks the very root and principle of the religious life, namely, obedience, and I see in him enough of that spirit of obstinancy and disobedience which unless they are irradicated [*sic*] will lead him some day or another to

abandon the religious life and seek his salvation among the
secular Clergy where there are fewer restraints and more
liberty but less security than in a religious body.

Moore, "Beginnings," p. 5-6; AASF, LBR(1a), 214-17, Riordan to
Searle [San Francisco], July 23, 1909, copy.
    Moore was determined to represent his position to Riordan. "I
would call upon you before going," he wrote before departing for
Chicago,

> were it not that I understand from Fr. Wyman that your
> Grace does not wish it .... I would remove a false
> impression, which I believe you have in regard to me. In
> spite of appearances, I was not an instigator of the article in
> the Sacramento *Bee*

Some months later, Moore was able to deliver to Riordan his
explanation through a mutual friend, Father Walter Elliott, C.S.P. The
reason for his dismissal, replied the archbishop, was not "your spirit of
disobedience or ... obstinacy in your opinions — I could have easily
dealt with these ...." The decisive cause was the removal of the
name-plate which Moore had himself confessed as "altogether
unjustifiable" and the sensational article in the Sacramento *Bee*. "When
this was brough[t] to my attention," Riordan concluded, "I considered
your usefulness as a moral and religious teacher of the students of the
University at an end, and I accordingly asked for your recall." NC,
Moore to Riordan, Berkeley, July 29, 1909; LBR(2a), 41-42, Riordan
to Moore [San Francisco], January 21, 1910, copy.
    73 NC, Searle to Riordan, New York, July 28, 1909.
    74 AASF, LBR(1a), 249-52, Riordan to Hughes [San Francisco],
November 27, 1909, copy.
    75 NC, Hughes to Riordan, New York, August 7, 1909.
    76 AASF, LBR(1a), 478-79, Riordan to Hughes [San Francisco],
November 27, 1907, copy.
    77 NC, Hughes to Riordan, New York, December 10, 1909; AASF,
LBR(2a), 9-10, Riordan to Hughes [San Francisco], December 16,
1909, copy.
    78 AASF, LBR(2a), 275-78, Riordan to Mackay [San Francisco],
January 19, 1911, copy.
    79 Moore to the writer, Burgos, Spain, May 25, 1963. Manuscript
Collection at the University of San Francisco (hereafter cited as USF,

MC), "Father Yorke's Sermon at Bishop Cantwell's Jubilee," *The Leader* (San Francisco), June 21 (?), 1924, preserved in one of Yorke's scrapbooks.

80 AASF, LBR(4a), 173-77, Riordan to Mackay [San Francisco], December 12, 1912, copy.

81 *Ibid.*, LBR(3a), 199-200, Riordan to John B. Casserly [San Francisco], October 6, 1911, copy.

82 *Ibid.*, LBR(4a), 448-49, Riordan to Mrs. Myles P. O'Connor [San Francisco], March 7, 1913, copy.

83 *Ibid.*, LBR(2a), 307-309, Riordan to Elliott [San Francisco], January 26, 1911, copy.

84 *Ibid.*, LBR(4a), 173-77, Riordan to Mackay [San Francisco], December 12, 1912, copy.

CHAPTER TEN

1 AALA, Riordan to Mora, San Francisco, January 21 and March 31, 1893; these documents were sent to the writer through the courtesy of the archivist, the Monsignor Francis J. Weber.

2 San Francisco *Call*, July 29, 1900, p. 31.

3 P.N. 01/44198, Riordan to Ledochowski, San Francisco, n.d. (registered at Propaganda on May 6, 1901.)

4 *Ibid.*, Ledochowski to Riordan, Rome, May 13, 1901, copy.

5 P.N. 02/18621, Riordan to Cardinal Camillo Mazzella, San Francisco, May 13, 1896.

6 P.N. 02/49485, report of the Meeting of the Consultors and Irremovable Rectors . . . . San Francisco, March 14, 1902, signed by John Prendergast as secretary. The exact tally of votes was as follows: Montgomery 7; Grace 3; James Cleary 3; Peter Yorke 3; Bishop Thomas Conaty 2; Monsignor Thomas F. Kennedy, Rector of the American College in Rome, 1; Father Richard P. Brennan, pastor of Mission Dolores Church, San Francisco, 1.

7 *Ibid.*, Riordan, Grace, and Scanlan to Ledochowski, San Francisco, March 22, 1902.

8 P.N. 02/49485, Martinelli to Ledochowski, Washington, D. C., April 22, 1902.

9 P.N.02/51071, report of the general congregation of September 1, 1908.

10 ASMS, Montgomery to Magnien, San Francisco, January 26, February 23, and March 1, 1880. An appreciative sketch of

Montgomery's life is Francis J. Weber, *George Thomas Montgomery: California Churchman* (Los Angeles, 1966).

11 *Sadliers' Catholic Directory . . . 1885* (New York, 1885), p. 137; *Sadliers' Catholic Directory . . . 1887* (New York, 1887), p. 136.

12 *Monitor*, February 14, 1903, p. 16.

13 Riordan's letterbooks indicate that he had left San Francisco on Easter Monday, April 24, 1905, and returned sometime in mid-December.

14 AASF, LBR-14(439), Montgomery to Joseph Scott [San Francisco], May 11, 1905, copy.

15 AASF, LB-21(282-283) [Cantwell or Ramm?] to George A. Burkley [San Francisco], January 22, 1907, copy. Accounts of Montgomery's last days in the San Francisco *Chronicle*, January 11, 1907, p. 1; *Monitor*, January 12, 1907, pp. 1, 8.

16 AASF, "Archbishop Montgomery" File, Falconio to Riordan, Washington, D. C., January 11, 1907; Gabriels to Riordan, Ogdensburg, New York, January 11, 1907; Stang to Riordan, Fall River, January 11, 1907; McQuaid to Riordan, Rochester, January 11, 1907.

17 AASF, LB-21(337-338), Riordan to the Right Reverend Michael J. Lavelle [San Francisco], January 31, 1907, copy.

18 The account of Montgomery's delay in coming north is entangled with the complicated appointment of Bishop Conaty as his successor. Riordan had kept his coadjutor in southern California some five months after his appointment to San Francisco — part of a series of deft maneuvers to weaken local candidates and to assure the appointment of his Own. The full story is told in pp. 325-31.

19 AASF, LB-22(274-275), Riordan to Grace [San Francisco], March 27, 1907, copy.

20 AASF, LB-22(148-149), Riordan to Conaty [San Francisco], March 14, 1907, copy; LB-21(337-338), Riordan to Michael J. Lavelle [San Francisco], January 31, 1907, copy; and Lavelle to Riordan, New York, February 6, 1907.

21 ACUA O'Connell Papers, Riordan to O'Connell, San Francisco, April 18, 1907.

22 P.N. 07/78456, Minutes of the Meeting of the Consultors and Irremovable Rectors, San Francisco, August 16, 1907; Minutes of the Meeting of the Bishops of the Ecclesiastical Province of San Francisco, San Francisco, August 21, 1907; "Notulae" of each candidate compiled by Riordan, Also AALA, Riordan to Conaty, San Francisco, June 13 [1907].

23 A helpful sketch which emphasizes Hanna's early life may be found in Robert F. McNamara, "Archbishop Hanna, Rochesterian,"

Rochester History, XXV (April, 1963), 1-24; for documentation, see the same author's *The American College in Rome, 1855-1955* (Rochester, 1956), *passim*. A briefer account may be found by Hanna's former secretary in San Francisco, the Right Reverend Thomas F. Millett, in the *New Catholic Encyclopedia* (New York, 1967), IV, 914-15.

24 ACUA, O'Connell Papers, Riordan to O'Connell, San Francisco, December 28, 1903.

25 AASF, "Earthquake Letters," McQuaid to Riordan, Rochester, April 24, 1906, and his printed circular classified under "Bernard."

26 AASF, LBR (1a), 22-23a, Riordan to O'Connell, [San Francisco], January 20, 1909, copy.

27 Archives of the Diocese of Rochester, Riordan to McQuaid, San Francisco, April 4, 1907; hereafter cited as ADRo. These papers were provided through the courtesy of the Reverend Robert F. McNamara.

28 ADRo, same to same, San Francisco, April 18, 1907.

29 *Acta Sanctae Sedis*, XL (1907), 593-652.

30 P.N. 07/78658, Breen to Marini, Rochester, September 18, 1907. For a brief sketch of Breen's life, especially after his departure from Rochester, see Benjamin J. Blied, "Rev. Andrew E. Breen, D. D., Priest, Professor, Author," *Salesianum*, XLVIII (October, 1953), 172-79. The material in the Propaganda archives does not further identify Monsignor Marini. At the time of these negotiations there were two in Rome to whom Breen more likely communicated his letter, namely Antonino Marini, archivist and *scrittore* of the Consistorial Congregation and *camerlengo* of the clergy of the Diocese of Rome; and Niccolo Marini, consultor of the Congregation of Studies and *sostituto* in the Secretariate of Briefs. Of these two, the latter would seem to be more directly interested in Hanna's orthodoxy. (*La Gerarchia Cattolica, Anno 1907* [Rome, 1907].) Lagrange's comments may be found in the *Revue biblique*, IX (1900), 161-62, and XV (1906), 164-65.

31 ACUA, O'Connell Papers, Duffy to Hanna, Yonkers, New York, January 8, 1905.

32 The completed four-part series appeared as Edward J. Hanna, "The Human Knowledge of Christ," *New York Review*, I (October-November, 1905), 303-76; (December, 1905-January, 1906), 425-36; (February-March, 1906), 597-615; III (January-February; March-April, 1908), 391-400.

33 P.N. 07/78658, Gotti to Falconio, Rome, October 22, 1907, copy written and signed by Gotti.

34 *Ibid.*, Falconio to Gotti, Washington, D. C., October 15, 1907. Gotti's letter to Falconio had left Rome on October 22, and this above letter of Falconio's arrived at Propaganda on October 25. From the testimony of his students, Lépicier is reported to have borrowed the first copies of the *New York Review*, and on detecting what he conceived as errors he began a series of lectures at the Urban College which were eventually published under the title, *De Stabilitate et Progressu Dogmatis* (Rome, 1908.) Though Hanna's name was never mentioned, Lépicier had openly attacked his articles in the *Review*, the *Catholic Encyclopedia*, and the *American Journal of Theology*. (McNamara to the writer, Rochester, August 13, 1964.)

35 P.N. 07/79242, Lépicier to Gotti, Rome, registered at Propaganda on December 2, 1907. Contrary to Falconio's report, Lépicier established that he had never in a public lecture referred to Hanna by name because such had not been his custom, and he believed it was inopportune to question "one of the more distinguished scholars of His Eminence, Cardinal Satolli . . . ."

36 P.N., Lépicier to Gotti, December 31, 1907, printed copy.

37 AASF, LB-24(306), Cantwell to Peter S. Casey [San Francisco], October 9, 1907; ACUA, Minutes of the Board of Trustees of the Catholic University of America, XXXVIII Meeting, November 13, 1907, p. 156.

38 P.N. 07/79088, Riordan to Gotti, San Francisco [Washington, D. C.], November 7, 1907.

39 ADRo, Riordan to McQuaid, Washington, D. C., November 8 [1907]

40 ACUA, O'Connell Papers, Riordan to O'Connell, New York, November 19, 1907.

41 ADRo, Riordan to McQuaid, Washington, D. C., [November 14?, 1907].

42 *Idem.*

43 P.N. 07/79172, McQuaid to Merry del Val, Rochester, November 12, 1907. McQuaid forwarded virtually the same appeal to Gotti. P.N. 07/79316, McQuaid to Gotti, Rochester, November 20, 1907.

44 ACUA, O'Connell Papers, Hanna to O'Connell, Rochester, December 4 [1907].

45 P.N. 07/79607, Hanna to Gotti, Rochester, December 16, 1907. Propaganda's reaction to this document was recorded in the words of Riordan: "Dr. Hanna's 'Declaratio' has been received and Cardl. Gotti is much pleased with it," ADRo, Riordan to McQuaid, Rome, January 1 [1907].

46 AACL, Lawler to De Becker, St. Paul, December 3, 1907.

47 P.N. 07/79284, Gibbons to Gotti, Baltimore, November 18, 1907; P.N. 07/79420, Ireland to Gotti, St. Paul, November 29, 1907; P.N. 07/79419, Ryan to Gotti, Philadelphia, November 26, 1907; P.N. 07/79441, Glennon to Gotti, St. Louis, November 27, 1907. Riordan was under the impression that Archbishop Farley of New York had sent an appeal to Rome, but the archives of Propaganda Fide have no record of such a message. If Farley had reneged on his promise, it was probably due to the fact that he wished to avoid deeper personal involvement in the modernist controversy since the *New York Review* allegedly bore his *imprimatur* — although it did not appear in print.

48 ACUA, O'Connell Papers, Riordan to O'Connell, Rome, December 11, [1907].

49 ADRo, Meehan to McQuaid, Rome, December 17, 1907. Dom Aiden Gasquet, an English Benedictine and later cardinal, was a well-known ecclesiastical historian.

50 ADRo, Riordan to McQuaid, Rome, December 27 [1907]; and January 1 [1908].

51 *Ibid.*, Meehan to McQuaid, Rome, January 12, 1908.

52 P.N. 07/79688, a note reading: "Adunanza Gen. del. 13 Genn. 1908, Sul coadiutore all'Archivescovo di S. Francisco. Non proposita."

53 ADRo, Riordan to McQuaid, Rome, January 13 [1908]. In this hasty letter, Riordan shielded his bitter disappointment; and his reaction to the congregation's move was better recorded in Meehan's report to McQuaid which evidently resulted from a conversation with Riordan. "Archbishop Riordan is disgusted with the Italian methods," began Meehan,

> The Cardinals in the meeting ... would do nothing after twelve o'clock. Meeting[s] are held from ten till twelve, and at twelve nothing more could be done. They had to have their lunch.

Ibid., Meehan to McQuaid, Rome, January 19, 1908.

54 ADRo, Riordan to McQuaid, Rome, January 4, 1908.

55 ADRo, Brandi to McQuaid, Rome, December 28, 1907.

56 ADRo, Meehan to McQuaid, Rome, January 4 and 12, 1908.

57 UND, MC, Hudson Papers, X-4-F, McQuaid to Daniel E. Hudson, C.S.C., Rochester, February 18, 1908. Hudson was long the editor of *Ave Maria* at the University of Notre Dame.

58 Rochester *Democrat and Chronicle*, January 14, 1908, p. 12.

59 P.N. 07/80321, Breen to Gotti, Rochester, January 15, 1908. The anti-Hanna resolutions signed by the seminary's student body and sent to Rome may be found in the Rochester *Democrat and Chronicle*, January 15, 1908, p. 13.

60 *Giornale d'Italia*, January 20, 1908, p. 4; available at the Biblioteca della Camera dei Deputati, Rome. Meehan sent this issue to McQuaid with the comment: "Everything gets out here." (ADRo, Meehan to McQuaid, Rome, January 22, 1908.) The American press, it may be noted, had already taken notice of the affair, especially Hanna's failure to receive the appointment at the Propaganda's meeting of January 13, 1908. E.g., *Catholic Telegraph* (Cincinnati), January 16, 1908, p. 8.

61 ADRo, Meehan to McQuaid, Rome, January 22, 1908.

62 *Freeman's Journal* (New York), February 15, 1908, p. 5: also P.N. 07/80946, a clipping from a San Francisco newspaper.

63 UND, MC, Hudson Papers, X-4-F, McQuaid to Hudson, Rochester, February 18, 1908.

64 ADRo, Meehan to McQuaid, Rome, January 19, 1908.

65 Edward J. Hanna, "The Human Knowledge of Christ (IV), " and "The Power of the Keys (I), " *New York Review*, III (January-February; March-April, 1908), 391-400, 561-68, a combined issue. It may be further noted that three years later there appeared in the *Catholic Encyclopedia* a judicious article on "Penance" by Hanna and in 1912 an amendation inserted among the *errata* to correct his provocative sentence in the article on absolution. See the *Catholic Encyclopedia* (New York, 1911, 1912), XI, 618-35; XV, 776.

66 AASF, Meehan to McQuaid, Rome, March 9, 1908. *Acta Sanctae Sedis*, XLI (1908), 141-42.

67 AASF, Meehan to McQuaid, Rome, March 10, 1908.

68 AASF, McQuaid to Riordan, Rochester, March 23, 1908.

69 ADRo, Meehan to McQuaid, Rome, April 4, 1908.

70 AASF, Satolli to Hanna, Rome, April 5, 1908.

71 AASF, McQuaid to Riordan, Rochester, April 17, 1908.

72 P.N. 07/81671, Hanna to Gotti, Rochester, April 24, 1908; AASF, Hanna to Riordan, Rochester, April 24, 1908.

73 AASF, LB-26(123-124), Riordan to Falconio [San Francisco], April 23, 1908, copy. Falconio strongly seconded Riordan's request to Propaganda although he inferred that Riordan had no preference among the candidates. (P.N. 08/81827, Falconio to Gotti, Washington, D. C., May 10, 1908.)

74 AASF, LB-26(130, 132), Riordan to McQuaid [San Francisco], April 24, 1908, copy.

75 P.N. 08/81831, Riordan to Gotti, San Francisco, May 1, 1908.

76 *Acta Sanctae Sedis*, XLI (1909), 431.

77 AASF, Genocchi to Riordan, Rome, July 4, 1908.

78 AASF, LB-27(9), Riordan to Cantwell [San Francisco], August 4, 1908. Cantwell was much beloved by Riordan, who had earlier that year given him $1,000 toward a trip to Europe. (AALA, Riordan to Cantwell, San Francisco, May 5, 1908.) Even in late August, when Hanna's star had fallen, Cantwell sent highly optimistic reports to San Francisco, telling the archbishop that according to Gotti, "the appointment to assist you in your arduous labors in California would be made without fail at the first meeting of the Congregation in September, he felt sure in the manner satisfactory." There was an addendum in Cantwell's account, however, for at this point the cardinal was looking for another petition from Riordan. (AASF, Cantwell to Riordan, Rome, August 22, 1908.)

79 P.N. 08/81886, Breen to Gotti Rochester, May 13, 1908. Also, P.N. 08/82159, same to same, Rochester, May 30, 1908; P.N. 08/83209, same to same, Rochester, August 13, 1908.

80 The article was published in 1906, but two years later Hanna admitted that it had been written "six years ago." (AASF, Hanna to Riordan, Oswego, New York, August 28, 1908.) It possibly was an extensively revised article since a number of citations listed works published as late as 1904 and 1905.

81 Edward J. Hanna, "Some Recent Books on Catholic Theology," *American Journal of Theology*, X (January, 1906), 179, 181. P.N. 08/80891, Lépicier, "Proposizioni erronee estratee dal'articolo del Dr. Ed. Hanna . . . ," registered at Propaganda on March 21, 1908.

82 AASF, Genocchi to Riordan, Rome, August 5, 1908.

83 AASF, Gibbons to Riordan, Rome, August 2/10, 1908.

84 AASF, LB-27(107-108), Riordan to Conaty [San Francisco], August 24, 1908, copy.

85 AASF, Hanna to Riordan, Oswego, New York, August 28, 1908.

86 P.N. 08/82851, report of the general congregation of September 15, 1908; *ibid.*, Gotti to Falconio, Rome, September 22, 1908, copy.

87 AASF, LB-27(204-209), Riordan to Cardinal Sebastiano Martinelli [San Francisco], September 14, 1908, copy; *ibid.*, LB-27(241-242), Riordan to Hanna [San Francisco], September 24, 1908, copy. The ten archdiocesan consultors and irremovable pastors who drafted the priests' *terna* were: John J. Prendergast, William B. O'Connor, Thomas McSweeney, Patrick E. Mulligan, Edward P. Dampsey, Patrick J. Cummins, Lawrence Serda, Michael D. Connolly,

Peter S. Casey, and Peter C. Yorke, Possibly the one name which had not been suggested by Riordan but which had received one vote was Peter C. Yorke. (P.N. 07/78456, Minutes of the Meeting of the Consultors and Irremovable Rectors, San Francisco, August 16, 1907.)

88 AASF, LB-27(191-193), Riordan to Falconio [San Francisco], September [11] 1908, copy.

89 AASF, LB-27(173-174), Riordan to Ireland [San Francisco], September 11, 1908, copy.

90 AASF, Cantwell to Riordan, Paris, August 25, 1908.

91 AASF, An undated clipping attached to the letter below from Ireland. Cf. footnote 95.

92 P.N. 08/83625, Riordan to Gotti, San Francisco, September 15, 1908.

93 AASF, LB-27(204-209), Riordan to Martinelli [San Francisco], September 14, 1908, copy.

94 AASF, Ireland to Riordan, St. Paul, September 27, 1908.

95 AASF, LB-27(253-254), Riordan to Ireland [San Francisco], September 29, 1908, copy. Riordan shared his colleague's harsh views of Seton. Were "such dirty work" traced to him, Riordan told Ireland, Seton would be forced to leave Rome, for the authorities were "sick and tired" of his presence and activity there. "Of course we know he is practically out of his mind and is not responsible for what he says," lamented Riordan, "but people in this country do not know this." (*Idem.*)

96 AASF, Cortesi to Riordan, Rome, November 14, 1908.

97 P.N. 08/83625, Gotti to Riordan, Rome, October 6, 1908, copy.

98 AASF, LBR-27(324-325), Riordan to Ireland [San Francisco], October 21, 1908, copy.

99 AASF, LB-27(369-370), Riordan to Cerretti [San Francisco], November 2, 1908, copy.

100 AAB, 85-L-9, Keane to Gibbons, December 18, 1888.

101 ADR, Riordan to Keane, Paris, January 4 [1889].

102 ADR, Nugent to O'Connell, Liverpool, July 6, 1900.

103 ACUA, O'Connell Papers, Riordan to O'Connell, Rome, December 11 [1907].

104 AAB, 105-J-1, Riordan to Gibbons, San Francisco, June 11, 1907.

105 AASF, LB-27(357-358), Riordan to Lavelle [San Francisco], October 29, 1908, copy.

106 AASF, LB-27(369-370), Riordan to Cerretti [San Francisco], November 2, 1908, copy.

107 AAB, 106-L-1, Riordan to Gibbons, San Francisco, November 4, 1908.

108 AAB, 106-L-2, same to same, San Francisco, November 4, 1908.

109 AAB, 106-L-8, Gibbons to Riordan, Baltimore, November 10, 1908, copy.

110 AAB, 106-L-14, same to same, Baltimore, November 20, 1908, copy.

111 *Monitor*, January 2, 1909, p. 1; AASF, LBR(1a), 3, Riordan to Gibbons [San Francisco], January 13, 1909, copy. A copy of O'Connell's acknowledgment to Riordan reads: "Letter of appointment received this morning. Wishing you [a] very happy New Year. Obediently yours, D. J. O'Connell." (ACUA, Dougherty Papers, O'Connell to Riordan, n.p., n.d.)

112 ADR, Riordan to O'Connell, San Francisco, September 21, 1895.

113 AASF, LBR(1a), 105, Riordan to Riordan [San Francisco], March 19, 1909, copy.

114 AASF, LBR(1a), 104, Riordan to Kennedy [San Francisco], March 19, 1909, copy.

115 *Monitor*, April 17, 1909, p. 1.

116 AASF, LBR(1a), 22-23a, Riordan to O'Connell [San Francisco], January 20, 1909, copy.

117 AASF, LBR(3a), 169-70, Riordan to Falconio [San Francisco], September 16, 1911, copy; LBR(2a), 190, Riordan to Sister M. Louis O'Donnell, O.S.D. [San Francisco], December 12, 1910, copy.

118 AAB, 99-H-6, Gibbons to O'Connell, Baltimore, December 17 [1910]; this letter is misdated and misfiled as 1901.

119 AASF, LBR(2a), 270-72, Riordan to Keane [San Francisco], January 17, 1910, copy.

120 AASF, LBR(1a), 498-99, Riordan to Riordan [San Francisco], December 10, 1909, copy.

121 AASF, LBR(3a), 219-20, Riordan to Riordan [San Francisco], October 24, 1911, copy.

122 AAB, 109-V-1, Gibbons to Riordan, Baltimore, November 23, 1911, copy, *personal* and *confidential*. An account of the negotiations for O'Connell's transfer to Richmond may be found in John Tracy Ellis, *Gibbons*, II, 443-44.

123 AAB, 109-V-6, Riordan to Gibbons, San Francisco, November 29, 1911; 110-B-12, same to same, San Francisco, January 23, 1912. AASF, LBR(3a), 340-41, Riordan to Riordan [San Francisco], January 26, 1912, copy. Riordan was guilty of a common error in believing that O'Connell was a native American. His auxiliary had actually been born at Donoughmore in County Cork, Ireland. (Colman Barry, *The Catholic University of America, 1903-1909: The Rectorship of Denis J. O'Connell* [Washington, D. C., 1950], p. 1.)

124 AASF, LBR(3a), 374-77, Riordan to Riordan [San Francisco], February 23, 1912, copy.

125 UND, MC, Hudson Papers X-4-g, Riordan to Hudson, San Francisco, July 28, August 19, and November 27, 1911; and X-4-h, same to same, San Francisco, February 24, 1912. Also, AALA, Riordan to Conaty, San Francisco, February 5, 1912.

126 AASF, LBR(3a), 439-40, Riordan to Hanna [San Francisco], April 9, 1912, copy.

127 AAB, 110-H-1, Riordan to Gibbons, San Francisco, April 3, 1912.

128 AASF, LBR(3a), 473, Riordan to [De Lai, San Francisco], June 8, 1912, copy; AAB, 110-L-6, Riordan to Gibbons, San Francisco, June 10, 1912.

129 AASF, LBR(4a), 8-10, Riordan to Ireland [San Francisco], October 11, 1912, copy.

130 AASF, LBR(3a), 507-508, Riordan to Riordan [San Francisco], June 28, 1912, copy.

131 AASF, LBR(3a), 619-20, Riordan to Sister Mary Augustine O'Hay [San Francisco], August 29, 1912, copy.

132 AASF, LBR(4a), 29, Riordan to Bonzano [San Francisco], October 23, 1912, copy.

133 AASF, LBR(4a), Riordan to Hanna [San Francisco], October 25, 1912, copy.

134 AASF, LBR(4a), 43-44, Riordan to Ireland [San Francisco], October 25, 1912, copy.

135 AASF, Archbishop Hanna File, ms. of Cantwell speech, typescript; Rochester *Herald*, December 5, 1912, p. 11.

136 *Monitor* December 28, 1912, p. 1.

137 AASF, LBR(4a), 239, list of appointments for Hanna.

138 AASF, LBR(4a), 116-18, Riordan to Hanna [San Francisco], November 18, 1912, copy.

CHAPTER ELEVEN

1 AAB, 84-I-3, Keane to Gibbons, Richmond, April 11, 1888. An excellent series of monographs on the early years of the university have been published: John Tracy Ellis, *The Formative Years of the Catholic University of America* (Washington, 1946); Patrick H. Ahern, *The Catholic University of America, 1887-1896: The Rectorship of John J. Keane* (Washington, 1949); Peter E. Hogan, *The Catholic University of America, 1896-1903: The Rectorship of Thomas J. Conaty* (Washington, 1949); Colman J. Barry, *The Catholic University of America, 1903-1909: The Rectorship of Denis J. O'Connell* (Washington, 1950).

2 ACUA, Garrigan Papers, Keane to Philip J. Garrigan, Vice-Rector of the Catholic University, Paris, November 27, 1888; AAB, 85-L-9, Keane to Gibbons, Rome, December 18, 1888; ADR, Riordan to O'Connell, Paris, December 24, [1888].

3 ACUA, Keane Papers, Riordan to Keane, Paris, January 4, [1889].

4 ASMA, Magnien Papers, Riordan to Magnien, San Francisco, November (?), 1890. ACUA, Riordan to Keane, San Francisco, February 28 and March 6, 1891. For an interesting autobiographical account of Ramm's conversion, see the *Monitor*, July 3, 1897, pp. 6-7; July 10, p. 10.

5 ACUA, Keane Papers, Riordan to Keane, San Francisco, April 2, 1891.

6 *Ibid.*, same to same, San Francisco, February 4, 1890. Keane showed Riordan's letter to Archbishop Ireland, who was amused at the latter's references to St. Paul and Peoria. "His theories are pleasing," wrote Ireland,

> I wish they were more easily found true in practice. He is completely mistaken as to the resources of the Dioceses of the West. All the Archbishops in the country could not find fifty thousand dollars in the Peoria Diocese or a hundred thousand dollars in the diocese of St. Paul.

(*Ibid.*, Ireland to Keane, St. Paul, February 20, 1890.)

7 ADR, Keane to O'Connell, Washington, D.C., January 5, 1894. Evidence of large subscriptions from Mrs. Peter Donohue and Mrs. Parrott is found in ACUA, Keane Papers, Riordan to Keane, San Francisco, April 18, 1894, and October 16, 1895; Garrigan Papers,

Riordan to Garrigan, San Francisco. In the following year, Gibbons unexpectedly met in Germany Judge O'Connor, now a close friend of Keane, who was disposed to give the university $500,000, provided that a small interest from it be paid to him while he and his wife were alive. "I think the proposal ought to be accepted," the cardinal advised. "It puts at the disposal of the University an immense sum in a few years, for he is over 70 and his wife, an invalid, over 60." (*Ibid.*, Keane Papers, Gibbons to Keane, Munich, July 8, 1895.) A detailed account of Keane's mission may be found in the San Francisco *Chronicle*, February 12, 13, 15, and 19, 1894.

8 ACUA, Keane Papers, Riordan to Keane, San Francisco, April 18, 1894.

9 AAB, 94-R-6, Keane to Gibbons, Chicago, October 7, 1896.

10 ACUA, Garrigan Papers, Keane to Garrigan, San Francisco, October 11, 1896.

11 ACUA, Minutes of the Board of Trustees of the Catholic University of America, XXI Meeting, October 21, 1896, pp. 60-61.

12 Extensive treatment of the agitation during Conaty's regime may be found in Hogan, *op. cit.*, pp. 167-72.

13 AAB, 100-B-3, O'Connell to Gibbons, Rome, October 6, 1902; also *ibid.*, 99-W-5, Charles P. Grannan to Gibbons, Rigi-Scheidigg, Switzerland, August 20, 1902.

14 ADR, Riordan to O'Connell [The Hague], August 31, 1902.

15 ADR, Gibbons to O'Connell, Baltimore, September 1, 1902.

16 ADR, Keane to O'Connell, Dubuque, September 26 [1902].

17 ADR, Riordan to O'Connell, Louvain, September 11, 1902.

18 ADR, [Grannan] to O'Connell, Louvain, September 14, 1902; same to same, Rotterdam [September] 18, 1902.

19 ADR, Riordan to O'Connell, The Hague, September 23 and 28, 1902. The Province of San Francisco would name O'Connell behind Conaty on the list of candidates to succeed Montgomery. (APF, P.N. 02/53360, Riordan, Grace and Scanlan to Gotti, San Francisco, December 27, 1902.) A hint of Riordan's actual preference of O'Connell's candidacy for Los Angeles appeared when the archbishop told him that the bishops placed Conaty first on the *terna* "because he is a Bishop and considered it infra Dig. to put him second." Again, however, this may serve only to illustrate Riordan's diplomany. ADR, Riordan to O'Connell, San Francisco, December 30 [1902].

20 AAB, 100-C-4, Riordan to Gibbons, Rome, October 29, 1902, cablegram. ADR, Gibbons to O'Connell, Baltimore, November 29, 1902.

21 ADR, Ireland to O'Connell, St. Paul, October 31, 1902.

22 ACUA, Minutes of the Board of Trustees of the Catholic University of America, XXVII Meeting, November 12, 1902, p. 102. Propaganda had requested Riordan to investigate certain accusations related to Bishop Spalding's candidacy for Chicago. See pp. 341-46.

23 P.N. 02/51449, Giovannini to Luigi Vecchia, Secretary of Propaganda, The Hague, September 15, 1902; *ibid.*, Giovannini to Gotti, The Hague, September 26, 1902, copy. P.N. 02/51674, Giovannini to Gotti, The Hague, September 30, 1902. It would not be until after Christmas that Montgomery would acknowledge the notice of the appointment and accept it. (P.N. 02/53311, Montgomery to Gotti, Los Angeles, December 26, 1902; signed as Bishop of Monterey-Los Angeles.)

24 It was on November 2, 1902, that Riordan actually named Harnett as administrator of the diocese, but the appointment was not delivered until January 16, 1903. (AASF, LB-7 [408], statement of Riordan, January 16, 1903, copy.) The text of Riordan's signed memorandum at Propaganda reads as follows:

> Hodie scilicet die secunda Novembris A.D. 1902, Nominavi Ad. Rdm. Dm. P. Harnett, dioecesis Montereyensis ac Angelorum, Vicarium Generalem, ejusdem dioeceseos Administratorem sede vacante.
> +Patritius G. Riordan

(P.N. 02/52069, Riordan to Gotti, Rome, November 2, 1902.) Harnett's acknowledgement is in AASF, Harnett to Riordan, Los Angeles, January 26, 1903. It is not clear to the writer who governed the Diocese of Monterey-Los Angeles from December 26, 1902, to January 16, 1903.

25 ADR, Ireland to O'Connell, New York, December 7, 1902.

26 P.N. 02/52069, Riordan to Gotti, Rome, November 2, 1902.

27 Los Angeles *Herald*, October 30, 1902, p. 1.

28 P.N. 02/53069, report of the consultors' meeting, Los Angeles, December 12, 1902, signed by them and endorsed by Riordan. Uncharacteristically, Riordan did not have this document translated from English for Propaganda, another handicap for the consultors.

29 ADR, Riordan to O'Connell, San Francisco, December 30 [1902].

30 P.N. 02/53360, report of the provincial meeting of December 18, 1902, addressed to Gotti and signed by Riordan, Scanlan, and

Grace, San Francisco, December 27, 1902. The evidence has raised serious problems, indicating that Montgomery's status was irregular. In Rome's view, he had delayed his formal resignation from Los Angeles until after both the consultors' and bishops' meetings. It appears that through Riordan's design, votes had been taken on a see which was not technically vacant. Interestingly, Montgomery's resignation dates from December 26, 1902, the day before the report of the bishops' meeting was sent to Rome. Hence, in the report the bishops could legitimately describe Montgomery's see as then "vacant," though his status at the time of voting is unclear. Once he was clearly no longer an ordinary, Montgomery later endorsed this report and strongly recommended Conaty's appointment. P. N. 02/53322, Montgomery to [Gotti], Los Angeles, December 30, 1902; signed this time "Coadjutor Elect."

31 P. N. 03/53329, Mora to Gotti, Sarria, Spain, January 7, 1903; P.N. 03/53101, Adam to Gotti, Barcelona, December 30, 1903.

32 P.N. 02/53048, Hawe to Gotti, Los Angeles [December 31, 1902].

33 P.N. 02/53069, Riordan to [Satolli], San Francisco, December 31, 1902; P.N. 03/53514, Riordan to Gotti, San Francisco, January 4, 1903; P.N. 03/53549, Falconio to Gotti, Washington, D.C., January 12, 1903. For the petition [December 27, 1902], see P.N. 02/53327.

34 P.N. 03/54025, report of the general congregation of March 9, 1903.

35 ACUA, O'Connell Papers, Riordan to O'Connell, San Francisco, April 9, 1903.

36 ACUA, same to same, December 4, 1903.

37 ACUA, Files of the Board of Trustees, "Report of the Special Committee," April 9, 1902. For extensive treatment of the Waggaman affair, see Barry, *op. cit.*, pp. 71-108.

38 AASF, LB-9(417), Riordan to Maes [San Francisco], December 16, 1903, copy. ACUA, O'Connell Papers, Riordan to O'Connell, San Francisco, December 28, 1903.

39 ACUA, O'Connell Papers, same to same, Greenwich, Connecticut, June 5, 1904.

40 ACUA, O'Connell Papers, same to same, Greenwich, Connecticut, June 6, 1904; quoted in Barry, *op. cit.*, p. 85. This document was not to be located in ACUA.

41 ACUA, O'Connell Papers, same to same, Montreal, June 23, 1904.

42 ACUA, O'Connell Papers, Dougherty Papers, George A. Dougherty to O'Connell, Washington, D.C., June 29, 1904.

43 AASF, "Catholic University" File, Gibbons to Riordan, Baltimore, August 27, 1904. *Ibid.*, LB-12(127-128), Riordan to Gibbons [San Francisco], September 13, 1904, copy. Riordan eventually agreed to a personal subscription of $5,000. *Ibid.*, LB-13(288), Riordan to O'Connell [San Francisco], January 10, 1905, copy. Evidently, Riordan's impatience at the implementation of this suggestion was known to Gibbons. In his acknowledgment, the latter expressed his thorough agreement with the archbishop "about the necessity of doing something to conciliate the Germans and since securing your letter I have already taken some action." (*Ibid.*, "Catholic University" File, Gibbons to Riordan, Baltimore, September 21, 1904.) Invitations to join the Board of Trustees were sent in 1906 to Sebastian G. Messmer, Archbishop of Milwaukee, and in 1907 to Henry Moeller, Archbishop of Cincinnati.

44 AASF, LB-12(339), Riordan to O'Connell [San Francisco], October 25, 1904; LB-12(344), same to same [San Francisco], October 26, 1904; LB-12(351), Riordan to Maes [San Francisco], October 27, 1904; also LB-12(388-394), Riordan to Spalding [San Francisco], November 5, 1904, copies.

45 When Riordan offered his resignation nine years later, it was again declined. (AASF, Gibbons to Riordan, Washington, D.C., November 29, 1913.) When Pius X sanctioned in 1903 the annual collection for the university on the first Sunday in Advent, Riordan complied by publishing a circular letter which reprinted the pope's letter of approval. Despite papal support, Riordan had placed little faith in these programs, telling Spalding that he expected poor results for such collections, to which, he added, "until we take some efficient means of bringing the University and its work to those Catholics who can afford to give a goodly sum of money, its progress must be very slow." AASF, LB-9(306), same to same [San Francisco], November 20, 1903, copy.

46 AASF, LBR(2a), 351-54, Riordan to Ireland [San Francisco], March 1, 1911, copy.

47 AASF, "Catholic University" File, Maes to Riordan, Washington, D.C., November 19, 1904.

48 McQuaid to Corrigan, Rochester, October 3, 1896; cited in Zwierlein, *op. cit.*, III, 241.

49 ACUA, Garrigan Papers, Keane to Garrigan, San Jose, California, November 19 [1896].

50 ADR, Charles P. Grannan to O'Connell, n.p., n.d.

51 P.N. 97/24630, Edward Fitzgerald, Bishop of Little Rock, to Ledochowski, New Orleans, July 14, 1897.

52 P.N. 97/24820, Riordan to Ledochowski, San Francisco, July 23, 1897; P.N. 97/25523, Ireland to Ledochowski, St. Paul, August 20, 1897.

53 P.N. 97/25523, Gibbons to Ledochowski, Baltimore, August 10, 1897; P.N. 97/25449, Keane to Ledochowski, Washington, D.C., September 14, 1897. For other details about Keane's candidacy for American sees, see Ahern, *Keane*, pp. 241-43, 276-77, 301-309.

54 P.N. 97/25857, report of the general congregation of November 15, 1897.

55 P.N. 98/31474, Brondel, Glorieux, Edward O'Dea, and Christie to Leo XIII, Portland, Oregon, November 17, 1898.

56 P.N. 99/32060, Sebastiano Martinelli to Ledochowski, Washington, D.C., January 3, 1899.

57 P.N. 98/31862, Riordan to Ledochowski, San Francisco, December 17, 1898.

58 P.N. 99/32449, Gibbons to Ledochowski, Baltimore, January 24, 1899. Christie's appointment by Propaganda occurred on February 6, 1899, whereas Gibbons' letter was not registered at the congregation until the following day, a fact which was also mentioned by Keane. ACUA, Bouquillon Papers, Keane to Magnien, Rome, February 11, 1899.

59 ACUA, Bouquillon Papers, Keane to Magnien, Rome, February 11, 1899.

60 P.N. 99/32147, Cardinal Francesco Satolli, *Relazione con sommario*, "Sulla elezione del nuovo Arcivescovo di Oregon (Stati Uniti di America Settentr.)," February, 1899, p. 5.

61 P.N. 99/32147, report of the general congregation of February 6, 1899.

62 P.N. 00/38302, Henry Cosgrove, Bishop of Davenport, to Ledochowski [Dubuque, March 15, 1900] ; P.N. 00/38412, Cosgrove, Richard Scannel (Omaha), Thomas Bonacum (Lincoln), and Thomas M. Lenihan (Cheyenne) to Ledochowski, Davenport, Iowa, March 22, 1900.

63 AAB, 98-U-6, Gibbons to Rampolla, Baltimore, April 15, 1900, copy in French. P.N. 00/38744, Rampolla to Ledochowski, Rome, April 30, 1900.

64 P.N. 00/38497, Katzer to Ledochowski, Milwaukee, April 2, 1900.

65 ADR, Riordan to O'Connell, Paris, April 18, 1900; Ireland to O'Connell, St. Paul, April 4, 1900.

66 ADR, Riordan to O'Connell, Paris, April 29 [1900].

67 P.N. 00/38793, Riordan to Ledochowski, Paris, May 3, 1900; Spalding to O'Connell, Paris, May 3, 1900.

68 P.N. 00/39617, report of the general congregation of July 9, 1900.

69 The *terna* report by the bishops of the province listed Spalding, *dignissimus*; Montgomery, *dignior*; and Daniel Riordan, *dignus*. P.N. 02/51287, Report of Spalding, John Janssen (Belleville), and James Ryan (Alton) Chicago, July 24, 1902, translation.

70 ADR, Riordan to O'Connell [The Hague], August 31, 1902.

71 APF, Chicago File (1903), no P.N., Allegatio A, no. 3, Spalding to Francesco Marchetti, Peoria, July 25, 1902. Monsignor Marchetti was an auditor at the apostolic delegation.

72 ADR, Hugh P. Smyth, pastor of St. Mary's Church, Evanston, Illinois, to O'Connell, March 19 and June 25, 1901; Thomas Vincent Shannon to O'Connell, Chicago, September 16, 1902.

73 ADR, Smyth to O'Connell, Evanston, July 24, 1902. See also same to same, Evanston, August 21, 1902; and the Archives of the Diocese of Rockford, Muldoon Diary, entry for July 24, 1902.

74 APF, Chicago File (1903), Martinelli to Ledochowski, Washington, D.C., 1902; reprinted in Francesco Satolli, *Relazione con sommario*, "Sulla nomina del nuovo Archivescovo di Chicago, " December, 1902, pp. 24-29.

75 APF, Chicago File (1903), Allegatio C. no. 6, Riordan to Frederick Z. Rooker, New York City, August 6, 1902. Monsignor Rooker was a staff member of the apostolic delegation.

76 APF, P.N. 02/52124, Riordan to Gotti, Rome, October 28 and 29, 1902.

77 P.N. 92/1066, Satolli to Ignazio Persico, Secretary of Propaganda, Washington, D.C., December 20, 1892.

78 John Lancaster Spalding, "Catholicism and A.P.A.ism," *North American Review*, CLIV (September, 1894), 278-87.

79 P.N. 04/9458, Rampolla to Ledochowski, Rome, September 20, 1894.

80 P.N. 04/9458, Satolli to Spalding, Washington, D.C., September 7, 1894, copy.

81 P.N. 02/52375, the Baroness von Zedtwitz to Gotti, Paris, August 17, 1902; same to Satolli, Paris, August 17, 1902. The first published account of this phase based on documentary materials is David F. Sweeney, *The Life of John Lancaster Spalding* (New York, 1965), pp. 308-309.

82 P.N. 02/52375, Riordan to Gotti, Paris, November 9, 1902; same to Satolli, Paris, November 9, 1902. Ten years later Riordan recorded a

lengthy and harsh appraisal of Gwendolyn and Elizabeth Caldwell, concluding that both sisters were "partially insane." AASF, LBR(3a), Riordan to Daniel Riordan [San Francisco], September 10, 1912, copy.

83 P.N. 02/52375, the Baroness von Zedtwitz to Satolli, La Chartreuse, Switzerland, November 9, 1902.

84 P.N. 02/52375, Riordan to Satolli, Maynooth College, Ireland, November 15, 1902.

85 AACL, Maes to Jules De Becker, Covington, Kentucky, December 16, 1902.

86 ADR, Riordan to O'Connell, San Francisco, December 30 [1902].

87 ACUA, O'Connell Papers, Ireland to O'Connell, St. Paul, August 4, 1903.

88 AASF, LB-9(306), Riordan to Spalding [San Francisco], November 20, 1903, copy.

89 APF, P.N. 01/41832 and 01/43743, Satolli, *Relazione con sommario*, "Sulla elezione del nuovo Vescovo di Portland (Stati Uniti)." William O'Connell, *Recollections of Seventy Years* (Boston and New York, 1934), p. 212. For further details on O'Connell's loyalties during his rectorship, especially during the Spanish-American War and the Americanist controversy, one should read discriminatingly Robert F. McNamara, *The American College in Rome, 1855-1955* (Rochester, 1956), pp. 368-76.

90 P.N. 01/43743, Ledochowski to Cardinal Sebastiano Martinelli, apostolic delegate, Rome, May 29, 1901, copy.

91 P.N. 01/47626, O'Connell to Ledochowski, Portland, Maine, December 28, 1901.

92 P.N. 03/57074, Williams to Gotti, Boston, September 16, 1903.

93 P.N. 04/61197, "Verbale Conventus Consultorum dioecesis ac Rectorum Inamovibilium," Boston, April 4, 1904, endorsed by Williams and by Richard Neagle as secretary; *ibid.*, "Verbale della riunione dei Vescovi della Provincia di Boston per la nomina del coadiutore," Boston, April 9, 1904, signed by Williams and by O'Connell as secretary; *ibid.*, Falconio to Gotti, Washington, D.C., May 25, 1904.

94 P.N. 04/61216, O'Connell to Falconio, Boston, May 23, 1904.

95 P.N. 04/60704, O'Connell to Merry del Val, Portland, Maine, April 17, 1904.

96 P.N. 04/60384, Alesandro Ceppi *et al.* to Gotti, Boston, April 8, 1904.

97 P.N. 04/61185, Daly to Satolli, Boston, May 12, 1904.

98 P.N. 04/60835, Supple to Gotti, Cambridge, Massachusetts, April 28, 1904; same to Merry del Val, Cambridge, April 26, 1904, copy.

99 P.N. 04/60827, Cummins to Merry del Val, Boston, May 3, 1904.

100 P.N. 04/62219, report of the general congregation of August 22, 1904. See also *ibid.*, Cardinal Sebastiano Martinelli, *Relazione con sommario*, "Sulla nomina del Vescovo Coadiutore con futura successione a Mons. Williams, Archivescovo di Boston," pp. 4-5.

101 For details on this portion of O'Connell's career, see John E. Sexton, *Cardinal O'Connell, A Biographical Sketch* (Boston, 1926), pp. 37ff; and Robert H. Lord, John E. Sexton, and Edward T. Harrington, *History of the Archdiocese of Boston* (New York, 1944), III, 476ff.

102 AASF, O'Connell to Riordan, on board the *Korea* approaching Honolulu, October 17, 1905.

103 P.N. 92/1576, Cardinal Serafino Vannutelli, *Relazione con sommario*, "Sopra la cessione di due Scoule Parrochiali dell'Archidiocesi di S. Paolo alla Commissione Scolastica governativa," April, 1892, p. 3. P.N. 93/2916, Cardinal Ignazio Persico, *Relazione con appendice*, "Sulla questione scolastica negli Stati Uniti di America," May, 1893, p. 3.

104 AALA, Riordan to Conaty, San Francisco, June 13 [1907]; P.N. 08/79688, Martinelli, *Relazione con sommario*, "Sulla scelta dei Candidati per l'ufficio di Coadiutore a Mons. Riordan Archiv. di S. Francisco," January, 1808, pp. 1-2

105 Jules De Becker, "The Rt. Rev. Bishop William Stang," *American College Bulletin* [Louvain], V (April, 1907), 49-56.

106 P.N. 05/69589, Williams, Thomas Beaven (Springfield), John S. Michaud (Burlington), Michael Tierney (Hartford), Stang, and John B. Delany (Manchester) to Gotti, Boston, December 7, 1905.

107 AASF, Stang to Riordan, Fall River, January 22, 1906.

108 P.N. 06/69816, report of the general congregation of January 22, 1906.

109 AASF, LB-17(399-400), Riordan to Byrne [San Francisco], February 14, 1906, copy. Most of the documentation in the rest of this chapter is derived from AASF, and this symbol will not, therefore, be used when a letterbook is cited.

110 AASF, Stang to Riordan, Fall River, February 27, 1906. AACL, Stang to De Becker, Fall River, March 16, 1906. After the selection of the candidates in 1904, John B. Delany, Bishop of

Manchester had addressed identical appeals to Cardinals Merry del Val and Gotti, denying the validity of these *ternae* and professing O'Connell as the fittest condidate. The Bishop of Portland, according to him, possessed the qualities needed for the coadjutorship, and, he added: "His devotedness to the Holy See and his anxiety to carry out her least behest have excited admiration among those who love Rome, but have moved others to unreasonable animosity in his regard." (P.N. 04/62688, Delany to Gotti, Manchester, August 28, 1904; P.N. 04/62689, Delany to Merry del Val, Manchester, August 28, 1904.) To De Becker, it may be noted, Stang confided a sad epilogue to what he had repeatedly styled the "Boston affair." "Mgr. Harkins is well& happy: 'loquens contritus est,'" he wrote. "The first time that the Boston Coadjutor appeared officially before the Suffragans was to bury his best & only friend, the young Bishop Delany of Manchester. What a terrible lesson!" (AACL, Stang to De Becker, Fall River, June 22, 1906.) Delany had died on June 11, 1906.

111 P.N. 06/70646, Falconio to Gotti, Washington, D.C., February 21, 1906.

112 LBR(2a), 68-69, Riordan to Riordan [San Francisco], February 24, 1910, copy.

113 LBR(2a), 393-95, same to same [San Francisco], March 24, · 1911, copy. Many reasons have been ascribed to O'Connell for having removed the society, but in the opinion of a member of the last Sulpician faculty, Benjamin F. Marcetteau, S.S., the archbishop, a former Rector of the American College, preferred the distinctive Roman system of managing seminaries to the Sulpician plan. (Interview with Louis A. Arand, S.S., Washington, D.C., August 1, 1964.)

114 LBR(1a), 406-½, Riordan to Ireland [San Francisco], November 1, 1909, copy.

115 LBR)3a), 231-32, Riordan to O'Connell [San Francisco], November 14, 1911, copy.

116 LBR(3a), 233-34, Riordan to Riordan [San Francisco], November 14, 1911, copy.

117 LBR(3a), 244-45, 255-56, same to same [San Francisco], November 18 and 25, 1911, copies.

118 LBR(3a), 280-81, same to same [San Francisco], December 21, 1911, copy.

119 AASP, Riordan to Ireland [San Francisco], December 17, 1913.

CHAPTER TWELVE

1 AASF, LBR(3a), 82-83, Riordan to Riordan [San Francisco], August 3, 1911, copy. Most of the documentation in this chapter is derived from AASF and this symbol is not, therefore, used when a letterbook is cited.

2 LBR(5a), 186-87, Riordan to Léon Verwilyhen [San Francisco], December 27, 1913, copy.

3 P.N. 02/52375, Riordan to Satolli, Maynooth College, Ireland, November 15, 1902.

4 ACUA, O'Connell Papers, Riordan to O'Connell, San Francisco, April 14, 1903.

5 LB-13(273), Riordan to Riordan [San Francisco], January 9, 1905, copy.

6 ACUA, O'Connell Papers, Riordan to O'Connell, San Francisco, January 10, 1905.

7 AASF, "Catholic University of America" File, O'Connell to Riordan, Washington, D.C., January 18, 1905.

8 LB-27(173-174), Riordan to Ireland [San Francisco], September 11, 1908, copy.

9 LBR(5a), 57-59, Riordan to Spalding [San Francisco], October 29, 1913, copy.

10 LBR(5a), 61-62, Riordan to Riordan [San Francisco], October 29, 1913, copy.

11 LBR(2a), 270-72, Riordan to Keane [San Francisco], January 17 [1911], copy. Details on Keane's last days may be found in Patrick Henry Ahern, *The Life of John J. Keane, Educator and Archbishop, 1839-1918* (Milwaukee, 1954), pp. 353ff.

12 LBR(2a), 293, Riordan to Riordan [San Francisco], January 27, 1911, copy.

13 LBR(2a), 295-96, Riordan to Ireland [San Francisco], January 27, 1911, copy.

14 LBR(3a), 105-106, Riordan to Riordan [San Francisco], August 16, 1911, copy.

15 LBR)3a), 204-205, Riordan to Riordan [San Francisco], October 13, 1911, copy.

16 LBR)3a), 507-508, same to same [San Francisco], June 28, 1912, copy.

17 LBR(3a), 513-14, Riordan to Gibbons [San Francisco], July 3, 1912, copy.

18 LBR(6a), 245-46, Riordan to Ireland [San Francisco], December 23, 1914, copy.

19 AASF, Gleason to Ramm, Palo Alto, California, July 1, 1911.

20 San Francisco *Chronicle*, August 23, 1911, p. 5; LBR(3a), 118-19, Riordan to Crowley [San Francisco], August 26, 1911, copy.

21 USF. MC. Hunt Journal, pp. 71-78. The involved question of the Teamsters' Strike has been treated in Cronin, *op. cit*.; Robert Edward Hennings, "James D. Phelan and the Wilson Progressives of California," an unpublished doctoral dissertation, University of California, Berkeley, California, pp. 33-36; and Roy Swanstrom, "The Reform Administration of James D. Phelan, Mayor of San Francisco, 1897-1902," unpublished master's thesis, University of California, Berkeley, California. In the teamster's strike, Yorke played a significant role in supporting unionism and in opposing Phelan, who had ordered the city police to protect the nonunion teamsters. According to Hennings, Yorke's public denunciation of Phelan in 1901 was "by far the most serious check to his career," and from this experience, Phelan entered upon a political eclipse which lasted for ten years until he began early to espouse the cause of Woodrow Wilson. *Op. cit.*, pp. 36ff. For details consult Joseph S. Brusher, S.J., *Consecrated Thunderbolt: Father Yorke of San Francisco* (Hawthorn, New Jersey, 1973).

22 P.N. 02/49704, Keane (Dubuque), Henry Cosgrove (Davenport), Richard Scannell (Omaha), Thomas Bonacum (Lincoln) to Ledochowski, Dubuque, February 25, 1902, copy. This report in Latin characterized Yorke's relationship with Riordan as "infessus," while Cardinal Francesco Segna in his Italian summary translated it as "ostile."

23 *Leader*, January 11, 1902, p. 4.

24 ACUA, Thomas Shahan Papers, Riordan to Shahan, San Francisco, January 15, 1902.

25 P.N. 02/51071, Riordan, Montgomery, Grace, and Lawrence Scanlan to Ledochowski, San Francisco, March 23, 1902. For details on Yorke's attack on the Catholic University of America see Peter E. Hogan, *The Catholic University of America, 1896-1903: The Rectorship of Thomas J. Conaty* (Washington, D.C., 1949), pp. 115ff.

26 [P.N. 02/54025] Riordan to Diomede Falconio, Los Angeles, December 12, 1902. It may be noted that in negotiating for a coadjutor after the death of Archbishop George Montgomery, the diocesan consultors and irremovable rectors gave one vote to Yorke. (APF, P.N. 07/78456, "Minutes of the meeting...," San Francisco, August 16, 1907, endorsed by Riordan as president.)

27 AASF, Yorke to Riordan, March 14, 1903.

28 Santa Barbara Mission Archives, Yorke to Falconio, Oakland, July 2, 1906, copy; and the reply of Vitalis Feldman, O.F.M., n.p., n.d.

29 ACUA, O'Connell Papers, Riordan to O'Connell, San Francisco, December 7 [1906].

30 *Ibid.*, Riordan to O'Connell, San Francisco, April 18, 1907.

31 ACUA, Keane Papers, Riordan to [Keane], n.p., n.d. No doubt, this last comment referred to accusations in the San Francisco press that the construction company owned by Yorke's brother Frank had defrauded the city in a paving contract awarded through the Schmitz-Ruef interests.

32 ACUA, O'Connell Papers, Riordan to O'Connell, San Francisco, December 7 [1907].

33 LBR(1a), 19-20, Riordan to Falconio [San Francisco], January 20, 1909, copy.

34 LBR(2a), 351-54, Riordan to Ireland [San Francisco], March 1, 1911, copy.

35 AASF, Riordan to the Clergy of San Francisco, San Francisco, October 12, 1909.

36 USF. MC. Hunt Papers, Yorke to Joseph Harrington, n.p., October 15, 1909. The nature of Yorke's severance from the *Leader* has been debated. Several authorities contend that he remained the active spirit behind it. The tone of the weekly was, nevertheless, uncharacteristically pacific at least between 1910 and 1913, a development perhaps due partly to Yorke's personal fidelity to the promise. See Sister Catherine Julie Cunningham, S.N.D. "The Irish Republicanism of Peter C. Yorke of San Francisco, 1916-1922," pp. 20-21.

37 AASF, Gleason to I. T. Martin, Palo Alto, California, June 26, 1911, copy.

38 AASF, Yorke to Riordan, Oakland, California, July 12 and 17, 1911.

39 AASF, Yorke to Ramm, Oakland, July 17, 1911.

40 AASF, File of the Sisters of the Presentation, Denis O'Connell to Riordan, Washington, D.C., October 16, 1911.

41 AASF, "Detective Report," p. 36.

42 AASF, Kenna to Riordan, San Francisco, October 25, 1911.

43 *Leader*, December 21, 1912, p. 1.

44 AASF, Yorke to Riordan, Oakland, October 17, 1913.

45 LBR(4a), 693-94, Riordan to Sullivan [San Francisco], September 19, 1913, copy.

46 Walter McDonald, *Reminiscences of a Maynooth Professor*, edited by Denis Gwyn (London, 1925), p. 213.

47 AASF, Bonzano to Riordan, Washington, D.C., October 31, 1912, copy.

48 LBR(4a), 100-10, Riordan to Bonzano [San Francisco], November 15, 1912, copy.

49 AASF, Scanlan to Riordan, Hot Springs, Arizona, February 3, 1913.

50 AASF, Bonzano to Riordan, Washington, D.C., February 5, 1913, copy.

51 LBR(4a), 388-89, Riordan to Daniel Riordan [San Francisco], February 14, 1913, copy.

52 AASF, Thomas Kearns to Riordan, Salt Lake City, March 5, 1913.

53 LBR(5a), 578-81, Riordan to Edmund M. Dunne, Bishop of Peoria [San Francisco], July 28, 1914, copy.

54 AASF, Bonzano to Riordan, Washington, D.C., December 22, 1914. Scanlan died in 1915, succeeded by Joseph S. Glass, C.M.

55 A splendid study of this issue may be found in William J. Battersby, *The Christian Brothers in the United States, 1900-1915* (Winona, Minnesota, 1967).

56 Archives of the Generalate of the Brothers of the Christian Schools, Rome (hereafter cited as AGCB), Riordan to the General Chapter, San Francisco, February 20, 1897. Six other prelates who registered their opposition to the brothers were Spalding, Gibbons, John J. Kain (St. Louis), Cornelius O'Brien (Halifax), Patrick J. Ryan (Philadelphia), and Patrick A. Feehan (Chicago).

57 AAB, 97-R-5, Minutes of the Meeting of the Archbishops, Washington, D.C., October 12, 1899.

58 William J. Battersby, *op. cit.*, p. 164f.

59 AGCB, unidentified memorandum [1899].

60 ACUA, O'Connell Papers, Brother Justin, F.S.C., to O'Connell, St. Louis, November 10, 1904.

61 *Ibid.*, Riordan to O'Connell, San Francisco, March 26, 1906.

62 *Ibid.*, same to same, San Francisco, September 13, 1907.

63 LBR(5a), 143-45, Riordan to De Lai [San Francisco], December 30, 1913, copy.

64 AGCB, Alexis François, F.S.C., Procurator General to Imier of Jesus, F.S.C., Rome, November 20 and 30, 1914; December 2, 1914; January 20, 1915; and June 26, 1920. Not until 1923 did the Holy See request the Institute to adjust its rule.

65 LBR(6a), 71-72, Riordan to Riordan [San Francisco], October 9, 1914, copy.

66 LBR(2a), 305-306, same to same [San Francisco], February 3, 1911, copy.

67 LBR(2a), 316-17, same to same [San Francisco], February 13, 1911, copy. Actually Ryan had been senior to Riordan, having succeeded to the See of Philadelphia on June 8, 1884, six months before Alemany's retirement had become effective.

68 LBR(2a), 322-23, same to same [San Francisco], February 17, 1911, copy.

69 LBR(5a), 57-59, Riordan to Spalding [San Francisco], October 29, 1913, copy.

70 LBR(5a), 179-180, Riordan to Anna Sheehan, R.C.S.J. [San Francisco], January 9, 1914, copy.

71 LBR(5a), 203-204, Riordan to Riordan [San Francisco], January 20, 1914, copy; *Monitor,* January 24, 1914, pp. 1, 8.

72 *Ibid.,* January 2, 1915, p. 1.

73 AASF, Scrapbook: "Abp. Riordan's Death and Funeral," pp. 3, 13.

74 San Francisco *Chronicle,* December 28, 1914, p. 1.

75 *Monitor,* January 2, 1915, pp. 1, 8.

76 LB-10(57), Riordan to Mrs. Cryan [San Francisco], January 10, 1904, copy.

77 LB-14(57), Riordan to Lathrop [San Francisco], February 3, 1904, copy.

78 LBR(3a), 199-200, Riordan to John B. Casserly [San Francisco], October 6, 1911, copy.

79 M. D. Connolly, "Personal Recollections of the Late Most Reverend Archbishop Riordan," *Monitor,* Christmas, 1915, pp. 6-8.

80 Peter C. Yorke, "Essentially a Churchman," *Leader,* January 2, 1915, p. 4.

81 *Blue and White* (Sacred Heart College, San Francisco), V (November, 1908), p. 4.

82 AASF, Riordan to Patrick E. Mulligan, Paris, November 9, 1902, telegram.

83 AASF, William Bourn to Riordan, San Francisco, March 11, 1911.

84 LBR(3a), Riordan to Nichols [San Francisco], October 2, 1912, copy.

85 ASMS, Havey Collection, Jean-Baptiste Vuibert to Edward Dyer, Menlo Park, August 31, 1903.

86 Moore to the writer, Burgos, Spain, November 6, 1965.

87 ADR, Hugh P. Smyth to O'Connell, Evanston, August 21, 1902.

88 AASF, Merry del Val to Riordan, Rome, May 29, 1909; Ramm's notes recording the transfer of the cathedral administration, February 1, 1913.

89 Peter C. Yorke, *Altar and Priest* (San Francisco, 1913), p. 328.

90 LBR(5a), 124, Riordan to Yorke [San Francisco], December 17, 1913, copy.

91 LBR(2a), 378-81, Riordan to Gibbons [San Francisco], March 14, 1911, copy.

92 AASF, Gibbons to Riordan, Baltimore, April 17, 1911.

93 AASF, Tyrrell to Riordan, Richmond, York, December 29, 1905.

94 AASF, same to same, Storrington, Sussex, June 23, 1909.

95 LBRC1a), 206, Ramm to Tyrrell [San Francisco], July 20, 1909, copy. In Riordan's judgment, however, this was a favor personal to Tyrrell, for when the English scholar died in the following month, the archbishop discouraged his young associate from coming to California. (*Ibid.*, LBR[1a], 296-97, Ramm to the Reverend Edward Schmidt [San Francisco], August 9, 1909, copy.) Curiously, Maude D. Petre, Tyrrell's literary executrix, acknowledged Ramm's first letter of July 20 which quoted Riordan's sentiments, but she made no references to the archbishop's offer in her book, *Autobiography and Life of George Tyrrell* (London and New York, 1912).

96 AASF, Scrapbook: "Abp. Riordan's Death and Funeral," p. 26, Spalding to Daniel Riordan, Peoria, January 6 [1915], copy.

THE SOURCES

1 See Thomas J. Brennan, "Archbishop Riordan," *Records* of the American Catholic Historical Society of Philadelphia, XXVI (1915), 47-54.

2 Interviews with John Manning, M.M., an official at Propaganda, Rome, November 28, 1964.

3 The writer is grateful to Mr. Debevec for a helpful précis entitled, "Propaganda Fide Archives: Disposition of the Papers to 1893." For further details see John B. McGloin, S.J., "The Roman Propaganda Fide Archives," *Church History*, XXXIII (March, 1964), 84-91. Father Kovalsky has also published two helpful guides to the Propaganda archives, the first being a listing of its holdings and the latter a catalogue of the important personnel attached to the congregation since its inception: *Inventario dell'Archivio Storico della S. Congregatione "de Propaganda Fide"* (Beckenried, Switzerland, 1951); *Serie dei Cardinali Prefetti e dei Segretari della Sacra Congregazione "de Propaganda Fide"* (Rome, 1962).

4 An idea of the holdings may be found in Francis J. Weber, "The San Francisco Chancery Archives," *Americas*, XX (January, 1964), 313-21. A brief overview of Catholic collections in the United States is Thomas T. McAvoy, C.S.C., "Catholic Archives and Manuscript Collections," *American Archivist*, XXIV (October, 1961), 409-14.

5 AASF, LBR(3a), 244-45, Riordan to Riordan [San Francisco], November 18, 1911, copy.

6 For a general description of the contents of this depository, see John Tracy Ellis, "A Guide to the Baltimore Cathedral Archives," *Catholic Historical Review*, XXXII (October, 1946), 341-60.

Index

For clarity, most personal and institutional titles have not been capitalized; and most persons have been identified in their last post during Riordan's lifetime.

The sequence of entries follows the pagination.

A

H

Hague Conference, First, proposes principle of international arbitration, 213; establishes the Permanent Court of Arbitration, 224; vindicated by the work of the Hague Tribunal, 243.

Hague Tribunal (Permanent Court of Arbitration), the, considered for the Pious Fund claims, 223-24; establishment, 224; panel of arbitrators selected, 225-26; litigation before and decision, 230-31; Vatican excluded from participation, 232; vindicated the Hague Conference, 243.

Halligan, Thomas, pastor of St. Mary's Church, Chicago, appointed as Duggan's procurator, 25; in open conflict with Dunne, 26; as diocesan administrator, 35, 38.

Hanna, Edward J., Riordan's coadjutor, 385; appointment delayed to San Francisco, 255-56; Riordan nominates as coadjutor, 281-82; named professor at St. Bernard's Seminary, 282; writings associated with modernism, 284-89; reluctantly makes a defense, 288-89; Propaganda postpones consideration of the case, 290; publishes two orthodox articles in the *New York Review*, 294; sends his second submission, 296; Breen's persistent opposition to, 297; an old article surfaces and disqualifies his candidacy, 298-300; thanks to Riordan for support, 300; Riordan explains Hanna's selection, 302; not at first a part of Riordan's renewed campaign, 313; nominated and appointed as auxiliary, 314-15; consecration, 315-16; reception in San Francisco, 316; Riordan's later reflection on the appointment, 317-18; seeks to make effective the compromise on the teaching of classics in Christian Brothers' schools, 383; statement at Riordan's death, 387; sermon and final prayers at the obsequies, 388.

Hanna, Mother Anne, R.S.C.J., Edward Hanna's sister, receives Riordan's story of her brother's appointment to San Francisco, 317-18.

Harkins, Matthew, bishop of Providence, leading candidate for the Boston co-adjutorship, 349-54, passim.

Harmonized Exposition of the Four Gospels, A, study by Breen reviewed in the *Revue biblique*, 284-85.

Harnett, Patrick, Rev., vicar general in Los Angeles, receives appointment as diocesan administrator too late to help his own candidacy, 328-29; a petition to Rome in his favor, 329; has first place on consultors' *terna*, 329; dropped from the bishops' list, 330.

Harriman, Edward Henry, executive of the Southern Pacific Company, member of the Finance Committee of Relief after the earthquake, 251.

Harrington, Joseph T., manager of the *Leader*, publishes a "Detective Report" on Yorke, 373.

Hawe, Patrick, Rev., priest in Los Angeles, organizes the petition in favor of Harnett's candidacy, 328.

Hay, John, U.S. secretary of state, cousin of Ralston, 219; orders negotiations with Mexico regarding claims to the Pious Fund, 219; public commitment to settling the claims, 220; approached by Riordan, 221-22; recommends international arbitration to Mexico, 223-24; insists on additional counsel at the Hague Tribunal, 228; declines to reopen the case despite the mixed decision, 231.

Hayward, California, residence of Yorke's mother, 147.

Hennessy, John, archbishop of Dubuque, death, 339.

Henry, John Quincy Adams, minister, conducts anti-Catholic meetings, 141.

Hibernians, Ancient Order of, under attack, 180-83; establishes a chair of Gaelic studies at the Catholic University, 368-69.

Hickey, Thomas F., coadjutor bishop in Rochester, selected by McQuaid, 280.

Hill, David J., assistant U.S. secretary of state, receives Ireland's petition

I

J

Y

Z

San Francisco Ferry Building and Flames